SOUTHERN CROSS

ALSO BY
CHRISTINE LEIGH HEYRMAN

*Commerce and Culture: The Maritime Communities
of Colonial Massachusetts, 1690–1750*

*Nation of Nations: A Narrative History of the American
Republic* (with four coauthors)

SOUTHERN CROSS

The Beginnings of the Bible Belt

CHRISTINE LEIGH HEYRMAN

ALFRED A. KNOPF
NEW YORK
1997

THIS IS A BORZOI BOOK
PUBLISHED BY ALFRED A. KNOPF, INC.

http://www.randomhouse.com/

Library of Congress Cataloging-in-Publication Data
Heyrman. Christine Leigh.
Southern cross: the beginnings of the Bible
Belt / Christine Leigh Heyrman.—1st ed.
p.   cm.
ISBN 0-679-44638-9 (alk. paper)
1. Southern States—Church history.   2. Evangelicalism—
Southern States—History.   I. Title.
BR535.H47   1997
277.5′081—dc21   97-6354   CIP

Manufactured in the United States of America
First Edition

To Thomas Calvin Carter

Contents

Acknowledgments

Eudora Welty described her beginnings as a writer by recalling that "Day-dreaming started me on my way, but story writing, once I was truly in its grip, took me and shook me awake." On a good day, I can see my-self somewhere in the middle of that process—happily imagining that story writing is taking hold of me; on a bad day, I feel myself slipping from its grasp. But always, I am sustained and challenged by three friends—historians by trade, story-tellers by some higher calling—whose way with the past rouses those in the present to wonder and reflect. First among them is Edmund Morgan, who has squandered many hours over the last twenty-five years teaching me almost everything that I know and much more that I'm still trying to learn. Then there is James West Davidson, who encourages me to keep trying, even while pretending that he's doing nothing of the sort. And there is Richard Godbeer: some years ago I tried to teach him, and ever since he has been retaliating. All three would be embarrassed by any fuller praise of the many ways in which my work has benefited from their formidable knowledge, inimitable grace, offhand generosity, and lethal wit.

Before beginning the research for this book, I had worked only on early New England, so it took some doing to find my way into the South. Those who especially helped me to make that change are Michael Johnson, who warned me against assuming that evangelicalism won acceptance among southerners as readily as it did among Yankees, and Rachel Klein, who encouraged me to cast this book as a study of the entire South rather than focusing on a particular state or community. A great many other special-ists in southern history shared their expertise on matters that ranged from where to find what in the archives to the best ways of seasoning grits, for all of which I thank Lacy Ford, Stephanie McCurry, Patricia Montgomery, Miles Richards, and Fredrika Teute. I am also indebted to Allen Stokes and Herbert Hartsook at the South Caroliniana Library, and to John Brunswick and David Langenberg at the Morris Library of the University of Delaware, as well as to the many other professional librarians who helped me to track down both manuscript collections and obscure printed sources at the Perkins Library of Duke University; the Regenstein Library at the University of Chicago; the Southern Historical Collection at the University of North Carolina, Chapel Hill; the Virginia Baptist Historical Society at the University of Richmond; and the Virginia State Historical Society.

I figured out what this book was about at the National Humanities Center, a sylvan mecca where an impeccably professional staff headed by their director, W. Robert Connor, treats every scholar like a treasure. After a year of being spoiled there as a fellow, I eagerly returned for three summers as an instructor of seminars for high school teachers on American religious history, organized by Richard Schramm, Carolyn Jackson, and Crystal Waters and funded mainly by the National Endowment for the Humanities. During our long morning classes and informal sessions after lunch, I learned more than I taught, from both the participants and my fellow instructors—Randall Balmer, Grant Wacker, and, most particularly, Donald Scott, a wonderful teacher and an ideal critic.

As it happened, these summer seminars fell during the years in which I was working research notes into chapters. For much of that time I was able to devote myself to writing, thanks to grants from the American Council of Learned Societies and the John Simon Guggenheim Foundation; I also benefited from the semester at the Shelby Cullom Davis Center at Princeton University, to say nothing of the kindness of its then-director, Natalie Zemon Davis, and her assistant, Kari Hoover. And I am most particularly indebted to my colleagues at the University of Delaware, David Pong, the chair of the History Department, and Mary Richards, the dean of the School of Humanities, who arranged for both sabbatical leave and additional financial support.

I have been equally fortunate in those people who encouraged me by commenting so knowledgeably on various chapters in progress. That long list includes Steven Aron, Richard Beeman, Michael Bellesiles, Ira Berlin, Anne Boylan, Betsy Brown, Peter Brown, Jon Butler, Catherine Clinton, Drew Gilpin Faust, Emily Grosholz, Dirk Hartog, James Henretta, Bernard Herman, Peter Kolchin, Bruce Mann, John Murrin, Alison Olson, Harold Selesky, Neva Specht, Steven Spector, Sean Wilentz, and

Michael Zuckerman. Jane Garrett, my editor at Knopf, helped me to complete this book with her irresistible mixture of savvy advice, uncommon sense, and offbeat jokes, while my copy-editors, Sarajane Herman and Melvin Rosenthal, alerted me with superhuman tact to many sins against the English language.

That leaves only those people who make it easy for me to write and easier still to stop. My parents, Robert Heyrman and Verona Monfils Heyrman, made a point of never asking me when this book would be finished, while my sister, Anne Hart, quite credibly feigned interest in my southern evangelicals, claiming to find them almost as fascinating as her Hellenistic Jews and early Christians. I have been as generously indulged by Richard Carter, my brother-in-law, and my niece and most beguiling muse, Rachel Elizabeth Speer, both of whom drew on their command of the Bible to help me locate some of the passages that open these chapters. Meanwhile, my friend Lisa Keamy showed her loyalty by refusing to humor me in any way—the perfect tonic for instilling in others some measure of her own courage and confidence. Finally, there is my husband, Tom Carter, who likes to claim that he contributed to this book merely by correcting my spelling through several drafts. We both know better. Our life together is what I long dreamt of being awakened to, so this book is for him.

SOUTHERN CROSS

Prologue

CANAAN'S LANGUAGE

Behold, the Lord is riding on a swift cloud and comes to
Egypt; and the idols of Egypt will tremble at his presence,
and the heart of the Egyptians will melt within them. . . .
In that day, there will be five cities in the land of
Egypt which will speak the language of Canaan and
swear allegiance to the Lord of hosts. One of these will
be called the City of the Sun.
—ISAIAH 19:1, 18

MARY MACDONALD raised her children to fear the Lord. The
mistress of a large plantation in the South Carolina low
country, she nurtured the fledgling souls committed to her
care with a daily regimen of family prayer and Bible readings, moral
admonition and spiritual advice. Even when her children left home to
attend school or visit relatives, she kept up her oversight of their spiritual
progress in long letters. In 1814 she pressed "Sweet little Catherine," then a
twelve-year-old schoolgirl, to consider "what will you do when death
comes and cuts your body, this proud and haughty body, down to be consigned to the tomb, there to be food for worms,—it is so vile and sinful it
deserves no better, but what will become of your immortal part, the soul
cannot die, it must ascend to God to receive its doom." True, Catherine
was still more child than woman, but not too young, in her mother's view,
to be warned that death stalked life, and that judgment would be as swift
as hell was terrible, for "if you are not united to Christ . . . infernal fiends
will stand ready to drag you down to outer darkness . . . no hope of
release, torments eternal." To avert so awful a fate there could be only one
recourse: "Come then, my dear," she implored the girl, "believe in Jesus,
go to him and say, 'Thy word teacheth me . . . that I am a lost undone
creature by nature and I have added and made myself more vile by prac-

tice. . . . Holy Father I ask in Jesus Name that faith which shall purify my sinful wicked heart.' "[1]

Thus did a devout Baptist and loving mother prepare her daughter for that crucial passage into the accountability of adulthood. Catherine needed to realize what mattered most in life; and for evangelicals like her mother, that was the rebirth of the fallen soul, the regeneration of the corrupt heart. Without that inward change, one that divine grace alone could effect, MacDonald believed her children would neither find true comfort on earth nor enjoy eternal happiness in heaven. Although saving faith came only at the behest of divine mercy, they could still seek that favor by submitting their minds, hearts, and wills to God. Such was the essence of evangelical faith, and self-abasing inwardness was a defining feature of its temperament. MacDonald's concern to foster humility in her children, to teach them to approach the Lord with awe and trembling, guided all her counsel. For only by chastening the proud self might they experience the profound spiritual transformation that would make her words meaningful to them in a new way—sounds and signs suddenly resonant because they conveyed a truth now affirmed by the heart. Only by an anguished "conviction" of personal wickedness followed by the joyful release of "conversion," the assurance of having received the grace to believe in Jesus, would they learn "the language of Canaan."[2]

That understanding of what made men and women truly religious unified all evangelicals in the early American South, a diverse group composed mainly of Baptists, Methodists, and Presbyterians. While differing over which theological beliefs most closely conformed to biblical teachings, and how best to organize their churches, all spoke the language of Canaan. Rather than a distinctive form of speech, the phrase was a metaphor evoking the new awareness into which believers were initiated by undergoing repentance and rebirth. For some, conversion transpired slowly, stealing over them as the winter of spiritual despair waned almost imperceptibly and the tender shoots of faith sprouted; upon others it burst like a sudden summer, forcing a luxuriant bloom of assurance in their barren souls. The places in which those epiphanies occurred—under a "lonesome, hanging rock" or on a "beautiful white sandbank"—became sacred to the individuals affected, sites that they visited for decades afterward. Sometimes entire neighborhoods of devout souls revered as consecrated ground, as the "very gates of heaven," the simple settings of outdoor "camp meetings," clearings ringed by trees where the words of preachers had struck home to many hearts. But if individuals experienced the progress toward salvation as a solitary process, its results made them conversant with others who, by their own singular pilgrimages, had also come to learn the common language of Canaan.[3]

So powerful were those experiences that the faithful believed they could be communicated even among those who did not share the same native language. They attested that men and women who spoke only broken English—immigrants recently arrived from Germany and slaves lately brought from Africa—sometimes found faith after listening to sermons preached in English. By that same alchemy, a future evangelical preacher claimed to have found solace in his spiritual agony from a German immigrant "who had experienced religion," and "understanding fully my condition, had me carried to his house," where he prayed over him in a medley of English and "Dutch." So transcendent, too, was the force of Canaan's language that even those who had literally no tongue to speak nor ears to hear could somehow convey its accents. Among them was a man, "always deaf and dumb," who, as another preacher witnessed, "by signs, will give a good experience of grace, both of his conviction, conversion, and his progress in the service of the Lord."[4]

But Canaan's language did not pass as the lingua franca among most of Mary MacDonald's contemporaries in the South. For all the barriers that it surmounted, many men and women regarded those captivated by its cadences as speaking in an incomprehensible tongue. To such people, as one evangelical expressed it, "conversion and the work of grace in the soul appears . . . a strange work, and the language of Canaan as foreign as if it was Hottentot or Chinese." It is impossible to gauge how many among them were hostile to evangelicalism, how many wary, how many merely indifferent. But, taken together, they comprised a majority of southerners well into the nineteenth century.

It is almost as impossible to know precisely how many souls evangelicals claimed. But by the most generous estimate, less than one-fifth of all southern whites over the age of sixteen and fewer than one-tenth of all African Americans had joined Baptist, Methodist, or Presbyterian churches by the 1810s. There were, of course, many more southerners of both races who attended evangelical worship but stopped short of seeking church membership. Yet even taking them into account, those who regularly sought out evangelical preaching probably did not exceed half of the South's white adult population until the 1830s. More impressionistic evidence from the letters and diaries of both the clergy and lay people suggests that those estimates may even overstate the extent of evangelical influence. In other words, almost a century elapsed between the 1740s, when evangelicals started actively proselytizing in the South, and the middle of the nineteenth century, when they may have won the attention, if not the allegiance, of a majority of southern whites. Among blacks, acceptance came more slowly still, and only with the emergence of a distinctive Afro-Christianity, a fusion of evangelical teachings and surviving elements of West African religious traditions.

The surprise, of course, is that evangelicals struggled for many decades to prosper among whites in the South. So long has this region been regarded as the cultural hearth of evangelicalism in the present-day United States that it takes some doing to imagine a past that was radically different, a time when a diverse, contentious spiritual culture seemed unlikely ever to become the "Bible Belt," let alone its proudly proclaimed "buckle." But much of what follows is an effort at doing just that—recovering a world marooned from living memory in which evangelicals, far from dominating the South, were viewed by most whites as odd at best and subversive at worst. As for the rest of the story told here, it focuses on how evangelicals, most of them members of Mary MacDonald's generation, wrestled to change those perceptions.

Evangelicals approached this challenge with an overwhelming sense of urgency, in large part because they felt beset by enemies on all sides. Even if that had not been the case, the evangelical temperament might have made it seem so; but, as it happened, circumstances in the early South justified their feeling of being an embattled minority. In her efforts to set her own children on the way of the cross, Mary MacDonald waged a fierce struggle against one of those influences hostile to her faith, the enlightened learning that attracted her bookish elder daughter, Maria. Despite two brushes with death, Maria persisted in an "obstinate careless temper," trusting more to the sages of ancient Athens and Rome than to the messiah from Nazareth. "Were you to spend as much time in studying the character of your Redeemer, as you do in studying virtuous characters among pagans and heathens," Mary chided, "you would find it more to your account, though you were denounced as fool by the worldly-wise." But she was determined that "your disobedience ought not to prevent my doing my duty," and spelled out in no uncertain terms the choice before her daughter: "the Bible tells us there are two characters, the righteous and the wicked—there is no alternative—to one or the other you must belong." Here is the starkly dualistic cast of mind so typical of evangelicals: Men and women whose search for transcendent meaning diverged from their own, strangers to "that change without which you can never enter the kingdom of God," were, in MacDonald's eyes, "enemies to God." "You must meet them," she warned Maria, "as devils and damned spirits."[5]

Such demons assumed many forms in the early South, but few more beguiling than that of Thomas Jefferson. Nothing could have been more contrary to his private convictions than evangelical religiosity—its prizing of feeling more than intellect, its veneration of biblical revelation as a truth higher than reason. A deist for much of his life, a Unitarian during his later years, and an arch-rationalist always, Jefferson held that the head rather than the heart should dictate an individual's beliefs. He dismissed the Bible as a collection of myths and derided the notion of a trinity as "Abracadabra." Jesus was a mere mortal, albeit one whom Jefferson came to regard as a moralist superior to any other of antiquity's sages, pagan or Jewish. As for eternal outcomes, he gave the matter little thought, but once speculated that each person's fate would be decided by whether their life had benefited humanity, not whether they believed in a divine Christ. Had he been inclined to dwelling on death rather than life, to defining instead of deploring formal religious creeds, Jefferson remarked, "my fundamental principle would be . . . that we are to be saved by our good works, which are within our power, and not by our faith, which is not in our power." Here was a judgment repugnant to evangelicals, but wholly in keeping with Jefferson's confidence in mankind's innate "moral sense," the ethical compass implanted in each individual heart by a benevolent deity. It followed that he nurtured the youthful souls within his family circle in ways that departed sharply from those of Mary MacDonald. The venturesome curiosity that so alarmed her in Maria was the very trait that Jefferson encouraged in his daughters, as well as his nephew, Peter Carr. "Fix reason firmly in her seat," he urged that young man, "and call to her tribunal every fact, every opinion," even unto questioning "with boldness . . . the existence of a god." Contemptuous of playing upon youthful fears of death or emotional estrangement to compel conformity to any particular point of view, he also called upon Peter to approach religious inquiry with dignified courage, because if a God existed "he must more approve the homage of reason, than that of blindfolded fear."[6]

Dangerous as they were, clever devils like Jefferson made up only a small minority of southerners even by the opening of the nineteenth century. It was not those who, placing their confidence in the powers of enlightened human reason, posed the chief threat to the progress of evangelical churches. For all the vehemence with which evangelicals denounced such "infidels," they recognized that the greater obstacle to their success lay less in a minority committed to expanding the mind's scope than a majority committed to enjoying the body's delights. Incarnate demons of this sort—"worldlings," as they were known among those who most certainly were not—were men and women who shunned evangelical inwardness and asceticism as morbid seriousness.

The largest number of southern churchgoers in that group were Anglicans, members of the colonial Church of England who later came to be called Episcopalians. Their religious training schooled them in the essential doctrines of Christianity—the divinity of Jesus, the authority of the Bible, the promise of life after death. Their sense of what it meant to be truly religious, like Jefferson's, emphasized the importance of men and women leading upright lives by exercising reason and learning self-restraint, but permitted pursuing many customary pleasures—indulging in the thrill of a hunt, the sociability of a tavern, the lure of a fiddle. Indeed, they were mystified that anyone would choose to live otherwise: In the 1760s, when the newly converted evangelical Devereux Jarratt refused to drink and dance with his Anglican kin and neighbors, "they allowed that all people ought to be better than they were—but they thought I had overshot the mark and carried matters quite too far." "We all ought to be good," his friends allowed, "but surely there can be no harm in *innocent mirth*, such as dancing, drinking, and making merry." More than thirty years later, the same sentiments were voiced by one Mr. Hooks, "a Church Man [Anglican] very Morral," who shrugged off the scolding of William Ormond, a Methodist preacher, by insisting that "it was a pleasure to him to see his daughters dance."[7]

Just as jolly and far more numerous than Anglicans were those southern "worldlings" who did not worship regularly with any church. Such men and women could be found everywhere in the South, but they may have been most numerous in areas newly settled by whites as migrants filtered into its vast western country—the western parts of Virginia and the Carolinas before the American Revolution, Kentucky and Georgia in the years preceding 1800, and, during the opening decades of the nineteenth century, Tennessee, Alabama, Mississippi, and Missouri, as

well as the southern parts of Ohio, Indiana, and Illinois. Much to the chagrin of Wilson Thompson, a Baptist minister in a raw southern Missouri
community in the 1810s, most of his neighbors convened on Sundays not
at the local church where he preached but instead at "Hubbe's mill." In
this popular "place of assembly," his neighbors observed the Sabbath by
"hunting, sporting, and shooting at marks, horse-racing, jumping and
foot-racing." A good deal of drinking took place as well, so that by late
afternoon, the festivities got even rowdier, "some fighting, some swearing,
and some playing tricks, such as knocking off each other's hats, and cut-
ting bridles and saddles." A few years later, an English Quaker visiting the
southern Indiana frontier observed that Christmas Day "was spent by one
set of the *religionists* in hearing a sermon and prayers which lasted from
breakfast till nightfall," while "another set of people . . . [was] busy in
cooking wild turkeys, and dancing in the evening," festivities presaged by
"young men [who] had their rifles out, and were firing *feux de joi[e]* all the
preceding evening."[8]

So it could be said that evangelicals faced their most formidable challenge not in the few southerners like Jefferson who wanted children to
think, but rather in the many who wanted them to dance. Their ranks
included both some who belonged to nonevangelical churches like the
Anglicans and a much larger group who had only the most tenuous ties to
organized Christianity and preferred it that way. Moreover, as late as 1822,
Jefferson sanguinely predicted that the future would go his way—that
most southerners, led by their boldly inquiring young men, would come
around to his own religious views and embrace Unitarianism. In his hopes
lay Mary MacDonald's fears, that her children's generation, enchanted by
enlightened learning, would embrace the delusions of Unitarianism, or,
lured by the dance, descend into even grosser forms of worldliness and
infidelity. But it is only hindsight that makes Jefferson's confidence seem
so farfetched and MacDonald's concerns so laughable. For when he
effused and she fretted, it was anything but certain that Canaan's language
would come to be so widely spoken in the South. How that happened
remains a matter to be explained.[9]

To UNDERSTAND that remarkable transformation, it is best to go back
to the beginning. Evangelicalism came late to the American South, as an
exotic import rather than an indigenous development. Its distinctive religious ethos dated back to the Reformation and strongly imbued the sensi-

bility of many early Protestant groups—the Puritan reformers of England and Continental pietists like the Moravians of Bohemia. Colonists carried the evangelical tradition to British North America during the seventeenth century, particularly to New England and the Mid-Atlantic, where it gained renewed strength through a series of religious revivals in the 1730s and 1740s known as the First Great Awakening. That wave of revivalism also swept Protestant Europe, where it swelled the numbers of German pietist sects, lent an evangelical cast to many Presbyterian churches in Scotland and northern Ireland, and inspired the Methodist movement to reform the Church of England. It was nothing less than a new age of faith arising to counter an age of reason.[10]

But before the 1740s, little of this religious ferment affected the South. There the Church of England had been trying to strengthen its influence since the first decades of white settlement, a time when the rigors of this life fixed the minds of most people on the next but gave few the luxury of making elaborate arrangements to prepare for it. It was only during the latter half of the seventeenth century that Anglican efforts finally yielded a growing number of churches, clergy, and congregants, mainly in the Chesapeake colonies of Virginia and Maryland. Even so, every southern colony hosted a variety of religious groups. There were tiny enclaves of Jews in South Carolina, Georgia, and Maryland, which also claimed a small Roman Catholic population. Larger numbers of nonevangelical Protestants like German Lutherans and English Quakers settled from Delaware to Georgia, as well as some Presbyterians and Baptists. Anglicans ultimately secured the advantage of being the established church in every southern colony, but they commanded the loyalties of most churchgoers only in the Chesapeake. In short, for most of the colonial period the South was a mosaic of religious groups, with Anglicans enjoying the strength of numbers in the upper South and the edge of state support everywhere.

That situation changed dramatically as a result of two developments in the middle of the eighteenth century. First, settlers began to spill south and west of Pennsylvania, pushing into the Shenandoah Valley of Virginia during the 1740s, into the backcountry of the Carolinas and Georgia during the 1750s and 1760s, and later into adjacent Kentucky and Tennessee. These newcomers came mainly from the ranks of Scots-Irish Presbyterians and German pietists like the Moravians, Dunkers, Mennonites, and Schwenkfelders. In addition, the recent evangelical revivals in the northern colonies and Britain inspired some converts to become missionaries to the American South. In the late 1740s, Presbyterian preachers from New York and New Jersey began proselytizing in the Virginia Piedmont; by the 1750s, a group known as the Separate Baptists moved from New England to central North Carolina and quickly extended their influence to surrounding colonies; and in the late 1760s, the first English Methodist missionaries began preaching in Delaware, Maryland, and Virginia. All of those migrants and missionaries carried into the South the conviction that spiritual rebirth was essential to salvation, and the most militant among them, the Baptists and Methodists, aimed at nothing less than teaching all southerners the language of Canaan.[11]

That would require, of course, convincing lay people that no other path could lead to salvation—especially not the one plotted by their only formidable competitor for souls, the Church of England. Compared to evangelicals, Anglicans made less stringent demands on the inner resources of individuals: belonging to the Church of England did not require testifying to a conversion experience or submitting to an ascetic discipline. Nor was any premium placed on strict doctrinal conformity, for Anglicans had little taste for dogmatism and tolerated differences of opinion on many points of theology. Instead, their clergy encouraged a temperate, practical piety among the laity through liturgical observance and moral admonition. Many southern whites found spiritual satisfaction in hearing intoned the familiar, stately cadences of the Book of Common Prayer, the basis of Anglican worship, and, in some larger churches, savoring the sublime music of choirs and organs. They took consolation from carefully crafted sermons emphasizing the reasonableness of Christianity, the benevolence of God, and the moral capacity of humankind. And they drew assurance from frequent allusions to the divine origin of a social hierarchy that set rich over poor, men over women, and white over black.[12]

It became the goal of evangelicals, then, to persuade both the Anglican faithful and the unchurched that resting content in this kind of Christianity entailed a dangerous complacency. They derided the Anglican emphasis on ceremonialism as an empty outward show and condemned that church's elaborate rituals, holy day observances, and set prayers as "popish" relics. Charles Woodmason, one of the few Anglican missionaries in the early southern backcountry, complained that on Christmas Day in 1766 Presbyterian leaders in one frontier South Carolina settlement refused him use of the common meetinghouse to conduct the

Anglican liturgy, which they referred to as "the Mass." His attempts to celebrate All Saints' Day and Good Friday met with similar charges that such practices "savour'd of Popery," and that he was a "Romish Priest in disguise." That was bad enough, but what brought out the worst in the Presbyterians, in Woodmason's view, was his effort to celebrate the Anglican rite of communion. After one service, Presbyterians broke into the chapel and smeared the communion table with excrement.

Anglican parsons came in for equally undignified treatment. Evangelicals offered caustic commentaries on their sermons, which they dismissed as spiritless moral homilies, and even more acerbic appraisals of their private character. By their lights, all Anglican clergymen were fox-hunting, whist-playing, Madeira-tippling, money-grubbing wastrels who failed to impose a stricter morality on the laity because their own lives would not bear looking into. In a typical dismissal, William Watters, a Methodist preacher, recalled the two parsons of his Anglican boyhood in Maryland as "immoral men" with "no gifts for the ministry; if they *received* their salary they appeared to think little about the souls of the people. . . . [I]t was the mere mercy of God that we did not all fall into hell together."

Such judgments, of course, were anything but dispassionate or disinterested. It is true that the best and brightest young Anglican divines did not rank a career in the American colonies as the summit of their aspirations, so the South became the last resort for some clergymen of indifferent talents. But charges that those parsons combined the worst traits of Falstaff and Polonius reflect mostly the evangelicals' rigid measure of what it meant to be religious rather than the realities of clerical leadership in southern parishes. So to Richard Dozier, a Virginia Baptist layman, the local parson's failure to insist on the necessity of rebirth became evidence of his tepid piety, and the same luckless fellow's opinion that "fiddling and dancing were not criminal so that it was not carried to excess" convicted him of gross moral laxity. Yet such strictures show only that Anglicans did not share with evangelicals the same religious sensibility or ascetic moral code, not that the general run of their clergy lacked either fervor or rectitude.[13]

Beyond trying to discredit Anglicanism as a religious option, early evangelicals trained their preachers' energies on backcountry districts, where the colonial Church of England was weakest and the greatest number of people were unchurched. Rather than drinking to excess or dallying unto scandal, the besetting sin of the Anglican clergy was the lackluster vice of sloth, which caused them to neglect the needs of men and women in those remote areas. In their indifference to concerns of western settlers they mirrored the attitude of the coastal gentry, the ruling group with whom they identified and whose dominant position they defended. There were a handful of Anglican ministers in the South like Charles Woodmason, who condemned the "Inattention and Indolence" that kept most of their colleagues from venturing into the backcountry, but such criticisms shamed few into forsaking their snug parsonages along the coast. Meanwhile evangelicals, most notably the Baptists and Methodists, were raising up young clergymen who became the shock troops of their churches, a vast cadre of itinerant preachers intent on recruiting souls in every community, no matter how distant.[14]

The success of such efforts seems to be confirmed by the sheer numbers of new evangelical churches formed before the American Revolution. By 1776, their members outnumbered Anglican communicants in every southern colony. It was not that the Church of England had failed to expand—they established more than one hundred new congregations in the South between 1750 and 1776. Yet evangelicals enjoyed even more vigorous rates of growth, with the Presbyterians and the Baptists each founding about two hundred new churches over the same period. In addition, an entirely new group, the Methodists, who had begun to proselytize in the South only a few years before the Revolution, established thirty-eight congregations by 1776, most in Maryland and Virginia. Even so, impressive as those gains appear, evangelicals had cause only for cautious optimism. At most their membership included just 10 percent of the adult white southern population in 1776, and only a negligible percentage of African Americans. More important, the largest single group of evangelicals in the South on the eve of the Revolution was the Presbyterians, which suggests that what swelled evangelical ranks was the flood of Scots-Irish migration into the region rather than an influx of native-born southerners into their churches.[15]

OVER THE SAME decades, evangelicals had recognized as much, taking their first measure of the challenge before them. Among the obstacles they faced were lay loyalties to Anglicanism, which stubbornly persisted even in the face of evangelical pillorying. Indeed, evangelicals enjoyed little or no success before 1776 in those areas where the Church of England was strongly entrenched. Most telling on this point are the recollections of

Devereux Jarratt, a member of Virginia's Anglican clergy, but one of the few who welcomed the first Methodist reformers springing up in their midst. As an evangelical partisan, Jarratt painted a damning portrait of his church's failure to meet the spiritual needs of the laity. Yet even he admitted that the local Anglican church of his youth in the 1750s drew "a great many people" every Sabbath, despite being served by a parson who habitually mumbled from a prepared text and, being nearsighted, always appeared to be addressing the pulpit instead of the congregation. That lay commitment endured in the face of such discouragements Jarratt attributed to the narrow-minded prejudice which he saw embodied in an Anglican couple of his acquaintance, Jacob Moon and his wife. According to Jarratt, when told of his conversion, they laughed off his sudden fondness for *"new light cant,"* and insisted that, "being *Church people* [Anglicans], . . . they . . . could listen to nothing but what came through that channel." But in fact, the Moons' attachment to the Church of England involved much more than unquestioning assent to familiar forms of religious authority, for it was in their household that Jarratt first came across the sermons of George Whitefield, one of the founders of Methodism and a model for him later in life. Evidently the Moons had explored their religious options and decided to hold fast to their Anglican faith. To be sure, some lay people stayed within the fold from family tradition or sheer inertia. But there were plenty of other ordinary southerners who, like the Moons, adhered to the Church of England because its religious teachings, no matter how soporifically droned from the pulpit, met their standards of what it meant to be a good Christian.[16]

Those standards could be strict. Ironically, the most reliable testimony to Anglican rigor issues from those men who became the South's leading evangelicals during the latter half of the eighteenth century. Many ministers, especially among the Methodists but also among the Baptists and the Presbyterians, a generation that came of age immediately before the Revolution, were raised by Anglican parents. True, their private journals and published memoirs abound with sweeping assertions that in the South of their youth, "Religion . . . appeared to be universally neglected," and "It was almost a miracle to find a man of real piety." But the force of such generalizations is undercut by their recollections of the devotional regimen of Anglican mothers, the stern rectitude of Anglican fathers, and the common parental practices of teaching young Anglican children to read with the Bible as their primer, drilling them in the catechism, and stocking their households with books of sermons and other religious treatises. Some Anglican families attended Sabbath worship so regularly that one future Methodist recalled being able from a tender age to "repeat much of the morning service by heart." And if Anglican parents indulged and even encouraged their children's desires to dance and play musical instruments, they meted out severe punishments for swearing, gossiping, and lying.[17]

But it was not only the satisfactions that many southerners drew from Anglicanism that balked the ambitions of pre-Revolutionary evangelicals. An even more daunting obstacle was the view, widely shared by both the humble and the great, that some of these insurgent churches undermined the stability and unity of southern communities by challenging the hierarchies of class and slavery that properly kept people apart, while preaching against the customary pleasures that occasionally brought people together. In those matters not all evangelicals were held to be equally guilty, and least among them the Presbyterians. Most of their clergy were, from the outset, as conspicuous for their tact in dealing with the Anglican gentry as they were forbearing on the issue of slavery. And while they urged upon their members a code of conduct that allowed for less latitude than that prevailing in Anglican circles, they could almost pass as bon vivants compared to the Baptists and Methodists. Perhaps most important, even during the pre-Revolutionary period, Presbyterians largely restricted their ministries to Scots-Irish settlements, focusing their efforts on maintaining the faith of migrating families and converting the children of the faithful. The same could not be said of early Baptists and Methodists, who proselytized so widely as to make it common knowledge that they were guilty on all counts of fomenting division within southern neighborhoods.[18]

Consider the crisis that engulfed one Virginia community in 1771 after John Dupuy's curiosity led him to the prison where two Separate Baptist itinerants, William Webber and Joseph Anthony, had been jailed for disturbing the peace. Whatever he saw or heard at the prison prompted Dupuy to ask his sister's husband, John James Trabue, to open his home to the preaching of a third Baptist itinerant, John Waller. Trabue refused, his opinion being that the Separates were "false teachers," and that "we ought not to be Dreven [driven] about with every wind of Doctrain [doctrine]," especially since "we had a good establishment and a good parson and all at peace." Allowing the Separates to preach, in Trabue's view,

would only "give offense" to the Anglican church and Colonel Archibald
Cary, one of the county's leading gentlemen and the justice of the peace
who had ordered the imprisonment of Webber and Anthony. But the
pleas of Dupuy along with pressure from some of his neighbors finally
persuaded Trabue to compromise: He agreed to allow Waller into his
home to sing hymns, pray, and give his views on the Bible—while seated
in a chair. Under no circumstances was the itinerant to stand and expound a biblical text, for that would be accounted unlicensed "preaching," a violation of colony law. (Like most Separate Baptist ministers,
Waller refused to apply for a license to preach, claiming that his certifica-
tion came from an authority considerably more august than the colony
government.)

Despite these precautions, Trabue's worst fears were realized within a
matter of months as religious contention engulfed his Piedmont community. Baptist itinerants came flocking, drawn there not only by the hospitality of his wife, Magdalen, who made their household a center for their
proselytizing, but, perhaps more important, by the inhospitable ways of
Colonel Cary, who, at least in his dealings with the Baptists, epitomized
the dim-witted Anglican squire. When the Baptists appeared, Cary tried
to stop their preaching by threatening them with prison; to his chagrin,
they seized the chance for a few months of martyrdom. Nor did imprisonment silence the itinerants: they preached through the bars, and when
Cary, in desperation, built a brick wall around the jail, they shouted louder.
All in all, the Baptists could not have invented an opponent more accommodating than Colonel Cary or a stage more admirably suited to drama-
tize their endurance and determination. For that spectacle alone, "great
congregations flocked to hear them."[19]

Gentlemen like Colonel Cary had many reasons for despising evangelicals like the Separate Baptists. Magistrates who tried to restrain their
ministry met with stark defiance and rank insolence. Elsewhere in Virginia, when another gentleman, one Colonel Harwood, ordered John
Leland to desist in mid-sermon, that Baptist itinerant "gave a heavy stamp
on the floor and told him in the name of God to forbear . . . [making] no
more of [him] than if [he] had been a dog." Such open shows of disrespect to gentry authority would not do at all. But it was the subtler forms
of disregard from evangelicals that proved harder to bear. When Baptist
preachers won adherents and formed churches, the converts drew themselves off from those gatherings where the most affluent and powerful

families customarily impressed upon their lesser neighbors those attributes that made them the rightful rulers of society. On Sabbath mornings,
when the sumptuously dressed gentlefolk seated themselves in the front
pews of Anglican chapels, evangelicals were not present to witness the
spectacle, but were observing the Lord's day among themselves. Neither
could evangelicals be found dancing at balls held in the great houses or
drinking there after militia musters or otherwise enjoying the gentry's
hospitality. Nor did they frequent horse races and cockfights, where
gentlemen proved that blood told even among their animals. Evangelicals
scorned all of those pastimes, thus sounding a silent reproach to all those
proud displays by which the great buttressed their authority. There were
louder reproaches, too: those ringing denunciations of slavery, the very
basis of gentry domination, that issued from the mouths of some early
Baptist and Methodist preachers.[20]

OBNOXIOUS AS Baptists and Methodists were to many members of the
Anglican gentry, many white southerners of lesser means liked these religious upstarts no better. Among them were the aforementioned John
James Trabue—a planter of middling means descended from French
Huguenot refugees—and most of his neighbors. As Trabue's son Daniel
recalled, the Separates "weare [were] held in contempt by most of the
people." Nor was it only members of the gentry or Anglican clergymen
who violently opposed early evangelicals: After the Baptist preacher James
Ireland was arrested in Culpepper County, Virginia, a "considerable
parade of people" followed him to the jail, shouting "such vollies of oaths
and abuse as if I were a being unfit to exist on the earth." When he
attempted to preach from his prison cell, gangs of mounted men galloped
through the crowds around the jail, shaking clubs over their heads and
whipping any blacks in attendance. Everywhere in Virginia east of the
Blue Ridge Mountains, Ireland concluded, the harassment of the Baptists,
although sometimes instigated by Anglican ministers, "received the hearty
concurrence of their parishioners." Devereux Jarratt agreed, noting the
"general prejudice" of Virginians "against dissenters, and in favor of the
[Anglican] church."[21]

Part of what inspired that antipathy in ordinary people was their
concern for preserving harmonious relations with the gentry. It was for
good cause that men like John James Trabue believed that "Their [There]
was a wo[e] prounanced [pronounced] against them" who disrupted the

peace of a county by challenging the authority of gentlemen like Colonel Cary. Middling planters like Trabue and men who ranked below him may have deferred to their betters more from necessity than admiration, but they recognized that no good could come from giving them "offense." Gentlemen dealt out the fate of lesser mortals in their varied roles as magistrates who judged cases of petty crime and debt, as merchants who marketed the crops of yeoman and tenant farmers and supplied them with British manufactured goods, as creditors who could extend loans for years, and as neighborhood patriarchs who often supplied food, medical assistance, and employment to needy households. Yet even when livelihoods were not at stake, many southern whites objected to trespasses against the deference due to men of rank and learning. James Ireland discovered as much when he tried to debate a Shenandoah Valley parson, only to find that many people were outraged by the "presumption in such a youth as I, to enter into an argument with the teacher of the county." Whenever Ireland seemed to have scored some telling point against his adversary, Anglicans in the audience interrupted to assist their parson with some passage from the Bible to confute the uppity Baptist.[22]

But it was more than their impulse to honor or conciliate the better sort that made many ordinary southerners so wary of evangelicals. Indeed, what many feared more deeply were the ways in which evangelical moral codes and ritual practices estranged their converts from the community of their peers, neighborhood networks of yeoman and tenant farming families. Evangelicals drew people away from the familiar settings of sociability in rural counties—horse races and taverns, barbecues and balls. They taught their adherents to regard drinking and joking, gambling and dancing, fiddling and cockfighting not as innocent amusements that made strangers into neighbors but as sinful frivolities that set men and women on the path to hell. Those who embraced that ascetic discipline avoided the company of those who had not, and, after a while, their censoriousness caused their friends and neighbors to shun them. After joining the Baptists, James Ireland noticed that some of his "old companions in vanity" deliberately avoided meeting him "under the apprehension that they would be subjected to admonition or reproof." An understandable reaction, for, as he added, "I rarely suffered any of them to pass without one or the other." Even those drawn to evangelicals voiced some uneasiness, like the young Marylander Ezekiel Cooper, who, when he began worshipping with the Methodists, "felt strangely, and . . . almost afraid to speak or do any thing lest they should see cause to reprove me for wrong-doing." But the memory of such feelings did not stop Cooper, once he joined their church, from displaying so much "earnestness . . . that it was seldom that any of my acquaintances would sin within my sight or hearing." Converts even altered their appearance in ways that dramatized their singularity. They shed "all ruffles, bows, rings, and feathers," adornments once prized but now despised as worldly vanities. Pious women hitched up bodices to conceal their cleavages; men cut their long hair.[23]

As the paths of evangelicals diverged from those of their neighbors and friends, friction often resulted. Those tensions surface in the recollections of Mary Avery Browder, who was persuaded by Devereux Jarratt's ministry "to pray and leave off many things which I formerly thought innocent amusements." When her sisters and a woman "who had been as a Mother to me" discovered her new religious seriousness, their anxious defense was to tease, wanting "to know if I was Jarratifyed." Young Mary, "who could not bear to be slighted by them," temporarily abandoned her Methodist convictions. Similarly, John Brooks recalled that the introduction of Methodism to his corner of rural Georgia divided the entire community. Before the Methodists made their influence felt, he observed, "the young people . . . went to frolics and danced" and participated in games "connected with all our corn shuckings, log rollings, and harvestings." But when the new converts "quit all those plays and frolics and spoke against them as sinful . . . they were laughed at and opposed by all." Sometimes, too, differences over religion provoked violence. One Virginian, outraged when his son-in-law invited Baptists to preach at the family plantation on Christmas Day in the 1770s, "roused perhaps twenty rugged young fellows, a number of whom came armed with instruments of death, to drive all before them." Once fists started flying, the preachers beat a judicious retreat, whereupon the assembled crowd turned the meeting "into a great Christmas frolic."[24]

Southern whites recognized in evangelicalism a stark alternative to the region's traditional culture based on conviviality and competition. Baptists and Methodists modeled their churches on the primitive Christian communities of the New Testament, fellowships knit together by emotional intimacy and spiritual equality, godly discipline and self-abasement. They were meant to be refuges from what evangelicals regarded as a false and harsh world dominated by materialism, rivalry, and aggression. They believed that their communions would lead ordinary people toward lives of greater security and satisfaction by providing them with emotional support, moral guidance, and peaceful ways of settling personal differences. Encouraged by like-minded Christians, converts would learn to supplant excess with simplicity and to prize self-denial above self-assertion. But while that promise of putting personal fulfillment and social order on a radically new foundation beckoned some southern whites, it left many more unmoved. Attachment to familiar pleasures and forms of sociability settled the views of some men and women, but what shaped the reservations of others was not sheer hedonism or reflexive conservatism. It was rather that they doubted whether evangelical churches could promote local unity and fellow feeling more effectively than impromptu neighborhood gatherings to dance and drink, joke and carouse.[25]

Such misgivings drew added strength from Baptist and Methodist ritual practices, which were not only alien but exclusionary. The defining ritual of the Baptists—full-immersion baptisms of adult believers—drew the most notice from those outside their communion, responses ranging from curiosity to fear. The mass baptisms that followed revivals afforded a truly riveting spectacle: new converts, men in the lead, lined the river's edge, solemnly awaiting the minister, who laid his hand on the head of each individual and prayed aloud for each person, "according to . . . age and circumstance." Then came the culminating moment when, after the converts waded into the river, they were tilted backward and briefly submerged by preachers. It was that ritual climax, commonly known as "being dipped," the sight of a "watery grave" closing over the faces of believers before they resurfaced, sputtering but reborn, that inspired the greatest fascination and horror among non-Baptists. Before William Hickman and his neighbors in tidewater Virginia learned anything else about the Baptists, they knew that "they would take people and dip them all over in water!" That news warned off another Virginian, John Goode, who had been advised by an Anglican neighbor to "take care of the Baptists, for . . . they will not rest till they dip you." Even men and women who were drawn to the Baptist faith singled out that initiation as the greatest obstacle to their joining the church. Some dispelled their reluctance by searching the Bible for passages confirming the deity's preference for believers submitting to being completely soaked rather than merely "sprinkled." Others never overcame the sense of ritual danger shrouding the ceremony, heightened by the fact that, in some cases, converts christened in infancy were to be rebaptized. No doubt those worries moved

Abram Clark of western Virginia to warn the Baptist preacher John Taylor, "I love your preaching, but you shall never dip me."[26]

Many other rituals practiced within the circle of early Baptists, especially some Separate Baptist churches, struck nonbelievers as bizarre and intimidating. There were gatherings of the faithful presided over by ministers, for the "taking of experience," during which men and women recounted their conversions. To an Anglican observer like Charles Woodmason, such performances were "ludicrous"—and when accompanied, as they sometimes were, by accounts of visions and revelations, downright "blasphemous." He blasted the credulity of Baptist ministers, themselves "a sett of Mongrels," "hearing all this Nonsense for Hours together, and making particular Enquiries, when, How and Where, in what Manner, these Miraculous Events happened . . . a String of Vile, cook'd up, Silly and Senseless Lyes." There were also ceremonies within pious Baptist households known as the "devoting of children" in which ministers laid their hands on the heads of all young people, black and white, from infancy to adolescence, and prayed for them by name—"a dry christening," as non-Baptists joked. In those rituals and others within Baptist churches, the constant was physical contact that sometimes crossed the lines of gender and race—whenever they met, members exchanged "the right hand of fellowship" or the "kiss of charity," and on special occasions washed each other's feet, anointed the sick, and ordained ministers by the "laying on of hands." Many southerners outside the fold concluded that Baptist men and women touched one another entirely too often, and their frequent resort to ribald innuendo about supposed evangelical licentiousness signaled that discomfort.[27]

The ritual emphasis of the Methodists fell less on touching than on talking, but their practices were no less unsettling to outsiders. Like the Baptists, the Methodists administered baptism and the Lord's Supper, although their clergy baptized only children and unchristened adults and always with a minimum of ceremony—by dipping or sprinkling depending on individual preference. The only other practice shared by both churches entailed the public recounting of religious experiences at gatherings that the Methodists called "love feasts." Admission to those meetings was usually restricted to members, because, as the Virginia preacher Jesse Lee explained, "it was thought improper to have many people among us where we were speaking of our experiences and the deep things of God." The same secrecy shrouded "class meetings," the most novel feature of Methodist ritual and the center of their devotional life. A Methodist church might contain any number of "classes" segregated by sex, race, age, and marital status, each consisting of about a dozen members who met often to confide their spiritual trials and triumphs. At the very least, the exclusivity of both class meetings and love feasts stirred speculation among southerners outside the circle of church members. One Tennessee man confessed to spying on a love feast by gaining access to a loft through the roof, because "My curiosity was up to the highest pitch to know what they were doing in there." But in many others, such mysterious goings-on bred suspicion and resentment. As early as 1772, the Methodist itinerant Joseph Pilmore admitted that many "are apt to speak many disrespectful things of our *private meetings*," while as late as the 1800s, John Brooks noted that "The shutting of doors in class-meetings and love-feasts, and turning all others out . . . gave great offense to all and was much spoken against."[28]

FOR THOSE REASONS alone, early evangelicals met with resistance from white southern colonials of every class. But then, most unexpectedly and, by evangelical lights, providentially, the American colonies declared their independence from the British Empire. After 1776, most Anglican clergymen fled the newly proclaimed republic for England, leaving most of the lay faithful without ministers to conduct public worship or administer the sacraments. In the ensuing decade, every southern state dismantled its Anglican establishment; the Church of England not only lost its legal and financial privileges but also bore the stigma of being linked with the spurned and defeated parent country. Although Anglicanism survived, resuscitated in 1789 as the Protestant Episcopal Church, it never regained anything approaching its former strength in the South. Thus did the twist of fate that brought victory to American rebels dispatch the only serious rival to evangelicals in the South. No longer were Anglicans in any position to compete for the religious loyalties of unchurched southerners—indeed, they were hard-pressed to hold their own parishioners, perhaps as many as 146,000 men, women, and children. Bereft of a clergy and desperate for any Christian ministry, many fell back on evangelical churches as their only option. While Presbyterians and Baptists prospered from that windfall, the Methodists, still nominally a reform movement within the Church of England, were ideally positioned to scavenge stranded Anglicans. Even after 1784, when American Methodists formally became a

distinct denomination, the Methodist Episcopal Church, the old identification with Anglicanism lingered in the minds of the laity and continued
to assist their expansion. Such were the circumstances that spurred the
rise in evangelical church membership in the years after the Revolution:
By 1790, about 14 percent of southern whites and nearly 4 percent of
blacks belonged to Baptist, Methodist, or Presbyterian churches.[29]

But underlying that spurt of growth lurked something less gratifying to
evangelicals. Throughout the latter half of the eighteenth century, their
gains in the South had resulted in large part from Scots-Irish migration
before the Revolution and the demise of Anglicanism in the wake of independence. In other words, evangelicals had yet to show much strength
among the South's large unchurched population, white or black. Just how
much evangelical growth had hinged upon the shift of migration southward and the rupture with Britain is betrayed by their sluggish progress in
the quarter century after 1790, when, without strong competition from
any other churches, the combined membership of Baptists, Methodists,
and Presbyterians inched up to just 17 percent of the white population and
8 percent of the black. It was this uncertain state of affairs that lent so
sharp an edge to Mary MacDonald's fears for her children and so ebullient
a note to Jefferson's opinion that Unitarianism would triumph among his
countrymen within a generation. And, right up to the present, it poses a
puzzle: Why was it that evangelicals, although now vested with every
advantage, still struggled to claim the soul of the South?[30]

Warfare and migration may have impeded evangelical proselytizing.
During the American Revolution, vicious partisan strife between rebels
and loyalists seared the Carolina backcountry; in the 1790s, contests with
Native Americans kept the Ohio Valley frontier in turmoil; mobilization
for the War of 1812 briefly affected parts of both the western country and
the upper South. And in the same decades, the flow of southerners to
the frontier offered an added challenge, since places of worship often lay
miles from most settlers' homes, sometimes over terrain broken by
swollen rivers, dismal swamps, and dense forests. Under those circumstances, many southerners had little regular contact with organized Christianity of any kind, and some came to revel in being thus reprieved from
religious observance. Among them was one Abraham Pruitt, a migrant to
Kentucky, who shocked a visiting Presbyterian preacher by allowing that
"He be darned if he had said his prayers since he left old Carolina." On the
other hand, whatever disadvantages evangelicals faced due to the ravages

of war and the upheaval of migration may have been offset by the tendency of those disruptions to heighten lay needs for the consolation and community that joining a church could provide. Preachers everywhere in the backcountry remarked on the great numbers of people who, whenever the chance arose, flocked to sermons delivered by clergy of any faith. And by the end of the eighteenth century, both the Baptists and the Methodists had created an itinerant clergy whose far-flung travels allowed those churches to follow the drift of population into the western country.[31]

There were other circumstances, too, that should have yielded more impressive gains, particularly to the Baptists and Methodists. Those confrontations, so unsettling to some southern whites—evangelical preachers defying gentleman magistrates and debating Anglican parsons—ended with disestablishment and the advent of full religious toleration. Thereafter, the Baptist and Methodist clergy assiduously cultivated goodwill among the ruling gentry by affirming their support for the established hierarchy that awarded power and privilege to those with wealth and influence. While evangelicals surrendered none of their distaste for the high-stepping, hard-drinking, fancy-dressing ways of proud ladies and gentlemen, most ministers now approached the gentry by cajoling and conciliating rather than threatening and denouncing. And now, too, preachers boasted eagerly and often of attracting new members, willing listeners, and gracious hosts among the rich and respectable.[32]

That hope of wooing gentry support, along with pressure from many of the lay faithful in their own churches, also muted evangelical testimony against slavery. On this issue, the vanguard of opposition consisted mainly of clergymen who, even before the Revolution, sparred with laymen and -women who either owned or hoped to own slaves. By the 1780s, it was plain that the latter would have their way and that evangelical churches would shape their policies accordingly. Among the Baptists, although some preachers and even the occasional church denounced slavery, no decisive steps were ever taken to bar slaveholders from membership. The Methodists at first showed greater determination, but they did not maintain it. In 1784, the newly constituted Methodist Episcopal Church capped more than a decade of fiery antislavery preaching in America by passing a rigorous set of rules to purge its membership of slaveholders. But within a matter of months, a whirlwind of opposition, stirred up mainly by the southern laity, swept away all of the new restrictions except for one forbidding members to engage in buying or selling slaves with the intention of keeping them in bondage.[33]

Evidently such changes assured those southerners who had the greatest stake in the existing social order. During the last decades of the eighteenth century, ever-increasing numbers of gentlefolk and small slaveholders joined evangelical churches, and by the opening years of the nineteenth century, the membership of most fellowships probably represented a cross-section of white society. But although evangelicals succeeded in winning as much acceptance among the prosperous as among the poor, they were not able to command the loyalties of a majority among southern whites until well into the nineteenth century.[34]

Herein lay the hazard of evangelical fortunes. What long persisted as the primary obstacle to their success in the South was not that they were shunned by the better sort but that they were long held at arm's length by most of those less exalted. While it is true that early Baptists and Methodists drew mainly southern whites of no more than modest means, it is equally true that most people of that sort did not join evangelical churches. Nor did the misgivings of the many who stayed away arise only, or even mainly, from lingering fears that evangelicals might antagonize the gentry, embolden the slaves, and shatter the fragile solidarity among friends and neighbors. Other concerns, anxieties just as powerful and even more enduring, sustained lay resistance to evangelical teaching and practice for many decades.

The full scope and force of that opposition has long eluded detection, because there is so little direct testimony before the 1830s from any but the South's wealthiest men and women. Lacking the luxuries of time and, often, literacy, to say nothing of paper and ink, most of the common folk did not keep diaries; some painfully composed occasional letters to kinfolk, but little of that correspondence survives. The sole exceptions are the early evangelical clergy, a group drawn mainly from middling families of farmers and artisans: some Baptist preachers and many more Methodists kept journals in which they tirelessly chronicled their lives among the laity. While a surprisingly large number have found their way into archives, they do not yield easily to the reader. Most are weatherbeaten books no larger than the palm of a hand, their stained, brittle pages packed with daily entries scrawled in a tiny, cramped hand, a barely legible script blotted with phonetic spellings, idiosyncratic punctuation, and mystifying abbreviations. These serve to identify the authors as itinerant preachers, mainly young men, marginally literate and only recently raised from the ranks of the laity, usually scribbling in haste by candlelight before being claimed by fatigue. What they record is utterly mundane and completely absorbing: extraordinarily direct and detailed accounts of their encounters with white southerners sometimes devoted to but more often confused about, wary of, or outraged by evangelicalism. The voices of people silenced by obscurity in a world that has slipped far away from the present echo in every entry.

Taken together, what they tell is why southern whites of all classes so long kept their distance from evangelicals. Present, although not predominant, in those pages are disgruntled laymen and -women who complain of Baptist preachers insulting local grandees or Methodist ministers condemning slavery. But far more common are middle-aged farmers who storm that young Methodist preachers have disputed their authority over the household or turned the heads of their wives, and distraught matrons who fret that their newly pious daughters now shun unconverted kin, or that their once boisterous, swaggering sons have sunk into seeming madness from fear of hellfire and the devil. In sum, what held the center of lay concern, what aroused their sharpest fears, were the ways in which Baptists and Methodists struck at those hierarchies that lent stability to their daily lives: the deference of youth to age; the submission of children to parents and women to men; the loyalties of individuals to family and kin above any other group; and the rule of reserve over emotion within each person. Because Baptists and Methodists threatened the most fundamental ways in which ordinary people structured their neighborhoods, their households, and their very selves, these churches drew lay suspicion for nearly a century. Misgivings widely shared by southern whites focused on the prominence of young men and of women of every age in Baptist and Methodist churches, the prizing of religious fellowship over the family, the rejection of prevailing ideals of masculinity, and the demand for introspection and self-revelation. Indeed, for all those reasons, many lay people were more disposed to locate early Baptists and Methodists on the radical fringe, along with such other despised groups as the Quakers and Shakers, than in the respectable mainstream of Protestant Christianity.

There was, then, nothing inevitable about the triumph of evangelicalism in the South. In fact, reimagining it as a religious movement that faltered at first by failing to compel the loyalties of ordinary men and women raises the question of how—and how completely—it later succeeded. Finding full and satisfying answers will doubtless lead other historians further into the nineteenth century than this study ventures, but the beginnings of that story are told here by reckoning with the members of Mary MacDonald's generation. For her contemporaries, Baptists and Methodists whose adult lives spanned the pivotal opening decades of the nineteenth century, were engaged in their own reimagining of the evangelical tradition. Those men and women knew what they were up against and why. And they realized that the future of their churches in the South depended on more than yielding ground to gentlefolk and slaveholders. It would require winning humbler folk as well, by altering, often drastically, many earlier evangelical teachings and practices concerning the proper roles of men and women, old and young, white and black, as well as their positions on the relationship between the church and the family and between Christianity and other forms of supernaturalism. As a result, evangelicalism looked much different in the 1830s than it had in the 1790s, and far different than it had in the 1760s. And to white southerners, it looked so much better that the proportion of evangelical church members among them rose appreciably between the 1810s and the 1830s—gains that could have come about only by an influx of unchurched men and women. This is the truest sense in which southern evangelicalism was a dynamic and popular movement: It was being reinvented during the very decades that it took root in that region, transformed by the demands of laymen and -women and the responses of clerical leaders. Southern whites came to speak the language of Canaan as evangelicals learned to speak with a southern accent.[35]

1

RAISING THE DEVIL

Then Jesus was led up by the Spirit into the wilderness
to be tempted by the devil. . . . the devil took him to a
very high mountain, and showed him all the kingdoms
of the world and the glory of them; and he said to him,
"All these I will give you if you will fall down and worship me." Then Jesus said to him, "Begone, Satan!"
—MATTHEW 4:1, 8–10

WILLIAM GLENDINNING pressed a razor against his pulsing
throat and awaited the worst. He did not even try to pray,
that recourse having failed since he had first sunk into
despondency more than a year earlier, in 1784. For the likes of him, he
knew, there could be no mercy now, even though heaven's gate once had
seemed within his reach. Only a few years after emigrating to the Chesapeake in 1767, Glendinning had been saved, plucked by his conversion to
Methodism and the call to preach from an obscure, rootless lot as a jour-
neyman tailor. A sawed-off, scrawny Scot whose speech rolled off his
tongue in a thick burr, he struck Methodist leaders as less choice a recruit
than the beefy, native-born farm boys who could withstand the rigors of a
traveling ministry, and less choice still than the stray scions of genteel
families who might lend the church some respectability. But with all the
determination of one accustomed to being underestimated, Glendinning
set about proving his worth. During the years spanned by the American
Revolution, he spread the Methodist message throughout the Chesapeake.
And despite the strain of constant travel, preaching, and pastoral work,
Glendinning, eager to grow in wisdom and grace, steeped himself in study
of the Bible and learned theological treatises.

That ambition, alas, became his undoing: It "brought my reasoning mind into many philosophical inquiries more curious than useful, and which are too deep for the short line of human reason to fathom." He came to question the divinity of Jesus, the reality of original sin, and "whether the scriptures were the truths of God." Such exertions took their toll on a constitution already wracked by chronic rheumatism; insomnia robbed him of rest, and even sleep, when it finally came, offered no true repose but rather dreams of "going over dreary mountains and falling into bottomless abysses." Glendinning gradually overcame his religious doubts, but only to become haunted by the fear that such "atheistical inquiries" had cost him eternal life. From within there rose a voice that intoned, "Hence apostate—away thou damned spirit," and when he closed his eyes, "let the night be ever so dark, all would appear like dismal flaming brimstone burning around me." Feeling "like an outcast, from the face of the Lord," he "became stripped of all, but entire enmity against the Most High, and all that appeared sacred." By June of 1785, he was violently agitated, spewing curses and babbling blasphemies; he stopped preaching and spurned offers to pray. He had surrendered to the stark despair that, shortly thereafter, drew a razor's edge to his sweating neck.

Glendinning did not slit his throat, but neither had he hit bottom. By November of 1785, some influential Methodists in the Chesapeake had concluded that he needed to be either treated by doctors or, that failing, quarantined from the faithful. So they tied him up and spirited him across the border to North Carolina, a place in the South then akin to what Rhode Island had been earlier in New England—a remote exile for those whose religious eccentricities embarrassed more sober Christians. When medical remedies failed, Glendinning was committed to an isolated plantation owned by John Hargrove, a Methodist layman, and left marooned with his inner demons. The chief among these devils did not remain within for long. One stormy night, suddenly beset by the sense "that *Lucifer* was near," Glendinning threw open the Hargroves' front door, stared out into the pelting rain and howling wind, and, with a surge of horror, "saw his face: it was black as any coal—his eyes and mouth as red as blood, and long white teeth gnashing together." In the weeks that followed, the devil reappeared often, and Glendinning's frantic outbursts on those occasions created such commotion that John Hargrove moved his charge from the family's home to a separate cabin, thus completing his isolation: "[S]o lost to all human creatures, was I, that if I did not see, or hear any, I did not know that there was any other being on earth but myself."

For the next two years, Glendinning entertained few visitors except Satan. So he came to know that prince of demons intimately, down to every detail of appearance and demeanor. Now Lucifer appeared mainly by day, sometimes accosting him in open fields or orchards, at other times approaching the cabin's door or perching atop its roof. Male in gender, dark of hue, the devil stood about five feet in height, his body "bigger than that of any living person, and about 15 or 18 inches from the ground there appeared something like legs and under them feet, but no arms or thighs." There was "a ridge round the top of his head" from which there sometimes shot out *"something like a horn"*; balls of fire flamed from his eyes, and "when he moved, it was as an armful of chains rattling together." On one occasion, he "appeared like a four-footed beast, as large as a calf a year old, and seemed to have large wings." He also "made smoke to rise" about his person, which, his host speculated, he accomplished by eating dust.

Familiarity with this dusky presence did nothing to diminish Glendinning's terror. Sometimes the stalking demon drove him into the Hargroves' house, where Lucifer "followed me . . . from one room to another." On such occasions, "I would beg some of the family to stand by me, and would loudly mention the name of the LORD to him," whereupon the devil trembled and disappeared. Useful as such self-exorcisms proved, their effect did not endure: His tormentor always returned, intending, as Glendinning feared, to carry him off bodily "down to the pit." The terrible dreams continued, too, in which "I would feel as if pitched off the spot on which I lay, into the flaming gulf . . . as if the fallen angels had me in their arms, and [were] fastening the chains of misery round me." Desperate, Glendinning once again tried and failed at suicide, this time by weighting himself with a stone and jumping into a creek.

Strictly speaking, Glendinning saw himself not as "possessed" by a devil who afflicted from within but rather as "obsessed" by a devil who assailed from without—a distinct but kindred torment. Apparently he exhibited none of the more extreme symptoms of some medieval and early modern demoniacs, those who were convulsed by bodily contortions, seizures, and paralysis while expelling unexpected objects from otherwise unassuming orifices. Yet he did endure many other afflictions common among victims of diabolical possession—a conviction of utter sinfulness and certain damnation, bouts of blasphemous raving, an inability to pray, an impulse to desecrate the sacred, attempts at suicide. If not literally possessed by the devil, Glendinning's chief terror nonetheless arose from expecting that at any moment Lucifer would claim full property rights to his prey, both soul and body.[1]

The plight of their former colleague inspired pity and terror among the southern Methodist clergy. James Meacham, who preached during 1790 within the precincts of the Hargrove plantation, noted in his journal "a Tragical Scene, the Sho[c]king condition of W.G." Their opinions varied about the source of his distress: It may have been the revenge of a body drained by exhaustion, a brain disordered by excessive study, or nerves frayed by spiritual anxiety. Then again, perhaps Glendinning's wayward theological speculations actually had, as he believed, raised the devil. For Meacham, the matter remained a mystery: "Is it possible that Satan can have the power to change the right reason of a Human Soul, up in the dark caverns of distraction? or is it a constitutional disorder?" Whatever the cause, the consensus among his colleagues was that Glendinning had been driven, by something or someone, stark raving mad. "He is like a Man Fatally void of Rational reason," Meacham observed, "he is fearful."[2]

But frightening as Glendinning in his madness may have been, he became even scarier, at least to the Methodist leadership, in the sanity, or semblance thereof, that returned to him by the early 1790s. What brought him back from beyond the brink remains as imponderable as what had pushed him toward it, but the awful dreams ceased, the accusing voices stilled, and the timeless hell of inner torment released its captive. Sleep returned, a reprieve soothed by dreams of being restored to his better self and respected role in a godly community, "of being with human creatures . . . standing up and speaking for the Lord, to great numbers of people." Lucifer, too, made his last appearance at a spot sacred thereafter to Glendinning as "*my mount, or the Mount of Olives,*" forever shrinking back into hell when his victim pronounced the potent exorcism that "he could not hurt me, and that I was not afraid of him,—and that his power was limited." Better still, it now occurred to Glendinning that "*it yet lay in my power to do much for the LORD OF HOSTS,*" a hope confirmed one day when, while returning to his cabin from the fields, "these words were applied, with divine power to my mind, 'Thou art my Son, this day have I begotten thee.' Such a ray of divine glory then beamed forth on me, that I had a clear evidence of my sonship in the favor of God." Heartened by these assurances, Glendinning left his solitary cabin on the Hargrove plantation, resumed his ministry in the Chesapeake, and requested reinstatement in the Methodist clergy.[3]

But hearing of these developments did not dispose his colleagues to regard Glendinning as a man rested and ready for service. On the contrary, most refused to credit his recovery, mainly because he not only continued to insist on having entertained Satan but even celebrated his passing through that "very singular state" as a badge of spiritual virtuosity and divine favor. Worse still, he had resumed preaching as an independent itinerant, broadcasting throughout the upper South his encounters with the Prince of Darkness. Worst of all, he then committed those stories to print, his memoir easily attracting a publisher eager to turn sensationalism into sales. The work appeared in 1795, serving up all that its author promised in the preface—"scenes of horror," "depths of misery and wretchedness," and "sufferings . . . dreadful and unparalleled," all "extremely uncommon and wonderful." That and much more he delivered, not only in the pages that followed but also in the sermons that he preached—much to the dismay of Methodist leaders—to large crowds throughout the Chesapeake.

Southerners read Glendinning's memoir or flocked to hear the man himself for many reasons. True, his tales of a visible devil struck some as the stuff of spooky spectacle, the latest installment in a "wonder lore" of portents, prodigies, and apparitions served up by the popular press on both sides of the Atlantic for centuries. But if some members of his audience hoped for nothing more than delicious frissons and cheap thrills, many others were more idly curious or insufficiently entertained. Some of those soberly inquiring souls were devout Christians, men and women who received his narrative in the spirit he intended—as an assurance that their God was a mighty fortress, proof against the forces of darkness. Yet many others among the earnest did not regard Glendinning's testimony as an inspiring spiritual odyssey. They understood it instead as exactly the opposite: a cautionary tale exposing the risks of embracing Methodism, or, for that matter, any evangelical faith. That required little doing, for what held the center of Glendinning's story was a potent, terrifying Lucifer, a specter conjured up by a convert's spiritual intensity turning in upon itself. Indeed, whether or not members of his audience credited his encounters with the devil, none could doubt that Glendinning's descent into despair bore an unmistakable connection to his fervid, and characteristically evangelical, religious inwardness.[4]

Therein lay the deepest threat posed by Glendinning. This renegade Methodist preacher lent credence to the dangers that many southerners already detected in evangelical religiosity. In his horrific evocations of how that peculiar spirituality bred distraction and bedevilment, both the critical and the credulous of all classes found confirmed their fears about the risks of following the Methodists or the Baptists. Indeed, decades before Glendinning's revelations—as soon as evangelicals began aggressively proselytizing in the South—their unique demands on the hearts and minds of their converts had aroused deep and widely shared misgivings. Many southern whites, both humble and great, believed that evangelicals, by this unsparing emphasis on mankind's sinfulness, hell's torments, and Satan's wiles, estranged men and women from the strong and decent parts of their personalities and plunged them into fathomless inner darkness. From that fall there could be no easy recovery, for, as Glendinning's case attested, self-alienation snuffed out social identity and ruptured communal bonds. All that leavened the isolation of such anguished souls was the company of demons "black as coal" who abided within and sometimes walked the earth. Those were the devils that Glendinning had raised—and that evangelical leaders spent the decades surrounding the turn of the century trying to put behind them.

IN BEARING witness to William Glendinning's account of his sufferings, many southerners felt less the horror of the novel than the shock of the familiar. What rose in their mind's eye were images of friends, neighbors, and family members alarmingly transformed, rendered almost unrecognizable by their engagement with evangelicalism. To be sure, most men and women drawn to the Methodists or Baptists did not attempt suicide or see the devil. Even when people did suffer distress induced by religious concern, it was not usually because they had, like Glendinning, imbibed skepticism from learned books and then despaired at their want of faith. But if the inner agonies attending his way of the cross were singular, Glendinning's morbid intensity was not at all unique among the evangelical laity.

It was expected that all who committed themselves to evangelical faiths would engage in a close study of the Bible and in constant inward scrutiny. They would explore, regularly and relentlessly, the darkest recesses of their hearts, experience overwhelming guilt and remorse, and search their souls for signs of repentance. Nor did that discipline end once those men and women felt the stirrings of hope, for such assurances might prove premature or false. Some Baptists, after weeks or months of conviction climaxed in the release of seeming conversion, then spent years searching for the marks of spiritual progress that would confirm their having been truly saved, not victims of vain imaginings or a passing "hell fright." Methodists maintained the same rigor after conversion, enforced by the caution that converts could "backslide" and thus lose eternal life, as well as by the belief that the choicest saints would experience "sanctification," a "second blessing," which freed them forever from sin.

That regimen of anxious introspection aimed mainly at inducing and sustaining certain states of feeling. True, the process of conversion also involved giving intellectual assent to evangelical creeds: Most crucially, in a moment of epiphany, the reasoning mind grasped that depraved humanity deserved no gentler fate from a just deity than eternal torment. But always, the head followed the heart's lead: What led men and women to accept that proposition as a stark truth were not the reflections of the dispassionate mind but the inclinations of the engaged emotions. Typical of the triage of feeling practiced by evangelicals is Mary Avery Browder's report of her inner pilgrimage to her Methodist pastor in a letter of 1777. When her mounting sense of guilt began to ease, Browder entertained the fleeting hope that she had been converted. But almost instantly, she dismissed so smug a prospect: "No, I had not suffered enough, I was not worthy." Then, in good evangelical fashion, she prayed to feel again the depth of her sinfulness, believing that conversion could occur only after she banished any sense of false assurance. Less effectively, Browder also tried "reasoning with unbelief," a reliance on the impotent intellect that consigned her to a spiritual limbo in which "I could neither feel the burden of sin nor know that my sins were forgiven." Only after several weeks did the suspense of inner confusion shatter in "a feeling sense of my sins being forgiven," when "God broke my heart, turned stone into flesh."[5]

That intensely inward spirituality was well known to northerners, whose ranks had included many evangelically inclined Baptists, Congregationalists, and Presbyterians since the seventeenth century. But it was foreign to most of Browder's contemporaries in the late-eighteenth-century South. Among those mystified was one woman who, on discovering that her devoutly Methodist daughter spent nights praying instead of sleeping, "caught her about the neck, and told her to go to bed, for there was no occasion for so much ado about religion." Such reactions were common. Most white southern churchgoers of that era had been reared in the Anglican church, which practiced an entirely different style of devotionalism, one emphasizing liturgical observances like attending Sabbath worship and receiving communion. In the course of those public rituals, Anglican pulpits rang with sermons calling parishioners to upright behavior, which meant observing moderation in every vice save obsequiousness to social superiors. But no Anglican parsons, except those few tinctured by Methodism, urged the necessity of undergoing a spiritual rebirth by scouring the Bible and inquisitioning the soul. Even Quakers, a substantial minority among southern Christians before the Revolution, who rejected the Anglican reliance on outward ceremonies and encouraged their followers to nurture the "light within," did not share the evangelical emphasis on monitoring the inner life in the hopes of experiencing a transforming conversion.[6]

So it comes as no surprise that most white southerners were taken aback by evangelical ways—particularly the reactions of those struggling under conviction. Even in his old age, William Mead still remembered his wonder at witnessing, as a young Virginia Quaker in the 1750s, the agonies of his future brother-in-law, the first person he had ever known to experience an evangelical conversion. Half a century later, many were still transfixed by the spectacle: Shortly after 1800, when a Kentucky man came under conviction, the news brought neighbors flocking to his house "through sympathy and curiosity to see a man distressed on account of his soul." The same impulses drew huge crowds to camp meetings, where preachers were obliged to set rules to keep gawkers from standing on benches and "idle spectators" from crowding the repentant at the altar. Then, too, mass behavior at evangelical gatherings in the South, especially during the fifty years following the Revolution, would have been regarded as singular anywhere in the Anglo-American world. As in the American North and Britain, there was much sighing, sobbing, and trembling, but there was much more shrieking, shouting, writhing, and "falling"— stricken souls collapsing on the floor under the weight of remorse and sometimes lapsing into trancelike states. Those displays of collective enthusiasm, astonishing even by evangelical standards, long commanded the curiosity of southerners. Like many of his contemporaries, the Virginian John Taylor attended his first Baptist meeting only because "the people hallooed, cried out, trembled, fell down, and went into strange exercises," and "my object was to see and amuse myself at all this, as I would at other sport." But the charm of that novelty faded when one of his friends suddenly "broke out into a flood of tears and a loud cry for mercy . . . I stared at him for a while with awful wonder."[7]

Less fortunately for evangelicals, what the laity first greeted with awe and wonder often gave way to fear and loathing. Their unfamiliarity with the process that began with conviction and, for some, climaxed in conversion, often led southern whites to confuse the onset of religious seriousness with physical illness. When his wife showed alarming symptoms of some mysterious distress, one Chesapeake husband "was for having the doctor" until his spouse demanded to see a Methodist preacher. Even those suddenly overtaken by remorse sometimes mistook malaise of the soul for sickness of the body: one western Virginia farmer, John Goode, felt so certain of his imminent death after being shaken by a Baptist sermon that he insisted a local gentleman compose his will. Even more commonly, concerned onlookers identified both the despair of the repentant and the zeal of new converts as fearful harbingers of derangement, if not outright proofs of insanity. Indeed, among many southerners before about 1800, it passed as common report that Baptists and Methodists first made mad those whom they purported to save. That concern prompted one Georgian to warn his brother, a budding Baptist, of the family's opinion that religious "excitement was going too high for me, and continuing too long to be safe." It prodded a Maryland Anglican father, fretting over his Methodist-besotted son, to fear that the boy might be "going beside" himself. And it haunted a Maryland mother when her son, newly stricken by his sinfulness, confided that he harbored thoughts of suicide and could not sleep because "I thought the earth would open and swallow me up."[8]

Nor was it only lay critics of evangelicalism who were concerned by the dangers lurking in its consuming inwardness. The Baptist and Methodist clergy knew from their own experience that sustained religious excitement could produce both physical debility and emotional imbalance. Exhausted by his itinerant ministry and inner struggles, John Williams, a Virginia Baptist, confided to his journal of feeling "unwell and unable to preach," as well as being "tempted to talk out in a dreadful manner." His fellow Virginian, the Methodist William Ormond, disquieted by "some strange exercise of mind" that left him unable "to tell my own feelings," worried that "I am about to have a Nervous Disorder," for "I find I cannot bear much deep Study nor severe exercise of mind." It is possible that knowledge of Glendinning's troubles sharpened Ormond's fears for his own sanity; more certainly, firsthand observation of the tormented Glendinning spawned James Meacham's morbid interest in madmen. Among them was another Methodist preacher who, sometime in 1793, lapsed into distraction, a condition Meacham attributed to "extreme Study and anciety [anxiety] of mind, which I think has in a measure intoxicated his brain that he is not at this time Master of himself."[9]

The distress that they often met with among devout lay people also heightened the clergy's sense of the dangers lurking along the way of the cross. Pastors as well as preachers, they carefully noted in journals or later recalled in memoirs the spiritual progress of many individual souls, the majority of whom did not enjoy an easy pilgrimage to heaven. On the contrary, most men and women who joined evangelical churches experienced emotions that ranged from acute doubts to nagging scruples about their inward state, virtually all when they came under conviction, and many, intermittently, for years after their conversions. It was the business of the clergy to counsel that legion of troubled Christians who, worn down by poring over the Bible or traveling miles to attend sermons, suffered in body and mind. James Meacham consoled several Methodist sisters who, consumed by the quest for holiness, fell prey to what he called "the hystericks." The same obsession also claimed men, like young Robert Garreau, who, "under great distress on account of his soul," had "reduced abundantly" and could "neither work nor eat"—symptoms that prompted his Methodist neighbors to warn their preacher that they were "afraid he would fall into despair." Indeed, John Goodlet, a Kentucky physician, was often called upon to treat people tormented by what he, like Meacham, diagnosed as the "hysterics," the most severely afflicted being the wife of one Captain Greathouse. After prescribing medicines that did nothing to alleviate her symptoms, Goodlet insisted on a closer observation of his patient, and the Captain and his lady lodged with him for a few days. As Goodlet then witnessed, the woman "would walk and wring her hands from morning to night," insisting that "God had forsaken her entirely"; she "saw so clearly the justness of God in condemning her and so fully anticipated the torments of hell that She gave up trying to pray." Neither the good Presbyterian doctor nor the Baptist Greathouses doubted that those sufferings arose from a spiritual struggle rather than some physical ailment. Their only recourse was to watch and pray for grace to intervene before hopelessness drew the woman toward a darker fate.[10]

That danger was never far from the minds of the clergy. From his long

Baptist ministry among Kentuckians, John Taylor had learned that pro-
longed anxiety over salvation could unhinge the reason of his parishioners. Souls so imperiled included his own sister who, fearing "that there
was no mercy for her," went without food or sleep for a month and "it
really seemed as if she would go deranged." Even more alarming was one
Mrs. Thomas Reese, whose "desperation" led him to believe that "she
might commit some personal violence upon herself." The same fears beset
Methodist preachers like Thomas Haskins, who could do nothing to console a woman in "continual torture of mind" that left her "often tempted
to Blaspheme and to hate her Children." It was usually southern men,
however, whose inner demons drove them to act out their violent impulses. Among them was a Methodist blacksmith who, concluding that
"his sins were so enormous . . . as to exclude all hope of pardon," took up
a sledgehammer and "gave himself a blow in such a manner that it laid the
brain open to view." When that did not suffice, he then "ran to the garden
fence and struck his head against the post . . . and was found by the family
weltering in blood." As much set on self-destruction was a Baptist who, a
few days after confiding to a preacher that he suffered from "a burning
fire" in his brain and a temptation to curse God, "blowed out his brains
with a gun."[11]

Lay people whose spiritual intensity detoured into despair instead of
yielding to conversion occasioned constant worry among the clergy. But it
was at least as unsettling when men and women who had once felt firm in
their faith suddenly lost that confidence and "backslid" into unbelief.
Their number was legion among early southerners, and it was with palpable relief that some shed sanctity to resume the pleasures of insouciant
sinning. But others later regretted turning "willfully against God." Among
them was John Adam Granadd, a Methodist preacher popular among Virginians before being "led away by a gay community." When he came to
repent that betrayal, Granadd concluded "that he had sinned against the
Holy Ghost" and then spent five years wandering along the canebrakes of
the Cumberland River, "till he was reduced to a mere skeleton" and "his
bright intellect appeared like an expiring lamp." Still others fell from grace
much against their wills, unbeckoned by the lure of the world. Such a one
was Philip Webber, a former Baptist minister in Kentucky whom his colleague Joseph Gregg found, in 1796, "in one of the most fearful, uncomfortable states of unbelief short of absolute despair," even though he had
not "ever lived according to the course of this world." He refused Gregg's

offers of prayer, claiming that "he [Webber] could say words, but could not pray," and insisted, weeping, "I am gone. I am gone!" The encounter left Gregg so shaken that he confided to his journal feeling "fatigued and unwell" the day afterward, doubtless from wondering, "Is this the man I heard preach, more powerfully to me than an angel, before (probably) I was twelve years old? Whence is it that I am now preaching, and him wringing his hands . . . ?" Left unspoken, but tugging at Gregg's sleeve, was the question of whether he might someday share Webber's fate. The notorious declines of such preachers only confirmed what the devout knew from their daily struggles and what unbelievers had witnessed as well: that conversion did not reprieve all who experienced its transports from anxiety over salvation.[12]

In other words, to seek evangelical rebirth was to court daunting emotional risks, as even their clergy acknowledged. And while some who observed kin and friends come under conviction were inspired to emulation, many others shrank back, appalled at the toll it exacted. Characteristic is the reaction of one German Quaker who looked on with terror as his wife, a recruit to Methodism, became so preoccupied by the fear of an eternity in hell that she neglected their children and appeared, even to the Methodist preacher Benjamin Abbott, "like one going distracted." When she finally experienced conversion, her husband "burst into a flood of tears, and said, if my wife, who had been so good, had to undergo such distress, what will become of me?"

If that line of lay reasoning worried preachers, what concerned them even more was the outrage of families who misunderstood the sufferings of those under conviction. Enter one household, where a frightened mother had spent the night watching her adolescent son suffer what Benjamin Abbott assured her to be the boy's spiritual awakening. Yet the mother feared otherwise—that her son's agonies had brought him to the brink of death. "Away with you," she stormed at Abbott. "I want no more of you here. . . . I want no more of your being born again." Unfortunately, Abbott chose this inopportune moment to press the matter. He asked the woman, an Anglican, if she had been born again, to which she replied that being christened as an infant and later taking communion "made [her] a member of Christ's mystical body." That, of course, fell far short of what evangelicals understood as spiritual rebirth, prompting Abbott to point up her confusion: "My dear mother, you were born blind and are so the present moment." She would have none of this from the Methodist preacher who had driven her boy mad: "Away with you—I want no more of you here."[13]

Often, too, resentment at what evangelicals wrought spilled outside of family circles and embittered entire communities. Typical was the furor stirred up in one western Maryland settlement in 1781 when an elderly couple sank into such "deep distress" from Methodist preaching that they committed their possessions to a bonfire, agreeing that "old things must be done away [with] and all things must become new." Neighbors arrived in time to salvage some of their goods, and then called for the imprisonment of Freeborn Garrettson, the clergyman whom they blamed for the old pair's bizarre delusion. More than a quarter century later, a similar scandal tainted the Methodists in one southern Ohio town when a local matron emerged from a long period of "black despair" to declare "that she was Jesus Christ, and took it upon her, in this assumed character, to bless and curse any and all that came to see her." To the horror of family and neighbors, she then refused food or drink and died within two weeks "without ever returning to her right mind." Convinced that the Methodists had authored her gruesome fate, many in the community made "a great fuss," but, as her pastor Peter Cartwright added, "they were afraid to go far with it, for fear the Lord would send the same affliction on them."[14]

DESPITE ALL that bedeviled the progress of evangelical pilgrims, some southern whites judged those risks worth the reward. By braving the passage from conviction to conversion, they found their ultimate questions met with answers that brought consolation and inner peace. Their initiation into evangelical culture culminated in the creation of an inner bedrock of assurance about their life after death that endured despite occasional periods of doubt and distraction. Harrowing as the first shock of repentance may have been, for many that spiritual novitiate stood in memory as a horror never to be repeated. Even months and years after the ecstasy of conversion had given way to occasional bouts of spiritual "sluggishness" or "deadness," the fervor of their early faith persisted, sometimes even rekindled. Such men and women never banished doubt altogether, but few lived out their days on an emotional edge, and even if religious intensity waxed and waned, a belief in their ultimate redemption never departed. Committed evangelicals also drew strength from the sense of participating in a cosmic spiritual drama, an ongoing struggle between God and the devil, which was sweetened for them by the certainty that they had cast their lot among the winners. Accepting the faith delivered to the saints meant never having to wonder again whether existence held any meaning, for every individual triumph over sin advanced the kingdom of God, furthered the providential plan for the unfolding of human history, and cast its mite into the mounting treasury of cosmic triumph.

For that reason, even though the process of repentance demanded a radical self-abasement, it also fostered a profound sense of individual importance. Humbling as it was to sound the depths of private wickedness, that plunge into the self also persuaded sinners of the utter singularity of their experience. Those struggling for assurance often alluded to searching for biblical passages or sermons that directly addressed their particular "case," by which they meant a mixture of guilt, doubt, and fear unique to themselves. Moreover, to enter evangelical circles was to find those thoughts and feelings elevated into matters of uncommon and abiding interest—not only to oneself but to an entire religious community. For some southerners—those who happened to be black in a society ruled by whites, poor in a society that bowed to wealth, female in a society dominated by males, young in a society that honored age—being taken seriously was always a novelty, and often an irresistible seduction.

But the immersion of evangelicals in a world of feeling left many other southern whites uneasy. Indeed, it often tried the patience of their closest connections, even when those intimates shared their faith. A telling measure of its costs emerges from the memoirs of Wilson Thompson, who was reared in a Baptist enclave in Kentucky during the last two decades of the eighteenth century. Two formidable relatives dominated Wilson's childhood and much of his adult life, men whose approval he constantly sought. The first was his father's half-brother, James Lee, a Baptist elder who entered Wilson's life at birth, when his parents, fearing for their baby's health, called upon the preacher to pray. Lee did that and a good deal more: "[D]uring his prayer . . . he received such full assurance [of Wilson's survival] that, rising from his knees, he boldly said to all present, that the child would be a man for God, to preach the Gospel." Here is epitomized the evangelical style: Lee's spontaneous expression of and utter trust in the truth as revealed to his heart. It should be noted, too, that this pronouncement effectively shifted the attention of kin and neighbors from the worried parents and sick infant to the preacher. And when Wilson did begin to thrive, Lee gained added authority within the family, a claim on both his nephew and the boy's parents: He gave "a special charge to my father respecting my education," and shortly thereafter, the couple joined the Baptist church.

But James Lee's influence within the family circle was greeted with mixed feelings by the other important man in Wilson's life, his father, Closs Thompson. Meeting the demand to educate Wilson lay well beyond the means of this struggling tenant farmer, and that failure left Wilson resentful, for "when I commenced preaching I could not read a chapter nor a hymn intelligently." Then, too, Closs had been reared as an Anglican and remained, unlike his Baptist-bred half-brother, mistrustful of sudden, strong emotion. It was not that Closs was a remote or uncaring father— far from it: When the youthful Wilson exhibited the first promptings of conviction, he urged the boy "to tell him all my feelings." But as a man guarded in his own emotions, the father strove to instill the same caution in his son. Closs sensed, too, the weight of familial expectation bearing down on the boy, a burden made heavier because only weeks earlier many cousins of Wilson's age had joined the church. He worried that his son might be pushed into membership by peer pressure or, perhaps recalling the circumstances attending his own entry into the Baptist church, by the insistence of James Lee. So Closs advised Wilson to wait, to "test" his faith. But within days of hearing out his father, Wilson waded into the murky shallows of a Kentucky river as James Lee announced that "I am now about to baptize one who will stand in my place when my head lies beneath the clods of the valley." The new convert was then thirteen years of age.

Wilson proved an apt successor to his uncle in more ways than one. He, too, was obsessed by inner preoccupations and often thrust them to the center of his kinfolks' lives. In young adulthood, his agonizing over whether to enter the ministry left him so wasted and distraught that his parents insisted that he sleep in their room, and an aunt, devout evangelical though she was, scolded him for "troubling" both his relatives and the church. After the family moved to southern Missouri in 1810, Wilson, now a newly minted preacher, grew so morose over his failure to win converts that he brought his wife and infant son to his parents' home and there took to bed until he experienced a "revelation" that he would preside over a great revival. To this prediction, the long-suffering Closs replied, with the counsel he may have wished he had given James Lee years before, that "We may have many feelings when the mind becomes excited, and we may feel very different, in a short time afterward, when that excitement dies away; and we should not feel, nor speak positive so soon, but take a few days to see whether these sudden impulses prove true and permanent." But even though the revival came to pass and its converts included one of Closs's brothers, Wilson snatched defeat from the jaws of victory: He told his family, and quite possibly the entire church, that "God, the father of the family, has used me in this way; but He is now done with me, and is dropping me out of his hand." Shortly thereafter, drained by years of coping with Wilson's demons, his wife suffered a severe breakdown.[15]

It fell to Wilson Thompson's lot to find himself caught in the middle of whatever tensions existed between his father and James Lee. The impossibility of pleasing both men left him with lasting insecurities, anxieties that echoed in the morbid suspicion that he was used rather than loved by his "fathers" in heaven and on earth. But if his conflict was unusually acute, his immersion in that inner drama was not at all uncommon among evangelicals. To be sure, they urged introspection as a means of transcending the self and channeling energies into advancing God's kingdom on earth. Even Wilson Thompson, although well into midlife, finally recognized that being so wholly involved with himself had kept him from being devoted to God. But it proved all too easy for other converts to succeed at that to which their faiths did not aspire—to become so transfixed by the drama of emotion and impression, dream and revelation, unfolding within that they grew oblivious to the world without, save for its uses as a stage for dramatizing those feelings. Not all evangelicals were so exquisitely self-absorbed, but most men and women who joined the Baptists and Methodists shared something of Wilson's impulse to explore and reveal emotion.[16]

It was a temperament that repelled many southern whites. Some, like the Anglican-reared Closs Thompson, had been raised in faiths that valued greater reticence, while others learned self-containment in the dear school of childhoods disrupted by parental death and remarriage. Consider the recollections of one James Potter Collins, a native South Carolinian whose spiritual pilgrimage reversed that of his contemporary Closs Thompson: Early in life, Collins left the Presbyterian faith of his father and became skeptical of all organized religion. That may have been an oblique way of easing his disappointed hope of entering the ministry, a future thwarted when his father remarried following the death of James's mother. More children resulted from this new union, which made it impossible for his father to provide James with the college education required of future Presbyterian clergymen. Beyond that, his stepmother so favored her natural children that she went as far as naming one boy "James," after which the rest of the family referred to her stepson as "Potter." Being stripped of his patrimony and even his proper name in adolescence surely must have saddled Collins with insecurities rivaling those of Wilson Thompson, losses so keenly felt for the rest of his life that he could rehearse them in a memoir composed decades afterward. But at the time, Collins showed a restraint worthy of Closs. Instead of confronting his stepmother, he resorted to subtlety, needling her by pretending to court the same woman whom she favored as a wife for one of her own boys. And instead of reproaching his father, Collins lit out for the Georgia frontier. Even when the perfect moment for recrimination offered itself, Collins held back: On one of his visits home in 1792, his father "gathered up several books on religious subjects, and presented them to me . . . enjoining on me to read them with attention," but the son "received them with a promise, that I would read and consider them, at the same time, caring little about it, for I had not imbibed the same notions on the subject of religion that he had, but did not show any signs of aversion to his advice."[17]

As Collins's memoir suggests, southern whites of humble status were neither incurious about nor unaware of their innermost feelings. Yet most made it their practice neither to dwell daily on those emotions nor to express them often. That temperament is poignantly captured in a rare moment of disclosure, one resulting from a chance encounter between a woman with means and status, Louisa Maxwell Holmes, and a woman who had neither. In the summer of 1816, when her carriage broke down on the road to one of western Virginia's posh spas, the mischance stranded Holmes in the rude cabin of a woman whose husband had succumbed to disease in Andrew Jackson's army camp at New Orleans. The two young widows struck up the fleeting intimacy that strangers sometimes share. Perhaps Holmes, out of some nervous impulse to seem sociable, blurted out her own loss, maybe even her hopes of a speedy remarriage with a suitable prospect now awaiting at the hot springs. Whatever it was that passed between them, her accidental hostess was emboldened to share confidences: She produced letters from her husband that astonished Holmes, being "filled with the warmest professions of real love and written in a style of tenderness and feeling much above anything I would have expected from persons in their rank." As that remark suggests, elite southerners like Holmes were more inclined to open expressions of emotion than were people of lesser rank, to whom such indulgences did not come easily or often. It was not mere snobbery but her awareness of the habitual reserve of ordinary people that made for Holmes's surprise at what the dead man's correspondence disclosed. As for his widow, she quickly withdrew after that moment of revelation, showing Holmes a quilt on which "she had worked to keep thoughts of the world from intruding too much upon her."[18]

Guarding emotion figured as one of many ways to lessen risk and disruption in a world where most people struggled merely to survive. The majority of white southern families, yeoman and tenant farmers who often lived on or near the margins of subsistence, took the precaution of planting enough of their acreage with food crops for home consumption before putting in tobacco and cotton for sale abroad, a practice that has been aptly described as "safety-first agriculture." Unable to afford slaves, they relied on the labor of family members, which meant producing large broods of children. Most families—husband, wife, and some five or six offspring—thus spent their days providing for basic needs and their nights clustered in log cabins with only a few rooms. Those hardscrabble lives of little privacy schooled most men and women to subordinate their individual needs and desires to the welfare of the family. So, too, did witnessing the fragility of existence. Even those families who staved off want could never forget that death stalked life, as disease, accidents, and natural disasters took their grisly toll. Nor did other threats to physical security ever stray far from their concerns: Whites knew that they needed to stick together and to keep their wits about them. Those in the lower South lived amid large concentrations of enslaved African Americans who resisted bondage with conspiracies and insurrections, arson and poisoning. Those in the western country lived in dread of Indian attack until the opening decades of the nineteenth century. All of those pressures impressed upon ordinary white men and women the importance of maintaining solidarity within kinship circles and communities—no matter what the inner cost to individuals.[19]

Small wonder, then, that many men and women decided that the satisfactions of inwardness so prized by evangelicals lay beyond their means. How could a life so well examined be worth living if life left unexamined was already hard enough? Crowded households set within a world of scarcity and danger did not permit most people the luxury of studying the

heart and speaking its impulses. Instead, those constraints inclined southerners to deflect their inner demands, to repress any emotions that might,
if openly expressed, estrange them from relatives and neighbors upon
whom their very survival often depended. True, not all those who chose
otherwise—who joined with evangelicals in giving free rein to feeling—
would bring upon themselves the awful fate that befell William Glendinning. But anyone in that world who probed the soul's recesses and shared
with fellow pilgrims what had been hidden therein might still raise many
devils best not conjured.[20]

IMAGINE, THEN, how southern whites felt when called upon not only to
search their souls but to impart what was yielded to African Americans. When evangelicals began actively proselytizing in the South, nearly a
century's worth of law and custom designed to protect slavery had
instilled in most whites the belief that blacks were bereft of the capacity
for elevated thought or feeling. But white converts, many of them wary of
self-revelation in any setting, were bound to share their feelings, doubts,
and vulnerabilities with their African-American brothers and sisters, most
of them enslaved. Both the emotionalism of evangelical gatherings and
church rituals of testifying to spiritual struggles and disciplining wayward
members imposed on many whites an unaccustomed—and disturbing—
intimacy with blacks. In Glendinning's report of being reduced by his
madness to the society of "demons black as coal," many southern whites
may have heard echoed their own fears of interracial communion.

It was not the numbers of African Americans within early evangelical
ranks that intimidated whites. Presbyterians and Baptists attracted few black
converts prior to the Revolution; in the decades that followed, despite the
added efforts of the Methodists, black membership in all three churches still
grew slowly. Even by 1800, under only 5 percent of all African-American
adults in the South had entered evangelical churches, mainly Baptist and
Methodist; at most, they accounted for one-third to one-quarter of members in individual churches. Nevertheless, joining in spiritual fellowship
with converts of another race, no matter how many, drew ambivalent
reactions even from the most committed white evangelicals.

To be sure, some lavished unstinting praise on individual slave converts. In 1762, James Gordon, a Virginia Presbyterian merchant, approvingly noted in his journal the dying words of one of his bondswomen,
who told her mother that she "hoped to see her in heaven"; a few days

later he came away from "much conversation" with a neighbor's male slave of "whose piety I have a great opinion." Among the Baptists and Methodists, clergymen often noted that blacks sometimes outnumbered whites at worship services, particularly in bad weather, or, like Nelson Reed, they singled out certain African Americans for "how sensible and feelingly they spake of the work of grace on their hearts." Others, like Jeremiah Norman, struck a more tentative note, but found cause for encouragement: After preaching to one black gathering, he was pleased that "2 or three . . . prayed of their own accord" in "broken sentences but they Seemed to come from the heart." Yet even as white evangelicals seized on such instances of devotion, the tenor of their comments conveys a certain defensiveness about the authenticity of black Christian commitment, as if they were amassing examples to sway a shadow audience of those more skeptical.[21]

Or, perhaps, to persuade themselves. Even those who spoke hopefully of winning black souls feared that some African Americans approached the churches not out of sincere conviction but only in search of diversion or an escape from work. Such suspicions made James Meacham hesitate when a black woman approached him for baptism until "I questioned her very close. She wept and cryed out for mercy." White evangelicals recognized, too, that some African Americans were drawn toward their churches only because of the antislavery sentiments voiced by some preachers. Meacham may well have wondered whether it was his notoriety among slaveholders that, as he meditated in a granary one night in 1793, brought him face-to-face with a black man "who fixt his Eyes upon me and said 'What have you got for me[?]' " A decade earlier, the same reputation drew a group of slaves to Nelson Reed to complain that "their masters never suffer'd them to go to hear preaching."[22]

Such efforts to enlist the churches in gaining leverage over masters confirmed white fears that what blacks "got" from evangelicalism were strategies for resisting slavery. So persistent was that anxiety, especially in the lower South, that mob attacks on African-American worshippers occurred well into the nineteenth century. Some masters cast all Baptists and Methodists, merely by virtue of their regular communion with bondspeople, as accomplices in subverting white supremacy. To be sure, the intensity of those suspicions waxed and waned: After drawing only a small audience of whites in the fall of 1793, Jeremiah Norman, to his great surprise, "heard that [at] the notion of the insurrection among the Blacks the People had made a vow against hearing the Methodists any more, but this I expect will soon decline." Even so, such concerns proved troublesome enough to white evangelicals to prompt gestures that positioned them on the side of the South's masters. One of many was the censuring of Sal, a black woman, by a North Carolina Baptist church in 1790, for attending church against the orders of her owner.[23]

White evangelicals also worried about whether blacks came into their churches willingly. So keenly aware was James Meacham that some devout masters enforced slaves' attendance at worship that he took heart when, conducting devotions on one plantation, "the Black people came in I believe of their own accord." Less encouraging was his encounter with a slave woman who, evidently at the insistence of her owner, presented her three children for baptism, but defiantly declared that "She did not fear nor serve God herself and she would not ingage [engage] to do that for others as She did not do for herself." Reluctant to baptize the children of a mother who "only Mocked God," Meacham relented only when the woman's mistress intervened, promising "to see to the raising of the children herself." In other cases, too, entire households of slaves joined churches at the insistence of pious masters, like Delaware's Henry Ennalls, whose conversion to Methodism inspired sudden imitation by "all his Negroes down to those but eight years old."[24]

Those episodes gave white preachers pause, but did not stop them from celebrating spiritual intimacy between the races, often by offering their own experiences as a model. Ezekiel Cooper, a Methodist preacher, re-called that during his youthful quest for salvation in the 1770s he "used to converse frequently with one of our Negro men, who was also concerned on this subject," while his Kentucky colleague, Benjamin Lakin, confided to his journal in 1795 that "my soul was fill'd with love while I had some conversation with a Black man about the dealings of God with his soul. He spake so feelingly and powerfully of the work of Grace . . . that it much affected me." Yet those very remarks, so redolent of preacherly admoni-tion, raise doubts about whether most white converts displayed the same eagerness in engaging their black brothers and sisters. Indeed, when such interracial exchanges did occur, they drew the clergy's notice, like James Meacham's rare report that at one Methodist gathering, "Some of the dear humble White sisters went out, with the dear black, and God poured his divine spirit and love upon them." Left unsaid was that such "humble" souls might not have abounded among white Methodists.[25]

If interracial communion remained more an ideal than an actuality, what fueled white reluctance, beyond their mistrust of black motives, was their sense of the distinctiveness of African-American spirituality. The Baptist preacher John Leland—while admitting that "many . . . can give clear, rational accounts of a work of grace in their hearts" and admiring the "zealous" quality of black preaching—believed that African Americans, most being illiterate, were "more exposed to delusion than whites are." He also found black Baptists to be "more noisy, in time of preaching, than the whites, and . . . more subject to bodily exercise, and if they meet with any encouragement in these things, they often grow extravagant." Methodist preachers, too, often commented on the "noisy" enthusiasm exhibited by black worshippers, particularly their common practice of interjecting shouts and cries during sermons. While some of the clergy tolerated and even reveled in that participatory style, many more were miffed at being interrupted or drowned out entirely by African-American congregations. Some white lay people took exception as well: At one racially mixed gathering, according to Jeremiah Norman, "one of the Blacks cryed aloud, which gave great offense to some."

The Methodists also shared Leland's view that blacks were more susceptible than whites to ecstatic responses. While speaking to about fifty African Americans one evening in 1781, Freeborn Garrettson "fear[ed] that Satan got an advantage of one," for "she fell down, thumped her breast and puked all over the floor," which prompted him to explain to the gathering that "they may be converted without falling down, or hollouring." Evangelical preachers were not strangers to such varieties of religious expression. Some whites in their congregations also shouted, cried out, fell down. Possibly more African Americans, as whites reported, reacted in the same ways still more often, but, just as possibly, clerical anxieties gave rise to that impression. Ecstatic responses unnerved many white preachers because they defied control; whenever mass enthusiasm gripped meetings of whatever racial composition, it threatened clerical dominance over the direction of worship. But, for obvious reasons, the spectacle of an audience of blacks seizing the spiritual initiative disturbed southern whites more than did similar behavior on the part of enthusiasts among their own race.[26]

Even more unsettling to whites than the ease with which the dynamics of black worship escaped their mastery was something more dimly sensed: the suspicion that the essence of African-American spirituality, although often expressed in forms familiar to white evangelicals, somehow eluded their comprehension. Could it be that when black worshippers wept and screamed, collapsed and sank into trancelike states, that such behavior meant something other to them than what it did to white evangelicals? Was it possible, even as blacks exhibited outward forms of religious engagement similar to those displayed by whites, that such responses arose from inward states of feeling and belief different from those of whites? Did those African Americans who seemed so fluent in the language of Canaan colonize its cadences to express spiritual truths of their own devising?

Most surely they did. And white evangelicals in the South could not have avoided those speculations, even if the clergy's perennial optimism precluded their dwelling on them. Because of that reticence and the absence of direct testimony from blacks, the processes by which the earliest African-American evangelicals adapted Christianity, as well as the changing contours of that sacred world, remain matters in which the vacuum created by a dearth of evidence has been filled by a flurry of speculation. It is certain only that, by dint of affinities between African and Christian cosmologies and forms of revelation, the first black converts started syncretizing the two religious traditions. By the middle of the nineteenth century, their successors had elaborated a distinctive Afro-Christianity, a religious mosaic that melded discrete survivals from disparate West African beliefs and practices with elements of evangelical Protestantism.

Decades earlier, however, its beginnings are intimated in brief but intriguing exchanges with African Americans as recounted by white evangelicals. In 1796, the Methodist Jeremiah Norman listened as an "old Negroe man" recalled "the Worship carryed on in Affrica," a ritual that he described as:

> for a nation to Collect on a Large spot of open ground while thus drawn in a circle 2 men goes round proclaiming to the others what they ought to do as their Duty. Then making their adoration to that great one above they then return to their respective employments Leaving one [illegible] man to take care of the place and things . . . in such cases they are sometimes routed [?] and taken [as slaves].

In fact, what this elderly slave's "memories" reveal is the merging of religions—a mingling of unmistakably West African traditions, like worshippers forming a ring in sacred precincts, with Christian elements emphasizing monotheism and moral exhortation. Some of his black contemporaries more self-consciously sought common ground with Christianity. When Stith Mead addressed blacks on a Georgia plantation in the 1790s, "one called April, late from Africa, was attentive to hear, and told me he had been religious in his country." Similarly, James Meacham, after asking directions from a black man working in the fields, began to instruct him in Methodism after discovering that "he knows nothing of Jesus," yet "saith he trys to Seek religion."[27]

To such seekers can be traced the origins of Afro-Christianity in the American South, and men and women of the same ecumenical bent numbered among the earliest members of biracial churches. But how did the white laity greet the prospect of entering into spiritual fellowship with people who, even as they entertained evangelical teachings, claimed to be "religious" already—presumably devotees of Islam or West African traditions? And how did whites regard the many blacks who, while attending their worship, even joining their churches, still adhered to some of their ancestral beliefs and practices? To ask those questions is to answer them, so the white clergy did their best to allay such anxieties by curbing any behavior on the part of black converts that betrayed the survival of West African spiritual traditions.

Among such white clerics was Freeborn Garrettson, who stood ready to reprove a Maryland slave woman who attended his sermon in 1783 most un-Methodistly bedecked, "her ears, nose, and hands . . . loaded with gold." He became readier still when the woman explained to him that she was "the daughter of a king," and proceeded to peel off her finery and "proferred her gold to one who would bury her decently [according to West African rites] when she died." Equally likely to incur clerical censure were black church members who conjoined the transports of evangelical conversion with the African religious phenomenon known as spirit possession or spirit mediumship. Look in upon one North Carolina Methodist gathering around the turn of the nineteenth century being brought to a halt when one "Aunt Katy," a slave woman, "with many extravagant gestures, cried out that she was 'young King Jesus.' " To the black worshippers present, the meaning of her claim was clear: being filled with spirit, in the context of traditional African religiosity, connoted a human medium being possessed by and thus speaking in the words of the spirits of deities or ancestors—but, in this case, Jesus Christ. The presiding preacher, Joseph Travis, knew enough to recognize that Aunt Katy's melding of the two traditions strayed beyond the bounds of the evangelical understanding of conversion. And he knew exactly what to do: he ordered her to be seated and then "publicly read her out of membership, stating that we would not have such wild fanatics among us, meantime letting them [the blacks in the congregation] know that such expressions were even blasphemous."[28]

Such hybrid beliefs ranked among the "delusions" to which John Leland and other early evangelicals judged blacks to be prone. But while Leland put down such deviations from orthodoxy to a want of literacy, he was only right by half: They also demonstrate the enduring power of ancestral religious traditions among southern blacks. Neither prospect, of course, could have eased the misgivings of white lay people. On the contrary, many concluded that belonging to evangelical churches enforced spiritual intimacy with African Americans who, even if they had not sought membership to spite or humor their masters, could muster at best only a dubious piety, flawed by both a dim understanding of the Bible and a strong infusion of non-Christian beliefs. Here were yet more grounds for misgiving, for white southerners to draw back from faiths that required members to spare themselves nothing in self-inquisition and to withhold nothing that the heart disclosed.

And there was another still. Because motives were murky and appearances deceiving, there could be no telling whether interracial gatherings, passing as a communion of saints, might not mask a congress less holy— an unwitting union with African Americans who owed their true spiritual fealty to darker entities in whose image centuries of tradition reputed them to be cast—demons "black as coal." If the devil had mattered less to white evangelicals in the South, it might signify little that they, like Christians of other places and times, identified Satan as "the black man" or as a "dark spirit." But the devil commanded nearly obsessive notice in early evangelical circles, and his dark prominence may have subtly undercut the cause of drawing whites into biracial churches. Less subtly and more certainly, southern evangelicals soon discovered that, no matter what his hue, the visible Lucifer raised by Glendinning was a presence with whom they could not indefinitely postpone a reckoning.[29]

SOUTHERNERS HAD always known something of Satan. From the beginnings of white settlement, courts formally indicted miscreants for being "stirred up by the devil," while, less formally, colonists of every rank invoked Lucifer's name when consigning their enemies to perdition. Yet this devil was a dim specter, not at all the vivid presence that cast a long shadow over early New England. Nearly absent in the teachings of southern Anglicans and Quakers, he remained at large mainly in figures of speech and bits of folklore. So it created no small sensation when evangelicals restored the power of darkness to the center of Christian belief, which they did decades before Glendinning's revelations. Indeed, as soon as evangelicals began in earnest to proselytize among southerners, Satan, in some form, suddenly seemed to be everywhere, a name that dropped easily and often from the lips of every convert. It was a novelty that drew universal notice, if not appreciation. One Anglican parson took great exception to the Presbyterians in his Virginia neighborhood for reviling their critics as "lumps of hellfire, incarnate Devils, 1000 times worse than Devils." And, as Jesse Lee recalled, when his colleague Robert Williams first brought the Methodist message to Norfolk in 1772, "the people were so little used to hearing a preacher say hell or devil, in preaching, that they thought he was swearing."[30]

This devil so ubiquitous in the lives of evangelicals was a dogged and cunning adversary. In every wrangle that divided their churches, the devout sniffed the sulfurous whiff of diabolical subversion; as one sister in a troubled Methodist society concluded, "I think the Devil is come down in this place and seeks to destroy our peace." In their every impulse to doubt faith or to stray from rectitude, the pious traced the imprint of a cloven hoof: "[T]he Devil often assaults me," another Methodist sister confessed, "I am just going into an ingagement, with the powers [of] darkness, I feel as if Ile die reather than yeald." Women and men alike depicted their spiritual lives as deeply personal, nearly physical, struggles with Satan. Thus Mary Avery Browder promised her pastor that the devil could claim her only if "he should tear me from the feet of Christ," while a young Methodist preacher, suffering "many sore temptations," felt as if "an Emasary [emissary] from hell had undertaken to overthrow me."

If there was something bracing in daily engagements with so formidable a fiend, evangelicals never underestimated nor ceased to fear the powers at Satan's command. Most agreed that it lay within the devil's scope to lead human beings astray by filling their minds with evil thoughts, images, and impulses. So intensely did some experience diabolical influences that they detected the demon's taunts resounding from within, like the Methodist Nelson Reed, who, while preaching, heard "[S]atan say to me—now how foolish do you look." Even sleep brought no escape from the devil's wiles, for, as James Meacham explained, Satan could "overthrow . . . precious souls" by controlling their dreams. Through such devices, evangelicals believed, the devil could not only seduce believers into doubt and sin but drive them to madness and mayhem. While working in his field, one Delaware Methodist saw Lucifer "in his bodily shape," and succumbed when "tempted . . . to curse God" and "den[y] the Holy Scriptures"; whereupon he "went into despair" and lay "months together without drinking." A Methodist woman, convinced that she had sold her children to Satan, "carried a razor in her bosom for three weeks with an intent, first to take the lives of her children (before the day came, that she thought the devil was to come for them) and then take her own life." Among the Presbyterians, Agnes Templin believed that a neighboring man had "cut his throat to pleas[e] satern [Satan]."

In short, an arch-fiend of tridentine might—as relentless as the Jehovah of the Old Testament, as familiar as the Jesus of the New, and as mysterious as the Holy Spirit—came to command frequent and fearful notice among the southern faithful. It could hardly have been otherwise, for evangelicals not only urged men and women to admit their weakness as abject sinners but then heightened their dread at such impotence by pitting them against a tireless and endlessly resourceful enemy. Consider the confession of John Craig, a western Virginia Presbyterian minister: While his wife was giving birth to their first child, he was suddenly filled with "the most bitter hatred . . . against the wife of my Bosom . . . and all of them that was with her that I could have wish'd house and all of them in it in one flame." Burning with "Rage and bitter Revenge against them," he "Saw my conduct was wrong and fain would have prayed to God to Deliver me from the power of Satan but could Not Express one Sensible Sentence." After several hours those feelings passed off, but what endured was Craig's conviction of the "inability" of humankind to combat "So powerful and cruel an Enemy."[31]

Small wonder, then, that lay strategies for quelling fear of Lucifer were as numerous as that demon's purported legions. Knowing God to be more powerful than the devil, some resourceful believers, even among the young, summoned benevolent spirits to their defense. Join the preacher Nelson Reed in the early spring of 1781, listening intently as one George Lewis, a Methodist layman, related the recent experiences of his twelve-year-old daughter, who woke him one night by crying "out in her sleep . . . that there was a black man coming to kill her." Responding in the manner of all sleep-deprived parents, Lewis soothed the child, "told her she was a dreaming and that nothing would hurt her." Perhaps vengeful black specters haunted his own dreams, but what was to be done about it? On the next day, however, the true identity of his daughter's dark tormentor emerged: While collecting sap from maple trees, she "saw a person very tall in white," who told her that "the black man she saw was the devil, but she need not be afraid of him . . . that he would keep him from doing her any harm . . . the devil would always be plauging [plaguing] her but she was not to mind him." Then her consoler revealed himself as "the spirit of God." All this the child confided to Lewis, who, skeptical at first, "charg'd her not to tell a ly, for if she did that black man would catch her." It seems that those children whom parents judged too tender in years to be told of slavery's horrors were not too young to be warned of the devil's sway. But now the girl knew how to protect herself. On the following morning, Lewis again heard his daughter talking in her sleep to Satan, "saying so you are come again you need not come, for I have got your Master. O Lord Jesus keep me from him."[32]

There were also more playful devices to tame the devil's terror. One appears in the ingenuity with which southerners spun out nicknames for His Satanic Majesty—"Old Horney," "Old Harry," and "Old Clooty." Still another ploy for dispelling awe appears in patterns of naming some of the more intimidating features of the southern landscape, particularly the topography of the western country: As early as 1755, one deep ravine in the Blue Ridge Mountains, "where the sun never penetrated," was known to travelers as the Devil's Three Jumps. Equally evocative is the ritual of "treeing the devil" that James Potter Collins witnessed at the meeting of a "curious sect" of evangelicals in the western Carolinas. According to Collins, one man alerted the congregation to the devil's presence within the house and then began scuffling with an unseen antagonist as the rest of the company shouted encouragement: "Well done, Johnny! Gouge him, Johnny! Bite him, Johnny!" To even matters up, another of the brethren urged on the devil ("Fair play, there shall no man touch! Hurrah devil! I'll stand to your back!"). In due course, the fight spilled outdoors and the devil fled up into a tree, "whereupon his adversary began barking up the tree, while the rest of the crowd threw sticks to make him jump off."[33]

Such lively rituals found no place in most southern evangelical churches, but their importance lies in pointing up the anxieties that beset more sober believers. Even those who sneered at "treeing the devil" still held Satan to be a real, if invisible, entity empowered to cloud the mind, warp the will, and corrupt the heart. More important, many others exposed to evangelical influences credited the devil's ability to take on corporeal form and menace his human prey. That was one of the lessons imparted by many evangelical parents to their children, among them one little girl of six who woke her Methodist parents "and told them she saw the devil and that he grinned at her"; the next morning, the child asked her mother "what she must do to be saved, for, said she, I am so wicked I am afraid the black man will come for me." Demons also strayed into the slumbers of young John Barr, a Presbyterian who, even in old age, vividly recalled a boyhood dream of the Last Judgment: "I . . . saw the earth teeming with its former inhabitants, the dead rising in every direction. Some had got on their feet—others appeared in a sit[t]ing position—whilst only the heads of some were to be seen above the ground." Then, after everyone was "disengaged from his clay," the "good folks ascended to heaven, and devils drove the rest toward hell."[34]

Nor was it only impressionable children who lived in dread of a literal devil. After playing the fiddle at a dance, Philip Mulkey, a South Carolinian who later became a Baptist preacher, "saw the Devil grinning at him . . . with fiery eyes." Terrified, he "swooned away," and "when he came to himself" grew even more frightened, "thinking the Devil would be permitted to take him bodily." Then there was William Tweedle, a Georgian old enough to be suspected of bigamy, who had been in "a strange way" ever since the night in 1799 when his then-wife awoke to find him "down on the Floor with his Stick fighting of [f] something." No element of playful release leavened that harrowing struggle, which left Tweedle unable to speak, although "He appeared to be in his Senses, could Wright [write]," and thus explained to his terrified neighbors that "It was the old Boy I fit [fought]. He got the best of me. I see him now. He is in me. I can't cast him out. I want to (or will) drown him with the Swine." Tweedle described his adversary "with great Eyes like fire," and "showed some present several bruises on his Body and told them the Devil made them; also showed us how the Devil seized him." Doubtless it occurred to William Ormond, the Methodist preacher called upon for counsel, that the torments described by Tweedle, an "uncommon wicked" man, might signal the onset of conviction, for his case was far from singular.[35]

Indeed, as evangelical pastors well knew, what sometimes accompanied the first throes of repentance was a sinner's sheer terror of being snatched into hell by a devil trying not to be cheated of triumph. One newly awakened man thus entered the diary of John Early, a Methodist preacher, in 1807, by "bellowing like a bull . . . for fear the devil would get him alive." A decade earlier, Stith Mead witnessed the same desperation in a young Virginia Methodist who, after coming under conviction one evening, feared that a disgruntled Satan had pursued him into the bedchamber. "Behold the approaching fiend," the young man cried to his nephew, who shared the bed. "Sleep not . . . the monster [is] Coming." Mead, lodged in the same room, "spake Billy be not afraid have faith in God—and changing beds . . . I said the D[evi]l shall not hurt you and no sooner was I in bed with him but I felt his palpitating heart thumping within and a cold sweat on his affrighted body." Nor were such terrors of close encounters with the Prince of Darkness confined to lay people of humble rank. Obadiah Echols, a prosperous Baptist planter, feared going to his private retreat to pray because a voice that seemed to come from "without" warned him that "you'll see the Devil." And Loveless Savidge, a piquantly named Baptist preacher, reported that similar fears so consumed a wealthy Georgia matron, who believed herself "the greatest sinner living," that "she could not bear a red garment in her sight, from its supposed resemblance to hellfire, nor anything black, as exciting an idea of the devil."[36]

Taken together, these reports display the range of opinion among the early evangelical laity about how real the devil was and what the devil could do. A few spoke of Satan in a purely figurative sense, as an emblem of the human heart's sinful inclinations. A greater number regarded Satan as an actual but invisible entity, who raised evil impressions in the minds of those awake or asleep. But still others—how many can only be guessed—either believed or at least entertained the possibility that, beyond those powers, the devil could take visible form and even inflict violence. It was not an anomalous notion, given the frequency with which other spirits took corporeal shape and accosted southern whites. Some were specters of the unquiet dead; one, a recently deceased Marylander, appeared before his former neighbor to announce that he had risen from hell to warn that "you will die in a few weeks and go there to[o]." Other spectral presences remained more mysterious: While fishing in a marsh on the Eastern Shore, one Solomon Evans "heard a noise somewhat like 'hah! hah!' and on looking that way, saw an apparition coming towards him, leaping like a frog," a ghostly presence that he later met "on lonely walks, and once saw . . . approaching his door."[37]

Glendinning, of course, hoped to tap that vein of supernaturalism in order to persuade still more southerners of the existence of a literal, palpable Lucifer. His long ministry had schooled him in the leverage to be gained by drawing men and women into a world ruled by demons and then touting the power of evangelicalism to set at bay those terrors. Although his reason may have wandered, this certainty never strayed: He believed that testifying to his torments by a visible devil would draw many converts. However incompletely restored to sanity, Glendinning was crazy like a fox. As he saw it, once lured into evangelical circles by curiosity, the laity could be held by the stark fear of seeing Satan.

Yet most of his clerical contemporaries shrank from such tactics. Indeed, it is surprising how few early preachers ventured opinions about whether the devil they so often invoked could actually be seen. Even as they carefully committed to their journals instances of lay people seeing or wrestling with the devil, most ministers usually withheld any judgment about whether Satan could assume bodily form. Doubtless their own uncertainties may have contributed to the clergy's reticence, but there is something studied in their vagueness, suggesting that preachers sensed that they might risk everything and gain nothing by taking a firm position on the question of seeing Satan. How much better, then, to allow the laity to believe in whatever sort of demon they chose, and for the clergy to leave the matter of Satan's scope as deliciously mysterious and comfortably muddled as it was. And so it might have remained, had not Glendinning's notoriety forced evangelical leaders to confront all that they stood to lose by giving the devil free rein.

GLENDINNING WAS not wrong in his conviction that scaring the devil out of southerners might enlist some on the side of the angels. But the man who succeeded Lucifer as his main adversary, Francis Asbury, was right. Armed with even more adamantine certainties drawn from even longer experience ministering to the southern laity, Asbury also had the advantage of being the leader of early American Methodism, which made him the arbiter of rightness in that church. It was Asbury, along with his fellow bishop Thomas Coke, who decreed that the Methodist ministry would remain closed to Glendinning unless he would agree never to mention in public what they delicately termed his "past exercises." In their view, his tales of seeing Satan "took the strength of imagination for realities," and, as Coke affirmed forcefully, "all such accounts of creatures having any intercourse with beings from eternity, [are] only imaginary."[38]

In the circumstances inspiring that summary pronouncement may lurk two fine ironies. The first is that Glendinning himself may not have believed in the Lucifer that he so vividly evoked. His whole account of diabolical obsession could have been a clever hoax or a desperate ploy to salvage a career shipwrecked on the jagged reef of his broken reason. Recall how deftly his narrative transforms a pitiable lunatic into a spiritual virtuoso, a soul so choice as to attract daily abuse from the Prince of Darkness before, by a potent exorcism, returning his tormentor to hell. Suspicion deepens, too, upon learning that Glendinning later joined the Unitarians, not a group conspicuous for harping on the terrors of diabolical encounters. Evidently the devil of rationalism that triggered his derangement claimed him in the end. Second, it is likely that Asbury's private opinions of the devil's power more closely resembled those professed, however artfully, by Glendinning than those expressed by Coke. The representative of a more sophisticated British Methodism, Coke visited America only occasionally; but Asbury, an immigrant out of step with the parent church after more than thirty years in America, may well have thought that the wayward Scot truly was possessed by the devil. "As for Glendinning," Asbury confided to another preacher in 1791, "I believe Satan is in him and will never come out." Nonetheless, even if he personally inclined toward the view that spirits, dark or bright, could assume visible form, Asbury judged it a risky business to focus lay attention on that sort of devil. So Glendinning had to go.[39]

At least partly underlying Asbury's resolve was the increasing concern of both Methodists and Baptists to cultivate the good opinion of the southern gentry, professional classes, and the most substantial members of the yeomanry. Their ranks included not only the wealthiest but also the most educated men and women in the region. Although enlightened learning had not permeated the upper strata of southern society by the 1790s, its influence had become sufficiently widespread to render Glendinning a figure of easy ridicule. Indeed, even a few men and women of lower rank were drawn toward the Universalists, a tiny church of Christian rationalists whose teachings denied both the existence of the devil and the

eternity of hell. Around the turn of the century, churches were occasionally obliged to expel the stray brother or sister who became tinctured by
Universalism, and one Baptist fellowship even took the precaution of forbidding any member to "countenance or encourage any man to preach,
who preaches the doctrine of redemption from hell." Aware of rationalism's inroads, Asbury worried that many eyebrows would be raised if
the ranks of Methodist preachers were revealed to include those who
insisted on having seen a chain-rattling, eyeball-flaming, roof-roosting,
dusky-winged Lucifer.[40]

Consider, as Asbury doubtless did, how the Methodist Hargrove
family, Glendinning's hosts in North Carolina, responded to his terror of
the devil. According to Glendinning, some members of that prosperous,
slaveholding yeoman family assured him that they, too, saw Lucifer—that
"they saw him go off, like a gust," or "that they had seen him on the top of
the cabin, or in the orchard, or some other place." But those remarks were
almost certainly meant to pacify a man whom they believed beyond
reason. As much is indicated by Glendinning's exchange with Mrs. Hargrove and one of his rare mortal visitors, Mrs. Leonard Sims, the wife of a
neighboring gentleman. When Glendinning announced that Lucifer
would take him bodily "down to the pit," Madame Sims stoutly objected
that "it could not be so." At that, Glendinning grew agitated and appealed
to Mrs. Hargrove, who, perhaps after shooting a significant glance at her
neighbor, declared that she "could not deny" having seen the devil. Other
Hargrove kin conveyed their disbelief directly—and so commonly that
Glendinning suspected that "a large black appearance" looming before
him on one occasion was none other than "one Argil Hanks," a Hargrove
son-in-law, wrapped "in a dark-coloured great coat, in order to frighten
me." Even the Hargrove children insisted on an empirical demonstration
of the devil's presence, among them the couple's two young daughters,
who, despite Glendinning's warning that the family should forbid any "to
come nigh me," in the event of another visit from Lucifer, brought supper
to his cabin one evening. When he claimed to hear the devil knocking, the
girls dragged him toward the door, saying, "*let us see if he can't take you,
and we will believe it.*" In other words, Hargrove kin and neighbors of
every age and sex variously soothed Glendinning, challenged him, even
baited him, but they did not take him seriously.[41]

Such skepticism among both comfortable yeoman clans like the Hargroves and gentry families like the Simses weighed heavily in Asbury's

decision to repudiate Glendinning. But it was even more urgent for the Methodists—and indeed, for all evangelicals at the turn of the century—to exorcise the specters that his testimony conjured for a far greater number of white southerners. These were mainly, but by no means entirely, men and women of humbler means—the nonslaveholding yeomanry and tenant farmers—who, knowing little or nothing of the new learning that banished demons from the natural world, still accepted what many of their betters and perhaps even some among their peers now shunned as superstition. It may have taken the advent of evangelicals to school those southerners in the fullness of Satan's sway, but many were already primed to receive that instruction by their sense of living in an enchanted universe. For such people, being exposed to evangelical teachings merely wove the dark threads of diabolism into what was already a richly hued tapestry of supernatural lore. Even as the Age of Reason was attaining its American meridian over Thomas Jefferson's study at Monticello, the powers ruling the world that many southern whites still inhabited were not the natural laws of a benevolent Deity but a panoply of mysterious and sometimes sinister forces. From settled coastal regions to scattered frontier enclaves, there could be found people of every class, color, and creed who entertained, with varying degrees of conviction, beliefs in the foretelling power of dreams and portents, in the efficacy of magic and witchcraft, and in the ability of spirits, benign or wicked, to take visible form. While it is well known that such beliefs played a powerful role in the sacred worlds of both Native and African Americans, less fully appreciated is their persistence among whites. But they, too, numbered among the many southerners who adhered to those varied forms of supernaturalism, often an amalgam of European, West African, and Indian lore, with no sense of their being incompatible with Christian teachings.[42]

The fascination with dreams was nearly universal. While some southern whites regarded them as curiosities, provoking a passing moment of apprehension or anticipation, those who held that either God or the devil could raise these "night visions" took them seriously as warnings and guides. John Craig, a university-trained Presbyterian minister in western Virginia, insisted that a "dream or vision" dating from his youth had revealed "as it were in a miniature the whole that has happened to me of any importance these thirty-five years yea the very place I have been settled." His self-taught colleagues among the Baptist and Methodist clergy put the same trust in their dreams, which variously predicted the death of loved ones, the remedies for sickness, the onset of revivals, and opposition to their ministries. Lay people, too, both evangelical and otherwise, took direction from what sleep disclosed. One Eastern Shore Methodist, long unable to give up his beloved violin despite churchly admonitions, finally found the resolve in a dream, whereupon he started from his bed, seized that "unruly member" (the violin, presumably), "ran out to a fence corner, and with one fierce blow broke the instrument to shivers." More prosaically, another southerner, gripped by the national mania for treasure hunting, dreamt that his dead mother told him where to find some "plates" buried during his childhood, which he then dug for successfully.[43]

Portents held the same purchase on the imagination of many southern whites. Entire neighborhoods were roused to terror and piety by earthquakes, solar eclipses, and the aurora borealis—natural wonders widely viewed as heralding the end of the world. More curiously, many people regarded certain birds as harbingers of death; hence Francis Asbury's musing over a young Maryland woman "in deep distress of mind, occasioned by the flight of a whip-poor-will close to her, which strangely led her to fear her end was nigh." Odd coincidences also invited some to ponder their possible meaning, like the "deistically inclined" carpenter in southern Ohio who reconsidered his doubts that "God can reveal things to men" when, in succession, three newly built coffins mysteriously fell apart—each collapse followed by another death in the neighborhood. Other omens carried a significance clear to all: "[A]mong white and coloured," one South Carolinian reported, "if any one appeared willing to die, and no remarkable incident (as a storm, etc.) occurred at the time, it was taken for granted that such a one had gone to heaven, no matter what had been his manner of life."[44]

If dreams and portents might reveal the shape of things to come, a repository of lore and charms fortified many men and women to meet present difficulties. Prudent farmers never started any task on "unlucky" Fridays, while those more daring tried to break droughts by digging an alligator out of its cave and turning the beast on its back. Magical cures for disease were as various as the woes they promised to remedy: Frontier Georgians held that the ravages of malaria could be controlled, among other ways, by looping a string around a fruit-bearing tree and, as the afflicted person shook during a bout of fever, tying it with a knot for every tremor. Southerners also turned to magic to account for life's misfortunes and mysteries. In 1745, when some cattle belonging to John Craig mysteriously sickened and died, he accepted the belief current among his western Virginia neighbors that witchcraft was responsible, "for I real[l]y thought then and Now that God had permitted Satan and his Emissaries to Destroy them." More than half a century later, many still invoked witchcraft to explain the inexplicable. In 1799, concerned members of one Virginia family summoned the Methodist preacher William Ormond "to see two little Girls that were in a Strange way," because "they were bewitched." Brantley York recalled that whenever people in his rural North Carolina neighborhood came together around the turn of the century, "the most prominent topic of conversation was relating some remarkable witch tales, ghost stories, and conjurations of various kinds."

Warding off threats of this magnitude—from witches who could transform themselves into any animal, survive any shot except a silver bullet, and even creep through keyholes—required more than the tricks of amateurs. In such cases, many southerners turned to professional practitioners of countermagic, white and black. There were "witch-doctors" who, for a price, would break any spell, as well as fortune-tellers who not only foretold the future but located lost objects. Among the many seeking their expertise was James Potter Collins, once he grudgingly concluded that witchcraft caused his chronic insomnia—although "I was once opposed to the belief, as much as any man living." What swayed Collins, usually nothing short of Melvillian in his wariness of confidence men, was the testimony of some respectable neighbors, confirmed by the advice of a local doctor, who suggested that his malaise might be the "African poison," also called "tricking," and allowed that he had seen two men cured by an "old African" conjurer.[45]

In short, the South that spawned the likes of Jefferson was still a culture steeped in supernaturalism. Knowing as much, Francis Asbury shared Glendinning's premise that many denizens of that enchanted world would be susceptible to the terror of a visible devil. But where Glendinning could see only opportunity beckoning, Asbury sensed disaster looming. He recognized that the strategy of stoking lay fears of such a demon could all too easily backfire if ordinary people concluded that evangelical affinities actually raised the devil, beckoning that dark spirit into the midst of believers and daring Lucifer to do his worst. Decades of itinerant proselytizing had only strengthened Asbury's concerns on that score. As his remarkable journal reveals, the bishop spent nearly all of his adult life touring America, mainly the South and its western country, lodging in the homes of the faithful, addressing audiences of every class and color, and quizzing his preachers about life among the laity. Those experiences enabled Asbury, perhaps better than any of his contemporaries, to understand both the satisfactions that evangelical faith afforded and the anxieties it induced. He had either met or heard of many men and women who feared that following the way of the cross might end in robbing them of every inner resource essential to survival in a harsh and hostile world. And among them were some whose greatest dread was that repenting their sins would rouse Satan to appear before their horrified eyes in their fields, their barns, their bedchambers.

What added to Asbury's concern were reports circulating throughout the late-eighteenth-century South that only uncommon—and unholy—powers could account for the effects evangelical preachers sometimes wrought upon individuals and audiences. One convert reported that upon first meeting Shubal Stearns, the first Separate Baptist missionary in the South, his gaze "made me feel in such a manner as I had never felt before. . . . I began to think that he had an evil eye and ought to be shunned." Suspicions of the Methodists ran deeper still; observe the reaction of one community in the South Carolina low country, where none "had ever heard of any one being stricken down, or led to cry for mercy," after one man, in the midst of a Methodist sermon, "commenced shaking like a leaf in the wind, and down he fell on the floor." His collapse convinced the entire neighborhood "that the power that attended Methodist preaching was something magical, or wizardly. . . . that the preacher was supplied with some strange powders, which he had wrapped up in his handkerchief, and during the exercises he gave it a flirt, and these powders fell on the men and women present."

Reports that preachers practiced not merely conjuring tricks but a "devilish necromancy" susurrated among the white laity everywhere in the South. They echo in rumors whispered on the wharves of Norfolk, that a visiting Methodist preacher had cast a spell on a ship. They quaver in the fear of a Quaker woman drawn to Methodism "that it was witchcraft, and that she was bewitched," and in the pledge of an Anglican man that "none of them [the Methodist clergy] should put a *spell* on me, to make me fall down and pretend to be converted." They resound in the outrage of some western Virginians who, after watching as their neighbors "fell to the floor as if they were shot" at a Methodist service, "gathered their friends and relatives up, and carried them out of the house, saying this was the work of the devil." Asbury's trained ear might even have detected something backhanded in the familiar compliment that silver-tongued Methodists could "preach the devil out of hell," if only because of hearing so often the angry charge that they "preached people down to hell and then left them there." In fact, at the opening of the nineteenth century, Asbury himself faced public charges of being "a sorcerer, a Wizard," leveled, to compound the embarrassment, by a former Methodist clergyman. His accuser, Jeremiah Minter, alleged that during a chance encounter with the bishop in the Allegheny Mountains, Asbury "cried aloud and raised the devil to help himself against me . . . in the exact form of a pale grey horse, and I saw him as plain as eyes could see for a moment. . . . Thus was F. Asbury dealing with and bowing down to and worshipping devils."[46]

So, Asbury knew to a nicety how supernaturalisms still pervasive in much of the South could as easily work against evangelicals as for them. Preaching the terrors of diabolism could reach a point of diminishing returns, especially in the face of widespread lay fears that their clergy "must be sent of the devil." While being credited with those powers made evangelical preachers men to be reckoned with, it did not place them in choice company, for the ranks of those believed to do more than dabble in the powers of darkness also included not only a handful of white witches and witch doctors but many more black conjurers and Indian shamans. There was the very real prospect that men thus reputed might frighten off more people than they attracted. It all added up to Asbury's decision that Glendinning had to go—less because he beggared the credulity of a select few steeped in rationalism than because he might scare off a majority who had suspended less completely, or not at all, the belief in an enchanted universe.[47]

Yet even as Asbury came to that conclusion, the danger of dispensing with a visible devil was not lost on him. Would the clergy's whittling down Satan to an unseen presence lead to other concessions, setting evangelicals on the slippery slope toward skepticism? Could the case be posed that starkly: no devil, no God? Doubtless, as Asbury pondered those questions, the shade of his spiritual father, John Wesley, rose in his mind's eye to reproach and warn, as he had in life, that most learned men in Europe "have given up all accounts of witches and apparitions as mere old wives' tales," for "they well know . . . that giving up witchcraft is, in effect, giving up the Bible; and they know . . . that if but one account of the intercourse of men with separate spirits be admitted, their whole castle in the air (Deism, Atheism, Materialism) falls to the ground." "I know no reason, therefore," Wesley concluded, "why we should suffer even this weapon to be wrested out of our hands."[48]

Weapon it was, and surrendering any advantage in the spiritual warfare that consumed his life was not Asbury's style. But experience had shown him its double edge, which threatened to cut so deeply into his cherished goals as to fix his resolve to rid American Methodism of Glendinning's devil. Yet he could deny neither the wisdom of Wesley's caution that any concession to rationalism might prove costly nor the shrewdness of Glendinning's insight that much could be gained by exploiting lay supernaturalism. So if Glendinning himself had to go, some elements of his missionary strategy might well be adopted by those whose lighter touch in striking the chords of wonder would achieve a more delicate economy of terror—enough to frighten people into evangelical churches instead of scaring them away.

Viewed in this light, the strange odyssey of William Glendinning becomes more than the story of a rogue preacher ousted into obscurity by an evangelical church bent on respectability. Just as his besetting demons evoke some of the starkest fears aroused by evangelicals during their earliest decades in the South, his repudiation illuminates one chapter in the story of how Baptists and Methodists refashioned their faiths to win greater acceptance among whites. That effort took place on many fronts, and ultimately it reconfigured an entire religious movement, forging the shape that evangelicalism has assumed not only in the South but elsewhere in the United States down to the present. It issued from an intricate interplay between resistance on the part of the white southern laity and efforts at adaptation led mainly by the Baptist and Methodist clergy. As early as the 1780s, that dynamic of challenge and response was yielding some important changes in the teachings and practices of both churches, but many of the most sweeping transformations unfolded in the decades after 1800. And among the most basic of these efforts at redefining evangelicalism during those years was the search for ways to assure wary whites that spiritual intensity would not prove to be their undoing.

Those strategies included, but went well beyond, stripping the Prince of Darkness of his power to take visible form. Indeed, the first and perhaps most fateful initiative involved pushing other "dark presences" to the margins of evangelical culture—segregating worship by race. Even from the outset of their ministries in the South, evangelicals had followed the Anglican practice of relegating African-American worshippers to the back of churches, upper galleries, or "sheds" attached to the side. When large numbers of whites turned out for preaching, blacks were excluded from the churches entirely, permitted only to stand outside and listen from under open windows. In the decades following the Revolution, the etiquette of racial separation became even more firmly entrenched. On many plantations, Baptist and Methodist clergymen routinely preached to slaves apart, especially after sunset released them from their work. On others, preachers prayed with white families in the parlor while slaves were permitted to listen from no closer than the kitchen. Methodist ministers also convened African Americans separately for class meetings, love feasts, and communion services. Even at outdoor gatherings like camp meetings, when more than one preacher was at hand, whites and blacks met in two groups. That drift toward distancing the races in worship settings both reflected and reinforced white evangelicals' retreat from any effort to ban slaveholders from their fellowship.[49]

A rare account of how blacks responded to being consigned, quite literally, to the fringes of fellowship, appears in the records of one troubled Tennessee Baptist church. By the hot summer of 1820, that congregation had grown so large that the pastor, one Brother Darden, asked "the Black people to go out of the meeting house and give place to the white People." They did not go quietly: African-American members objected to such high-handed treatment and made "some disturbance" before stalking out. A flurry of church meetings ensued, ending, predictably, with the white brethren voting "that the Black people are, hereafter, to give place or go out of the meeting house, when called upon or requested to do so." As the church's white clerk assured posterity, the black dissidents finally admitted their error in "leaving our communion in the manner they did," and thus was the dispute "satisfactorily settled." But in fact, many of the church's black members were neither contrite nor satisfied; one Luke was overheard by his master to say, "scratch his name off of the Book . . . that he never intended to have anything to do with religion any more, as long as he lived."[50]

Many black brothers and sisters in other biracial churches shared Luke's outrage at such betrayals of spiritual equality, and their disillusionment fueled the segregation of worship. As early as 1790, John Leland observed that blacks generally "put more confidence in [preachers of] their own color, than they do in whites," but failed to add that white prejudice promoted black preference for worshipping apart. Even by the end of the eighteenth century, pious slaves on some plantations met in the evening to pray, sing, and exhort, and others formed their own churches. In the decades after the Revolution, a growing number of such churches appeared, usually led by the region's swelling urban free black population and often drawing slave members from nearby plantations. Those separate black churches, mostly Baptist congregations, emerged mainly in cities like Richmond and Charleston, but as early as 1791, one group of Methodist slaves owned by a rural Maryland family had built their own meetinghouse.[51]

Many white southerners, including some evangelicals, cast a wary eye on black churches and informal worship within the slave quarters, fearing that such meetings might breed rebellion. Widely shared were the apprehensions that drove the white members of North Carolina's Flat River Baptist Church to oppose slaves meeting together for worship, "which perhaps may lead to licentiousness." The clergy could not discount such concerns, but they held fast to the comfort of having chosen the lesser of two evils. Suspect as separate black worship was to some white lay people, most preachers judged it less troubling than a "promiscuous" mixture of the races at religious gatherings. They saw, too, that their churches stood to lose influence among African Americans, some already alienated by their shabby treatment at the hands of white members, if they were also deprived of the liberty of worshipping apart. The denouement at Flat River demonstrates as much: White objections to slave meetings drew an angry outburst from Isham, a spiritual leader among that church's African-American members. Seeing what was at stake, the white brethren stopped short of prohibiting such gatherings, instead requiring black members to "obtain leave" in the future. Yet that concession did not keep black membership at Flat River from falling off sharply over the next decade.[52]

The drift toward segregated worship did not create a cordon sanitaire that prevented any religious contact between the races. For decades after the Revolution, whites flocked to hear African-American preachers, blacks accepted the ministries of whites, and converts of both races testified to their experiences before entire churches. But white evangelicals steadily limited occasions for the races to draw close together during worship, while other changes assured masters that the churches spared no vigilance in monitoring their black brothers and sisters. After 1800 it became accepted procedure in Baptist and Methodist churches to seek the permission of masters before accepting slaves as members. Nor did whites relax their oversight after admitting blacks to membership. African Americans were less likely than whites to face charges of misconduct in church courts, but if convicted they were far more likely to be expelled rather than merely censured or suspended for a period of time. What assisted imposition of such severe discipline on black members was the exclusion of African Americans from any authoritative role in church government. While some black evangelicals, usually men, had earlier enjoyed the privilege of voting in Baptist church deliberations, most societies had withdrawn that liberty around the turn of the century, arguing that "The degraded state of the minds of slaves, rendered them totally incompetent to the task of judging correctly respecting the business of the church." The message from the ruling white brethren could not have been clearer: They intended to keep their black fellows on a short leash, one that, at every stage of membership, might tighten the noose of mastery.[53]

Erecting barriers to interracial intimacy within the churches was part of a broader strategy to ease the white laity into accepting the demands of evangelical spirituality. Baptists and Methodists continued to emphasize the necessity of experiencing a wrenching rebirth, but they took new precautions to prepare people for its rigors. The main vehicles for conveying such solace were the published memoirs of the clergy, which began to trickle from American presses as early as the 1790s and then poured out after 1820. Appearing both in religious periodicals and books, in the form of autobiographies, hagiographies, and edited collections of journals and letters, all were freighted with diverse agendas. But the single feature common to such memoirs are descriptions of the varieties of inner struggle attending the way of the cross. All preachers rendered in meticulous detail their own progress from conviction to conversion, and most also included relations of similar spiritual passages among the laity.

Many clergymen shone as contributors to that endeavor, but among the best was John Taylor, a Baptist whose recollections of his youthful conversion in western Virginia and later ministry to ten Kentucky churches appeared in 1823. His own awakening began at the age of seventeen when, attending a Baptist gathering "with the same view, that I would have gone to a frolic," he felt the preacher's words "pierce my soul as quick . . . as an electric shock." Yet for a year afterward, Taylor clung to his former "vice and folly," because "the attaining of true religion seemed so perfectly out of my reach . . . and, as I was to be lost at last, I had better try to enjoy myself." Besides, "praying looked to me both awful and dangerous—awful for a sinner to approach an infinitely holy God, and great danger of offending God, more than to omit the duty." Hoping to overcome his fear of sacrilege, Taylor tried to reform his "external vices and read the scriptures a great deal," only to be persuaded that the "poor rags of my own righteousness" could not conceal the soul's corruption. He grew ever more despondent, believing that "the time had been when I might have been saved, but . . . it was now too late." For months, he ate little and slept less, whereupon "my father's family took the alarm that I had gone beside myself, and to tell the truth, I was driven to my wit's end, believing that I was sure to be lost, as if I was then in hell." Ceasing even to pray for mercy, Taylor "acknowledge[d] God's justice in my condemnation" and concluded that "no man ever saw and felt what I did, till just before God . . . sent them to hell . . . and that I should die soon." Even when the first stirrings of hope eased his sufferings, he suspected that "it was the Devil deceiving me." The same themes are adumbrated—with some variations—in Taylor's remembrances of the spiritual pilgrimages of Kentuckians under his ministry.

Such clerical narratives thus addressed every possible contingency attending repentance—the deepening sense of worthlessness and withering of hope, the physical debility and emotional paralysis, even the mental distraction and suicidal impulses. It was the object of Taylor and his colleagues to demystify those symptoms by presenting them as unexceptional, familiar stages in the morphology of conversion as experienced by many men and women. The clergy also emphasized that such struggles, no matter how harrowing or protracted, nearly always ended in the rapture of grace. Although private journals and letters permit of a less sanguine conclusion, in the devotional literature published after the turn of the century happy endings abound.[54]

And in this same literature of lay reassurance, preachers dealt with the devil. Specifically, they sought to dispel fears of Satan's ability to take visible form. The most telling evidence of that aim appears in the changing versions of his ministerial career produced by Freeborn Garrettson. A contemporary of Glendinning, Garrettson spoke pure southern owing to his origins as the educated, native-born son of a slaveholding Maryland family, people who could hold their heads high among the Hargroves and perhaps folks even grander. In short, Garrettson was what Glendinning was not: one of the golden lads of early American Methodism. As such, he was encouraged to publish his memoirs, a first edition in 1790, quickly followed by a second the next year. That commercial success owed much to Garrettson's spicing his narrative with stories of encountering supernatural entities, including the devil. As a young preacher struggling for sanctification late in the 1770s, he recalled seeing "with my bodily eyes a ghostly appearance, which in a few moments vanished away." Subsequently he began "falling into a visionary way," communing with both demons and angels, and once "saw the devil who appeared very furious; he came near to me and declared with bitterness [that] he would be the death of me . . . thus saying, he began pelting me with stones and bedaubing me with dirt, till I felt wounded almost to death." Finally, Garrettson confided, "without fear of man, though these things may appear strange to some people," he tussled with Lucifer himself, who "made his appearance" atop the preacher's bed. At first, "he felt like a cat; he then got hold of my pillow. I now believed it to be the fiend, and was not alarmed. I took hold of the pillow and pulled at it. I cried out, get behind me, Satan; and immediately he vanished."[55]

Those disclosures made Garrettson one of the few bold souls among the early evangelical clergy willing to assert that Satan could be seen, even combated. Most inconveniently, however, the only other preacher taking so public a stance in the 1790s was William Glendinning. Indeed, just as Garrettson was savoring the acclaim of authorship, Glendinning was relating his own dealings with the devil to southern audiences and preparing his narrative for publication. That goes a long way toward explaining why, when a popular evangelical magazine serialized his memoirs in 1794, Garrettson produced a version stripped of every reference to the apparitions and demons abounding in his first two editions. Obviously, the message had come down from Asbury that there was no room in the ranks of the Methodist clergy for anyone who could be confused with Glendinning. Garrettson duly toed the line and made the appropriate excisions; even so, Asbury exiled him to preach until the end of his days in New England and upstate New York.[56]

Garrettson's retreat on the devil's power set the tone for the memoirs of his colleagues that appeared in later decades. Indeed, throughout the first half of the nineteenth century, most evangelical clergymen took pains in all their public statements to dispel lay fears that Satan could assume corporeal presence. In recollections published in 1805, Benjamin Abbott, while admitting that the fear of seeing Lucifer in bodily form shrouded his own approach to conversion, emphasized that such terrors took shape from his overwrought emotions. And as late as 1856, Peter Cartwright related that, while under conviction, "it really appeared to me that he [the devil] was surely personally there to seize and drag me down to hell," but found solace in his mother's advice that such impressions were merely the "device" of a thwarted Satan.[57]

Even so, evangelicals did not put Satan behind them. While most men entering the ministry after about 1800 discouraged the view that the devil could take visible form, they did not categorically deny it. They could not. Ruling out that possibility altogether would not only have infringed on divine sovereignty but impugned some of the founding fathers of their churches in the South—men, unlike Glendinning, whose reputations for sanity and sanctity had survived their claims to entertaining Satan and whose days of ministering (and composing memoirs) lasted into the early nineteenth century. Besides Garrettson, those ranks included the barely literate Eastern Shore Methodist preacher John Thomas, who claimed that the devil had once hurled "a knot of pine wood at his head," as well as the western country's learned Valentine Cook, who insisted that he had crossed paths with Lucifer in the Allegheny Mountains and engaged him in an elaborate exchange reminiscent of a more celebrated temptation in a biblical desert.

What to make of such anecdotes challenged the ingenuity of younger clergymen who wrestled with the thankless charge of redacting the literary remains of their literal-minded elders. But some found a way to make the most of it. Cook's antebellum hagiographer, William Stevenson, summoned up enough nerve to take the devil by the horns, insisting that the old man's "rencontres with the prince of darkness" were meetings with "a real presence." But then he added, with a wink to his readers whose conversance ran more to French than to demons, that "it was this strong and palpable view of subjects that gave such an interest to all he [Cook] said." Few of Stevenson's contemporaries proved as deft, but all managed to convey the same message—that seeing the devil was simply a quaint eccentricity of their sainted elders, a curious artifact of a comfortably bygone piety. Indeed, what arises from their rendering of such "rencontres" smells less like the harrowing stench of brimstone than the subtler odor of condescension. Even without lapsing into French, their patronizing tone cued sophisticated readers not to shiver but to smile indulgently. As for those too simple to share the joke, there could be no harm in their believing that these venerable pioneers had faced down devils in the heroic past.[58]

Then, too, even as the devil receded from evangelical discourse as a visible presence, the devout continued to pay tribute to his sway as an unseen entity. Satan's power over the hearts and minds of individuals remained a matter beyond dispute. When one distraught Tennessee Baptist woman attempted suicide in 1812, the church readily set down her desperate act to "a weakening of mind and temptation of the wicked one." Undiminished, as well, was the conviction that the unrepentant were the devil's rightful prey, even if he no longer appeared personally to claim them in life. Well into the nineteenth century, Methodist preachers expelled the wayward from communion by publicly proclaiming that the church was "giving them to Satan." Above all, Lucifer was still a name with which to conjure general attention. When nineteenth-century ministers wanted to attract big crowds to their meetings, they often resorted to the proven ploy of promising "to preach from the words of the devil." Most likely, those lay people less steeped in Scripture felt suckered when such pulpit performances turned out to be nothing more sensational than sermons based on the biblical texts relating Jesus' temptation in the desert. A more titillating contribution to evangelical devil-exploitation was a best-selling tract first published in 1803 and provocatively titled *News from the Infernal Regions*, in which Caleb Jarvis Taylor, Kentucky Methodism's answer to Charles Brockden Brown, evoked a sinister conclave of demons scheming to destroy evangelicalism by encouraging animosity among rival churches.[59]

The strategy of toning down—but not dispensing with—diabolism's terrors reflects the broader repositioning of early-nineteenth-century evangelicals with respect to traditional forms of supernaturalism. Unlike their eighteenth-century predecessors, later generations of preachers openly dismissed beliefs in witchcraft and magic as "superstition," and many became notably more circumspect in weighing the import of dreams, portents, and visions. In part, those shifts register the emergence of a more mature and educated clergy among the Baptists and Methodists, men who prized acceptance among the South's well-read and well-heeled.

But these changes also suggest that evangelicals, feeling more secure in their influence by the early nineteenth century, now felt equal to the task of taking on all competitors who claimed leverage in dealing with the supernatural. Such was the determination that inspired one North Carolina Baptist association in 1825 to bar the faithful from seeking out "those who pretend to use the art of witchcraft or what is termed Conjuration for advice or relief in any case whatever." And in the evangelical campaign to weaken the hold of those wonder-workers on southern whites, there could have been few weapons more potent than the clergy's insistence that such credulity was confined to African Americans. As the Baptist minister Charles Colcock Jones suavely asserted in 1842, only blacks embraced the lore of "second-sight . . . apparitions, charms, witchcraft, and . . . a kind of irresistible Satanic influence. . . . superstitions brought from Africa [not] wholly laid aside."[60]

Yet even as they distanced themselves from the world of wonders, nineteenth-century evangelicals did not scruple to exploit the lay fears sustaining its sway. A classic instance appears in Peter Cartwright's account of fending off two young gentlemen who proposed to beat the daylights out of him for "giving their sisters the jerks." A sharp, spasmodic twitching of all or part of the body, "the jerks" often afflicted those overcome by emotion at evangelical gatherings of that era. One of his would-be assailants believed that Cartwright had wrought that effect by magic, having seen him "take out a phial, in which I carried some truck that gave his sisters the jerks." Waving the offending bottle—from which he chugged peppermint to ward off the bad breath that could blight any budding preacher's career—Cartwright threatened, "Yes; if I gave your sisters the jerks, I'll give them to you." This tale, probably told many times to chuckling audiences of the faithful before finding its way into his published memoirs, captures the Janus-faced quality of the new evangelical approach to traditional supernaturalism. Cartwright's intent in relating the story was to deride lay credulity and confute the image of Methodist preachers as a pack of conjurers, but it also reveals that he was not above playing upon lay belief in his preternatural powers.[61]

Many of his contemporaries, even as they scorned superstition and ruled out lay recourse to witch-doctors and fortune-tellers, also cast the clergy as powerful shamans who commanded skills that can only be called magical. Among those talents was controlling the weather: As one nineteenth-century biographer informed his readers, the early Virginia

Methodist preacher Joseph Everett, who happened to be preaching as a storm raged, "prayed for the thunder to come yet nigher." It came. He called out a second time, "O Lord send thy thunder still nigher!" With that "the house appeared to be ablaze with lightning," setting afire the piety of those present. Variations on such pulpit ploys remained current among nineteenth-century preachers like John Early, who exulted to his diary in 1808 that when the lightning flashed during one worship service, "I immediately got to my knees and told the people I would . . . pray that God in his great mercy would withhold the rain until we were done. The rain immediately blew over. . . ." Like many of his clerical contemporaries, Early also claimed the power to predict the future, on one occasion telling his audience of "the awful curse that would come upon them if they did not do better than they had, and that some would die before I preached there again." Given mortality rates in the early South, clergymen might venture such projections with real confidence; somewhat harder to understand is why some lay people took them as prophetic.

Perhaps it was because many of the faithful endowed men of God with even more awesome talents which ministers' demurrals only served to confirm. Some believed that preachers possessed an intuitive grasp of an individual's character, right down to detecting the darkest secrets of his or her past. Among them was a bigamist in the western country who confessed his sin after being converted by Henry Smith, being "fully persuaded that I knew all about him." The antebellum biographer of Valentine Cook likewise regaled his readers with tales of how some members of that preacher's western country flock believed that he could heal the sick by the laying on of hands, even though Cook "utterly disclaimed the possession of such power." Still, "there were some among the simple-hearted people of the country who . . . maintained he possessed the apostolic 'gift of healing' " and "insisted that he would lay his hands on the part where it was supposed the disease was located." Here is evangelical finessing at its finest: While disclaiming any faith-healing powers for Cook, assuring readers of his belief that "God alone could rebuke disease," it still left the impression that he was a shaman before whose touch sickness fled.[62]

Such were the strategies by which nineteenth-century evangelicals sought at once to uphold their respectability among the learned without surrendering their influence over less skeptical members of the laity. The clergy wanted to have it both ways—to discount the sway of demons and wonder-workers even as they played upon the susceptibilities of those who still inhabited a world shot through with marvel and mystery. It was a delicate business, an artful trimming intended to maximize their appeal to a diverse audience of southern whites. Even now its seamiest side haunts some quarters of American evangelicalism, taking perverse shape in the promises of charlatans to cure the sick and "expose" the ritual abuse of children by Satanic cults.

Nor was that the sole legacy of evangelicals who settled with the devils raised by William Glendinning by colluding, in some form, to leave them at large. Recognizing those demons as emblems of the terror that revealing the private self conjured for southern whites, evangelicals stilled such lay anxieties by moving darker brothers and sisters to the margins of church fellowship, even as they beckoned slaveholders to its center. This betrayal of spiritual equality cost far more in the currency of conscience than stealing a little of Satan's thunder, and as much echoes in the shrill defensiveness of Francis Asbury's famous retort that "I am called upon to suffer for Christ's sake, not for slavery." Yet that had become the calculus, simple and stark, of most southern evangelical leaders by 1800; nothing meant more to them than reclaiming white souls, and nearly any concession to the South's ruling race could be justified in the name of that end. It would require nothing short of that fierce, single-minded resolve to ensure that evangelicals would attain their goal, for the white laity's opposition to their early teachings and practices went well beyond warding off incursions into the sanctum of the self and shunning spiritual intimacy with African Americans. Much as those matters bedeviled evangelical progress before 1800, their cause also aroused resistance from southern whites who discerned in new faiths other challenges, equally fundamental, to their old way of life.[63]

2

THE SEASON OF YOUTH

Now his parents went to Jerusalem every year at the
feast of Passover. And when he was twelve years old,
they went up according to custom; and when the feast
was ended, as they were returning, the boy Jesus stayed
behind in Jerusalem. . . . After three days they found
him in the temple, sitting among the teachers, listening
to them and asking them questions; and all who heard
him were amazed at his understanding and his answers.
And when they saw him they were astonished; and his
mother said to him, "Son, why have you treated us so?
Behold, your father and I have been looking for you
anxiously." And he said to them, "How is it that you
sought me? Did you not know that I must be in my
Father's house?"

—LUKE, 2:41-49

WELL BEFORE and long after 1800, countless stories circulated
in the South of the marvels taking place wherever evangelicals met. It was said that some fell to the ground, slain by the
spirit of the Lord. There they lay, writhing, groaning, and crying in repentance, a few lapsing into trances from which they glimpsed heavenly glory
or future events on earth. It was said that others, smitten with spiritual
ecstasy, laughed uncontrollably, sang and danced to a music heard by no
one else. Still others, gripped by anxiety over their eternal fate, got "taken
with the jerks," their heads and upper torsos whipping back and forth in
hectic spasms. Of those who came to meetings for sport and left scoffing,
it was said that no small number suffered sudden deaths of exquisite
agony, screaming for mercy as devils bore their souls to hell. Of those
who came and found faith, it was said that divine grace often endowed
them with extraordinary eloquence. The least privileged members of

southern society—African Americans of every age and young white women, men, and children—found a voice to speak of spiritual truths that moved adults of both races to tears.

Many southern whites dismissed such stories as sheer invention or the delusions of overexcited imaginations and overheated emotions. Even among evangelicals there were doubters who dissected in clinical detail the varieties of religious ecstasy and looked for explanations in nature rather than the supernatural. But most of the faithful believed that the events being witnessed and rumored were miracles indeed, proof that the spirit of God wrought upon the souls of men and women in the South and its western country. Beleaguered as they were by the devil, evangelicals knew that they were beloved by God and regarded such astonishing behavior among their adherents as evidence of divine favor. Clergymen collected and published hundreds of firsthand reports in religious periodicals and autobiographical memoirs to silence the scoffers, persuade the curious, and edify the faithful.[1]

That body of southern evangelical literature drew its inspiration from two sources. The first was the lore of wonders, accounts abounding in marvels and miracles, prodigies and portents, which were published on both sides of the Atlantic during the early modern era. An eclectic genre, drawing upon any seeming intrusion of the supernatural into the normal order of the world, its repertoire included tales strikingly similar to the stories of lay religious experience compiled by southern evangelicals—the pious experiencing visions, disembodied voices, and forewarning dreams; the notorious meeting horrible deaths. The second source influencing the southern clergy were narratives of earlier religious awakenings in Britain and its American colonies published in the middle of the eighteenth century. Chroniclers like Jonathan Edwards, a perennial favorite among southern evangelicals, perfected for his many imitators the strategy of establishing the divine origin of revivals by emphasizing the more "surprising" features of lay religious response. Such surprises might take many forms, among them the rapidity with which spiritual excitement spread throughout neighborhoods or the abrupt and fervent conversion of many who had previously displayed indifference. But the most spectacular were precocious displays of piety exhibited by the young—the most memorable, in Edwards's recollection, being little Phebe Bartlet, a four-year-old girl in his parish whose preternatural sanctity made her, for a time, the dominant spiritual influence in her family.[2]

That same fascination with the young and the godly also found its way into the writings of southern evangelicals. Indeed, what often makes for the wonder in their lore is the youth of the main characters. There were young women who lay unconscious for hours and even days on end, their limbs rigid, their breathing barely discernible, who then rose to tell of sublime visions and astonishing revelations. There were children of both sexes who displayed sophisticated religious knowledge, along with the self-possession to command audiences of adults and reduce even the most hardened sinners among them to repentance. And there were men in their teens and early twenties who, often within days of their conversions, experienced an irresistible desire to spread the gospel and poured forth its truths with stirring eloquence.

If evangelicals exaggerated their numbers, such juvenile prodigies were not merely wishful inventions. Even so, the performances of youthful virtuosos were not quite so wondrous as the clergy claimed and many devout lay people believed. Then as now, children of even the tenderest years took in more than their elders suspected and possessed a talent for mimicry that they perfected when hidden from the prying eyes of adults. Thomas Cleland recalled that after a Methodist minister preached several times at his Kentucky grammar school during the 1780s, "The girls . . . held, through the summer, any playtime, religious meetings in the woods. . . . You might hear them at the top of their voices nearly a mile. One or two led in prayer, until all joined the outcry." Elsewhere in Kentucky at about the same time, Polley Woodfork and Hannah Graves, both fourteen, aped the style of spiritual counsel current among Baptist adults in their revival-rocked neighborhood. "After long setting up at meetings, in bed together," they would "weep and converse together chief of the night; and if one should drop to sleep, the other with bedewing tears, raising her warning voice, would say how can you sleep, when every drawing breath may terminate in eternal destruction." Keeping one another at this fevered pitch hastened the conversion of both, with Polley demonstrating, through a close observation of grown-ups, how even young people might come to recognize the marks of saving grace: "These girls sitting together, and Polley seeing something unusual in Hannah's countenance, exclaimed what ails you—receiving no answer, she then replied, Hannah you are converted!"

Boys, too, proved apt at imitating what they saw and heard among adults. Around 1800, one ten-year-old boy favored a Kentucky camp meeting with a pulpit trope that had been in vogue among evangelical preachers for at least fifty years. Held aloft by two men while exhorting a crowd, the boy dropped a handkerchief and cried, "Thus, O sinner, will you drop into hell unless you forsake your sins and turn to God." Just as expert was the group performance witnessed one evening by the Methodist preacher Philip Gatch, who overheard his three youngest grandsons singing and praying in another room of his home: "The eldest one came and leaned against the post of the door . . . and they began to pray for him, 'Lord send down the power; let it come!' He soon cried out, 'It has come!' and he fell on the floor. . . ."

It is likely, then, that the children who so impressed adults at religious gatherings were reprising performances rehearsed earlier for audiences of friends and siblings. The preaching talents "suddenly" shown by young men in their late teens and early twenties yield to a similar explanation. Long before he stunned his local Baptist church with a torrent of eloquence, Jeremiah Jeter relieved the monotony of pushing a plow on every bleak Monday morning by repeating the sermon, "with all its intonations," that he had heard the day before. "This I did," he admitted, "not from any special fondness for preaching or any expectation that I should become a preacher, but merely because it was the most pleasant intellectual exercise within my reach."[3]

To describe such displays as studied is not to discount the religious feelings professed by the young people involved. But it is to acknowledge that evangelicalism presented bright, sensitive children in the rural South with rare opportunities to stimulate their imaginations and engage the attention of both adults and peers. Occasionally, evangelical parents sensed as much, and, for that reason, resisted admitting children under the age of sixteen to church membership. When displayed by African Americans, spiritual precocity sometimes aroused even greater mistrust among whites: In 1823, one Kentucky church voted unanimously to defer baptizing two slave children, aged eight and ten, "fearing they might some way have picked up what they stated [in testifying to their experience] to the church." But more often, both devout parents and preachers encouraged spiritual virtuosity among the youthful and even the very young. In 1778, Methodist Nelson Reed credited the authenticity of the conversion of an eleven-year-old girl in Virginia, viewing her piety as an invitation "to let all adult persons blush," while his colleague James Jenkins boasted of awakening several South Carolina children, "I think none of them . . .

more than fourteen years old." The adult members of one Kentucky Baptist church around 1800 also expressed unqualified enthusiasm when a local revival produced a flood of young converts, remarking that "It looked like the latter days of time, to hear children of eleven or twelve years of age, give such deep and clear relations of experience, as to almost surpass, and certainly to astonish the old members."[4]

Evangelical leaders knew that the young held the power to shape the religious future of the South and its western country, regions where over half the white population was under the age of sixteen. And while most of the adult faithful preferred to regard juvenile piety as solely the result of supernatural intervention, the clergy recognized the role played by peer pressure. Accordingly, they shaped strategies of recruitment that targeted children and adolescents. The Methodists formed "classes" within some congregations that consisted exclusively of children, and others for young, single men and women in their later teens and mid-twenties. Preachers also sought to convert the most popular youths in every neighborhood, hoping that others would follow them into the churches. James Jenkins recalled that the young people in one South Carolina community were "so clanned together it was difficult to make a breach among them." So he set out to sway "the sort of captain among them, in their wildness and fun; and we often said, if we could catch him, we should get all the company." The Baptists used the same tactics: Jeremiah Jeter was persuaded to join that church after a preacher detected his influence over his peers, "among whom I had been a leader in amusements and in mischief."[5]

That array of evangelical devices succeeded with many others, setting off a spiritual domino effect among neighborhood networks of young people. The power of peer example to induce religious seriousness emerges in countless instances of siblings, friends, and schoolmates being drawn together into Methodist and Baptist churches. While affectionate ties among youths of the same sex may have been the most common channels for transmitting spiritual commitment, bonds between brothers and sisters and attachments between sweethearts also helped to draw young people into the churches. During one long Kentucky winter in 1779, as Daniel Trabue and his friends huddled in the cold woods and waited for game to approach a salt lick, one of his companions wished them all back "in old Virginia," where "At this very time their is preaching at Dupuy's [Baptist] Meetinghouse. So many pretty Girles there." Jeremiah Jeter, too, confessed that his first stirring of conviction dated from a western Virginia revival gathering in 1821, which he had attended in the hope of being "amused with a young lady of my acquaintance." Once caught up by the contagion of religious enthusiasm, some young people came to regard "getting religion" as a point of pride, even a contest. Jeter, for one, was mortified to learn of "the conversion of a young female friend, who was awakened . . . after I was," whereupon "my ambitious purpose of outstripping my companions in the celestial race was not only abandoned, but remembered with shame." Less apologetic about vying with other adolescents for spiritual attainment was his contemporary Brantley York, whose "friends were constantly bringing news to me that this one and that had obtained religion. . . . Finally they told me that every penitent had obtained religion but myself—not perhaps, less than fifty in number. . . . I had become willing . . . to suffer anything in order to be relieved of the burden which seemed intolerable to be borne."[6]

It is on the conversion of such young men that the lore of southern evangelicalism, understandably, lingers. Although most children and young women enjoyed only a fleeting local fame at evangelical religious gatherings, young men comprised the ranks from which evangelicals recruited a clergy. Those promising male converts came to be called "young gifts," a term connoting the consensus that they possessed unique spiritual talents and had been bestowed upon the churches by an approving deity. In both senses, they embodied the glorious future of evangelicalism.

Presbyterians profited least from the young gifts raised up in their midst. Most church leaders insisted that all those called by God to preach required the weightier imprimatur of a classical education at Princeton or, at least, a few years in a backwoods academy dispensing rudimentary knowledge of Latin and Greek. That requirement discouraged many young men, who had neither the money nor, they feared, the ability, to master the mysteries of ancient languages and academic life. Their reticence made it impossible for the Presbyterians to train and field a large number of ministers quickly and to fill pulpits as the population moved southward and westward. As a result, Presbyterians in the South generally confined their postwar evangelism to enclaves of receptive Scots-Irish settlers and fell far behind in the competition for new members.[7]

By contrast, the Baptists and Methodists emerged in the decades after the Revolution as the South's strongest evangelical churches, in part because both groups dispensed with a formally educated clergy. They regarded inner claims to divine appointment as sufficient authorization, the truth of which would be tested when young men apprenticed as itinerant preachers. No time was lost when a young gift rose up within their midst. Among the Baptists, that promising young man was first encouraged to open public religious meetings with a prayer or to close them by delivering an exhortation or leading the congregation in a hymn. He might also be urged to expound on passages read aloud from the Bible at household gatherings of family and neighbors. If he completed those exercises satisfactorily, he was then licensed to preach, and, if he proved his mettle in the pulpit, could expect to be ordained as an "elder" (as they styled their ministers) within a few years. The Methodists cultivated an eager recruit by licensing him to exhort or appointing him to serve as class leader and then urging him to accompany an itinerant on his rounds for a few months. If a young man showed the makings of a minister, he was assigned to a circuit and received "on trial" into the "traveling connection" of itinerant preachers. After two years, if he proved his worth, he was admitted to their itinerancy in "full connection."[8]

Not only were the Baptists and Methodists able to marshal more preachers than the Presbyterians, they were prepared to use them more effectively. While most Presbyterian clergy were settled ministers, serving a particular congregation (or two or three neighboring churches), many young Methodists and Baptists began their ministerial careers as itinerants, traveling and preaching both to established congregations and gatherings of the unchurched. That mode of deploying their clergy enabled the Baptists and Methodists to reach an increasingly dispersed population—the tens of thousands of southern families who, during the postwar decades, filtered southward into the Georgia frontier and swarmed westward into Kentucky, Tennessee, and southern Ohio. Drawing mainly on young, single men as itinerants also ensured an inexhaustible supply of cheap and enthusiastic evangelists, a group attuned to the concerns of the lay faithful, especially younger men and women, from whose ranks they had recently been plucked.

Fresh-faced youths also drew the merely curious to religious meetings. The spectacle of a "boy preacher" caused as much of a sensation at the turn of the century as it had in the 1740s when George Whitefield first claimed that title. Popular acclaim for John Crane, who from the age of nine attracted large audiences in middle Tennessee, won him his first circuit at sixteen, while Jacob Young, at the comparatively ripe age of twenty-six, swelled with pride when another Methodist minister rode away after hearing his sermon shouting "Young Whitefield! Young Whitefield!" At the same age, Jeremiah Norman noted that his sermons brought out "perhaps more than would have been if they had not the expectation of hearing the young performer." Prodigies bowled over the Baptists, too: After twenty-one-year-old Wilson Thompson wowed a Kentucky congregation in 1810, a senior minister dubbed him " 'the beardless boy,' by which appelation I was spoken of for some years." Jeremiah Jeter in later life recalled that when he was traveling with another young Baptist preacher in western Virginia in the 1820s, "It was represented that two Bedford plowboys had suddenly entered the ministry and were turning the world upside down," exciting "almost as much interest as a dancing bear."[9]

In itself, the process of culling novice preachers from the ranks of young male converts stirred local excitement. William Watters, who joined the Methodists in 1771 and soon thereafter entered the itinerancy, reported that, in his Maryland neighborhood, "my conversion was . . . much talked of, as also my praying in a short time after without a book, which, to some, appeared a proof that there was a notable miracle wrought on me indeed." Decades later, the appearance of likely prospects still aroused the laity's interest: In 1810, Martha Bonner Pelham in southern Ohio gossiped to her sister-in-law in Virginia that a "smart revival" among the Methodists had yielded one young male convert "who is expected to make a preacher." When novices proved their powers to evoke strong emotions, congregations rejoiced, like the Methodists of one Kentucky society who came away from Jacob Young's first sermon "bathed in tears," so gratified that "they clustered round me, shook my hand." And when his contemporary Thomas Cleland showed talent as an exhorter at a local religious gathering, "it was noised abroad that ' little Tommy Cleland' . . . had commenced *preaching*," and his neighbors eagerly sought him out to speak and pray in private homes and to offer spiritual counsel to troubled souls.[10]

Most men singled out as young gifts at first professed their unworthiness. Undeniably sincere in his humility was the fledgling Methodist itinerant who, as he confided his fears to Francis Asbury after retiring for the night, trembled so much that "the bed shook under him." Among the Baptists, Wilson Thompson hesitated even to enter the pulpit, fearing that "it was too sacred a place for me," and quailed at "the very thought of attempting to preach before the old and wise men of the Church, and before preachers." Such worries prompted the young Methodist Philip Gatch to test his preaching skills in Pennsylvania rather than his native Maryland neighborhood, feeling that "it would be less embarrassing to me." But after displaying due modesty about assuming so great a calling, most novices threw themselves into the Lord's work with the untiring energy and unflagging zeal of all youthful aspirants. Often within a matter of months, the same young men who had agonized over entering the clergy were casting themselves as latter-day apostles, boasting of their heroic sufferings for the faith and their skill in winning new converts.[11]

For a more direct sense of that transformation, enter an evening conclave of Virginia Baptist preachers in 1771, and find them entranced by John Waller's story of being roughed up by an Anglican parson and several gentlemen. Afterward, Waller, by his own account, returned to his congregation and preached with such power that "he could scarcely feel the stripes for the love of God, rejoicing with Paul that he was worthy to suffer for his dear Lord and Master." Another young minister who modeled himself on that apostle, the Methodist Stith Mead, regularly dispatched what he called epistles to congregations on his first circuit in western Virginia in 1792. In return he received and carefully preserved glowing letters from his converts, including Robert and Hannah Chambers of Greenbrier County, who believed that ministers like Mead "will be the most Beloved by the true Disciples of Christ upon Earth," the recipients of "the greatest reward in Heaven." Meeting with opposition could be just as heady, as twenty-two-year-old John Early discovered in 1808 when a justice of the peace in North Carolina threatened to bar him from preaching at the courthouse. "Persecution surely has got almost as high as possible against me without putting me in prison or whipping me," he proudly noted in his diary in 1808. The enemies that he had made won the almost martyred Early a full measure of popular curiosity, if not support; wherever he preached, "people flocked out in crowds, saying 'we want to see and hear this Early.' "[12]

However well they may have succeeded, southern Baptists and Methodists did not set out to create a cult of youth. Even though congregations prayed for young gifts to be raised up from their ranks, even though multitudes thronged the sermons of "boy preachers," evangelicals never took the position that religious virtuosity resided exclusively or even mainly in the young. But their clergy and pious lay people did create a climate within churches that celebrated youthful adepts. The working of wonders among the young at once attested to divine approval of evangelical aims while also advertising their affinities with the primitive Christian church. And in practical terms, Baptists and Methodists had set themselves an ambitious agenda of proselytizing a predominantly youthful population spread over a vast territory. Such a goal dictated their reliance on a traveling clergy, which meant that much of the energy fueling the engines of evangelism would come from men who had spiritual conviction, physical stamina, and, in some cases, financial support from their families. In practice, then, young preachers were endowed with extraordinary authority as spiritual models and religious leaders.

The luck of the Baptists and Methodists in tapping young men's zest and zeal seemed too good to be true—and, of course, it was. Ironically, the youthful clergy who bolstered their ability to attract adherents also contributed to the strife within those churches that ultimately drove many away. The strategy of relying on young recruits that had served so well when it came to staffing their ministries and drawing audiences proved less effective when it came to retaining converts and keeping peace within congregations. Although culled out of the laity and by the laity, young preachers quickly came to regard themselves as entitled to deference from the laity and even from older ministers. Their claims to preference, sanctity, and authority rested not on superior education but instead on a combination of the willingness to endure physical hardship, the power to preach sinners to repentance, and, in the case of the Methodists, the right to rule in the church. Such expectations on the part of young preachers set the stage for what followed—a sharp, protracted generational conflict in a culture in which age still commanded honor and deference. The years of turmoil that ensued not only alienated some of the faithful but kept many unchurched white southerners from joining their communions. It was a chastening experience, one that left many wondering whether their abundance of young gifts might not be, after all, the Trojan horse within the citadel of evangelicalism.[13]

Consider, then, the case of the Methodists. The predominance of young men in their itinerancy began with the American Revolution. In the wake of war, nearly all of the older and more seasoned preachers, relatively recent arrivals from England, returned to the parent country. Those left behind to maintain the Methodists' fledgling churches were mainly preachers in their twenties and early thirties, most of whom either had been born in the colonies or had lived there since adolescence. Their nominal leader and one of only two English itinerants who remained in America, Francis Asbury, had reached the ripe old age of thirty-one in 1776. Meeting with his fellow Virginia itinerants in 1778, Edward Dromgoole, then aged twenty-seven, had ample reason to feel "as if we were like a parcel of Orphans destitute of parents. No old Preacher to direct or guide us." The passage of time did not remedy that problem; few gray eminences graced the Methodist itinerancy until well after the turn of the century. Annual salaries were barely sufficient to support a single man, and because preachers depended for their pay on collections from the faithful, the sums actually received often fell short of those promised. The church made no regular provision for preachers' wives and children until 1796, and even then granted only modest allotments. As a result, most men left the itinerancy and "located" soon after they married, their places taken by even younger men, most in their early to mid-twenties. As probationers, the new recruits preached under the immediate supervision of men not much older or more experienced—other itinerants assigned to the same circuit who, in most cases, had themselves only recently been received into full connection. Both groups answered to "presiding elders," the most senior among the itinerants, who oversaw the several circuits within their "conferences" but paid only occasional visits to each circuit. In other words, most Methodist itinerants in the early South were men in their twenties and early thirties who had little guidance from preachers of greater maturity or seasoning. To the lot of those young men fell hardships and duties that taxed their powers as well as the patience of the laity.[14]

The challenges began when the bishops who headed the Methodist Church assigned each itinerant to a circuit. Most circuits took between four and six weeks to "go round," and the rigors of riding through rugged terrain on poor roads in every sort of weather quickly wore down even the hardiest of men and left their mounts rickety and lame. There were dangers, too, as Jeremiah Norman discovered when assigned a circuit along the North Carolina coast. Sometimes he could reach his preaching appointments only by navigating swollen creeks in tiny boats—or crossing paths with "Allegators." One surly brute stretching a scaly five feet Norman had to beat with a stick "until I was sure there could be no more life in him, broke some bones in his head, and he seemed to be useless"—

only to be ridiculed later by expert locals who insisted that so substantial a reptile could not have succumbed to so puny a weapon. Nor were two-legged creatures always more welcoming when preachers approached. Usually itinerants changed circuits annually, so they arrived as strangers and were often met with hostility or suspicion for that reason alone. In 1795, Henry Smith found Kentuckians wary of "these traveling preachers," for "we know them not, nor from whence they came." North Carolinians could be just as prickly: One who encountered John Early on the road in 1810, upon learning "that I had no abiding city . . . said I was either a gambler or a Methodist preacher." More than a habitual mistrust of outsiders made for such chilly receptions. Shady characters posing as preachers caused so much trouble among the laity that the Methodists took to issuing certificates to authenticate the identity of their itinerants.[15]

Tension did not always subside once itinerants became more familiar with their circuits. Traveling from one preaching appointment to the next, they rarely lodged at inns or taverns but relied on the hospitality of the faithful. Ministers and their horses arrived at private homes hungry and weary from the day's journey, and sometimes both required more than food and shelter. Their journals catalogue the cycle of sufferings to which the flesh was heir—sinus headaches and nagging colds brought on by changeable weather in spring and fall; heat exhaustion from long rides in steamy summers; chilblains and frostbite from fording icy rivers in bitter-cold winters. In all seasons, they were beset by intestinal ailments, sometimes brought on by viruses contracted in close lodgings and, in other instances, by too trusting an indulgence in the local cuisine. As a result, sick preachers could end up imposing on lay hospitality for days or even weeks while Methodist sisters nursed them back to health. For the brethren, the trouble and expense came on those many occasions when itinerants' horses ran off, obliging hosts to spend days scouring the countryside or finding another luckless beast to continue the circuit. Even when preachers kept their health and their horses, they could be finicky guests, liable to complain about the exuberance of young children or the mirth of other adults. After one long night of being serenaded by "abominable Songs, and ho[a]rse laughters, and high hallows, at other times blowing the still cap," a sleepless James Meacham vowed never again to lodge in any home harboring a distillery.[16]

But itinerants demanded even more when acting in their ministerial capacity. Besides preaching at least once at each stop on their circuit, they also admitted new members to fellowship. Unlike the Baptists, the Methodists did not restrict their membership to those who had experienced conversion, but admitted men and women who were still struggling for that assurance. Even so, membership could not be had merely for the asking, and itinerants held the exclusive power to receive or refuse those seeking it. Young preachers could be particularly ruthless about separating the sheep from the goats: In one Maryland neighborhood, Thomas Haskins, just turned twenty-two, "had several applications from persons to join . . . but joined none."[17]

In each neighborhood on their circuits, itinerants also conducted class meetings, at which they encouraged members to relate their spiritual trials and triumphs and inquired into breaches of morality. Rewarding as those meetings sometimes were, they could turn sour when members and lay "class leaders" bridled at being corrected by young preachers. As Jeremiah Norman discovered, some of the faithful came to class meetings in less than a humble spirit, having "made their boast, that the preachers should not examine them." Among such feisty souls was a woman who, when chided by John Early for dancing at a wedding, "p[er]emptorily replied I had no business to catechize her for such little things as that." Indeed, sometimes what lay class leaders led were local revolts against censorious preachers, like the man who "took huge offense" when reproved by Thomas Haskins and then "refused any more to meet the class." Itinerants retaliated, often with the weapon wielded by James Jenkins, who dealt with one truculent South Carolina society by expelling half its members.[18]

Young itinerants prayed hard for more patience, a virtue, to be sure, sorely wanting in their ranks. Zeal made them intolerant of human frailty and rigid when it came to enforcing morality; youth inclined them to regard both traits as strengths. To make matters worse, as newcomers to the places where they preached, they lacked crucial knowledge about individual personalities, kinship networks, and patronage ties. Perhaps worst of all, these self-righteous young strangers came armed with absolute power to expel members from Methodist churches. Until 1800, the procedure for dealing with lay people suspected of wrongdoing provided for their being tried before the church or a select number of its members, but the laity's role in that tribunal was limited to "giving advice and bearing witness to the justice of the whole process." Determining the accused member's innocence or guilt was left entirely to itinerants, who wielded "the whole authority of both judgment and censure."[19]

That power, mixed with moral certitude and ignorance of local circumstances, could make for explosive consequences. By chastising the great,
itinerants often succeeded only in alienating both those prominent sinners and their humbler neighbors, who took the part of leading families
out of either loyalty or fear. In 1794, for example, James Jenkins expelled
"an old member of the church, whose conduct had been very disorderly,"
only to find himself "exposed . . . to much hatred and persecution in the
neighbourhood as he had been a class-leader." Similarly, by disciplining
one member of a family, itinerants might embitter the culprit's entire
circle of kin against the Methodists. Such were the wages of William
Ormond's expelling one Jane Baker after hearing gossip that she "had
Danced and spent part of a Night at a still house." On the preacher's next
visit, her father demanded to know who had informed against his
daughter and then threatened a lawsuit. But like most of his colleagues,
Ormond did not shrink from the fray: "Let him try it; I am not so easy
Scared." That kind of feckless courage was all that sustained itinerants
when facing the most thankless of all cases—scandals that divided families
belonging to the same Methodist church. Thus find young William
Capers sometime in 1808, wishing that he were anywhere other than
Chester County, South Carolina, where a woman faced church trial, most
likely for sexual misconduct. "Her father-in-law and the connections on
that side generally believed her guilt; her husband held her to be innocent,
and was partially deranged on account of the affair; and all the society and
most of the people in the neighborhood were intensely enlisted for or
against the accused." Judged guilty, she was duly expelled by Capers, upon
which "a riot ensued and considerable violence." As he left the meetinghouse, one woman displeased with both the verdict and the young
preacher shrieked "at the top of her voice, 'He had better go home and
suck his mammy.' "[20]

There were times, too, when itinerants' judgments disrupted the peace
of local churches by defying forces more formidable than wealthy planters
and more legion than a phalanx of kinfolk. James Jenkins stumbled into
such a situation when he encountered "an old lady" in one South Carolina
class meeting whom everyone else knew to be a witch. When he asked why
other members "suffer her to stay in class," his informant explained, as if
to a simpleton, "Suffer her! why we are afraid of her . . . and he went on to
tell of the poor woman's cows she had shot with hair-balls, or a great
many of them fired at once, she had killed in a moment every fowl in the

yard of some poor woman whom she had a grudge against." But lay alarm did not move Jenkins; here was no witch, he decided, but only someone who "looked as if she might have been struck with a hair-ball herself." Jenkins did object, however, to her stout refusal to join the Methodist church, for "No stranger, meaning no one not a member of the Church could be allowed to stay in during the class-meeting." Finally he confronted the old woman, and as he led her out of the class, "she shook herself with a strange, wriggling motion, not unlike a turkey in the sand, muttering something like boo, boo, boo, woo, woo, woo." He was amused, but others witnessing her performance knew a witch's curse when they heard one, and felt the "terror of her anger was upon us, and what would she not do, poor old woman?" Jenkins believed that he went down in local memory as being "very bold for such a young man," but more likely he was recalled as merely reckless by the laity, who neither shared nor welcomed his daring.[21]

It was not just preachers' censure of the potent few that could raise lay hackles. They protested when whites of any class whose moral lapses commanded general sympathy received summary justice from itinerants. Many were the instances like that recorded by Jeremiah Norman in which preachers declared "the necessity of expelling one from society" over the opposition of a laity "unwilling to part with the person." But always, the insistence of the clergy carried the greatest weight, and members duly "submitted as the rule was violated." That determination to prevail over lay sentiment stiffened the spine of twenty-seven-year-old James Meacham when he suspended a man who had fallen behind in repaying his debts to other church members. "The Brethren is much griev[e]d about it," Meacham noted, "but none of this turns me from my aim to keep up Discipline. . . . I struck him out in time of Class Meeting. . . . [I]t was like a Sword to them all but I kept my course, my mind is fixt." When one Brother Taylor intervened on behalf of the offending man, Meacham allowed that "he [Taylor] led me in the light of things I never had been inform'd of before which brings a Spirit of true Sympathy in my Soul for him [the suspended debtor]." Yet even after learning of those extenuating circumstances, Meacham stuck to his decision until the expelled man "came to me . . . and begged that I would not Shut him out of doors among the Sinners but Suffer him to Sit in Some part of the Meeting House, with the Christians . . . and said O my dear Bro[ther] am I cast off for ever." To that heartfelt plea, Meacham finally relented enough to advise him "to keep humble and Submit to God and his preachers and he should not be rejected, O how my poor heart did weep, but I turned my back to him and went to my horse. . . ." Such situations could lead to lasting bitterness: In the name of extracting submission, itinerants levied unsparing judgments on the laity, and many who suffered from such stringency or looked on with regret would never forgive or forget.[22]

Even so, some of the problems young preachers encountered would have defied the wisdom of far more experienced ministers. Since no matter was too private or delicate to be discussed at class meetings and then submitted to ministerial discretion, itinerants often found themselves in the unenviable position of sifting through contradictory reports of sexual scandals in order to punish the guilty parties. On one occasion, William Ormond baptized a bastard infant presented by a man named Joiner and his wife who alleged that the child's father was one Anthony King, only to be sought out later by the Widow Smith, who claimed that the baby had resulted from her adulterous affair with Joiner, which Mrs. Joiner now sought to conceal. Ormond thereupon washed his hands of the whole matter, telling Widow Smith to apply to the courts to prove her claims of motherhood. But more often, such sensational charges led to investigations by the clergy and committees of members, sometimes followed by church trials. Individuals and sometimes entire families were left tainted by scandal, even when those accused were vindicated. Imagine the humiliation of one Sister Angel, who listened in 1792 as William Ormond invited her class to discuss whether she suffered from a venereal disease or only a vaginal discharge. Or the resentment of parents who, after Jeremiah Norman condemned "Bundling . . . as an evil practice, not fit to be among Christians," found their adolescent children hauled before the church in a trial yielding testimony "the equal of [which] I have seldom heard."[23]

Just as common were heated conflicts between itinerants and lay people over the church's policy on slavery. Although by 1784 the Methodists had given over efforts to bar slaveholders from their fellowship, some preachers, especially younger men, persisted in pressing their antislavery views on the laity and vigorously enforced the remaining prohibition on buying and selling slaves. They seized every opportunity to preach against the evils of bondage, distribute antislavery tracts to the societies within their circuit, and urge individual masters and mistresses to free their slaves. On some occasions, the laity lent support to that testimony: Much to James Meacham's admiration, a Virginia woman rose at a meeting on Christmas Day 1791 and blasted the hypocrisy of some of her fellow Methodists, "apparently . . . as happy as the saints in Heaven," who kept their slaves "half starved and nearly naked." But more often, laymen and -women met their preachers' strictures against slavery with stony defiance. After one of the brethren lectured Meacham that "we [Methodist itinerants] ought not publicly to preach or exclaim against it [slavery]," they "parted without reconciliation." Even more obdurate was the sister who, reproached by Meacham for abusing her slaves, insisted that "she would still do the same if they would not work"; when he warned that "she might not expect to continue in communion with us," the woman shot back that "she could serve the Lord out as well as in."[24]

All preachers shared the concern that attacks on slavery would alienate both members and prospective converts. While even James Meacham admitted that any mention of "oppression" from the pulpit immediately dampened spiritual fervor among whites in southern congregations, Devereux Jarratt, who believed that masters had Scripture on their side, issued the same warning even more emphatically. "I think they [slaveholders] ought not to be put upon a level (as they are now) with *horse thieves and Hogstealers, Knaves,* etc.," he warned, "nor to be insulted at every turn with the odious Names of *Oppressors, Rogues,* etc." The chief culprits, in Jarratt's view, were young preachers, "Men, who are as incapable of discerning or judging in these Matters as a Schoolboy Almost." A decade later, in 1795, Jeremiah Norman echoed Jarratt's sentiments, denouncing one fellow itinerant, "a rigid defender of liberation," for saying that "he has Preached all slaveholders to Hell and cannot redeem them again," and another "implacable enemy to Slave holding" for being "a most stubborn tempered man."[25]

No matter what issues they confronted, what complicated the task of enforcing discipline was that itinerants annually switched circuits. Preachers had no sooner developed some acquaintance with the families and local conditions on one circuit than they were dispatched to another, often hundreds of miles distant, to begin the process all over again. Then, too, taking on a new circuit often entailed defending—or challenging—the decisions of one's immediate predecessor. Despite the efforts of the Methodist Church to set forth uniform standards of discipline, itinerants sometimes differed in their enforcement of certain policies, especially those pertaining to slavery. In a typical instance, Meacham expelled a male member for buying a slave, only to learn that the offender had been excommunicated earlier for the same offense and then reinstated by his predecessor on that circuit. The clergy also diverged in their judgments on matters pertaining to sexual morality: William Ormond complained about being scheduled by another itinerant to preach a funeral sermon for a young woman's illegitimate child, "for it is likely the Child was made contrary to the Will of God."[26]

While disciplining the faithful sometimes exceeded the skills of itinerants, they often felt even more inadequate when it came to advising those struggling for spiritual assurance. Many shared the insecurities of Nelson Reed, who, "when I got amongst old and deep experienced Christians . . . was frequently tempted to think I had no grace, that I was not accepted of them and therefore could not be profitable to them." Especially daunting to novice preachers were those church members who had experienced what the Methodists called "sanctification" or "the second blessing," a profound inner assurance that all of one's sins had been forgiven. After listening to a North Carolina woman recount her sanctification, Freeborn Garrettson, then twenty-five, wistfully admitted that "I likewise knew I was not in possession of it."[27]

Awareness of their deficiencies drove young itinerants to devote the few days when they were not traveling and preaching to a regimen of prayer, meditation, and reading, mainly the Bible and the writings of John Wesley and other evangelicals. Ashamed of his lack of formal education, Jacob Young prickled when a family with whom he lodged quizzed him on his knowledge of the Bible, ancient history, and English grammar. The untutored Peter Cartwright was stung when "a regular graduate in theology" tried to embarrass him publicly by "speaking Greek," but marshaled the wit to reply with his smattering of German, which his adversary took to be Hebrew. "My idiars [ideas] are but shallow yet," James Meacham admitted as he began his first circuit—and his spelling also left something to be desired.[28]

Such insecurities made young preachers acutely sensitive to the most trivial challenges to their dignity. While the Methodist clergy disdained levity on any occasion, snickering from the congregation during their sermons mortified novices. Nelson Reed, for example, confided to his journal the shame of being "laught . . . in the face" once by a man, at another time by a woman, and, on one dark day, by an entire congregation. John Early seethed over a fellow who perused a newspaper during his sermon, while Benjamin Lakin, galled by a young man who "began to crack nuts" against the side of the meetinghouse, took grim satisfaction in the youth's untimely death. The same and more found their way into Jeremiah Norman's journal, a veritable litany of insults inflicted by congregations who displayed their "Bad manners" and "ill breeding" by laughing, talking, and daydreaming. Once even his horse conspired against Norman's efforts to hold an audience's attention, the animal getting entangled in the bridle and falling with a loud thud. ("I went on calmly.") But Norman's supreme embarrassment came cloaked in seeming glory: Just as he was inducing due solemnity in his hearers by preaching from the text "thou art weighed in the Ballences and found wanting," he noticed "a Youth of About 17 or 18 . . . with a vessel of water standing at my Left hand . . . the People seeing him thus standing several of them . . . broke out into immoderate Laughter." Norman soberly "proceeded on weighing them," but with so many dissolved in helpless giggling, he was "forced twice to complain of them before I gained my point."

Itinerants particularly loathed being halted in mid-homily by lay people with a talent for talking back. Typical was the garrulous old man who nettled Nelson Reed by rising from the pews to challenge his doctrine, and another fellow who announced that the Sabbath would be better spent if "people wo[u]ld stay home and make corn for their families." Those who took courage by stopping at stills before attending sermons also proved inspired antagonists. In 1783 one such man, before staggering out of the meetinghouse, punctuated Thomas Haskins's description of hell by crying out, "I fear we shall all be there too soon." In Kentucky, another inebriate parried Benjamin Lakin's reproof by declaring "that if he had whiskey he could stand well enough before God," while, somewhere in South Carolina, a tipsy heckler more modestly declared himself equal to young William Capers by swearing "lustily he could beat me at preaching all hollow, and if he were in my place he would go home and never try again."[29]

Challenges from mischievous teenagers, cantankerous farmers, and rowdy drunks were trial enough, but flippancy from young women stung the worst. When one Eliza Scott defied and bested James Meacham before a large western Virginia congregation, he salved his bruised ego with a long journal entry, rendering their exchange verbatim: There at the front of the house sat the redoubtable Eliza, she of "Stern countenance," bedecked in her finery ("very bear [bare] about the Breasts"). Her constant laughing and whispering during his sermon drew several patient "reproofs" from Meacham and as many tart rejoinders from Scott, who got the last word: "I came to see and be seen, and not to hear your nonsense if you can preach why don't you preach."[30]

If clashes with the defiant could plunge itinerants into purgatory, comeuppance from the devout left them lower still. Men and women with high standards for preaching and pastoral care peppered novices with advice, which, however well meant, devastated young preachers, who, even without lay prompting, devoted pages of their journals to scrutinizing their performances and detailing the congregation's responses. One hot August week in the Chesapeake, Thomas Haskins simmered over local Methodist families who expected that he would visit each of them before traveling to his next appointment ("the Methodists are in some things an inconsiderate people ..."). Then he preached, after which some of the same church members who sought his company complained "of my speaking too low," while others "said I took a text [from the Bible] I did not know how to manage." "This is very possible," the battered Haskins allowed, but "how hard is it . . . to fall under the crit[ic]ising lash or reproving nod to every pretender to religion, without feeling some degree of resentment." John Early bridled, too, upon being told that some North Carolinians "did not like such fiery preaching as I preached," especially when "I hollered very loud and stamped with my foot." Among his candid critics was an elderly Methodist who "told me that he heard another man preach on the subject that I preached on that day and he preached a much greater sermon than I did."[31]

Not only the pulpit skills of itinerants but their private lives came in for close scrutiny by the laity—right down to their manner of dress. After preaching to a congregation in the winter of 1797, Jeremiah Norman was approached by "a poor man . . . to inspect my Pantaloons. . . . Stooping down peeping [at] the kneeband [he] Said we have been disputing whether these were all in a piece or not but they are one." Irked that his audience had attended more closely to his britches than his sermon, Norman retorted, "I suppose Sir you did not dispute which of you would get to Heaven first or who would get the Most Religion." But the man replied simply that "there arose no such dispute among them." While novel tailoring may have inspired such innocent curiosity, other men and women searched their itinerants' apparel with eyes peeled for foppish affectations, genteel pretensions, and other telltale signs of the clergy taking on airs that set them apart from the laity. Among them was one James Tarrant, a man "very much averse to the use of the Umbrella among the Clergy." Since Norman "carried one constant I wished to hear at once all that he had to say in condemnation of that, or those that used them." And whether he wanted to or not, William Capers heard out an "eminently pious" South Carolina man stricken by the preacher's suspenders: "O, they make you look so worldly; and I know you ain't worldly neither, but do pull them off." So he did.[32]

The potential for graver scandal lurked in lay watchfulness over preachers' sex lives. Being mostly young, single, and thus, by church fiat, unavailable, itinerants were also irresistible to some southern coquettes spoiling for a challenge. Preachers, too, seem to have sensed that this romantic aura—a mystique less that of childlike innocence than of sensuality withheld—enhanced their charisma, spiritual or otherwise. Most recognized that exploiting such an advantage could involve them in situations rife with the potential for misunderstanding, embarrassment, or outright ruin. But even those men who tried to hold themselves above suspicion by keeping female admirers at arm's length found themselves vulnerable to rumors or worse. One young Virginia itinerant, Josiah Cole, was suspended from his circuit after a young matron charged that he had raped her, and he "could not prove the contrary." His colleague, James Meacham, suspected the woman and her kin of concocting the story to punish the preacher for disciplining a member of their family, but it took months of investigation and a church trial before Cole finally cleared his name. Alert to a like peril, John Early took swift action when, on North Carolina's Outer Banks in 1808, tongues wagged of his "courting a wicked widow." He threatened "if I found out who started it [the gossip] I would make them sick of it." Two years later a Methodist church in southern Ohio served by Hector Sanford teemed with news of his upcoming nuptials, a surprise to at least one of his flock, "as I thought he thought of nothing but preaching." For his part, the embarrassed Sanford "thought people would have had more manners than to talk about his marriage."

But since people would talk, itinerants took every precaution to protect their reputations. Made wiser by the troubles of Josiah Cole, James Meacham made journal entries about wooing his future wife in a code devised specifically for that purpose. Stith Mead also behaved with impeccable discretion when he received an unsolicited love letter in May of 1793 from a young Methodist woman who described herself as his "unworthy captive" and "wounded lover" and urged him to meet with her. He did nothing—until several months later when, in a second letter, she begged him to "carry me in the arms of prayer before the Lord" and expressed her determination to be united with him in heaven if not on earth. Flustered by her resolve but sufficiently flattered to save both letters, Mead scribbled redundantly on the bottom of her second note that "This young lady was a personable well looking person. . . . I had an interview personally—in the presence of a male member of the Church and parted—respecting her for her friendly regard." And when the future wife of John Johnson wondered at his seeming indifference, her female friend advised that "Preachers avoid courtships as occasions for scandal, and make very few words answer for that business." Johnson's intended was even more mystified when, after proposing in 1813, he still "paid no more attention to me than he did to the dogs." When she complained of his neglect he replied that "Any interchange of views we may have in the future, must be in writing."[33]

Hard as the lives of young itinerants were, sitting under their occasional ministry could be just as trying to even the saintliest of the faithful. More burdensome than the demands that entertaining preachers made on the often slim resources of lay households was bearing with an ever-shifting cast of inexperienced young men whose zeal often exceeded both their wisdom and their compassion. Such were the circumstances that bred deep resentments among mature white lay people, particularly men habituated by regional custom to speak and act with unquestioned authority and to be received with deference. Those increasingly embattled relations between older church members and callow itinerants are nowhere more poignantly depicted than in the journal of Jeremiah Norman, who spent his twenties traveling nearly everywhere in the South of the 1790s. Throughout, the problems that his youth posed for the laity are as evident as his inability to deal effectively with their discontent. It was when some older members of a congregation interrupted his sermon in the fall of 1793 that Norman first "made some discoverys that the aged did not like to be Eaquiled [equaled] by the young: much more to have them their teachers." "But," he huffed, "I do not regard their crittycism." A month later, bombarded by lay complaints about his rigid enforcement of discipline, the young preacher first took refuge in anger ("I was much alarmed to hear what Hell could invent"), followed by self-pity ("I see that the more labor spent for People's Good the less love is paid back"), and capped by pique ("I am resolved shall not again trouble them"). But trouble them again he did. A few years later and no further along on the learning curve, Norman took it upon himself to correct an "old Lady" who "pretends to believe that a young person cannot be as religious as an old person." Alas, he set her straight: "I told her that religion was not confined to age sex or circumstance." Then he tangled with a venerable North Carolina gentleman: After "giving him Sufficient evidence of his mistake," to no avail, "I said Sir you are an older man than I therefore I will not contradict you again and tell you that you lie." At that backhanded display of deference, his adversary "shewed the utmost rage . . . threatening what he would do to any man that would make him a Liar in his own house"; Norman, oblivious to his breach of decorum, smugly confided to his journal that he had "at Last carryed my point."[34]

It was on generational conflicts such as these that the laity's complaints turned. What troubled them was not that authority over Methodist churches resided in the clergy as a group rather than the membership as a whole. If that had been the case, disaffected Methodists could simply have defected to the Baptists, whose churches were ruled by the laity. But Methodist malcontents were not Baptist wannabes. On the contrary, many were former Anglicans habituated to the sway of clerical authority—as one expressed it, "by tradition as well as by sentiment." The problem was that, while most of the faithful accepted the right of clergy to rule, many believed that itinerants were, in every sense, too green to wield power effectively—too young, too unseasoned, and too unfamiliar with the intricacies of local alliances and kinship networks. Those sentiments were most strongly voiced by white husbands and fathers, masters on whose ears it fell hardest to hear "beardless boys" pass summary judgment on wives who gossiped or daughters who danced, or to find themselves upbraided for putting off creditors or buying slaves by a self-righteous stripling who had never shouldered the task of making his own crop. Writing to his son-in-law John Owen in 1791, Daniel Grant hinted at the trouble brewing between Georgia's laity and several itinerants, whom "the people generally receive with Love, though they have to bear with them in many things, as they are young in the work." By 1795, William Watters more bluntly warned another Methodist preacher that "a good deal of uneasiness" had been occasioned in his Virginia neighborhood by young preachers "keeping in and turning out [of societies] who they pleas[e]" without allowing members "to have anything to say in the business."[35]

Well before 1796, leading Methodists knew they faced a formidable problem. But in that year, Francis Asbury and Thomas Coke, who headed the church as its bishops, finally admitted, in a triumph of understatement, that "our ministers who have the charge of circuits may not be always so aged and experienced as we might wish them to be." Recognizing the problem, however, did not prod Asbury and Coke to embrace the Baptist expedient of making church governance more participatory. They believed that a laity empowered to influence decisions on admission and expulsion would result in worldly connections tainting church membership: family members would favor their own kin; clients, debtors, and the poor would fear offending patrons, creditors, and the rich. "To give . . . the authority of judging and censuring offenders to the private members of a church," the bishops warned, "would be to form a court which in innumerable instances would have the strongest temptations to partiality."[36]

Brave words, but not those that the faithful wanted to hear. Indeed, the "partiality" that the bishops wanted to keep from tainting the churches was precisely what many lay people longed to introduce in the name of promoting local peace. Unlike peripatetic bishops and itinerants, the laity lived out the length of their days amid relatives and neighbors, customers, clients, and creditors in communities whose very sinews were knit by ties of kinship, reciprocity, and patronage among whites of different classes. Theirs were the lives disrupted when the delicate equilibrium of local alliances was upset by itinerants whose uninformed decisions sent shock waves through neighborhood networks. Imagine the consequences if a novice preacher took it into his head to refuse membership to a wealthy planter because he had sold a slave or to expel his wife from church because she had hosted a ball. Those thus offended could exact their revenge by demanding that their whole circle of kin and clients break off fellowship with the Methodists, or by refusing to extend credit or hire out slaves or rent land to those who stayed within society. Such catastrophes were readily conjured by a worried laity, and whether realized or only anticipated, compelled many to conclude that young preachers should show greater respect for the superior experience of long-standing church members, especially older white men. In short, the problem facing the Methodist clergy was that their church's organization endowed youth with an authority traditionally reserved for men of a certain race, age, and standing in southern communities. It was a fine irony, then, that lay concerns for honoring those entrenched local hierarchies were expressed in demands for the "democratizing" of Methodist Church governance.

Just as generational conflicts sharpened tensions between itinerants and the laity during the decades before 1800, they also divided the Methodist clergy itself. Although itinerants have attracted greater historical notice, there was a second group, known as "local preachers," within the Methodist clergy. Usually older and married, these men supported their families through secular employment but occasionally preached and otherwise ministered to the faithful in their neighborhoods. Men entered the "local connection" either by moving up from the rank of class leader or by "locating" after some years in the itinerancy. By 1799, there were 850 in the United States, many more than the 269 itinerants. As a group, local preachers also surpassed itinerants in age and experience, but not—and here was the rub—in power and prestige. As salaried, full-time professional preachers, itinerants ranked as the princelings of the church; they alone admitted and expelled members, and they alone were eligible to attend, deliberate, and vote at the General Conference, which the bishops convened every four years to decide church policy. In fact, their sway over the churches extended even to expelling those local preachers whom they judged wayward.[37]

Those discrepancies of status and power between the two tiers of the Methodist clergy made for no end of trouble. To be sure, many located men generously assisted in preparing young aspirants to enter the traveling connection, thereby earning the lasting esteem of many of their protégés. And itinerants often praised those local preachers who could deliver stirring sermons or who recruited prospective church members in frontier districts before circuits had been formally established. But many local preachers resented their second-class status and bristled at any hint of an itinerant's disregard. In 1795, one confessed to becoming angry when an itinerant took communion himself before calling local preachers to the table, seeing that as a sign that "the Local Station was not in esteem with the Travelling as [they] ought to be." Most aggrieved, perhaps, were former itinerants who, reduced to the rank of local preachers, felt disdained by their brethren who remained in the traveling connection. After he located, James Jenkins complained that "the treatment I have received in a few instances from the traveling preachers would have driven me from the church, had I been at all disaffected toward it." Indeed, for Jenkins that demotion was too much to be borne, and after raising his family, he reentered the itinerancy, wishing "to die among the brethren."[38]

Generational strife among the Methodists grew even more divisive when a bitter personal rivalry between two leading ministers ruptured into outright schism. James O'Kelly, a native Virginian who had built a large lay following during his long ministry, gradually came to realize that his star within the church's universe had been eclipsed by a younger colleague, Francis Asbury—Bishop Asbury after 1784. That disappointment inspired O'Kelly's sudden epiphany in 1792 that Methodist church government was tyrannical; he duly formed a splinter group, bearing the catchy name of "Republican Methodists." Seeking to broaden his appeal, O'Kelly quickly tapped into the resentments festering among both the laity and local preachers. He derided itinerants as "Boys with the Keys . . . these striplings must rule and govern Christ's Church as master workmen; as though they could finish such a temple." Those salvos produced the popularity he sought, at least for a time: In the mid-1790s, Methodist fellowships hemorrhaged several thousand members and lost an uncounted number of local preachers, mainly in southern Virginia and northeastern North Carolina. It is not without significance that O'Kelly, aged about fifty-eight when he founded his new church, was known, affectionately and otherwise, as "the old man."[39]

O'Kelly's challenge to the Methodists was short-lived, but it scared itinerants into surrendering some of their power. Although they refused to grant local preachers or laymen any role in the General Conference other than as spectators, new rules passed in 1796 and thereafter steadily limited eligibility to participate in its sessions to the more senior itinerants. In the same year, the General Conference also began to institute changes that narrowed the scope of all itinerants' disciplinary authority over both local preachers and lay people. They revoked the absolute power of itinerants to expel local preachers, vesting that authority in tribunals of other local preachers, whose judgments could be appealed, but only by a body consisting of both traveling and local preachers as well as leading laymen. The General Conference left no doubt about what had inspired that change: "By this mode of trial we are desirous of showing the most tender regard to our local brethren. . . . [W]e would not have so important a character as that of one of our local brethren even touched to its disadvantage, by only one preacher, who possibly might be younger than the accused." Finally and perhaps most important, in 1800, the General Conference stripped itinerants of their exclusive right to sit in judgment over the laity. New procedures for the trial of church members instituted that year turned church committees, which before had only advised in discipline cases, into juries in which a majority determined the accused person's guilt or innocence. Itinerants who dissented from the decision of the lay majority had the right to appeal any contested case to a higher body, but the discretion of a lone itinerant could no longer sweep any member from the Methodist church.[40]

Curtailing the powers of itinerants went some way toward soothing both lay Methodists and local preachers. But while their influence had been reduced in both individual churches and the councils of the General Conference, young men still predominated in the itinerancy, and lay concerns about their behavior persisted long after 1800. What stoked the anxieties of many believers like Baltimore's Thomas Chew, who entered the nineteenth century still shaking his head over "the inexperience of many of the Preachers," was the unchastened cockiness of itinerants like John Early. All of twenty-five when he took over a North Carolina circuit in 1811, Early boasted of his readiness to "make use of my pruning knife with some crooked disciples," and promised "I should not bend to half-hearted Methodists." He was as good as his word; within a few weeks he had locked horns with one Dr. James Keys, who took great exception when Early hauled his wife before the church for wearing a gold ring. Denouncing the preacher as a mere "novice," the doctor then "carried his stout wife off in a great rage." Disposing in his journal of Keys as "an Irishman," and hence given to "prolix and satirical speech," Early more decorously assured the church that "perhaps the Doctor would do better when he cooled off." He did not. Instead, Keys singed the fingers of Edward Dromgoole, a former itinerant and one of North Carolina's most beloved local preachers, with a sulfurous denunciation of Early's "disrespect." There stood his zaftig consort, "in as plain attire as any woman could appear in, wrethin [writhing]" before the unrelenting Early, "an ignorant, stubborn coxcomb; whose place would be best fill[e]d at the end of a plow . . . as swoln [swollen] and as big as the frog in the fables . . . looking as big as an Eastern nabob." "Tis a great pity," the doctor concluded, "that we can't have some old experienced men among us, who are acquainted with the rules, and the feelings of mankind." Other lay people agreed, some also scoring Early's high-handed treatment of local preachers. They circulated what he labeled "a large, vulgar, sarcastical and unlawful piece of writing against me" in one neighborhood after he instigated the church trial of a popular local preacher; a few years later, another disgruntled local preacher thoughtfully compiled a long list of lay grievances against Early and then presented it to the itinerant's superiors.[41]

Such disaffection showed that the reforms instituted by the General Conference only a few years earlier had not gone far enough. James Keys voiced a fear commonly held when he predicted that unless steps were taken "to lop the extravagances of young preachers," members would desert the Methodists in droves. He advised setting aside a day at annual regional conferences to instruct "young and inexperienced preachers"— or doing away with the itinerancy altogether and relying entirely on local preachers. But experience since 1800 had shown that stronger measures were needed than a few days of training for young preachers, and experience even before 1800 had shown that the itinerants assembled at the General Conference were not about to embrace Keys's radical suggestion that they abdicate in favor of local preachers. These same itinerants would also have been quick to point out that no greater harmony reigned within churches in which young preachers held no formal authority, settled clergymen bore the burden of pastoral work, and lay people governed. That lesson the Methodists had learned well—not from their own experience, but by watching the Baptists.

IF THE METHODISTS erred by vesting too much power in young preachers, the Baptists did not make the same mistake. The Baptists also recruited their clergy from the ranks of recent converts, and they encouraged those young men to itinerate, but there the similarities end. After individual churches licensed young Baptists to preach, no centralized church body assigned them to travel within any defined region for any specified period of time. Instead, licentiates set their own itineraries, sometimes evangelizing within their home counties and sometimes venturing farther afield. And for many, itinerating was occasional rather than constant because, like all the Baptist clergy, they received no salaries. Lacking that support, they either relied on the generosity of their families or worked at secular employment for some part of each year. After a few years, some licentiates sought ordination as elders, which enabled them to administer the sacraments, and within a few more years, they might be called by individual congregations to serve as settled pastors.

Their itinerant years thus marked not a career pinnacle but an apprenticeship for young Baptist preachers. Elders might also travel to preach and baptize in remote places, but most did so less frequently than did their younger colleagues. Unlike the Methodists, Baptist ministers did not lose standing within the church when they curtailed or ceased their traveling and accepted a settled pastorate. And unlike the Methodists, Baptist itinerants—as well as the rest of their clergy—enjoyed no formal powers superior to those of laymen. Governance of the congregation and the discipline of members resided exclusively with the brethren. The sole responsibilities of young Baptist itinerants were passionate preaching and, once they were ordained, examining and baptizing new members.[42]

The advantage of the Baptists' approach was that it drew on young men's popular appeal while according them no leverage over the laity. That lack of formal authority minimized friction between novice preachers and more mature church members, although it did not entirely preclude eruptions of lay resentment. Youthful itinerants often demanded a measure of deference that lay people like Joseph Bishop granted only grudgingly. A hunter in middle Tennessee and a lifelong Baptist, Bishop dismissed one preacher in his neighborhood as a "self-conceited young man, who must be heard first and all the time in society." Still more irksome were pastoral visits—his claiming the best chair in any house, expecting to be seated next to women at meals, "returning the sugar spoon to its place well slobbered," and blowing pipe smoke into the faces of other guests. "Though I could not help noticing all this," Bishop added, "I said nothing: he was a preacher."

Lay Baptists also echoed Methodist worries about whether young bachelors showed sufficient maturity as spiritual leaders and finesse as preachers. As early as 1773, concerned members in one Virginia congregation debated whether it accorded with the Bible for "an unmarried man" to hold the pastorate of a church. And as late as 1803, a lay Baptist historian railed against the number of "unqualified" young rustics in the clergy's ranks. But however aggravating the deficiencies of Baptist preachers may have been, church policy limited the extent to which they could antagonize the laity. Unlike early Methodist itinerants, Baptist ministers, no matter how senior, held no power to admit or expel church members. Instead, a majority of lay members in each church made those decisions, drawing on their expert local knowledge to calibrate what risks might be incurred by rejecting some individuals for fellowship or excluding others from communion.[43]

But if lay rule saved the Baptists from making the mistake that so bedeviled the Methodists, it contributed to their making another and equally fateful error. Although young men neither dominated the Baptist clergy nor domineered over the laity, their influence still churned up trouble in many churches. Those difficulties arose because the early Baptists did not develop any means for systematically dispatching their clergy, particularly their young preachers, over a broad geographic area. This failure both impeded Baptist missionary efforts and left many congregations bereft of ministers for long periods. And, far worse, it set the stage for ferocious generational struggles within the Baptist clergy in those churches with an overabundance of preachers. Whenever a revival stirred a congregation and young gifts emerged from the ranks of new converts, tensions arose between older ministers and younger men recently ordained or licensed.[44]

Typical of these troubles was the contest between newly ordained James Ireland and the aged Daniel Marshall over the pastorate at South River Church in Virginia's Shenandoah Valley. In the wake of a revival there, those lay people who attributed their recent awakenings to Ireland's preaching pushed for naming him pastor; Marshall's converts, meanwhile, insisted on honoring their own "spiritual father" with that accolade. The pastorate finally went to Ireland, but lingering bitterness among the losing faction persuaded him to relinquish the honor to his rival and move on to another church. South River reprised the same divisive drama after a later revival in the 1770s, when Marshall collided with the rising star of another young convert-turned-preacher, Joseph Redding. Their competition, as one Baptist chronicler decorously put the matter, renewed "great excitement" among church members and propelled Redding's retreat to an even more rugged part of western Virginia, "where he had a great opening for preaching."[45]

Such clashes seared many southern Baptist congregations, flash fires ignited by the spark of cyclical revivals. All too often, in the view of veteran elders, young converts who took up the call to preach stayed too close to home to begin their ministries and ended up challenging more seasoned clergy for the loyalty of the faithful. One of several young preachers produced by a western Virginia revival in 1821, Jeremiah Jeter recalled that "Some of the older preachers looked with suspicion, if not with jealousy, on the popularity of their younger brethren." For their part, many young aspirants had no choice except remaining within their home congregations, since they lacked either the independent means or family support to defray the costs of itinerating farther afield. With no fund for supporting the itinerancy of young licentiates and no formal mechanism for channeling them into communities lacking preachers, many Baptist congregations weathered recurring generational wrangles within the clergy that splintered churches into factions.[46]

Baptist churches also fell prey to division because there was no way to ensure that elders who had married and settled would be evenly spread among congregations. A single church might end up with as many as four or five ordained ministers—a situation that took its toll when more than one coveted the pastorate. In 1785, for example, the newly formed Clear Creek Baptist Church in Kentucky counted among its thirty-odd members no less than four ordained ministers, two of whom had been pastors of Baptist churches in Virginia. The youngest of the contenders, John Taylor, dreaded the prospect of Clear Creek choosing a pastor, for he had "seen much trouble at times in Virginia . . . where there was a number of preachers." To make matters worse, the two former pastors who now belonged to Clear Creek had migrated to that part of Kentucky with some of their Virginia parishioners, heightening Taylor's fears that "we should have a heavy church contest [about] which of them should be the pastor."

To Taylor's surprise, the congregation elected him—a dark horse commended by the fact that, unlike the other candidates, he had no kin or former neighbors in the Clear Creek church and had converted few of its members. Since Taylor had no special constituency, he became acceptable to all—for exactly one year. Then, less surprisingly, Clear Creek's members fell to feuding over discipline and doctrine, conflicts endemic to the independent-minded Baptists and often compounded by migration. Raw settlements in the western country usually spilled southern families from several different congregations into a single new church, whereupon disputes over fine points of theology or the proper conduct of church business quickly surfaced among the laity, with many surplus ministers ready and eager to spearhead the coalescing factions. In the case of Clear Creek, some of the disaffected laity rallied behind a disappointed candidate for pastor and formed themselves into a separate church. Many other churches endowed with the same excess of clerical talent were ruptured by separations and schisms. As John Taylor sadly observed in 1823, "divisions, factions, schisms, and heresies, both in doctrine and practice, has brought them [the Baptists] very low."[47]

Besides fostering factionalism among the laity, the competition among Baptist preachers claimed collegiality as another casualty. William Hickman's boast aside that Baptists could be singled out in any company "because they love one another," the hallmark of their elders was that they seldom let slip any chance to size up their fellows, especially younger men, and find them wanting. Whereas Methodist preachers quickly developed, both privately and in print, the dark art of damning with faint praise, the Baptists skewered their rivals without resort to polite subterfuge. Hickman himself overflowed with unloving appraisals of novice preachers in his Virginia neighborhood during the 1780s. There was Josiah Rucks, who in his zeal chastised one young lady for wearing stays, but later in life "became dressy . . . and was pretty much of a fop" before he went off to North Carolina and "married rich." And there was Theodoric Boulware, an elder in the Ohio Valley, who may have flinched at finding himself dismissed in John Taylor's published memoirs as the sort of minister who "has a greater aptitude to trim hypocrites than to invite poor sinners to come to Christ."

For his part, Taylor professed the opinion that preachers should be tough enough to take criticism from all quarters. When the members of the Buck Run Church requested him to step out of the room while they debated whether to accept him as a pastor, he replied, "[I]f they could not look me in the face and speak what they thought on that occasion, they did not deserve a name in the house of God; and if I could not bear with patience whatever they might say, I did not deserve the name of gospel minister." But many of his colleagues could not abide by that standard. They did not welcome the prospect of years spent fending off rivals who seized on their every weakness, exposing their flaws as preachers, lapses as theologians, and misjudgments as pastors. Younger men felt chilled in the long shadows cast by older preachers, and senior men wearied of vying for leadership with each rising generation after every revival.[48]

The Baptist clergy and even some members of the laity were not slow to recognize all of these difficulties and seek some remedy for the generational strife roiling their churches. From the middle of the 1780s until the end of the century, Baptist associations, advisory bodies composed of ministers and laymen from neighboring churches, almost annually appointed committees to frame plans for what, with intentional vagueness, they called "encouraging itinerant preaching." In fact, these committees aimed at expanding the Baptist itinerancy, to which end they all produced essentially the same plan—that the association would appoint four elders and as many young licentiates as could be recruited to visit each church within their connection at least twice a year. The association would also schedule their preaching appointments and defray their expenses with voluntary contributions from the laity. In effect, Baptist associations sought to create a salaried, professional traveling clergy much like that of the Methodists.

Here, in the view of many associations, was the ideal solution. Advocates urged that such reforms would provide both preaching talent and access to the sacraments for congregations without settled pastors, while at the same time supplying missionaries to places as yet untouched by Baptist influence. They also argued that, as impartial outsiders, itinerants might serve as troubleshooters, mediating disputes in embattled congregations. Their presence would not intensify conflict within churches, for itinerants would not be permitted to baptize, except in places without any ordained minister, and would enjoy only advisory power as arbitrators. But at least as prominent among the reformers' aims was the unspoken hope that an itinerancy thus enlarged and reorganized would siphon off surplus preachers, especially younger men, from overstocked churches where they could only cause trouble, and channel them into underserved congregations where they might do some good.

But the majority of lay Baptists wanted no part of this ideal solution, and so they became part of the problem. All such plans proposed by associations were disposed of forthwith by the sovereign lay majority of the churches. What their associations advised was anathema to most Baptists because adopting such innovations would reflect favorably on the Methodists. First, those reforms would empower associations to appoint itinerants and coordinate their evangelism, a suspiciously Methodist centralizing of organization that many Baptist brethren scorned as an assault on the autonomy of individual churches. Second, and still worse in the laity's view, such reforms would create a "hireling clergy" in the form of salaried itinerants. It was bad enough that many associations seemed bent on devising ways to compel church members to contribute to the support of settled pastors. Time-honored Baptist tradition held that all their clergy should work at secular occupations, their livelihoods supplemented only by what church members offered freely, "and in no wise by taxation or any other compulsion." Yet in the 1780s, a number of associations pressed the churches to adopt various schemes for prying open the hoards of lay misers. One plan instructed deacons to bring remiss members before the church and to discipline them for "covetousness." Another required members to contribute according to their means and assigned expulsion as the penalty for withholding that tithe. But neither measure found favor among the Baptist laity. Indeed, their outcry quickly pummeled even the associations into admitting that all their suggestions to inspire increased support for settled pastors engendered "violent opposition" from member churches. And the same chorus of opposition greeted the associations' plans for a remodeled itinerancy, which an already resentful laity regarded as yet another sordid scheme to compromise the ideal of a self-sustaining clergy.[49]

The commitment to upholding rule by the laity of each sovereign church kept the Baptists from making the Methodists' mistake of surrendering discipline to the clergy. But that same commitment betrayed the Baptists into a different error, and then kept them from correcting it. If they had abided by the advice of their associations and launched a more ambitious itinerancy, Baptists might have reached more unchurched southerners in the distant western country and eased the friction between older and younger preachers in their established congregations. In fact, had they implemented those changes at the end of the eighteenth century, the Baptists would have created an organization roughly similar to the one Methodist leaders were striving to achieve by their reforms of the same decades—a more centrally coordinated itinerancy that made the most of young men's dedication while trusting nothing to their discretion. But, as it happened, the Baptist laity clung to their tradition—and their determination never to be confused with the Methodists.

So PASSED the season of youth among southern evangelicals—for many, a long winter of discontent. Since its difficulties admitted of no easy resolution, they lingered into the nineteenth century. For decades after 1800, as before, Baptists and Methodists struggled to remedy the weaknesses riddling their clergy. Change came slowly, when at all, because both churches discovered that solving their problems with preachers would require sacrificing some of the distinctive elements that defined their religious identities. Accustomed though they were to compromise on some matters like slavery, many of the clergy and laity dug in their heels when it came to jettisoning the singular features that distinguished one evangelical church from another. Belief that the Bible sanctioned no other way played no small part in sustaining their fierce allegiance to certain traditional practices that made Baptists and Methodists two identifiably distinct churches. But expedience also reinforced the resistance to change: Baptists and Methodists vied with one another for converts from among the unchurched by each touting their peculiarities as superiorities. That strategy would not be served if they obscured the differences by which ordinary people could tell Baptists and Methodists apart.[50]

Conservatism endured, virtually unchallenged, among the Baptists. After 1800, they continued to muddle through their familiar difficulties, which became ever more familiar. While they excelled at producing young preachers, the Baptists never instituted any system for distributing them to full advantage. And while their autonomous, lay-governed churches appealed to some white southerners, the absence of any authoritative higher body left the Baptists with no means of settling disputes among the clergy, generational or otherwise. So when preachers within the same church inevitably squared off against one another, their squabbles, just as inevitably, drew lay members into the fray. While the Methodists also wrestled to subdue the long-standing tensions between younger and older preachers, they could at least call upon the General Conference to mediate between the two groups. The Baptists could only wait and hope for a resolution after the blood-letting over contested leadership engulfed and then exhausted their churches. Given their abiding devotion to congregational independence, a veritable icon of lay adoration, the Baptists could not have handled matters differently and still remained Baptists.

Faced with that dilemma, the Baptists' best hope was that individual preachers and churches would learn by experience how to hammer out solutions to problems as they arose. And amazingly, events sometimes vindicated that trust in the ad hoc. Some churches, for example, learned to minimize factionalism by arranging for two or three men to share the honor and burden of the pastorate. Such was the course steered by one Georgia church in 1808 when young Norvell Robertson emerged as the likeliest choice for pastor, but some members hesitated because of the presence of "Saul Willis, an old preacher late from North Carolina." "They felt a delicacy in calling me over his [Willis's] head, as I was a young preacher," Robertson recalled, but the brethren then resolved the matter by naming the two as copastors. Preachers, too, developed a strategy to avoid contending for pastorates: They moved on. Saul Willis spent only one year enduring invidious comparisons with Norvell Robertson before leaving to head a new church in a more remote part of Georgia, while Wilson Thompson, within months of being licensed to preach in 1810, lit out from his Kentucky church, newly rich in converts aspiring to the ministry, for underserved southern Missouri. When his efforts there yielded a revival in 1812, Thompson immediately began seeking another pulpit in a preacher-bereft part of southern Ohio, where he moved with his family in 1815. Even John Taylor, who bragged of his thick hide, kept his bags packed. After quarrels broke out among the members of his awakened Kentucky church in the mid-1790s, Taylor ceded the pulpit to two other preachers and took his family to southern Ohio. After his Ohio church experienced a revival in 1802 and ended up with several preachers among its two hundred members, he did not wait for trouble to find him but resettled in yet another community. Historians have lauded the Baptist clergy for keeping pace with a moving population, but it might as justly be said that the cycle of church feuds following revivals dispersed their preachers across the continent. Fortunately for the Baptists, the new republic was a big country.[51]

While the Baptists improvised after 1800, trusting to the ingenuity of individual preachers and churches, some of the Methodists mobilized to effect a sweeping, uniform change in their ministry. Those reformers, primarily men who entered the clergy around the turn of the century, knew that something more needed to be done about their ever-green itinerancy. They also knew that Methodists could do everything more quickly than Baptists, because anything could be done at a stroke by the General Conference, which set policy for the entire church. Finally, they knew the very thing that needed to be done: Their itinerancy had to be leavened by a larger contingent of older men. Specifically, reformers wanted more men to grow gray in the traveling connection, to remain within the itinerancy after they married and started families. In their view, continuing to pare away at the power left to itinerants after the reforms of 1800 was impractical, even if the General Conference had been more amenable, because reducing the prestige of the traveling connection would only have diminished the church's ability to recruit young men to its ranks. And in any case, it was less the authority than the immaturity of Methodist itinerancy that drew censure from the laity.

But it was the reformers' misfortune that many of the lay faithful who deplored the preponderance of young itinerants deplored even more the idea of doing the one thing that might produce greater numbers of older itinerants—providing preachers with salaries large enough to support wives and families. No doubt sheer stinginess fueled lay opposition to higher pay for ministers, but so too did the widely shared pride in the Methodist itinerancy as a select brotherhood of self-denying virtuosos. One of the reformers, William Capers, irritably summed up that view by noting that "there had been an everlasting preaching . . . against preaching for money. . . . It had been reiterated from the beginning that we were eighty-dollar men . . . till it got to be considered that for Methodist preachers to be comfortable, would deprive them of their glory, and tarnish the lustre of their Methodistic reputation." He got it exactly right: Within the culture of early Methodism, the spiritual charisma of itinerants—and thus their claims to authority over the laity—was linked to their embrace of "holy poverty" and lives of extreme physical hardship and deprivation. Then, too, the Methodist association of itinerants' self-denial with their sanctity took on even greater importance because their main competitors in the South, the Baptists, habitually boasted that their self-sustaining clergy made no demands whatsoever on the laity for financial support.[52]

That image of an ascetic clergy appealed deeply to many of the faithful. While easing the consciences of tightwads within their midst, it also signified for more generous souls the distinctive essence of their church. For many of the devout, the renunciation of worldly comforts authenticated itinerants as successors of the biblical apostles, and thus reinforced the laity's sense of participating in a pivotal moment in Christian history being ushered in by the expansion of Methodism. Equally profound was the sway of that ideal among the young men who chose the lot of itinerant preachers. Their journals, which record with dreary regularity every encounter with illness and anxiety, penury and humiliation, figured for itinerants as testaments to their spiritual and physical stamina, an endurance that enhanced their religious stature. Not even cloistered monks could have produced more unrelenting chronicles of mortifying the flesh. Nor were such journals always exclusively private matters: Itinerants often exchanged them with colleagues or the lay faithful, a practice which gives rise to the suspicion that some preachers catalogued their exquisite miseries with an eye to outdoing one another in feats of holy self-abasement, whether coughing up blood, beating down lust, patching their clothing, burying their horses, or enduring the mockery of "worldlings."

The image of the itinerancy as a monastic brotherhood dictated for some Methodists, too, that preachers should remain celibate for spiritual as well as economic reasons. That conviction had been ingrained in many itinerants by Francis Asbury, the patriarch of American Methodism from the Revolution until his death in March of 1816. To be sure, Asbury's preference for a bachelor itinerancy resulted in part from his concern for economizing, as well as his opinion that the "encumbrances" of a wife and children distracted men from their ministerial work. But Asbury also believed that chaste bachelorhood was holier than the married state. When told that low salaries forced "involuntary celibacy" on the traveling connection, he exulted to his journal, "All the better." A lifelong bachelor himself, Asbury personally rescued several preachers who were teetering on the brink of matrimony and greeted the news of one man's nuptials by declaring that "I believe the devil and the women will get all my preachers." On another occasion he told a group of itinerants, "I would not give one single preacher for half a dozen married ones." In short, Asbury strove to fashion the itinerancy as a celibate brotherhood entitled to rule over the laity because they were purer, free from carnal attachments. That belief was the legacy of his own spiritual father, John Wesley, who had encouraged not only Methodist preachers but even lay converts to refrain from marrying if at all possible.

Asbury voiced those convictions often enough to persuade his itinerants that "it was considered a very impolitic step to enter the holy estate of matrimony." But some postponed their own marriages and disdained their wedded colleagues not from any fear of the bishop's displeasure but because they embraced his views. He scored his greatest success among the itinerants of Virginia, who were, as Jesse Lee remarked, "a band of inveterate and invincible old bachelors." When one of their number married, "he seemed to think that unless he could justify the act, he must lose caste among his brethren." As late as 1814, William Capers observed that "The general policy of the Church, sustained by the opinion of the majority of preachers and people, was against preachers' marrying, and therefore against any provision for the support of preachers' families which might encourage their marrying."[53]

Because of his unmatched stature within the church, Asbury's desire to model the Methodist itinerancy as a Protestant monastic order pledged to poverty and chastity forestalled, for as long as he lived, any efforts to change the character of that itinerancy. But as the great man grew more enfeebled, younger reformers awaited their opportunity and laid their plans. In their view, Asbury's ideal was one distinctive feature of Methodism best consigned to the past, despite its appeal to many of the laity. Adhering to that model had produced its share of celibate saints, Asbury chief among them, but it also continually yielded a clergy of mainly young, single men. And that, the reformers recognized, was a dubious and dangerous distinction for any church seeking broad support in a society ruled by white husbands and fathers and in a culture that honored age and experience. Unlike congregational autonomy, the distinguishing feature of Baptist organization that harmonized with the deeply localistic culture of the South, the singularity of early Methodist polity—its authoritative itinerancy dominated by youthful bachelors—sounded a jarring note in a time and place where mature, married men held sway. Such were the reflections that led reformers to gamble that raising support for itinerants would ultimately create the kind of clergy who could gain the Methodists far more adherents than they would lose.

In their urgency, Methodist reformers did not even wait for Asbury's corpse to cool before they began pressing the General Conference to adopt their strategies for aging the itinerancy. Leading that effort, ironically, was Asbury's successor as bishop and a man after his own heart, William McKendree, one of the Virginia itinerancy's confirmed bachelors. Nearly medieval in his mistrust of the opposite sex, he once personified the lure of the world as a seductive woman: "[H]er limb[s] are soft and delicate[,] her attire loose and inviting, wantonness sparkles in her eyes . . . and by the smoothness of her tongue [she] endeavors to deceive." Yet for all his misogyny, McKendree was a sharp-eyed pragmatist who had known for a long time what needed to be done and could now set about doing it. He threw the force of his office behind ensuring greater economic security for married itinerants and their families, warning the General Conference in 1816 of "our misfortune . . . to have a ministry always in its infancy." That body duly fell into line, raising the salaries of all itinerants from $80 to $100 and the allowance paid to their wives by the same amount; it also served notice of the church's intention to enforce an earlier recommendation that all circuits build or rent housing for married itinerants. Modest as these improvements in maintenance were, they proved sufficient to attain McKendree's end. Their effect was apparent even by the 1820s, as the proportion of older men within the traveling connection increased significantly.[54]

Schooled by their season of youth, both Methodists and Baptists learned the sobering lesson that within every seeming strength there skulks a weakness, within every shimmering promise disillusion awaits. Yet as that time passed into memory, church chroniclers eased the faithful into forgetting its trials by fashioning an idealized past of heroic triumph. Writing in the full flush of evangelical success in the South later in the nineteenth century, they romanticized early itinerants as the unexpected agents of divine providence, men who, clad in the armor of innocence and inspired by the deity, spread their faiths across a continent. But those who had weathered the season of youth knew that its story was not so simple, nor its moral so edifying. They knew that Baptist and Methodist churches had paid a high price for vesting so great a trust in preachers whose youth challenged the South's hierarchy of age. They knew, too, despite what Scripture prophesied, that the old and the mighty had not bent to the young and the righteous. And they came to recognize something else as well: that it was not solely the frailties of its messengers that aroused the resistance of southern whites to evangelicalism. It was the message itself that put lay people on their guard as they pondered the import of what early Baptists and Methodists believed to be the proper Christian way of ordering not only relations between old and young but also those between parents and children, husbands and wives.

3

FAMILY VALUES

Do you think that I have come to give peace on earth?
No, I tell you, but rather division; for henceforth in one
house there will be five divided, three against two and
two against three; they will be divided, father against
son and son against father, mother against daughter
and daughter against mother, mother-in-law against
her daughter-in-law and daughter-in-law against her
mother-in-law.

—LUKE 12:49‒53

THE SPIRIT of the Lord overtook Stith Mead somewhere near
Lynchburg, Virginia, at summer's end in 1789. There that young
gentleman, then twenty-two years old, had traveled from his parents' Georgia plantation to inspect his patrimony, a large tract in Bedford
County, where he had spent his youth. It came to Stith as a present, the
most recent of many bestowed by his indulgent father. Like all of William
Mead's other gifts to his brood of eight boys—the lessons in dancing and
fencing, the suits of fine clothes, and his own reputation as a man of
honor—the land was meant to provide the advantages essential to perfecting a southern gentleman.

No one could have known better all that was needed, for in William
Mead himself the model was made flesh. As a young officer in the Virginia
militia he had served with distinction in the fighting against the French
and Indians during the Seven Years' War. He had acquired acres in the
thousands and slaves in the hundreds while enjoying political preferment
as a surveyor, justice of the peace, and pillar of the Anglican vestry. Following the death of his first wife, Stith's mother, he wooed and won the
young widow Cowles, whose beauty and wealth any man might have coveted. Shortly after the Revolution he removed his family and his slaves to

the Georgia frontier, where he carved from the countryside near Augusta an impressive plantation called Cupboard Creek. By the late 1780s, he was arranging for his sons to enjoy lives of similar wealth, privilege, and respect. His eldest boys, Nicholas and Mahlon, had already settled on his land in Bedford County, and William planned the same future for Stith and his brother Samuel. He did not foresee that Stith would fall heir to another kingdom entirely.

Upon arriving in Bedford, Stith visited his relatives and renewed friendships with his former schoolmates. But in the company of those young men he found none of their usual conviviality. Instead, they talked only of the revival stirring the county that summer and their own spiritual struggles. Almost daily they took Stith to sample the eloquence of the Presbyterians, the Baptists, and the Methodists, and he, too, began to pray privately and sought out preachers for spiritual advice. His sense of sinfulness quickly became so oppressive and his fear of damnation so stark that he wept at religious gatherings. When he tried to contain his feelings, their force overwhelmed him. Twice he "fell"—the strength having seeped from his limbs, he sank to the floor, where he lay helpless, shrieking for deliverance. Shortly thereafter, Stith experienced the release of conversion. As he stood amid other "mourners" at a Methodist meeting, his face buried in a handkerchief and his mind deep in meditation on the crucified Christ, "the bleeding spectacle of divine mercy," a preacher's wife approached and asked if he was "happy." In a flash assent sprang to his lips, and Stith realized that faith had found him. "Quick as lightning my mourning was turned to joy, and all distress vanished from my mind— Heaven burst into my soul, and I was filled with joy and peace."

After that summer in 1789, Stith Mead was never the same. The young gentleman raised to dance and duel, to converse lightly and to dress gaily, had been reborn as a God-intoxicated Methodist, soon to become one of the most celebrated preachers in the southern itinerancy. And because of that transformation, the entire Mead family would never be the same— not if he had his way.

The changes in Stith started to unsettle his family even before conviction ripened into conversion. His Bedford County kin regarded the young man's newly sober demeanor with "suspicion," since he had "always been a great rattle and very jocular." Hoping to lift his spirits, his uncle's family teased him about his frequent absences to pray privately. But after his younger brother's conversion, Nicholas Mead became less amused—

especially upon learning that Stith had chosen his, Nicholas's, own parlor to make a first trial at public prayer. When Stith's eloquence prompted Nicholas's wife "to cry aloud from a sense of her sins," her outraged husband announced that "he would have no more praying," for "his wife was going to fall as it was customary among the Methodists," adding for good measure that within six months Stith "would be as bad a sinner as ever." Yet Stith's proselytizing did not go completely unrewarded. His younger brother, Samuel, who had accompanied him to Virginia, came under conviction, and by the time the two returned to Georgia in the winter of 1790, Stith not only hoped for Samuel's ultimate deliverance but also aimed to convert other family members at Cupboard Creek and surrounding plantations.

These transforming events of his youth Stith Mead set down and published forty years later, in 1829. But only at the end of his memoir, in two pages of close-packed print so small as to appear almost a footnote to the rest of the text, did he bring himself to disclose how the Georgia homecoming blasted his hopes of bringing all of the Meads into the Methodist fold. Barely able to recognize the two stricken souls who returned as the dashing boys who had departed less than a year before, other members of the Georgia Mead clan reacted with concern and then with anger. One of Stith's married sisters, Mrs. Gordon, tried to moderate his fierce rectitude by advising that "as I had embraced religion she wished me to continue, but did not see the necessity of giving up all the pleasures in the world." Continue he did, turning a mill owned by her husband, Colonel Gordon, into a makeshift meetinghouse in which he exhorted the entire neighborhood. Even worse, he drew crowds that included some of the Gordons' slaves, prompting the Colonel to complain that "I would spoil his negroes." Vexed by her husband's displeasure and her brother's constant pleas to "flee the wrath to come," Mrs. Gordon finally snapped at Stith that "if she would turn fool like me it would please me."

As his welcome expired among the Gordons, Stith turned to evangelizing his father's household at Cupboard Creek. At first his pious initiatives met with polite acceptance, despite the "Gay and frolicksome" tone set by his stepmother, who regarded "a Religious Idea or an Evenings Hymn" as devices for killing a dull night when livelier diversions were wanting. But Madame Mead's tolerance of her stepson waned on the evening he discovered her parlor abloom with the flower of Augusta's gentry, a rubber of whist in progress, and a fiddle on the table foreshadowing a dance. "Seeing so many of the *Devil's* instruments lying about" left Stith "a little intimidated," but did not stop him from striking up a hymn as soon as "they had stacked up the cards." The frosty stares with which the parlor party greeted his psalmody left him feeling "that all was not well."

While these episodes soured feelings toward Stith among some of his kin, what befell his brother Samuel in Georgia embittered Stith toward his family. Like most southerners, the Meads loved dancing, and their concern about Stith and Samuel may have suggested hosting balls as a happy antidote to the young men's dour asceticism. Samuel succumbed to the lure of those familiar revels, his religious seriousness dissolved by the beckoning strains of a fiddle.[1]

It could have been the economies of his printer rather than any deliberate design on Stith's part that consigned his family's opposition to Methodism to the fine print at the back of his published memoir. Even so, Mead surely wished to conceal the intensity of his relatives' resistance: His unpublished letterbook and journals contain many episodes of subsequent and increasingly heated conflict which he suppressed entirely in his memoirs. Those sources reveal that Samuel, after dancing away his religious convictions, went back to Bedford County and the future arranged by his father. They also place Stith in western Virginia by the summer of 1792. Now a Methodist itinerant, he rode the heady wave of a revival gathering momentum on his circuit. By then news of Stith's notoriety as the family prodigal had reached another of his older brothers, Mahlon. Stung by the disgrace to their father, Mahlon decided that what his brother needed was not a ball but a beating to avenge the insult and bring him back to his senses. But when Mahlon came to administer that remedy at a home where Stith was preaching, he "fell," evidently under conviction. Placed on a bed, Mahlon stared at Stith with eyes full of wordless fear and then made a sudden grab for his brother's throat and struck him several times. Finally subdued by Stith and his followers, Mahlon passed the night in agony, lurching to leap out of the window, trying to bite the watchers at his bedside, and screaming, "I am going to hell this moment. . . . O, that I should ever raise children that should say their father is gone to hell!"[2]

Bizarre though they were, Mahlon's struggles revealed his warring emotions: Stith's sermon had overwhelmed him with the fear of the Lord, yet he fought against being gathered into the Methodist fold, especially by a younger brother wielding the shepherd's crook. As Stith observed, his presence at Mahlon's bedside seemed to increase his torments. There is no mystery about what made Mahlon despair. If he surrendered to Stith's faith, he would shame the rest of the family, most particularly William Mead, a man already saddled with a son who believed his father was bound for hell. But if Mahlon rejected the stirrings of repentance, he feared his own damnation and the disgrace of his own children.

After an awful night, Mahlon's misery ended in his conversion, and Stith's hopes of reclaiming other family members rebounded. Mahlon even offered to join him in carrying the gospel back to Cupboard Creek. But with Samuel's backsliding fresh in his memory, Stith shunned the risk of bringing another brother home. He reckoned that the more prudent strategy, at least initially, lay in appealing to other family members far removed from the dancers at Cupboard Creek. That prompted a letter to Samuel in the fall of 1792, telling of Mahlon's conversion and warning that "you may be sure you will have hot Dancing in Hell." Mixing threats with appeals to brotherly affection, he asked Samuel: "How Long do you mean to Break my heart, and make mine Eyes over flow with tears. . . . I cant bear the thought of your being a Companion for Devils . . . in the Lake that Burns with fire and Brimstone." To leave no doubt in Samuel's mind about the consequences of continuing to neglect his soul, he concluded, "If you will go with me here is my hand if nott I bid you Adieu." And at the crack of doom, Stith promised, "I shall be a swift witness against you in the Day of Judgment If you don't repent your sins."[3]

Stith wished to be understood as a man capable of anything. Even as he appealed to Samuel's affections, he declared himself ready to banish all feelings of family loyalty, to renounce his backsliding brother in this life and the hereafter. That claim to emotional ruthlessness did not prove mere posturing. Other members of the Mead family felt its full force only a few months later, following Samuel Mead's sudden death during the winter of 1793. Convinced that his brother had died unrepentant, Stith plunged into a frenzy of recrimination directed mainly against his father, blaming him for the dance that sealed Samuel's eternal doom. "The Indulgeance of Fid[d]ling and Dancing has ever been your beset[t]ing Sin," Stith informed his grieving parent, "you are training them [your children] up for the DEVIL, to make them an heir of hell-fire." Legacies of every sort were much on Stith's mind when he wrote those bitter words. In the opening of the letter, he acknowledged benefiting from his father's reputation, "your respectable Character being so generally known that I find it a recommendation to me in various parts of the world." He also admitted his fear that "if I write thus; you will Disinherit me." But Stith made it plain that he held paternal legacies cheap compared to his spiritual patrimony. As for "The Honour that Comes from man, I seek it not." As for his father's wealth, "I had rather be disinherited of everything I possess, than to think of your Soul going to Hell."[4]

That letter must have left William Mead wounded and bewildered. His gently nurtured son broke a father's mourning to charge him with sending Samuel to hell and to reject the wealth and standing William wished to bestow on him. In his confusion and misery, William showed the letter to one Mr. Haynes, a Methodist neighbor acquainted with Stith, who assured the old man that his boy was "a good Christian." When Haynes asked to keep the letter, "to serve him as a sermon," William readily assented, perhaps relieved by the prospect of never reading its contents again. Then he wrote an extraordinary reply to his son, a letter as gentle as Stith's was cruel. He remarked on the "great satisfaction" he took in his son's letters and commended his loyalty to "the cause of God." He delicately eased the boy's worry of being disinherited by discussing arrangements to deed Stith and Mahlon additional land in Virginia. He made no mention of Samuel. Having lost one son to death, William did not want to lose another to a family quarrel. Possibly, too, he shared the Gordons' views that Stith was "deranged," and feared that if further provoked he might run "raving mad." More certainly, William held family unity in the here and now dearer than did his son. The old man had wearied of his children's wrangling over religion and hoped that soothing words might restore some peace.[5]

He misjudged. Stith continued to bombard Cupboard Creek with admonishing salvos while, as he put it, "manning up" for another visit to those kinfolk whom he called "strangers to the renewing spirit of God." Among them was J. M. Simmons, once a close friend and now the husband of his stepsister. Since joining the Methodists, Stith had broken off their intimacy, prompting a letter from Simmons filled with hurt and anger. "Have I deserved it at your hands . . . that I am to be left behind by you?" Simmons implored, and then wondered wryly whether Stith "fear[ed] a Contamination of principles, by Keeping Communion with a free liver." If so, he concluded, then "Away with all Your Religions. If this is to be the case—I bid you adieu."

In that same painful letter, perhaps to shield William Mead, Simmons warned Stith to stay away from Cupboard Creek until he learned to keep quiet about his religious views. Ignoring that advice, Stith returned in the summer of 1794. By now the hardships of riding circuit had left him so wasted that he seemed a veritable skeleton rattling out of the family closet—his emaciated frame draped in ill-fitting clothes, face pale and haggard, spirit unquiet. He commandeered his father's parlor long enough to preach at least one sermon, the results of which he set down tersely as "I came to my own and my own Received me not." Writing to his father a month later, Stith weighed in with the judgment that "all the time I was with you I never felt in my heart that you was a Regenerated Christian." When his father protested that he was "a good man," Stith retorted that William was "glewed to the world," attached to "sensual delights," including "the Association of the Augusta Gentlemen and Ladies." "Probably you say, you are Old and Experienced, and I am Young and foolish," he continued, anticipating his father's objections, "But I reply in the language of Young Elihu, 'great men are not always wise neither do the aged understand Judgment.' "[6]

Perhaps Stith now directed his appeals to his father because William was the only member of the Georgia family with whom he was still on speaking terms. But possibly he sensed even during his summer visit to Cupboard Creek that his words were beginning to take effect, for a letter to Stith in the fall of 1794 suggests that Samuel's death slowly ate away at William. Although he never alluded directly to Samuel's fate, William recounted the dreadful misfortunes and premature deaths that befell an Augusta minister who preached against the Trinity and a local lawyer "who acted as though God did not take notice of his profane and wicked life." In any case, William came under conviction sometime in that year and began attending the Methodist church in Augusta. Ten years later, in 1805, he experienced conversion, just months before his death at the age of seventy-eight.[7]

STITH MEAD'S memoirs, journal, and letterbook reveal in intimate detail the ways in which evangelicalism touched the members of one southern family in the 1790s. At one extreme is the quick susceptibility of Stith himself, his brother Samuel, and Nicholas Mead's wife. At the other extreme is the visceral hostility of Stith's older brothers, Nicholas and, initially, Mahlon, and his brother-in-law, Colonel Gordon. Other family members, although equally resistant to evangelicalism, strove for restraint. There is the tense, fragile forbearance of Stith's sister and his stepmother. Both felt obliged to endure Stith's newfound convictions, but gradually came to resent him, Mrs. Gordon for jeopardizing her role as a dutiful wife and Madame Mead for spoiling her reputation as a gracious hostess. Finally there is the incomprehension of those stung by his rejection, a pain barely concealed by Simmons's sarcasm and bravely cloaked by William's reserve.

Beyond that range of responses to evangelicalism within the family, what draws notice is the contrast between the content of Mead's published memoirs and the material in his journal and letterbook. Here is revealed what Mead chose to make public and what he strove to mute or keep private. He admitted into his memoirs, although mainly in fine print, the sharp opposition he encountered from some relatives, whom evangelical readers could easily recognize as stock villains—the furiously prejudiced Nicholas; the smug, slaveholding Gordons; and the frivolous, worldly Madame Mead. But he censored any mention of violent or protracted conflict with other family members—his assault by the tormented Mahlon and his failure to reclaim the backslidden Samuel, his permanent breach with Simmons and his agonizing struggle with William. These were relatives, too, whose responses to Stith's Methodist convictions were less easily caricatured and thus dismissed.

The principle of selectivity that shaped Stith Mead's memoirs was widely adopted by other early Baptists and Methodists who published spiritual autobiographies and biographies. Their accounts represent evangelical influence as irresistible once a single convert started proselytizing within the household. Typically, they depict pious wives and mothers or zealous adolescent sons and daughters embracing evangelical beliefs, encountering opposition from other relatives, but then, within a matter of days or weeks, winning over the entire family, sometimes even extended kin and neighbors. Chroniclers are emphatic about how rapidly resistance spent itself—after a flurry of threats and recriminations, unawakened relatives dissolved into tears of repentance, and kinfolk sealed their renewed solidarity by joining the church together. Their narratives, like Stith Mead's memoirs, mention neither those like the anguished Mahlon and the lost Samuel, nor those who, like William Mead, held to their doubts for years, nor those who, like J. M. Simmons, severed all ties with their converted kin and friends.[8]

To be sure, evangelical accounts of family conversions were not sheer fantasy: Kinship ties played a key role in the spread of religious affinities. Membership lists show that men and women related by blood and marriage often made up the majority in Baptist and Methodist churches. During revivals, that pattern of "spiritual tribalism" surfaces in the profile of new converts, predominantly young men and women often linked together in a tangled cousinry. Sometimes those newly awakened were the children of members; in other cases, young people brought their parents into the church. Even so, evangelical loyalties were at least as likely to divide as to unite white families living in the early South. Although the Meads' wealth and standing set them apart from the vast majority of white southerners, the wrenching struggles set in motion by Stith's conversion were common, contests reprised within the humbler households of small planters in the Carolina up-country and the Virginia Piedmont and the cabins of hunters and tenant farmers on the frontiers of Georgia and Kentucky. Among all classes of whites, as evangelicalism claimed the assent or curiosity of some family members, it left many others contemptuous, wary, or simply befuddled. For those to whom Canaan's language long remained an unintelligible tongue, the conversion of beloved relatives could lead to enduring emotional estrangement. Transformed by their newfound zeal, dutiful sons and daughters, affectionate siblings and spouses, came to resemble the reborn Stith Mead—remorseless, relentless, seemingly heartless in dealings with loved ones.[9]

It was an uncomfortable truth, and one that evangelical clergymen labored to obscure by both self-censorship and cockeyed optimism. Typically, one contributor to a Methodist periodical reported that after a western country revival many young converts returned to their homes and "declared Hell-fire to be the portion of their brothers and sisters, fathers and mothers, whom they supposed to be destitute of an interest in Christ." "This kind of preaching," he exulted, "produced in some places the most happy effects." But since "happy effects" on the household do not routinely issue from the transformation of obliging children into censorious adolescents, it is hard to imagine many such "some places." Preachers knew as much and more from personal experience. Yet few were willing to acknowledge publicly their own embittered familial relations, and fewer still with the frankness of John Taylor, who noted in his memoir that except for one uncle who shared his Baptist beliefs, "neither of us had ever heard of a truly religious person among all our connections, and each of us had been held in contempt by them all." Most, like Stith

Mead, confided the worst only to diaries or letters. James Meacham agonized because even his exemplary life as a Methodist itinerant had not inspired the rest of his family, all of whom remained "Spiritually deceased in Sin," while Jeremiah Norman, upon returning to visit his kin and neighbors, prayed for "favour in the sight of those who was formerly opposed to me," including his elder brother, "who was one of my greatest opposers when I commenced an Itinerant Man."

The divisions within families that the evangelical clergy privately acknowledged took on an even more ominous shape in the anxieties of the laity. When two of his adolescent sons converted to Methodism in the 1770s, one Maryland Anglican dreamed that "a sprout grew up through his house, and that its progress was so rapid he became alarmed for the safety of his house; he wanted to remove it, but was afraid to cut it down, lest the house should be destroyed by the fall." In 1815, a similar worry beset Ebenezer Pettigrew, a North Carolina Anglican, who shared with his wife the news of another relative's decision to join the Baptists: "I expect . . . that he will be dip[p]ed in less than six months," Ebenezer sighed. "Sally fumes and frets and abuses the baptists in full proportion to Clements and his Mothers praises of them. Such is the way to produce distress in a family."[10]

What lent particular force to fears of families divided by religion was the increasing dispersal of kinfolk to the western country. In the decades before the American Revolution and with gathering momentum thereafter, many southern families migrated to the successive frontiers of Georgia, Alabama, Texas, Kentucky, Tennessee, and the southern portions of Ohio, Indiana, and Illinois. While some wealthy planters like William Mead dispatched sons to patrimonies distant from their own plantations to extend family influence, other sons of the gentry struck out for the western country to assert their independence. In much greater numbers, men of more modest means and ambition left behind aging parents and in-laws in search of greater economic security. No matter what the motive, migration ruptured southern kinship networks, and many partings became permanent, save for infrequent visits. The pain of those separations pours out in letters exchanged by parents and children, brothers and sisters, cousins and in-laws whose shared lives had become a matter of wistful longing, expressed by anxious inquiries about the health and welfare of distant kinfolk, heartfelt pleas for relatives to resettle in their midst, and morbid fears of never being reunited in this life. In a society in which so many men and women felt the sadness of intimacy slipping away before distance, families were acutely sensitive to anything that might compound their feeling that kinfolk were becoming strangers.[11]

The Baptist and Methodist clergy saw as much with a clarity sharpened by their own rootless lives. And they devised spiritual remedies to meet the inner needs of southerners whose grief over being physically separated from relatives heightened their dread of emotional alienation. To sustain those who, fearing domestic turmoil, shrank from religious commitment, evangelicals taught that believers fulfilled their highest duty to family by trying to convert loved ones. An irresistible impulse to spread the gospel among unawakened kin, preachers urged, both validated the authenticity of the convert's own rebirth and met the ultimate responsibility to family. Beyond that, evangelicals emphasized that such efforts would restore an unbroken circle of intimacy in heaven. Preachers and pious lay people alike most commonly described paradise as an everlasting family reunion, an eternal recompense for the pain of earthly partings.[12]

For a sense of the urgency that those convictions aroused among evangelicals, review the campaign waged by the Methodist members of one family for the reclamation of Dr. John Owen, who, perhaps deliberately, lived distant from his devout relations in Halifax County, North Carolina. By 1811, those Owens nearer to heaven than Halifax had enlisted help from the Methodist preacher John Early, who described Dr. Owen as "a very friendly clever young man who has no religion." Not content with alerting Early, whose circuit included the doctor's neighborhood, the entire network of his Methodist kin liberally dispensed spiritual advice to both Dr. Owen and his unconverted wife, Mary. Her sister, Frances Goodwin, as well as John's unmarried sisters, Mildred, Isabel, and Mary Owen, sent long letters reminding the couple of the transience of earthly pleasures and the lasting happiness awaiting when all the family met again in heaven. John Owen, Sr., the doctor's father, reinforced their message, depicting eternal doom as perpetual isolation from loved ones by cautioning, "as you know how it is to be in a distant land without friends and among strangers may the knowledge of this cause you to reflect . . . how awfull must it [be] to enter on that state of being that is never to end without a friend. . . ." Even more fervent promptings came from Dr. Owen's married sister, Elizabeth Owen Anderson, whose scorched-earth tactics recall Stith Mead's efforts to reclaim his brother Samuel. As she lay dying in 1814, Elizabeth exploited that leverage to prevail with John and

Mary: "I charge you both meet me at the right hand of god," she declared in a final letter, "I view you in danger. . . . [L]et my dying words rest with you far[e]well till we meet in heaven." During the months after her death, Elizabeth's pious survivors redoubled their efforts to bring the couple into the evangelical fold, alluding often to her departing "in a rapture to the paredise of God." Among them was Frances Goodwin, who urged that such partings need not be permanent: "I fear we shall never meet in this world but could we be prepared to meet in a better the separation would be trifling."[13]

Hopes of rejoining their relatives in the hereafter exerted an equally compelling force among the Baptists. Enter the only world known to Wilson Thompson as a boy entering his teens around the turn of the century—a Kentucky settlement where most adults, including his uncle, a minister, and his father, a deacon, belonged to the local Baptist churches. Around the turn of the century a revival began to gather the children of those churches into membership, a circle of adolescent converts including many of Wilson's cousins but not, to his dismay, himself. Not wishing to aggravate the boy's distress, his father told Wilson to stay at home when the rest of the family attended the cousins' baptism. As his relatives set out for the church singing, Wilson remembered, "I really thought they were on their way to heaven. God was their Father . . . and Christians were their brethren and sisters. . . . and I thought as these Christians were now leaving me behind . . . so at the last great day they would thus ascend to heaven, leaving me to endure the just punishment due me as a vile sinner."[14]

The evangelical promise of restoring an unbroken circle of kin in heaven thus spoke directly to the needs of many men and women whose closest attachments were being sundered by westward migration. It countered, too, the image of evangelicalism as a sort of Pandora's box that, once opened within a household, unleashed discord among its members. Yet it did not answer so fully as to banish the deeper misgivings about evangelicalism and the family. Those lay fears, sharper and even more fundamental, arose from the widespread suspicion that many evangelical teachings undermined the integrity of white households and, at their most extreme, subverted the southern ideal of family. Indeed, even as churches relied on the bonds of blood and marriage to promote their progress, many other southern whites viewed those ties as being threatened, possibly even supplanted, by certain evangelical beliefs and practices. While often exaggerated, such concerns were not groundless. Despite evangelical assertions that they prized family unity in this life and the next, their early message and ritual practice did not unequivocally affirm the primacy of family loyalties and affections. On the contrary, Baptists and Methodists held their converts to standards of commitment that sometimes required neglecting temporal responsibilities to kinfolk in order to meet spiritual obligations.

Taught from childhood to accept that their primary identity and duty lay with the lineal family, many southerners could only regard with uneasiness, at the very least, any church that demanded an individual's ultimate loyalty. It could hardly have been otherwise in a culture in which the claims of blood, the integrity of the clan, and the continuity of the lineage exerted extraordinary force, one heightened rather than diminished by the centrifugal pull of migration. For that reason, even the most comforting and culturally resonant evangelical teaching, the assurance of redeemed kin meeting in heaven for an eternity together, could not entirely dispel the anxieties aroused by other aspects of their belief and practice. Put simply, evangelicals could not lay to rest the suspicion that, for all their professed fervor to reunite relatives in the hereafter, they did a poor job of showing devotion to families in the here and now.

It was the evangelicals' misfortune that the group most conspicuous for such neglect were also their most visible representatives in the early South—itinerant preachers. Although held up as spiritual virtuosos, these young men made choices about familial obligations that were troubling not only to the laity but even to themselves. Itinerants, especially among the Methodists, postponed courtship and marriage well beyond the age when most southern men were boasting of their contributions to the continuity of the lineage—making romantic conquests, marrying, and starting families. Instead of engaging the affections of suitable females, young preachers like Stephen Davidson scorned any man "who can give up the ministry for a woman, and can delight more in a lady's chamber than in his studies." Instead of greeting word of weddings with jokes and congratulations, many, like Freeborn Garrettson, met the news of their colleagues' marrying with resignation or ridicule. Upon learning that his own brother, a fellow itinerant, had wed, Garrettson felt "overwhelmed with sorrow," and even more determined "to live a life of celibacy." Instead of celebrating the joys of becoming husbands and fathers, they referred to wives as "Jezabels" and children as "encumbrances."[15]

Like the early Methodist clergy, some lay people also prized a bachelor itinerancy—not merely because it was cheaper but because they thought it holier. Among them was a devout Virginia woman who discouraged James Meacham from pursuing a romance by warning "that Satan could counterfeit love—and begged me to hold fast Celibacy." A pious Methodist couple showed the same preference when John Early told them of his impending marriage in 1814, registering an "anxiety which all but overwhelmed me with grief." Yet such lay responses were atypical; most white southerners without and even some within the evangelical fold were more likely to wonder at young men's seeming indifference to the pleasures of wooing, wedding, and begetting.

Join one Virginia family in the fall of 1793 as they offered Jeremiah Norman an evening's hospitality, including the company of their eligible daughter. As an opening gambit, she playfully foreswore her former resolve "not [to] look at the young men in time of preaching." Norman duly expressed himself "astonisht" at her readiness to be distracted from prayer. Taking that rejoinder as a challenge, if not an invitation, she pressed on, drawling that "it were mighty hard for a young woman to have religion," for "how could they Pray while the Beautifull young men were in their sight?" When these coy overtures evoked no warmer response from the young preacher than his ardent hope for her salvation, she rallied once more, asking archly, "[H]ow could you be in love with and courting a young woman and not be alooking at her in time of meeting?" But, alas, he again "exerted" himself to correct her opinions, and "at last she . . . gave way to my arguments that they were right"—perhaps with an inward sigh at having squandered an evening's wiles on so dismal a prospect.

The Methodist *Discipline*, of course, bound itinerants not to jump at such bait, but Norman appears not even to have noticed the dangling hook. Instead, this young belle practicing commonplace coquetry enters Norman's diary as "the most singular young woman that I ever saw in my life." Most likely, both the lady and her onlooking family were even more "astonisht" at Norman's "singular" inability to recognize a flirtation. Equally mystified were a lay couple of his acquaintance who, when Norman reached his late twenties, tried without success "every polite and decent method of introducing me to the married state." Twenty years later, John Johnson evoked the same frustration from a young Kentucky woman when he shunned the charms of feminine company after preaching at a private home and instead "went to his room and sat down to read, without seeming to notice girls or anybody else." "Well," she snapped, "he's a cool chicken."[16]

There was, of course, a prospect more troubling to more lay people than either the superhuman reserve or unfeigned obtuseness of some itinerants. Far more commonly, husbands and fathers feared that traveling preachers would find an outlet for their sexual energies in liaisons with their wives and daughters, a concern heightened by the physical intimacy of the small, crowded homes where preachers usually lodged. Knowing as much, Jeremiah Norman woke from a sound sleep one morning in 1796 horrified to hear "a woman's voice sounding from the Bed opposite me." Dreading that the episode would ensnare him in scandal, he admitted being "apprehensive, the People are not so wise as what they might be in such Cases." But most were, if not wiser, warier, among them the Tennessee Quaker who mortified Thomas Ware in 1787 by refusing his own hospitality, instead directing him to a neighbor, "whose wife is old and ugly." Nor did wedlock place itinerants above suspicion: Peter Cartwright had been married for several years and was approaching forty when one Kentuckian condemned him as "a very bad man, for all the women in the country were falling in love with me; and that I had moved on their passions and took them into the Church with bad intentions."[17]

By their own admission, most itinerants were not immune to temptation. The failure to repress sexual impulses fills their diaries, and hostesses doubtless came across telltale evidence when laundering their bed linen. Awakening one morning in 1783, Thomas Haskins "found I had had a severe and very bold assault by my fleshly enemy," and begged for deliverance from "what remains of Sin." Worry about those "assaults" is a constant refrain in the diary of James Meacham, who suspected that he "may have yielded in Some Measure in my heart" to "powerful Temptations of the flesh," thus causing "the rapped [rapid] tide of Nature to flow." He admitted that "Nature presses me hard to brak [break] . . . Selibacy, but I resist it." Invention followed in the footsteps of necessity: Freeborn Garrettson, determined to "suffer anything than feel the motions of sin," wrapped himself up in his great coat and slept on the floor. His colleagues, who agreed that "this body must be kept under," were equally dismayed when attracted to young women. Meacham's resistance held on one occasion when, dining at the home of a Presbyterian, "I met with a powerful Temptation here from one of the female seck [sex]." But he was "ashamed" to "confess" his weakness and feared some future encounter when he might be conquered by lust. His colleague William Ormond, worn down by several days of "a hard wressel [wrestle] with the Devil and my Flesh," began to see what brought St. Paul to the grudging conclusion that "it is better to Marry than burn."[18]

How deeply young preachers suffered the torments inflicted by the flesh and the devil is revealed by the antidote to desire chosen by Jeremiah Minter, who, at age twenty-four, had himself surgically castrated. What prompted that drastic renunciation was his intimacy with Sarah Jones— Virginian, Methodist, and married woman. They exchanged letters almost daily during the late 1780s, and her side of the correspondence suggests that something more than spiritual affinities set her feelings afire. "I love your soul my precious brother!" she once confided. "I am forced to stop, while my lap is wet with tears." Minter, too, felt the humidity rising, and so concluded that nothing short of becoming *an eunuch for the kingdom of heaven's sake*" would enable him "to devote myself entirely to the Lord in a single life, and never marry." Unfortunately for Minter, his secret somehow came to light, giving rise to even greater scandal than his alleged dalliance with Madame Jones, and he was expelled from the itinerancy. Francis Asbury knew enough about southerners to prefer rumors that his preachers seduced pious matrons to reports that they gelded themselves in the name of godliness.[19]

Other deviations from masculine duty, while less notorious than Minter's, also fostered anxiety among itinerants, hard feelings among their kin, and unfavorable notice from the laity. Young men who chose the lot of traveling preachers spent long periods separated from parents, many of whom resented what they regarded as an abandonment of filial obligation. Before he could enter the itinerancy in 1803, Peter Cartwright had to overcome the reluctance of his father, who rented a small farm in Kentucky and relied on the help of his strapping, eighteen-year-old son. As John Early prepared to return to his circuit in the spring of 1807, his ailing father burdened him by announcing that "he never expected to see me again in this world."

Some youthful itinerants, secure in their own righteousness, left families without a qualm, perhaps even welcoming the chance for release. In 1772, William Watters turned aside the pleas of his widowed mother, who offered him "all her worldly possessions never to leave her," by reasoning that his brothers "would pay the utmost attention to her" and recalling the words of Jesus Christ to one of his disciples, "let the dead bury the dead, but go thou and preach the kingdom of God." In a similar vein, when Jacob Young started on his first circuit in 1801, "I felt like I had forsaken the world, father, mother, brothers, sisters, and all my friends to follow Christ," he declared. "This was one of the happiest days of my life." But many more agonized over the conflict between serving God and sustaining family. In the fall of 1780, Nelson Reed returned to his parents' home near Alexandria, Virginia, to find his mother and two of his siblings desperately ill; although he had "little Expectation of seeing [them] again in the land of the living," Reed reluctantly resumed his circuit "with my heart full." His colleague James Meacham's anxieties took shape in a dream of his orphaned sister Polly "very sick . . . and complaining that she suffered for want of care being taken of her . . . expect that is a token she is no more." While some, like Reed and Meacham, persuaded themselves that they were following a higher calling, the high turnover within the Methodist traveling connection indicates that many of their comrades succumbed to the pressure of family responsibilities.[20]

If itinerants came up short as sons and siblings, even in their own judgment, they fared no better as husbands and fathers. While most early Methodist preachers stopped traveling once they wed, the minority of married itinerants offered spouses and children little in the way of company, comfort, or security. Boarding with relatives sometimes fell to the lot of itinerants' wives, but most followed their husbands from one circuit to the next, moving every year with a growing brood of young children. Many itinerants also called upon parents, siblings, or in-laws for help in supporting their families. Preachers' wives had no claim upon the financial support of the Methodist faithful until 1796, which was when the church also took its first grudging step toward assisting the widows and orphans of itinerants. Even after 1800, when many circuits began to build or rent housing for married preachers, accommodations were far from choice.

While husbands traveled, wives stayed home, coping with loneliness, poverty, and sickness. Consider the plight of Edward Dromgoole's wife, whose entire family, including herself, fell ill while her husband rode his circuit in 1794. By the time he returned, their young son Edward lay dead and another child died shortly thereafter. Dromgoole was so stricken with guilt that he located, much against his desire, for he found "the most peace of mind when I am engaged to save Souls." Other preachers persisted in traveling despite family troubles. When his son was severely injured in an accident, South Carolina's James Jenkins, pondering "whether to stay and nurse my child, or to go and do the work of the Lord, I at length determined on the latter." Benjamin Lakin displayed the same willingness to sacrifice those closest to him in the name of religious duty. By 1810, his wife, Betsy Roye Lakin, had become so enfeebled by the rigors of accompanying him on circuits spanning Kentucky that she asked him to locate. Lakin resisted, deciding that "I am not my own, But belong to God, the Church, and My Country."

The Baptists liked to boast that their own clergy, by engaging in secular occupations, did better by their families. In the 1820s, a horrified Susanna Johnson overheard one Baptist preacher criticize her husband, a Methodist itinerant, by wondering "Why didn't he [Johnson] settle down and go to work, and not drag a big family around the country to sponge a living off honest people that had to work for it." But in truth, the Baptist clergy also stinted their families. Like many of his colleagues, Wilson Thompson neglected his Missouri farm because of frequent preaching tours that took him far from home. Failing finances forced him to accept his father's generosity because his congregations upheld the Baptist insistence on a self-supporting clergy. After years of struggling with this hardscrabble life, far from her own family in Kentucky, Thompson's wife began suffering bouts of delirium and agitated depression; yet still he continued to itinerate, leaving his "despondent" spouse and their child in the care of relatives. Another Baptist minister, the Virginian Henry Toler, spoke candidly when he observed that "Preachers wives and Horses were the most miserable Creatures imaginable."[21]

The choices made by many preachers bespoke the evangelical conviction that the obligations to kin must give way before duty to God. No other claim could take precedence over saving oneself and warning others of the wrath to come—to fall under the sway of family attachments was to invite spiritual disaster. This was the fear that haunted one Methodist itinerant who doubted his sanctification ever since discovering, when his wife fell gravely ill, that "he could not give her up." It stalked Susannah Johnson, too, who angrily accused another preacher of trying to ruin her husband's standing among other itinerants by telling them that "he thought too much of his wife." Perhaps in their thoughts was the example of the venerable Valentine Cook, a Methodist itinerant turned Kentucky schoolmaster, who acquired in age the wisdom to recognize where his ultimate loyalties lay. On the morning when the New Madrid earthquake rocked the western country, Cook, convinced that the millennium had dawned, sprang from his bed and, clad only in his nightshirt, raced through the streets shouting, "My Jesus is coming." When his wife, Tabitha, followed him, crying, "O Mr. Cook, don't leave me!" he responded, "O Tabby, my Jesus is coming; I can't wait for you Tabby."[22]

By boasting of their disengagement from the consolations of hearth and home, paragons like Cook hoped to command both respect and emulation from other white southerners. But many outside the evangelical fold were repelled by the ways in which preachers' behavior set at nought the security and continuity of their own families, to say nothing of the threat that protracted clerical celibacy might pose to the purity of other people's lineages. Indeed, even those laymen and -women who regarded the clergy as heroic exemplars of unworldliness were unsettled by how sharply these godly men diverged from conventional masculine roles. Whether within or without evangelical churches, all partook of a regional culture that idealized men as providers, protectors, and progenitors; inevitably, they sensed the challenge from a religious movement that urged young men to devalue such responsibilities.[23]

In that course, as many of their elders believed, the rising generation of southern males needed no encouragement. Indeed, what made itinerants' claims to exemplary status so threatening was the willingness of many of their secular male contemporaries in the post-Revolutionary South to sacrifice family stability by making similar choices, embracing lives of constant geographic movement and economic risk. Planters, tenant farmers, and hunters might uproot and resettle their families several times as they shifted from Virginia or the Carolinas to Georgia, Kentucky, or Tennessee, and, in later decades, in Alabama, Indiana, or Texas. The rupturing of kinship networks became the casualty of peripatetic lives. And although the hope of making their families more economically secure most often inspired men to pull up stakes, that process was fraught with uncertainty, both for poorer men who tried their luck as squatters and for those of greater means who courted the main chance as speculators. In other words, itinerants' life-choices became a lightning rod for deeper cultural anxieties and the occasion for family conflict not only because they departed from the southern ideal of how male heads of household should behave but also because they embodied the reality of how a growing number of southern men actually behaved.[24]

SOUTHERN RESERVATIONS about evangelicals' commitment to family went well beyond misgivings about the private lives of itinerant preachers, for churches also called upon lay converts to sacrifice earthly attachments in the name of personal salvation and religious duty. That demand is starkly dramatized in the opening pages of John Bunyan's *Pilgrim's Progress*, the book that, after the Bible, commanded the widest readership among the evangelical laity. Here Bunyan's pilgrim, "Christian," stopping his ears to the pleas of his wife and children, flees his home in quest of the Celestial City, crying "Life! life! eternal life!" He never looks behind and never returns. It is a striking image of abandonment, and one that could have been etched in the memory even of illiterate men and women by a popular series of prints illustrating Bunyan's allegory. The Methodist preacher Edward Dromgoole owned the entire set and evidently displayed them on the walls of his North Carolina home. Bunyan's message was also updated by devotional literature, most notably the popular autobiography of Hester Ann Rowe Rogers, an eighteenth-century British Methodist, which went through several American editions before 1820. Throughout the memoir Rogers held up her willingness to break with relatives opposed to evangelicalism as the measure of her spiritual virtuosity.[25]

That model of religious commitment, far from being peculiar to evangelicals, has been invoked by a variety of Christian groups whenever and wherever they strove to make headway against a resistant majority. Its message of radical spiritual individualism was an effective means of sustaining new converts in withstanding family disapproval. But that same ideal also assumed an ominous cast in any culture, like that of the early South, steeped in loyalty to kith and kin. The suppression of family feeling exemplified by "Christian" and Hester Ann Rogers, made even more immediate in the lives of Baptist and Methodist preachers and held up for emulation by lay believers, seemed to many southerners to subvert what should be held most sacred. Among them was one woman who confided to the preacher Benjamin Abbott her fear that joining the Methodists would oblige her to desert husband and family in order to follow him.[26]

Not only evangelical teaching but church practice called upon southerners to subordinate family allegiance to religious duty. Baptists and Methodists required their faithful to submit to a collective discipline that could expose to public discussion the most carefully guarded secrets of households and kinship groups. Converts themselves might confess indiscretions, or churches and preachers, prompted by their own suspicions, might pry into private lives. Such revelations often resulted in other family intimates, whether or not they belonged to the church, finding their misdeeds the fodder for local gossip. Consider the cases that, within a few years, enlivened meetings of North Carolina's Flat River Baptist Church. In March of 1786, the church cited one Jacob Mooney for "having kept a girl in his house in a very unbecoming manner, and she has proved with child and lays it to him." Possibly the woman in question was Elizabeth Cooper, whose embarrassment was compounded by being expelled along with Mooney for fornication and bastardy. A few months later, church members discovered that another of their brethren, Joseph Traylor, had "attempted to commit the sin called sodomy . . . together with other things too indecent to mention here." The stir over these sensations had hardly subsided when, in 1790, another season of scandal erupted after the Widow Rogers accused Rebecca Swaney of lying to conceal her daughter's miscarriage by "saying she has the ague and fever." After several months of investigating both Rebecca and her daughter, who was not a Baptist, the church widened its circle of suspicion to ensnare Rebecca's husband, John Swaney, who now stood accused of countenancing their daughter's lover, Matthew Griffin, another nonmember, even to the point of "supporting them from his own house." Swaney "endeavored to excuse himself, pleading he could not help it," but the Flat River Church ordered him to "drive Griffin off by the next church meeting." Then they took up the case of whether to admit William Moore, whose first wife had run off with her lover, whereupon Moore had married another woman.

So it went, church scrutiny indiscriminately shaming both believers and nonbelievers by setting neighborhoods abuzz with speculations about the paternity of bastards, the objects of homosexual advances, the parties to heterosexual liaisons, and the legality of marriages. To make matters worse, some churches did not confine the discussion of such matters to meetings of members only but aired them before entire congregations which might include anyone living within about a twenty-mile radius. The discomfort of some at Flat River with that forthcoming practice inspired the church to debate in the fall of 1791 whether "private transgression be transacted publicly, or only before the church privately and not before the world." But the godly majority prevailed, insisting that such trials should continue to be held "in public before all."[27] Doubtless, as evangelicals claimed, such oversight discouraged behavior that threatened domestic harmony and financial security—drunkenness, infidelity, physical and verbal abuse, extravagance, gaming, and remissness in paying debts. Yet just as certainly, church surveillance exacted a toll on household peace and stability. To join an evangelical fellowship was to bid farewell to whatever vestige of family privacy had escaped invasion by the secular scandalmongers of southern communities. It was also to let clergy and church members, rather than family, decide the proper resolution of many intimate matters.

Beyond intruding into family troubles, early Baptists and Methodists called on their members to conform to standards of behavior that could directly affect the temporal fortunes of future generations. The least rigorously pursued of those standards, because it was the most unacceptable to white southerners, concerned slaveholding. By the 1780s, evangelicals abandoned efforts to exclude slaveholders from their churches, but for at least a decade thereafter some Methodist itinerants expelled members for buying or selling slaves, while some preachers among both Baptists and Methodists persisted in urging manumission as a Christian's duty. This message aroused lay opposition for various reasons, not least being the perceived threat to their children's and grandchildren's economic welfare, which was identified with the ability to retain or acquire slaves. When William Ormond urged one Methodist woman to write a will liberating her slaves, she replied that their future freedom depended entirely upon whether she bore children. "Lord keep the Women in a state of sterility if this is their scheme," he lamented in his journal. Conversely, and for the same reasons, James Meacham was astounded that a Virginia couple, although elderly and childless, continued to hold slaves.[28]

Those southerners who, prodded by evangelical teachings, freed their slaves faced a difficult task explaining their decision to family members, even those who shared their religious convictions. Richly suggestive of tensions among kin triggered by manumission are the struggles of Daniel Grant, the Methodist patriarch of an extended clan scattered between Georgia and North Carolina. By 1790, Grant had begun to consider ways of gradually freeing his slaves and preparing his future heirs for that eventuality. "I feel a great Struggle in my mind about it," he informed his son-in-law, John Owen, Sr., "the thoughts that my Postirety [posterity] may labour hard for a living, and perhaps not be thought so much of in the world as if they had Slaves to sett them off in a more grand and Easy way, these things Plead hard against it." Despite those concerns, Grant had become convinced that slavery was sinful, blacks being "human creatures Indued [endowed] with Immortal Souls capable of Everlasting happiness or liable to Everlasting misery as well as our Selves." Within the year Grant committed himself to manumission, devising an elaborate plan for freeing both adults and children when they reached the age of thirty-one.

Since Owen's side of the correspondence has not survived, it can never be known whether he tried to dissuade his father-in-law. But subsequent letters suggest that Owen objected: Grant took pains to justify his actions and urged his son-in-law, without success, to free his own slaves. A year after he began to implement his design, Grant related the death of a three-year-old African-American boy owned by his neighbor, adding that "I cannot grieve much at the death of a poor little black who perhaps were they to live, might have a life of greater suffering here but now it is Indeed free from its master and doubt not but happy forever." A few months later he reported on the fortunes of his former slave Sampson, an artisan who had set up his own shop on Grant's land. Freeing his skilled slave had cost "50 pounds at least clear money a year," he admitted, and Sampson was evidently celebrating his freedom by indulging in drink. Nevertheless, Grant assured Owen, "I am and have been well satisfied . . . having discharg'd a duty of such consequence toward a fellow creature." If Daniel Grant felt obliged to defend his actions even to a Methodist son-in-law, disappointed heirs among the unawakened must have harbored even graver doubts about how well evangelical convictions served the temporal security of the lineal family.[29]

More lingering misgivings about evangelical discipline were occasioned by their teachings on marriage, which, unlike the testimony against slavery, were more uniformly observed over a longer period of time. Both Baptists and Methodists urged their converts to choose spouses of the same faith. The reasoning, as summed up by Freeborn Garrettson, was that "those who married out of the Lord turned out but poorly," forsaking their religion. Since female members outnumbered males in both churches, the burden of this expectation fell hardest on women, with the penalties varying. The Baptists stopped short of expelling members who married nonmembers, but made their preferences plain. In 1783, the preacher Henry Toler described the marriage of one Virginia Baptist woman to a non-Baptist as "being tied to the limb of Satan." In the same year, a North Carolina association weighed in, more tactfully, with the same judgment, allowing that "We do not know that God's word does actually forbid such marriages [to unconverted persons]," but advised members "to comply with Christian marriages . . . for their own comfort and satisfaction." Methodist opposition was more emphatic. Until the turn of the century the *Discipline* mandated the expulsion of any member marrying "an unawakened person," by which was meant "one whom we could not in conscience admit into Society." It was unequivocal about the "fatal" results of such marriages: "They [the Methodist spouse] had either a cross for life or turned back to perdition." The clergy were instructed to discourage those unions by preaching "the apostle's caution, 'Be ye not unequally yoked together with unbelievers.'" and the laity were ordered "to take no step in so weighty a matter without advising with the most serious of the brethren." Enforcing that rule left itinerants with the disagreeable task of purging members for the sole offense of taking spouses who could not pass muster with the Methodists. In 1790, for example, James Meacham winced at expelling "one of our old Members, a Sister which had stood as a pillare in the Church of God for many Years, but now had Married a Man who is a Sinner."

Such teachings could only have alienated those nonevangelical men considering marriage or newly wed to Baptist or Methodist women. Nor could the prospects for future conjugal harmony—in a patriarchal society like the South or any other—have been enhanced by telling an affianced woman or bride to regard her partner as a rank "Sinner," "a cross for life," or, even more graphically, "a limb of Satan." And appointing censure or exclusion as the penalty for failing to learn that lesson lost both churches many members and potential adherents among women as well. Beyond those difficulties, strictures against "mixed marriages" encouraged some spouses to believe that they were obliged, upon conversion, to sever unions with unbelieving partners. In 1796, Jeremiah Norman was called upon to settle a dispute between two laymen about how a Methodist husband should behave toward his unawakened wife: "The one said, put her away for you must come out from among the Wicked, while the other said she was my Wife before I became Religious, She is mine still, no replyed the former you are not the man that you were when you Marryed you are changed you now pray for her but not own her as your Wife. . . ." Norman promptly delivered his view that "if the unbelieving Wife be pleased to dwell with her Believing Husband, Let him not put her away," an opinion loudly sustained by two laywomen who "soon attacked him that wished to put away his wife."

Methodist rules concerning marriage not only compromised spousal commitment but also challenged the authority of parents over their daughters. Although the *Discipline* affirmed that "in general" women should not marry without parental consent, it allowed generous leeway for defiance "if a woman believe it to be her duty to marry," or "if her parents absolutely refuse to let her marry any Christian." The purpose of such rules could only have been to support those young women who, having disappointed their kin by joining the Methodists, also aimed at evading parental dictates in matters of the heart. In effect, the church taught female converts to select their own spouses strictly according to personal inclination and religious affinity. For parents who hoped to bolster family fortunes by expedient marriages, vesting their daughters with such latitude was unwelcome to say the least.

Such efforts to enforce religious endogamy created private anguish by narrowing the field of potential mates for the faithful, especially women. But it courted disaster by trying to supplant the hardheaded calculus by which southern parents commonly sized up prospective in-laws with a single, unworldly criterion—religious like-mindedness. Throughout turn-of-the-century America, arranged marriages were giving way to matches based on romantic love and compatibility, but that cultural trend, like many others, proceeded more slowly in the South. In the late eighteenth century and even thereafter, many southern parents still subscribed to the view that marriages were not made in heaven but contracted after fathers soberly weighed how a proposed union would advance the wealth, prestige, and political influence of their lineage. The intervention of evangelical churches in that delicate judgment could only have been regarded as rank presumption. Yet the churches presumed as much, like the Methodist fellowship that expelled a South Carolina couple in 1799 after finding no basis for their opposing a son's marriage. And they paid a price, one doubtless accounted dear by the likes of Benjamin Lakin, who, in 1802, faced the thankless task of conciliating an irate father after a young Kentucky woman ran off and married without his consent.[30]

In short, early Baptists and Methodists made strict demands on the southern laity by the model of Christian commitment their churches upheld, the public discipline they imposed, and the teachings on slavery and marriage they enforced. In all those ways, evangelicals challenged the primacy of the family, undercut the privacy of households, and diminished the authority of husbands and parents. It was to their disadvantage, too, that in those respects, early Baptists and Methodists diverged sharply from Anglicans, the most numerous group of white southern churchgoers before the Revolution, but bore close affinities to a distinct religious minority in the region, one rapidly dwindling by the end of the eighteenth century—the Society of Friends. Not surprisingly, the Quakers found much to admire in the disciplinary practices of early Baptists and Methodists, as well as in their occasional testimony against slavery and warfare and their consistent preference for religious endogamy. More firmly committed to forswearing slaveholding than either the Baptists or the Methodists, many Quakers by 1800 had fled the South for the North-west Territory. The Friends also carried into the west their practice of "disowning" members for marrying non-Quakers, as well as their system of men's and women's "meetings" through which the church exercised exacting discipline over the families of believers. Those affinities with evangelicals, especially the Methodists, were not accidental, for some Quakers on both sides of the Atlantic were drawn into John Wesley's reform movement. In the South, Quaker influence was reflected in the esteem of many early Methodist preachers who praised the Friends as worthy of being emulated by their own adherents. Quakers often returned the compliment, praising the preaching of evangelicals and offering their hospitality to itinerants.[31]

But the nearer that mutual admiration drew evangelicals to the Quakers, the more were southern whites encouraged to identify Baptists and Methodists with a shrinking group of radical outsiders. As their testimony against slavery grew more insistent in the postwar period and as they deserted the South in droves, Quaker loyalties to the region seemed so tenuous that many suspected Friends of fomenting slave revolts. Under those circumstances, it did not bode well for Baptists and Methodists that, besides everything else that linked them with the Quakers, their common-alities of ritual practice displaced the family from the center of white southerners' lives.

EXCEPT for a Quaker, any southerner first glimpsing a Baptist or Methodist gathering would have been struck by the physical separation of men and women. Whether worship services were held within church buildings or at outdoor meetings, male and female members sat on oppo-site sides of a center aisle. Even on the frontier, where preaching often took place in small, crude cabins, groups of women and men clustered in discrete spaces. The Friends, of course, saw in evangelical seating arrange-ments the sincerest form of flattery, for Quakers not only segregated men and women within their meetinghouses but provided each sex with its own door for obtaining entrance. On the other hand, the Anglican-reared majority of southern churchgoers viewed that division as more like an affront, accustomed as they were to sitting in family groups either in enclosed pews or on benches. As much is disclosed by the remarks of a woman raised not as an Anglican but within another communion which practiced the same mode of seating families together. Christiana Holmes Tillson, who moved from New England to the southern Illinois frontier in 1818, found the scenes of Methodist worship among her new neighbors, almost all southerners, a stark contrast in every way to her native Congregationalism. What drew her particular notice was the separation of men and women during worship. Within the log cabin that served as her settlement's preaching house, she recalled: "Around the fire sat the mothers with their babies, while the 'young'uns' huddled down on the floor beside them. In the circle where we were put there seemed to be a mixture of all ages, though of but one sex; the lords of creation with their big boys occupying the back seats."[32]

This matter may seem trivial to late-twentieth-century churchgoers, who consult only whim or grace of exit when choosing where to sit at Sunday services. But women and men in the early South did not take the matter lightly, in part because the seating in evangelical meetings confirmed, among other things, the ties perceived between Baptists and Methodists and the Society of Friends. Within all three churches, the segregation of men and women at worship had the effect of blurring family connections, especially conjugal ties. It would have been impossible for any stranger entering a Baptist, Methodist, or Quaker religious meeting to pair spouses and match parents and children simply by scanning seating patterns—something that could have been easily detected in any Anglican chapel or Congregationalist meetinghouse. It was a division that signaled to many, as Tillson's disdain implies, a subtle devaluing of the natural family.

Another aspect of Baptist and Methodist ritual that echoed Quaker practice struck at kinship connections even more directly—the custom of converts denouncing their flawed upbringings by unawakened parents, usually Anglicans. The Virginian William McKendree recounted his boyhood delight in reading the Bible and praying in the woods, practices he followed until other members of his Anglican family "began to laugh at me . . . and finally laughed me out of my seriousness." Stith Mead also remembered his younger self as a spiritual prodigy, attending church with his Anglican parents so often that "I could repeat much of the morning service by heart." That early promise would have been snuffed out by "the sinful criminal act" of his father, who insisted on all his children training with *"Dancing and Fencing Masters,"* but for Stith's showing an aversion to fancy footwork befitting a future Methodist preacher: "[M]y father had to call for the rod of correction, before I would move in a dancing attitude." Peter Cartwright was far more modest about his youthful religious bent, perhaps because it stood little chance against so winning a sinner as his fiddle-loving, high-stepping father, who also presented the boy with a racehorse and a pack of cards.[33]

These highly stylized accounts of spiritual neglect, emotional abuse, or moral misguidance began to appear in the memoirs of southern evangelicals published after the turn of the century. But it is likely that such recollections of blighted youthful piety had become a staple of an oral tradition decades earlier, as individual converts publicly "testified" to their personal experience of divine grace at camp meetings, class meetings, and love feasts. All such testimonies, of course, only deepened the emotional distance between believers and family members who remained outside of evangelical churches. Even pious children whose tender years prevented their attesting publicly to parental religious neglect found their way into evangelical lore through the mills of local gossip. An improvement upon the mills of the gods, those connecting Kentucky Methodists during the 1790s ground both fast and fine, bringing to Benjamin Lakin's notice the story of a young girl, perhaps eight or nine years old, whose preternatural zeal may have outshone even that of Stith Mead. She implored her unawakened parents to pray for her, "telling [them] they ware [were] old enough to know how to pray, she was too young, and made her Mothe[r] read [the Bible] to her and her F[a]ther set by her and when he wanted to go away she would not suffer him, and told him he did not love to hear it but she loved it." When that "wicked man" declared his intention to send her to dancing school, Lakin learned, "the Lord prevented his design by takeing the child to himself."[34]

There has been some debate among historians about what southern parents wanted most from their children—unconditional love or unquestioning obedience. But whatever those hopes may have been, they were thwarted by how evangelicals urged their young converts to behave. To find that sons and daughters had openly criticized their upbringings could only have hurt parents yearning for affection, or humiliated those demanding respect. Beyond that, such public denunciations figured as a ritualized form of disengaging from family that recalled the peculiar observances of the Friends. Although no exact parallel existed among the Quakers, their ritual of disownment conveyed a similar message: Quaker parents assented to the decision of the meeting to exclude a grown child from fellowship for marrying a non-Friend—a generational reversal of young evangelical converts renouncing the ways of their parents. In both cases, natural ties were sacrificed to uncompromising religious purity, and family members who failed to subscribe to specific beliefs or codes of behavior were deemed unfit to share religious fellowship with and by their own kin. Like seating at public worship, the adoption of those unyielding standards among some evangelicals encouraged southerners to link Baptists and Methodists with radical groups like the Quakers.

WHAT DISTURBED southern whites even more than the ways in which early Baptists and Methodists acted like Friends were the ways fellow evangelicals acted like "family." In what appeared to many lay people as the ultimate betrayal of the bonds of blood, evangelical rhetoric and ritual practice broached the possibility of replacing the natural family with a religious fellowship that replicated kinship bonds. They not only taught their adherents that God was their father and that conversion made men and women his "adopted children," but applied familial titles and metaphors to describe relationships among believers as well. Baptist and Methodist preachers disdained the address of "Reverend" but invited being styled as "Father" or, even more familiarly, "Daddy." The faithful adopted that usage, and among many younger clergymen, the identification of older preachers with fathers was often literal. The Baptist John Taylor recalled that during his youth a senior minister treated him "as a father would a son," a kindness especially welcome since his own father rejected evangelical beliefs. In his maturity, Taylor himself invoked patriarchal authority to force Wilson Thompson to give his first sermon before a Kentucky Baptist association, thundering at the quailing young man, "Children, obey your parents in all things." Methodist preachers customarily called the young men whom they had recruited into the itinerancy their "sons in the gospel" and those laymen and -women whom they had personally converted their "spiritual children." In 1796, Francis Asbury designated Methodist bishops and presiding elders as "fathers in the Gospel" to the laity and described the preacher in charge of a circuit as a "tender elder brother." As late as the 1820s, the Methodist bishop William McKendree explicitly invoked the authority of parents over children to justify the right of the itinerancy to rule over the laity, declaring that "Children ought not to rule their fathers; but fathers to rule their children."[35]

Both clergy and laity also drew on a repertoire of images that represented church members as mothers and siblings. Borrowing a phrase current among the Quakers, Baptists and Methodists referred to older women who were remarkable for their spiritual attainments as "mothers in Israel," and all members enjoyed the distinction of being called "brothers" or "sisters" by fellow converts, a mark of intimacy of no small moment. Hence George Dale, a Kentucky Baptist flush with the freedom of his recent conversion, burst in upon his preacher's wife exclaiming, "[H]ow do you do sister Taylor; I am born again, I can now call you all brothers and sisters." It followed that Baptists and Methodists habitually referred to the church as their "home"; even new converts applying for membership used the formulaic phrase, "I want a home among you."[36]

Some white southerners were beckoned by the image of the church as a household in which spiritual siblings were nurtured by "mothers in Israel" and guided by preacher-fathers. Thus understood, Baptist and Methodist churches provided men and women with surrogates for the family members they had left behind—either physically, by the process of migration, or culturally, by virtue of their conversions. But identifying the church as a family also raised the possibility that affinities to spiritual kin might compete with or even replace the bonds of blood and marriage. A case in point comes from the Virginia Methodist James Meacham, who habitually distinguished his natural mother as "my aged mother in the flesh." With that turn of phrase, Meacham intimated that he had developed emotional ties at least as meaningful with the "mothers in Israel" in his Methodist network. If Mrs. Meacham knew of her status as a "mother in the flesh," she might be excused for resenting her competition or suspecting a distinction drawn to her disadvantage.[37]

Stith Mead's experience illustrates even more memorably the ways in which evangelical spiritual fellowship created alternatives to parents, wives, and siblings. During the same period that Mead's Methodist convictions were rending his natural family, he was forming fervid attachments to other members of the Methodist traveling connection, especially an itinerant his senior by a few years, John Kobler. As Stith distanced himself from his lineal family—a deliberate effort revealed in his editing letters to William Mead by crossing out "Daddy" and inserting the more formal "Father"—he transferred the full force of that self-thwarted intimacy to Kobler. By all accounts, Kobler epitomized the self-denying itinerant, volunteering to evangelize the western country, preaching by day and, by night, learning Latin and Greek and experiencing mystical transports. Mead was smitten with Kobler, who served as his spiritual lodestar and, more formally, as his occasional presiding elder and "covenant brother." A novelty introduced by Asbury, the covenant brotherhood paired itinerants as spiritual partners pledged to pray for one another in secret at the same time each day and to correspond at least twice a month.[38]

Mead seized upon that opportunity, including in long letters specimens of his religious poetry (page after unforgiving page of rhymed couplets) that he begged Kobler to revise—an undertaking that exceeded even that saint's capacity for holy masochism. At the end of November 1793, Mead wrote to express gratitude for Kobler's "great Condescention in receiving unworthy me into Band with you." "I esteem you as a Father," he continued, "willing to sett at your feet, open for instruction," for "Close Discipline is what I love." In the same letter, however, Mead expressed his fidelity to Kobler by citing a biblical passage referring not to filial but to marital bonds: "Intreat me not to leave thee . . . for whither though goes I will go," he wrote. "Thy people is my people and thy God my God . . . the Lord do so to me and more also if ought but death part me and thee." About two years later, Mead cast his attachment in even more frankly conjugal terms. Telling Kobler that, above all other itinerants, "none seems so much like my own flesh as yourself," he continued: "I love you with a pure love fervently . . . I dream of you; I dream of Embracing you, in the fond arms of Nuptial love, I dream of kissing you with the kisses of my Mouth. I am Married to you; O that I could see you and spend a few moments in Heavenly Converse together. . . ."[39]

Language so ardent inevitably invites speculation about the extent to which eroticism entered into Mead's attachment to Kobler. Since the Methodist itinerancy would not be the first or last clergy whose commitment to celibacy drew those attracted to members of their own sex, the prospect cannot be ruled out. True, many nineteenth-century men and women developed what have aptly been called "romantic friendships" with the same sex and expressed those attachments in passionate language celebrating both their emotional and their physical intimacy. Yet even set against those standards, Mead's dreams are pretty strong stuff, more

explicit and erotically charged than anything appearing in letters exchanged by his contemporaries.[40]

At the very least, the pressure to remain celibate encouraged many
itinerants to channel their carnal impulses away from young women and
redirect them, in some form, toward safer objects of desire. For one of
Mead's colleagues, Jesus Christ was the answer: when James Meacham
retired alone for the evening, he consoled himself by thinking that "the
arms of [Christ's] love compased me around." And when he woke one
morning, "my Master appear[e]d with all his Lovely Charms," and, on
another occasion, "I awoke and felt for my Jesus and found him Standing
by my Bedside. . . . [H]e turn'd Sweetly to my Imbrace." For Stith Mead,
John Kobler may have been the answer. Since on at least one occasion he
confessed to Kobler his difficulties with suppressing the desires of the
flesh, it would not be surprising if he sublimated those yearnings into a
spiritual infatuation with his covenant brother.[41]

No matter what drew him toward Kobler, Mead sought and found in
the Methodist fellowship emotional substitutes for his natural family.
Kobler came to represent for him an amalgam of father, brother, and wife.
Mead may have gone further than others in freighting the itinerancy with
the force of those attachments, but many of his colleagues found fulfillment in being part of what Freeborn Garrettson called "this happy
family." Like so many fond siblings, they dubbed fellow itinerants with
diminutives: to read their letters is to start at discovering that even the
starchiest of Williams and Jameses answered to "Billy" and "Jemmy," that
the redoubtable Mead passed as "Stithy" and the venerable Asbury as
"Franky." Asbury encouraged such intimacy, not only by devising the
covenant brotherhood but also by lavishing affection on young preachers.
A particular favorite, South Carolina's William Capers, he habitually
addressed as "Billy, sugar," and when that young man entered the traveling connection, Asbury hugged him, exulting to the senior Capers, "I
have got the baby!"[42]

The Methodists also offered to the lay faithful forms of association that
recalled the closeness of family circles. The tender searching and sharing
at weekly class meetings were, in some churches, supplemented with
"bands"—smaller groups of converts that offered even greater emotional
intensity. Like classes, bands differed from families in that their members
shared the same gender and marital status, but Asbury did not exaggerate
when he referred to them as "little families of love." Indeed, weekly band
meetings were conducted with an unsparing candor by members who felt

"full confidence in each other" and agreed to be "entirely open, so as to speak everything," including to tell and be told "all . . . faults, and that plain and home." In probing sessions of mutual criticism they shared "whatsoever we think, whatsoever we fear, whatsoever we hear" concerning one another, so that "we should come as close as possible, that we should cut to the quick and search your heart to the bottom."[43]

Both ritual practice and the association of fellowship and family thus sustained converts to early Methodist and Baptist churches. Separating the sexes at public worship obscured the painful absence of converts' unbelieving family members. Condemning their upbringings eased converts out of past lives embedded in kinship networks. Identifying the church as a family endowed converts with a new circle of spiritual kin, often one more sympathetic to their religious strivings than were relatives by blood or marriage. The power of those strategies, evident everywhere in evangelical correspondence, is distilled in a surviving 1796 letter from William Spencer, a young Methodist preacher, to a North Carolina matron, Mary Gordon. Though she was no kin to him by blood or marriage, Spencer nonetheless addressed her as "Mother" or "Mama," confiding that the "Lord has indeed fulfill'd his promise to me his poor Dust, who has left all to follow him," for in church fellowship and the hope of salvation, "I have Fathers and Mothers, Brothers and Sisters, houses and Lands in great Abundance."[44]

Such were the emotional buttresses built into a symbolic edifice of ritual and metaphor on which people like William Spencer and Stith Mead relied for the strength to break with kin and scorn paternal legacies. Yet while the blurring of church and family fortified the resolve of some converts, it warned many other men and women away from Baptists and Methodists. What troubled those wary souls was not only that evangelicals challenged prevailing ideals of family life but, even more fundamentally, that they aimed to transform—some would say, subvert—the understanding of family itself by forging a new kind of kinship based on spiritual affinities rather than blood and marriage. And what compounded that problem into a potential disaster for evangelicals was the presence in the South of other groups with equally elastic views of the family, two of whom inspired in most whites even greater fear and loathing than did the Quakers.

THE FIRST and most numerous were Indian tribes, whose resistance to white encroachment embattled many parts of the western country well into the nineteenth century. To replace relatives lost to warfare or disease, tribes like the Shawnee of the Ohio Valley adopted white captives into their families—sometimes adult men but mainly women and children. That custom and its consequences so transfixed southern whites that for decades before and after the Revolution hundreds of "white Indian" stories circulated in the region, becoming a staple in its folklore. What gave those tales their hold on the popular imagination was both the Indians' seeming indifference to shared blood as the basis of kinship and, even more strikingly, the strong emotional ties that often developed between white adoptees and their Native American families. Those bonds invited transfers of both affection and cultural identity, which caused many to resist being reclaimed by their white kin; even those captives who returned often found that enduring attachments to former Indian families plunged them into a limbo of uncertain loyalties.[45]

For kindred reasons, the Shakers aroused among white southerners the same horrified fascination. After splintering from English Quakerism in the early 1770s, Ann Lee and her followers first settled in New England and upstate New York and then spread to Kentucky and southern Ohio and Indiana, forming six communities between 1805 and 1820. Widely suspected of being British sympathizers in unholy alliance with the Ohio Valley tribes, Shakers were also propelled into the already crowded ranks of subversives in the new republic because of their hierarchical church organization, described by hostile observers as "authoritarian" and "papistical." Still more alarming to their critics was that the Shakers, going even further than the Indians with whom they were identified, constituted their "families" without any regard for lineage or marriage. The Shakers not only discouraged their members from maintaining close emotional ties to parents, spouses, and offspring; they also prohibited conjugal sex and raised children communally. By these measures they hoped to direct converts' primary loyalty to their religious fellowship. Adherents referred to each Shaker village as a "family," to one another as "brother" and "sister," and addressed elders and eldresses as "father" and "mother."

Their ambition, as one apostate expressed it, "to new model the whole human family," became the focus of mounting concern as Shaker villages sprouted in the western country and their numbers grew to a few thousand by the 1820s. Drawn into those novel families were not only stray Yankee migrants, which was bad enough, and orphaned white children, whom the Shakers adopted as readily as the Indians did white captives, but also young southern men and women coming mainly (and ominously) from the ranks of evangelical revival converts. A chorus of southern critics quickly rallied to condemn the Shakers, particularly for their disregard of natural affections. The diatribes most widely circulated in the western country, two pamphlets published in 1810 by Kentucky's Colonel James Smith, described in chilling detail how, after joining the Shakers, his own son deserted his wife, schemed to disinherit her, and dragooned their children into the sect. In the wake of these revelations, public outrage ran so high that on several occasions mobs attacked the Shaker village where Smith's son resided.[46]

The fascination with lurid tales of Shakers and white Indians reveals how powerfully westward migration had wrought upon the inner world of southern whites. Its impact, reverberating through the many rootless decades around 1800, fastened collective anxieties on families ruptured and allegiances to kin betrayed. Such a climate inevitably heightened mistrust of the Baptists and Methodists, who also urged their converts to invest their deepest loyalties in church rather than family. In that demand there echoed the alien accent of known subversives—Indians and Shakers—whose survival was sustained by the same disregard of blood and suppression of feeling toward lineal kin.

Possibly, too, evangelicals courted danger by virtue of what Baptists and Methodists shared with a third group of southerners who rejected blood lineage as the exclusive basis for defining their families. Far from being despised outsiders, they were the region's ultimate insiders: white slaveholders. Masters and mistresses routinely reached for familial imagery to express their relationship to the African Americans whom they held in bondage. Whether or not they were related biologically to their slaves, owners referred to household members of both races as "our family." Slaveholders also invoked that metaphor to justify their claims upon the absolute obedience of bondspeople, as well as their prerogative to interfere in the most intimate matters of slaves' lives. In other words, the South's masters believed that blacks owed their primary loyalty to the metaphorical family of the slaveholding household, a claim overriding all duties of African Americans to their natural families.

Since white southerners relied on the metaphor of family to uphold all relations of authority, too much might be made of the fact that both slaveholders and evangelicals turned that language to the same purpose. Nor should it be overlooked that men and women submitted voluntarily to the rule of their spiritual "kin" in evangelical churches while compulsion enforced the membership of African Americans in the "families" of slave-holding households. Even so, it may not have escaped the notice of some southern whites that, except for many slaves and a few Shakers, evangelicals were the only group in their midst bound to subordinate the duties owed the natural family to the demands of another "family" which asserted precedence.

KNOWING FULL WELL the southern laity's sensitivity to such family matters, the clergy of rival evangelical churches should have had the sense to avoid touching on that subject when engaging one another in debate. They did not. On the contrary, zeal claimed prudence as its first casualty in the ferocious competition for southern souls. Particularly after the Revolution, in a newly republican world stripped of religious establishments and loaded with a bounty of bereft Anglicans, there were no holds barred as Baptists and Methodists vied for adherents. Both shamelessly played variants of the "family card," each charging the other with undermining bonds between husbands and wives, parents and children. And that flurry of invective only confirmed many people in their misgivings about all evangelicals.

Baptist attacks often intimated that the Methodists' commitment to conjugal relations would not stand close scrutiny. In 1811, that familiar canard reached the ears of the Methodist itinerant John Early after a local preacher on his circuit, along with his young wife and children, defected to the Shakers. The apostasy created a sensation in their western Virginia community, with local Baptists exulting that now "all the Methodists who had religion would join the Baptists and the rest would join the Shakers." Even choicer grist for the Baptist mill was supplied by the castration of the Methodist preacher Jeremiah Minter. Although that scandal dated from the 1790s, its notoriety lingered for decades thereafter; indeed, as late as the 1890s, the Baptist Jeremiah Jeter's published memoirs rehearsed the circumstances of Minter's being "dissevered" from the Methodists. "His error can scarcely be considered so strange," Jeter archly allowed, "as it is . . . the same operation . . . performed to secure for the Pope's choir in Rome fine alto voices." Not content with linking Methodism and Roman Catholicism, Jeter also aired the opinion that it may have been Francis Asbury's preference for an unmarried itinerancy which inspired Minter's decision.[47]

For their part, the Methodists put it about that Baptist parents were unfeeling monsters who blithely consigned their children to hell. The basis for this fantastic charge was that most southern Baptists by 1800 had embraced Calvinism, one of the main tenets of which was that God had foreordained the eternal fate of every human being and that every person must struggle during this life to discover whether he or she was numbered among the "elect" predestined for heaven. Young children, of course, did not possess the capacity for experiencing religious conversion, and because they could not proclaim themselves as believers, they could not receive baptism. Inevitably, some died in infancy or early youth, leaving unresolved their destiny in the afterlife. That created a formidable obstacle to Baptist evangelism, especially among southern Anglicans, accustomed as they were to the practice of infant baptism. Among them were James Quinn's western Virginia parents, who feared "that their children would be shut out of heaven, and damned for want of the regenerating sacrament." Uncertainty tormented even devout Baptist parents stricken by the death of an infant or a small child, despite the insistence of some preachers that children who died before reaching the age of "accountability" went to heaven. By 1802, lay concerns prompted Baptist associations in both South Carolina and Georgia to render the opinion that "nonelect" children never perished prematurely, thus guaranteeing all who failed to survive a place in heaven. Neither association ventured to explore what that judgment might imply about young Baptists who clung to this life more stubbornly, nor did any Baptist church reconsider the wisdom of insisting so rigidly on the ritual importance of adult baptism. But assurances that only the good die young did not dispel the dread Wilson Thompson detected when he happened upon his Baptist mother and aunt as they fretted over the fate of his young cousin, newly dead. The women, he recalled, "seemed doubtful whether she [his cousin] had crossed the line of accountibility or not."[48]

In Baptist confusion lay Methodist opportunity, and preachers made the most of it. The Methodists, who rejected the doctrine of predestination, translated Baptist adherence to that tenet into an endorsement of "infant damnation." They portrayed all Baptists, blind captives of a perverse doctrine, as heartlessly chucking dead babies into hell. Perhaps to retaliate for Baptist aspersions on Methodist conjugal relations, John Early advertised throughout his circuits that, unlike some alleged Christians, the Methodists believed that all who died in childhood went to heaven. Like the Baptists' slur that Methodism was merely a halfway house on the road to celibacy, Methodist propaganda that the Baptists damned their own children persuaded some lay people. The Kentucky Methodist itinerant Benjamin McReynolds discovered as much, to his delight, during a summer's trip to Virginia in 1823, when he met up with a traveling Tennessean, who opined that "any man who says that there are Infants in hell not a span long ought to have his mouth mashed."[49]

It was the tinder of lay misgivings that stoked the fires of clerical debates over the family, the exchanges of sham charge and countercharge. But the clergy's opting for that shabby strategy only extended the life of those suspicions. The invective flung ever more furiously between Baptists and Methodists in the decades after 1800 etched more indelibly in many people's minds an uneasiness about what evangelical commitments augured for the continuity, temporal and eternal, of southern families. Even some men and women who disregarded the sensational charges recoiled from membership in evangelical churches, suspecting that no true Christians would behave so despicably, especially toward others who professed the same faith in Jesus.

Such were the elements of early evangelicalism, real and rumored, that left many southern whites of every class much troubled about the "family values" of Baptists and Methodists. Assurances that their fellowships strengthened family solidarity were belied by converts who broke with unawakened kin or exposed domestic troubles to church scrutiny. Pledges that their churches promoted family security were undercut by preachers who neglected their responsibilities as sons, husbands, and fathers, by masters who freed their slaves, and by young women who wed without parental consent. Promises of believers rejoining an unbroken circle of relatives in the next life might prove just as empty, given the readiness of these churches to provide converts in this life with surrogates for parents, siblings, and spouses. To be sure, some of the skepticism toward evangelicals that ruled southern whites well into the nineteenth century owed its strength to circumstance. Mass migration heightened fears of family estrangement, while groups like the Quakers and the Shakers pointed up where the logic of evangelical beliefs might lead. Yet much of the resistance they encountered was of evangelicals' own making, for they projected conflicting images of their churches' relationship to the family. On the one hand, they emphasized the ability of their faiths to enhance the unity of kin now and forever. On the other, devotional literature, church ritual, religious polemic, and real life provided an array of unforgettable counterimages—Bunyan's "Christian" fleeing his family; itinerants abandoning decrepit parents, ailing siblings, deranged wives, and dying children; husbands and wives sitting separately at public worship; Methodist men shunning sex; Baptist babies simmering in pits of brimstone. Drawn from what was read, heard, and observed, such counterimages became the staple of talk and speculation, gossip and scandal. In other words, the significance with which white southerners freighted family ties could impede the spread of Baptist and Methodist affinities as readily as it promoted them because of the ambiguity of early evangelical ways.

Given those fears and suspicions, the trumping irony is that southerners—and, indeed, all Americans—would come to regard evangelical churches as one of the bulwarks of the "traditional" family. Historical amnesia set in slowly as Baptists and Methodists gradually acknowledged the sources of lay concern and adapted their teachings and practices accordingly. Those changes proceeded in piecemeal fashion in the decades following the Revolution, a glacial pace guaranteed by the decentralized organization of the Baptists and the sway of purists in both churches. Only in the 1830s did the belief that evangelical Protestantism upheld the natural family in all things, both temporal and eternal, begin to assume the aura of a widely cherished truth, one that would be passed by antebellum southerners to succeeding generations.

Evangelicals began the effort to bring their version of family values into accord with white southern mores by retreating from their opposition to slavery. In the two decades after the Revolution, most Baptist and Methodist clergymen deferred to white concerns about their future heirs first by muting and finally by abandoning appeals for manumission. By 1800, only a few white southern preachers, mainly those resettled in the Ohio Valley, spoke out for the liberty of African Americans and the integrity of black families. Even the Methodists, though their *Discipline* still denounced slaveholding as an "injustice" and barred members from buying and selling slaves, arranged after 1804 to omit the entire section on slavery from editions sent to the South. Those measures did not entirely dispel the white laity's skepticism about the soundness of evangelical views, but the increasing prominence of slaveholders in their ranks, apparent even by the turn of the century, suggests that many were persuaded.[50]

The churches' determination to enforce religious endogamy had also given way by 1800, collapsing under the combined weight of women's defiance and men's objections. Unfavorable references to "mixed marriages" disappeared from the diaries and published writings of both Methodist and Baptist ministers, replaced by sympathetic anecdotes of saintly wives striving for the reclamation of godless husbands. No longer the objects of church contempt, women married to unbelievers were now recast as heroic sufferers for the faith. Revisions of the Methodist *Discipline*, which had formerly mandated expulsion for those wedding nonmembers, register even more sensitively the growing reluctance of that church to monitor marital choices. By 1796, the Methodists allowed their members the new latitude of marrying non-Methodists, "providing such persons have the form and are seeking the power of godliness." When that change failed to satisfy the laity, the church continued to liberalize their policy, declaring in 1804 their newly modest aim to "discourage" rather than "prevent" marriages of their members to unawakened partners. This concession apparently quieted lay concerns, and itinerants' journal entries thereafter make no mention of members or their families in dispute with the church over marriage.[51]

Those changes not only underscored evangelicals' new regard for the privacy and temporal welfare of white southern households, but also distanced them from the Quakers. As a practical matter, Baptists and Methodists saw that by following the Friends' teachings on slavery and marriage they stood to lose more prospective converts from the ranks of southern Anglicans and the many unchurched than they could hope to gain from the dwindling number of southern Quakers. And as the affinities between evangelicals and Quakers waned, so too did their mutual admiration. A younger generation entering the Methodist clergy after 1800 showed none of the readiness of their predecessors to praise the Friends as exemplars of Christian piety, while the Quakers themselves ultimately split into pro- and antievangelical factions. By 1811, in one North Carolina neighborhood, cordiality had shriveled to such hostility that the Methodist John Early was waging an open debate with "a cold, backsliding, Quaker preacher" who tried "to confute the common doctrines of the Gospel by his visions and superstitions."[52]

Evangelicals took even more vigorous measures to keep from being confused with the Shakers, contributing more than their mite to the early Republic's bulging treasury of attacks on that group. As early as 1810, the

Kentucky Baptist preacher Steven Ruddles and some Methodist itinerants came forward as willing informants for Colonel James Smith, supplying devastating charges for his anti-Shaker propaganda. It was Ruddles who eagerly told of treacherous compacts between Kentucky Shakers and the Ohio Valley Indian tribes, while the Methodists bore witness to the brutal separation of Shaker converts from their spouses and children. By 1826, Baptists and Methodists could take added satisfaction from the publication of *Shakerism Unmasked*, in which Kentuckian John Woods described his defection from that sect. The love lately lost between evangelicals and Friends lent an edge to Woods's recollection that what had drawn him to the Shakers was their appearance of "sober, orderly deportment, dressed in the plain, old-fashioned manner of the Quakers." Besides recounting how the Shakers urged him to leave his wife without any provision for her or their son, Woods disclosed that at one gathering of newly minted Shakers, a man trying to mortify the desire for his wife "openly and clearly" exposed "a certain part" while exclaiming, "This is my God!" Once converts had so indecently subdued their natural affections, as Woods went on to reveal, they became "spiritual sons and daughters" of Shaker elders and eldresses, whom they learned to obey "as simply as little children." The foil, of course, for the unnatural family of the Shaker village was the network of his Presbyterian and Baptist relatives in Kentucky to which Woods finally returned. Among these evangelical kin, his readers were to understand, men prized their independence, did right by their wives and children, and, if they were tempted to worship strange gods, repented more discreetly.[53]

Less sensational, but of more enduring influence in burnishing their reputation as defenders of the family, were evangelical efforts to domesticate the image of their clergy. By the 1810s, the rising generation of religious leaders among both the Baptists and the Methodists had embraced a more modern conception of the ministry as a profession, entry into which required formal training and merited better salaries. Traditionalists among both southern preachers and lay people resisted, clinging to the earlier view that the deity prized religious charisma over classical learning, and that preachers should show an indifference to outward estate befitting the lilies of the field. But their hopes of preserving a clergy pledged to apostolic poverty stood no chance against the lust for "respectability" raging among younger clerical leaders.[54]

By the lights of that generation, respectability required, among other things, a Baptist and Methodist clergy whose dress, manners, and command of polite learning would make them a worthy match for the Presbyterians and Anglicans. They pointed out that temporal concerns should not distract preachers from their studies and pastoral work, and that miserly salaries would not lure pious young talents away from law and medicine. But an equally important step toward becoming respectable, they urged, meant endowing preachers with enough of the good things of this world to ensure that devotion to the church would not mean impoverishing wives and children—or forgoing the pleasures of family life altogether. In other words, the assumption underlying the argument for better clerical support signaled a shift in evangelical thinking even more radical than the notion of preaching as a profession: It announced a new preference for preachers who were married men supporting families rather than young bachelors sponging off relatives and striving for sexual restraint. The prospect that better pay would create a clergy committed to domesticity helped to moderate, if not entirely overcome, both chronic lay stinginess and hoary prejudices against a "hireling ministry." It explains how Bishop William McKendree was able to persuade the Methodist General Conference to risk lay ire by raising salaries and providing housing for married preachers in 1816. It also accounts for why, at about the same time, some Baptist congregations, especially those in the more densely settled parts of the South, relented in their insistence on a self-supporting clergy.[55]

But perhaps the most impressive testimony to the resourcefulness of evangelicals in the South lay in their suspending disbelief that anything good might come out of the Nazareth to the North. By the 1830s, southern Baptist and Methodist church leaders were enthusiastically promulgating a notion that had originated among middle-class Yankee evangelicals, the so-called "cult of domesticity." Its hierophants identified the home as a church—an Edenic sanctuary tended by wives and mothers in which the seeds of religious and moral sensibility were incubated in children and the flowering of rectitude forced among husbands and fathers.

That image of the home as church struck root in the South as readily as the North, but for different reasons. The growth of commerce and industry that fostered the emergence of new domestic ideals among the northern middle class did not take place on a similar scale in the South. While increasing numbers of Yankee men spent their working lives in shops, offices, and factories, leaving women to manage homes and children, most southern husbands and fathers remained farmers whose households served as their workplaces. In short, antebellum southern homes did not become the sphere of women. Even so, identifying the home as a church appealed to southern whites because it restored moral authority to the natural family and mitigated evangelical churches' earlier, more exacting, claims on their members' loyalty and affection.

A number of changes in ritual practice accompanied the appearance of this new rhetoric in southern evangelical circles, among them altered seating arrangements within their churches. In yet another retreat from Quaker practice, some Baptist and Methodist congregations not only stopped segregating the sexes at worship but started renting pews to family groups. That trend, under way by the 1830s, affected mainly large, urban churches in the South, but met with much resistance among the Methodists, who feared that rental fees would drive away the poor. Still, the prospect of family members sitting together held sufficient appeal that even some rural congregations began setting aside sections within their churches for family seating.[56]

In an even more crucial concession, churches yielded back to the family that moral oversight once exercised by the faithful. While Methodist devices for spiritual monitoring—like class and band meetings—were falling into disuse by the 1830s, Baptist churches were also disciplining a steadily shrinking number of whites. And as clerks inscribed ever fewer pages of church books with the details of their members' waywardness, evangelical publications overflowed with pieces celebrating Christian nurture through the gentle expedients of household prayer and parental example. The withering of congregational discipline reflected the dawning recognition among evangelicals that church meddling in family matters was more likely to alienate than reform the laity. Members might still address one another as "brother" and "sister," but the churches sent an unmistakable message that religious fellowship would no longer rival the natural family's claim upon its members.[57]

Finally, the image of the home as church left its imprint on the ritual of converts deploring their lax religious training in youth. Formulaic laments continued to appear in published memoirs well into the nineteenth century, but those that found their way into print by the 1840s and 1850s drew a careful distinction between mothers and fathers. While fathers were still commonly rebuked for religious indifference or worse, mothers—or, in their absence, older sisters—now emerged as angels in the household, icons of moral uplift and spiritual wisdom.[58]

The new view of the home as a church that inspired all of those changes in ritual practice neatly inverted the older identification of the church as a home and its members as a spiritual family. To be sure, southern evangelicals did not stop using the language of family to describe their religious fellowships, but they found that using the language of religion to describe the home and family held a potent charm for southerners, who held no bonds more sacred. In both North and South, evangelicals favored the term "family religion" to denote the new spiritualization of the household. Yet that phrase, as it fell on southern eyes and ears, could have connoted a second, and supremely reassuring, meaning—that the family itself was an object worthy of veneration.

Important as these changes were, they did not exhaust the ways in which early-nineteenth-century evangelicals strove to conform their faiths to white southerners' sense of what sustained a family. For it was not the delicate ligaments of love alone nor even the fierce bonds of blood that they regarded as knitting the sinews of household integrity and order. Reinforcing those claims was something sterner—the absolute rule that husbands and fathers exercised over all their dependents—wives, children, and slaves. As a result, during the same years that evangelicals sought to persuade all white southerners that their churches ceded primacy to family solidarity and kinship loyalty, they also tailored their teachings to uphold, ever more unequivocally, the authority of male heads of household, particularly over godly women. These ever more rigid teachings on gender roles, along with their changing messages about familial order and the prerogatives of age, transformed the early Baptist and Methodist movements into the evangelical culture that later generations of Americans would identify as epitomizing "family values."

4

MOTHERS AND OTHERS IN ISRAEL

And Mary said,
   My soul magnifies the Lord,
and my spirit rejoices in God my Saviour,
for he has regarded the low estate of his handmaiden.
For behold, henceforth all generations will call me blessed;
For he who is mighty has done great things for me,
and holy is his name.

—LUKE 1:46‑49

SCATTERED ALONG that part of the Piedmont where Virginia bor-
ders North Carolina, a world of tobacco plantations and piney
woods in the 1790s, lived scores of godly women who watched for
James Meacham. A privileged few plantation mistresses may have set their
slaves the task of spotting his approach. But most, the hardworking wives
of small planters, looked for themselves: With eyes squinting from faces
on which the sun had set a spider's web of wrinkles, they scanned the
horizon. Weather, health, and the Lord permitting, the young Methodist
itinerant might appear at their door once every six weeks for a night's
lodging, but there was no telling just when he might turn up. Visitors of
any sort, of course, always made for more work, but to his hostesses
Meacham almost always came as a guest welcomed, even longed for. And
if, perhaps, the pulses of some marriageable daughters quickened at first
glimpsing the solitary rider, drably dressed and mounted on a rickety
nag, both of them covered with dust or spattered with mud, most of
their mothers and older female kin admitted only to feeling their hearts
warmed. It was fitting, as a mark of their regard, to make a fuss—
sacrificing the choicest fowl in the yard for his supper, settling him in the
chair closest to the hearth, presenting him with homespun shirts and
suits of clothes, and seizing upon any sneeze or cough to dose him with

homemade remedies. For here he sat in their midst for a few precious hours, brimming over with news of the world beyond their neighborhood, including the kingdom to come, offering them a brief reprieve from the isolation of their rural households and the monotony of their daily lives.

As the evening wore on, they awaited the moment when Meacham could turn his full attention to them. That time would surely come, too, for he always bestowed such regard on all his hostesses, no matter how worn with work or drained by childbearing, no matter how old or sickly. To be sure, the *Discipline* bound itinerants to shun the company of women. But even the sticklers among them read that rule as barring only intimacies with sloe-eyed, sweet-talking young belles, not with sober matrons, sedate widows, or confirmed spinsters. For "Sister B. a poor Timmed [timid] woman full of unbelief, Quier [queer] oppinion," her private moment with Meacham could not arrive quickly enough. As soon as opportunity offered, she blurted out the doubts and fears festering since his last visit. "Satan works some newfound maneuvers with her," he admitted. "I can't move her at all." But other women, no less impatient for his ear, yielded more readily as he attended to their sorrows and offered his counsel. Always he proved an alert listener: Long familiar with the religious views of one "aged woman," Meacham noticed immediately when she became "a little Tinctured with Calvenism." His probing soon revealed the problem: She confided that "all her friends and relatives with her Children are Baptists and they have Teased and dallied her so much that she hardly knows herself, but she assures me that the Methodists are her people and when only but See one of them She feels Quite another person."

On the other hand, there were those among his hostesses renowned as "mothers in Israel," women possessed of a sanctity so exquisite that they profited Meacham's ministry as much as they benefited from it. After preaching at one home on a hot August night in 1792, he exulted that "my Soul scarcely ever felt the like power before, such power Several rol[l]ed on the flour [floor] for Hours." "The Lord lives at this house," he concluded, beckoned thence by his hostess, one Sister N.M., "the most accomplished woman I ever saw." It was she who assisted Meacham in this work of grace, by praying, exhorting, or comforting those under conviction. Yet another female adept of his acquaintance, as Meacham offhandedly explained, owed her spiritual influence to having "one Angel that waited on her Continually." The heavenly companion that made her "a Wonder to Many" also qualified her to offer religious solace to Meacham himself. When he confided his struggle for sanctification, she assured him that "perfect love" would "cast out all fear." There was only one thing that distressed him about their dealings: "I could receive abundantly More Satisfaction in Conversing with her if She was not Deaf."

But perhaps the most celebrated virtuoso known to Meacham was one Susanna Williams, whom he visited in the winter of 1793, shortly after she "hath been in her 5th vision." Evidently the nature of her four earlier visions was too well known by her Methodist neighbors for Meacham to elaborate, but, being featured prominently in the fifth, he disclosed her revelations in detail. After "much private conversation," he learned that "she saw me in her vision and that I was in a good deal of distress and that I wrestled hard in prayer for happiness but could not obtain it." There was more: "this she said She could tell by my lights and that I was greatly cast down and dejected." For Meacham, Sister Susanna's vision was the final word, revealing "all of which I know to be a truth." For months afterward, the young preacher strove to "correct" what her revelation had disclosed by "getting more religion."[1]

Other godly white women everywhere in the early South enjoyed such intimate relationships with Methodist and Baptist preachers. Like Meacham's network of pious hostesses, they were drawn by the readiness of the evangelical clergy to credit their religious seriousness, to explore their views on doctrine as well as their spiritual experiences. When the young South Carolinian James Jenkins's conversion to Methodism prompted his mother, a Baptist, to stick up for her Calvinist beliefs, he called for help from the local Methodist itinerant. That preacher accorded due respect to Mrs. Jenkins's differing theological convictions, Baptist and female though she was, and spent an entire evening with her, debating the merits of her opinions and searching the Bible. One of her contemporaries in North Carolina, Mrs. Bryan, also engaged the preachers of her neighborhood in months of "talk about Religion" before finally disappointing the Methodist Jeremiah Norman with the news that "She has designed to be Baptized on the next visit of the Baptist ministers." Preachers not only regarded women's religious opinions as worthy of discussion but also endorsed their right to acquire the skills that would enable them to make independent judgments based on firsthand knowledge of the Bible. In 1779, the Methodist itinerant Nelson Reed condemned the parents of a young Virginia woman who confided in him that "she desire[d] to serve god but could not read."[2]

Nor could it have escaped the notice of pious women that preachers often credited them with the ability to divine the spiritual condition of others—claims that ministers never advanced for lay*men*. Among those ready to praise was William Hickman, who recalled that at his Virginia home in 1773, a young Baptist woman, "in passing by where I sat, and in a kind of ecstasy, said I was converted." Thinking that "she spoke unguardedly," he walked out into the yard, and "all at once the heavy burden seemed to fall off, I felt the love of God flow into my poor soul"; when he returned to the house, "the same woman cried out aloud and praised God." Nor did distance diminish the empathic powers of devout women. William Ormond marveled at "a secret connexion between Spirits—a kind of telepathy—that he experienced with one North Carolina woman around 1800. He was "uncommonly engaged in prayer" for her soul one evening, and although he was "about 24 miles from her," she later confided that "she heard me and that was the Night she got the Blessing."[3]

The clergy also believed that godly women might see as directly into the future as they did the human heart. In the 1790s, James Smith, a Baptist minister, visited one Kentucky woman who lay near death, burning with fever but still, he asserted, "perfectly in her senses." "I saw the Spirit of God," she told Smith, "and he told me I should live 12 days, and this is the last. I also saw the Evil Spirit, but he said nothing to me." Even more welcoming of such revelations were the Methodists, although their clergy did not credit every person who professed to be delivered of visions from the invisible world—not an insignificant number of citizens in the new republic. In 1772, Joseph Pilmore "spoke freely" with a Maryland woman who claimed to be "haunted by Ghosts," before concluding that " 'Tis likely this ghost, like ten thousand others, is nothing but the whim of a deluded imagination." Yet when the clergy identified bona fide seers, they were more likely to be women than men. While preachers believed that both sexes might have portents of the future revealed in their dreams, they tended to be skeptical of laymen claiming special knowledge from any other source. Laywomen far more readily won the clergy's endorsement of their spiritual powers. In 1783, for example, Thomas Haskins encountered a Maryland woman much like Susanna Williams, whom "I believe deep in piety . . . she proposes to have the Spirit of opening prophecies, and says in 42 months Christ shall reign on earth in his Saints, the wicket [wicked] to be destroyed, etc."[4]

Southern women of every age appear as visionaries, but the clergy, particularly the Methodists, often drew attention to those whose youth served to authenticate their bouts of religious transport. In 1789, William Ormond eagerly received news of a young woman "who tells that she had great views of Heaven and Hell when she lay for 13 Days without eating or drinking." After an ecstatic night meeting of Kentucky Methodists in 1802, Benjamin Lakin exulted that his new bride saw "a most butifull [beautiful] light that circeld [circled] all round us and we were in it." A few days earlier, at Cane Ridge, Lakin had seen with his own eyes a young Presbyterian woman who lay in a religious trance for nine days, "surely . . . the Lords doings and . . . marvalous in our eyes." And his colleague, James Finley, applauded the surge of religious interest awakened by one Eliza Hankins, who, after a camp meeting in 1812, fell into a trance, "lying insensible, showing no sign of life for 32 hours," then "jumped up singing and shouting. . . . Her face . . . lighted up with an unearthly radiance." She quickly became the object of intense curiosity: "Great multitudes, from a distance, flocked to see this wonderful thing. . . . [T]he whole congregation was overwhelmed, and we felt ourselves in the presence of a superior being, rather than that of an artless, unsophisticated country girl."[5]

Predictably, black female adepts did not always meet with as much encouragement from the white clergy. Indeed, some preachers were confounded by witnessing behavior on the part of African-American women, which, when exhibited by whites, they esteemed as marks of spiritual virtuosity. In 1778, the Methodist Nelson Reed found himself thus mystified after attending a funeral sermon in southwestern Virginia and finding a black woman "laying on the ground as if she was all but dead." "I went to her and wanted to talk with her but she could not talk," he continued, forbearing any direct comparison of her religiously induced trance with those common among white women in the same neighborhood. Reed concluded by hedging that "if there was any good done the Lord take the praise and glory." Yet by 1793, in the same part of Virginia, another Methodist itinerant was more receptive, celebrating the revelations of "an outlandish Black Woman" (a slave born in Africa), who seemed "wonderfully transported ah said she my blessed God I see you coming."[6]

Whatever their reservations about African-American female adepts, the early Baptist and Methodist clergy consistently credited the spiritual capacities of white women. Their support, too, went well beyond admiring the illuminations of seers. Through their earnest inquiries into women's thoughts and feelings, the clergy instilled in the female faithful a belief in the importance of their individual salvation, a confidence in their personal worthiness, and a sense of their spiritual and moral autonomy. And when some women, thus emboldened, joined evangelical churches over the opposition of husbands and fathers, the clergy colluded in their defiance. After one Virginia woman warned that if her husband learned of her admission to the Baptist church, "I know he will kill me," William Hickman baptized her secretly and even instructed his deacons to convey the Lord's Supper to her in private.[7]

Pious sisters could also rely on early Baptist and Methodist preachers to affirm that women of all ages and races might exercise their gifts by speaking before public, sexually mixed, religious gatherings. Thereby the clergy endorsed the view that acceptable forms of female spiritual expression went beyond fulfilling their private roles as dutiful wives, mothers, and sisters. Indeed, rather than advising women to restrict their influence to the uplift of their households, ministers encouraged them to display their talents in churches and religious meetings at neighboring homes. To assert themselves as authoritative public presences was an extraordinary liberty for women in a culture that otherwise required them to be silent and subordinate.

Women most often spoke at Baptist and Methodist gatherings by "prophesying"—that is, by relating their religious experiences to edify the faithful and encourage the hopeful. Thomas Rankin noted approvingly a young white Methodist woman in Maryland whose conversion in 1773 "gave her uncommon boldness to speak for [God], and to declare what he had done for her soul," while a quarter century later, Jeremiah Norman applauded "Sister Speight [who] got such a Blessing she was imployed a good while in telling of the greatness of the good work." Similarly, the Baptist preacher John Taylor celebrated his slave Letty, whose account of her conversion before his Kentucky church at the opening of the nineteenth century "was more striking to the assembly present, than the loudest preaching." Mature white female church members, both Methodist and Baptist, also delivered extemporaneous prayers at religious gatherings held in private homes, churches, and camp meetings. The most eloquent were asked to "exhort," calling the congregation to religious seriousness and moral reform with impassioned, often lengthy, declarations that took place before or after a sermon. No less a figure than Francis Asbury commended "our excellent Sister Jones," whose words "both in speaking and in prayer, were sweetly and powerfully felt" at a Virginia worship service in 1786, as well as "several holy women" who "spoke of the perfect love of God" at an Eastern Shore gathering. Women were singled out to exercise such gifts by congregational acclaim and with full clerical approval. It was a point of pride for Joseph Travis, another Methodist itinerant, that his mother's "talent in public prayer was rather extraordinary," and that "Many a time has she been called upon to conclude a meeting, after preaching, by a prayer." His colleague in Kentucky, Henry Smith, likewise observed that during a revival at the turn of the century, "all of our praying men and women were in great demand. . . . [T]hose who could sing and pray as though they would bring down Heaven's blessings by strong faith . . . were called upon."[8]

A few evangelical preachers hoped to win for white women an even wider scope for the public exercise of their spiritual gifts. Some early Methodists argued that white women should be permitted to preach, an oral performance distinct from exhorting in that it entailed expounding a biblical text. The inspiration for those views came, in part, from the practice of the first English Methodists, who allowed women to serve as local preachers. But a more immediate influence, as Stith Mead acknowledged, was the early Methodist clergy's admiration for silver-tongued southern Quaker women: "I have uniformly, since obtaining the true spirit of religion been, from my plain dress in apparel, taken to be one of that society by some of the Quaker Friends," he remarked proudly, because of "my aversion to National War and Negro Slavery, and acquiescence to female preaching." Yet Mead's enthusiasm for female preachers, if not wholly singular among southern evangelicals, was never widely shared by either the clergy or the laity. From their first appearance in the South, most Methodists as well as Baptists stopped short of endorsing preaching by women of any age or race. Although many women served as local preachers among Methodists in late-eighteenth-century England, and the ranks of upstate New York's early Baptists included a few female itinerants, there is no evidence that southern women, Methodist or Baptist, preached in their own neighborhoods or abroad. Among southern churches, only the Quakers permitted women to preach, and even within their ranks support for the practice among male Friends was withering rapidly after 1800.[9]

Early evangelical churches also strictly limited the participation of women in matters of governance. Lay Methodists, regardless of their gender or race, played no role in selecting preachers or, before about 1800, accepting new members and expelling wayward ones. By contrast, lay

Baptists—but only the brethren among them—exercised the full range of those powers, although some churches permitted white female and black members a role in their deliberations. While practice varied from one congregation to another, in most, African-American and white female Baptists were allowed to attend church meetings that decided the appointment of pastors and the admission and discipline of members. In some churches they had leave to express their views, present evidence, and even serve on committees investigating charges against a member of the same sex or race. But by 1800 nearly all churches barred both groups from voting, the exclusive and jealously guarded right of the white brethren.

It appears, too, that, by the last decades of the eighteenth century, the white Baptist brethren were steadily curtailing women's participation in governance. A few preachers, like Kentucky's John Taylor, urged their churches to appoint deaconesses charged with visiting the sick and dying, an office instituted by some of the first Separate Baptist congregations that fell into disuse shortly after the Revolution. But the ruling brethren were content to consign deaconesses to their past, along with voting rights for female members. In 1771, one North Carolina association advised its member churches that "it was not lawful" for the sisters to vote in church meetings—a ruling that suggests some women either enjoyed or claimed that privilege earlier. By 1794, a church belonging to the same association went still further, instructing female members "not to make motions in their own Person nor debate on the floor." By 1802, a Virginia association offered the same counsel, averring that "none but free white male members" could speak with an authoritative voice in matters of governance because white women, like underage sons and African Americans, lacked the independence to reach impartial judgments.

Most early-nineteenth-century southern churches shaped their policies accordingly, vesting rule and discipline firmly in the hands of the brethren. Yet the exclusion of women from governing powers was less an accomplished fact than a continuing achievement. White settlement of each successive frontier renewed such contests, and in some new western churches, the sisters triumphed. In the second decade of the nineteenth century, the brethren of one early Mississippi Baptist church thought better of their initial policy, which had allotted women "all the privileges of male members in the church," and informed them that "we consider it their duty to learn of the Apostle [Paul] not to speak in the church nor to usurp authority." But when the sisters resisted, the brethren relented. Elsewhere in the South, however, the brethren more often persisted and prevailed. It took some doing, if only because women made up the majority of white members in most churches. But done it usually was, and the clergy continued their delicate brinksmanship of encouraging public displays of female eloquence while denying that such shows of virtuosity entitled women to any right to rule in the churches.[10]

Careful as most were to keep women's charisma from translating into governing power in the churches, the clergy were keenly aware of the sisters' informal influence within congregations and entire communities. As the Methodist preacher Robert Roberts discovered, he could not even draw an audience in Harpers Ferry, Virginia, until he made a favorable impression on one "good lady," who then arranged for other local women to meet the itinerant by hosting a quilting bee. There Roberts delivered a sermon, after which "the quilting room preacher" became "the principal topic of table talk in several houses of the neighborhood." Ingratiating themselves with women and infiltrating local female networks of kinship and friendship also helped the clergy to gain the permission of some reluctant husbands to open their homes to evangelical preaching. Beyond that, women proved expert at dispensing religious advice, instruction, and support to kin and neighbors. Among the Methodists, pious matrons led those class meetings that were composed of young single women. Some women also commanded the presence to pacify churches wracked by the disputes of their stiff-necked brethren. Thus John Brooks acclaimed a woman who resolved a bitter rift in one Tennessee Methodist society around 1810: "She commenced exhorting the brethren to lay aside their prejudice and let us all be for God and the church. . . . The whole assembly, saints and sinners, commenced weeping as she talked. . . . The old brethren who had hardly spoke to each other for years, now rose and ran and embraced each other." Brooks was duly impressed, for "I had discovered from the time she commenced talking that she was a woman of great influence there."[11]

As James Meacham's experience suggests, the scope of women's influence often encompassed the clergy, especially young itinerants. Lodging with lay families afforded many opportunities for preachers and godly women to develop intense emotional bonds. These "mothers in Israel" frequently helped fledgling preachers through periods of doubt about their callings. When Henry Boehm questioned his fitness for the Methodist itinerancy, a pious sister on the Delmarva Peninsula advised him to stay on his circuit, for "You may lose your soul by such an unwise, hasty step," while his colleague Jeremiah Norman sought out an aged South

Carolinian who "seems like a mother in Isreal" and "gave me her blessing when I took my leave of her." And when Philip Gatch found that his pastoral duties left little time for training young Methodist itinerants, he directed them to his wife, whose knowledge of the Bible made her "the best preacher's nurse."[12]

Through contacts like these, a network of mutually sustaining relationships between devout white women and the Baptist and Methodist clergy emerged during the latter half of the eighteenth century and flourished for decades thereafter. In a variety of ways and for a range of reasons, each group nurtured and authenticated one another's claims to religious virtuosity. Preachers attended respectfully to the opinions and feelings of women, credited their intuitive and visionary powers, and encouraged their contributions at public religious gatherings. In return, women offered homely comforts and moral support, encouraging these insecure, impressionable young men to persist in their holy quest. That regard came as a deep satisfaction to ministers ranging from Jeremiah Norman, who boasted of the sumptuous feasts spread before him by Methodist sisters during the 1790s, to his colleague Edward Dromgoole, who preserved a letter from Sally Eastland confiding that "I acknowledg[e] it a task to talk to one of the Elders in Israel . . . I feel encouraged, tho a child to speake to one of the Lord's annointed." Even in his old age, John Taylor recalled that during his youthful itinerancy in western Virginia, one woman told him of dreaming, "a little before she first saw me . . . that the awful day of judgment was come, that Jesus Christ the great judge was present . . . to each individual he gave a book to read; with the judge were two men to direct the people how to use the books each person had. When I rode up to the meeting where the great assembly gathered, she knew at first sight that I was one of the men she had seen with the Saviour in her dream."[13]

Cultivating that sort of stature among the South's white women was crucial to the Baptist and Methodist clergy, particularly as their churches struggled to adapt in the face of lay resistance during the decades after the American Revolution. The youthfulness of most evangelical ministers, while often enhancing their appeal, also made their authority vulnerable to attack by older church members, especially white men who bridled when challenged by itinerants. In such contests, preachers often looked to godly women as mediators and allies. At the same time, the clergy was also striving to dispel lay suspicions about evangelical teachings concerning the family, and making a good impression on white wives and mothers was not a bad way to begin.

But that reckoning with clerical interest should not diminish the importance of what James Meacham so strongly felt: the shared intensity of religious commitment bonding early evangelical preachers and pious women. As he effused in his journal after spending a summer evening in 1790 with one of his mothers in Israel, "This is a good woman. I can feel her spirit. I love it." What reinforced such affinities was a shared subordination in the South's social hierarchy—for women because of conventions of gender; for young, single preachers because of the conventions of generation. Yoked by the commonalities of their experience, both evangelical clergymen and many of their female followers sought in their spiritual lives similar releases—ways to express and distinguish themselves, to find spheres for assertion and autonomy in a culture that denied such satisfaction to those it defined as dependent. Yet theirs was not an alliance that all southern white men deemed holy, a mistrust voiced even by some within the churches as well as those without. And for that reason, among others, many southern white women resisted being drawn toward evangelical faiths.[14]

ALTHOUGH the clergy rarely described any as outright "infidels," there were many southern women who rejected both evangelical preachers and their message. Few did so as forcefully as one woman on the Delmarva Peninsula, who came to a Methodist gathering armed with two pistols, intending to empty both into Freeborn Garrettson. More conventional was the resistance of a Charleston matron whom Jeremiah Norman approached in 1798, only to be rebuffed by her saying that, "having a Family to take care of," she "could not serve the Lord." Then, too, there were the likes of Madame Depew, a Kentucky lady "of a gay turn" who irked John Taylor by "encouraging balls . . . which had grown to such a h[e]ight . . . that the chief of the youth in the neighbourhood had become distracted." Although she regularly attended his preaching, she had no intention of allowing Baptist discipline to interfere with her pleasures, and so she roused other young women to the same defiance. "Mrs. Depew had endeavoured to strengthen her female disciples before they went to [Sabbath] meeting," Taylor fumed, "by saying to them, 'girls we shall hear enough of our dancing to day, but let us not mind what Mr. Taylor says, we are at liberty and will do as we please, let [him] say what he will.' "[15]

Still other women joined evangelical churches but then renounced their membership, braving preachers' displeasure. Such confrontations could be harrowing, as one young South Carolina woman discovered after mustering the nerve to tell Jeremiah Norman of her wish to withdraw from a Methodist society. When "She told me that She had considered all the consequences and was predetermined to go at any rate," Norman insisted that the entire congregation kneel to pray for this backslider, while another preacher "told her at last, if she was bound for Hell and Damnation, there was his hand. . . . [H]e must bid her farewell, saying I cannot go with you there, for I am bound for heaven." Still unmoved, the woman "appeared to give him her hand very deliberately," and the preacher rose "saying I am clear of your Blood." At that dreadful pronouncement, "There seemed a general Shriek all over the house," punctuated by Norman's cry, "Lord have mercy on a poor Judas."[16]

What steeled such women—both the impervious and the backslid—against clerical pressure was the conviction that they stood to lose more than they would gain by joining evangelical churches. Like southern men, many southern women were unwilling to forgo familiar sociable pleasures and submit to the churches' ascetic discipline. They also often shared with men a resentment of evangelical boy-preachers, reservations concerning evangelical teachings on slavery and marriage, and doubts about evangelical commitment to the family. Yet the tenor of female opposition discloses some concerns that were, if not entirely unique to women, matters that weighed more heavily with them than they did with men. Women were more inclined than men to describe the demands of evangelical churches as overwhelming and consuming, an attitude typified by the Charleston woman who believed that she could not be both a good wife and mother and a good Methodist. Indeed, most women who joined evangelical churches took to heart the commitment to reform their lives, and they were disciplined far less often than were male members. But some women buckled under this self-imposed rigor and sought release from membership before their moral endurance failed. That fear beset one woman who told Jeremiah Norman to strike her name from Methodist rolls because "she had so many crosses etc. she could not live as she ought."[17]

Possibly, too, their exclusion from church governance led some women to suspect that joining an evangelical fellowship only added another tier to the hierarchy of male authorities demanding their submission. Consider the case of Tennessee's Red River Baptist Church, where, by 1810, the brethren claimed absolute rule "to act in church order on all things that may come before them." On the one hand, the church's discipline afforded female members some measure of protection—occasionally from drunken and abusive spouses, more often against male neighbors who slandered or defrauded them. On the other hand, the brethren closely monitored women's private lives, particularly sexual and marital indiscretions. Their vigilance occasioned no formal complaint until 1820, when the church cited one William Johnston for separating from his wife, and the brethren, in an unprecedented step, voted to hold a private session to discuss his domestic troubles. At that, the sisters rose as one to protest their exclusion, creating such a stir that the church postponed the case and urged "the Brethren and Sisters . . . to labor for an Union of Sentiment on this Matter." When the women held their ground, Johnston, who could endure neither having his conjugal problems aired before the entire church nor causing such an uproar, withdrew from membership. Plainly, what outraged Red River's sisters was the brethren's shielding Johnston's failed marriage from scrutiny by the entire church—a courtesy that had not been accorded to Stacey Babcock, charged with deserting her husband; or Darcus May, cited for contracting a bigamous marriage; or Sally Johnson, accused of "whoring and lying." But if Red River's sisters agreed that sauce for the goose was sauce for the gander, the brethren differed and finally prevailed. Not only was Johnston restored to church membership in 1826, but the ruling brethren thereafter often convened apart to decide cases involving the sexual and marital misdeeds of male members, black as well as white.[18]

But if some women chafed against the confines and inequities of evangelical ritual, there were others who quailed before its promise of spiritual empowerment. Before the appearance of evangelicals in the South there had been no tradition of according women any kind of spiritual authority, save among the increasingly despised and dwindling Quakers whose female members spoke at mixed religious gatherings, evangelized as missionaries, and maintained separate women's meetings to enforce discipline. But while the South lacked a past replete with strong female religious figures, it had long been a culture steeped in misogyny, against which many women had become schooled, as their best defense, in habits of submission. To find themselves suddenly credited by the evangelical clergy with qualities that most other southern men either denied outright or doled out sparingly to the opposite sex—intelligence and judgment, fortitude and power—came to all southern women as a matter of no small wonder. But for some women that novelty did not serve as its own recommendation.[19]

To be sure, some women delighted in seeing the image of their possible, more powerful selves reflected in the esteem of preachers. Especially receptive were younger white women without husbands to please by playing dumb and docile, some of whom seized the moments before marriage to savor the heady joy of riveting notice on their religious performances. Eliza Hankins, the "unsophisticated country girl" whose trance so fascinated Kentuckians, belongs to that group, as does her contemporary Ester Morgan. That young woman first found fame among her North Carolina neighbors as "an expert in dancing," but when repentance seared her soul one Sabbath in the 1820s, she lost her love of frolicking—if not her hunger for holding the center of attention. Deliberately "conceal[ing] her state of mind from everyone," she waited for the occasion when its revelation would produce the maximum effect, which came a few days later at a dance: When "the music began, she dropped to her knees and began praying aloud." Her performance so terrified the revelers that "a greater part of them left the house and fled as for life," even the strutting young men. Among them, most likely, was the future husband to whose rule Morgan would soon bow, but that evening it was she who, however briefly, held the upper hand. Many decades later, one dancer who took to his heels that night recalled that "We went over fences and through corn fields . . . and as I heard the blades of corn cracking behind me, I felt certain that the Devil was right after me, and on reaching [home] . . . broke down the door and jumped into the bed without pulling [off] shoes, hat, coat . . . and were almost afraid to breathe, lest the Devil should hear us." But if young women seized their moment in the sun of public acclaim, most also knew that it would quickly pass. Ester Morgan may have found herself eclipsed later that evening, when male church members, including her father, a Baptist deacon, came rushing to the dance to conduct a prayer meeting.[20]

While the encouragement of clerical Pygmalions frequently launched young, single women, like so many Galateas, into spectacular but short-lived religious debuts, a smaller number of female adepts enjoyed lifelong local repute and sometimes flourished independent of an endorsement from any preacher or church. Emboldened by her mystical experiences, a woman on the Delmarva Peninsula informed the Methodist itinerant Freeborn Garrettson, "I know that you are a servant of God; but you cannot teach me, for I understand all the Scriptures, and I know what kind of death I am to die." Garrettson visited her a second time, hopeful for her soul but dismayed by her stubborn belief that "man could not teach her." Just as serene in her power was Susanna Williams, who did not regard James Meacham's approval as validating the truth of her visions. On the contrary, both understood the flow of spiritual authority to proceed in the opposite direction, from the accomplished virtuoso to the struggling itinerant. Even more remarkable were some adepts among African-American women who developed an unassailable confidence in their spirituality, despite the discouragement meted out by men of both races. When John Taylor's slave Letty first experienced repentance, she sought advice from two men—her master, perhaps significantly, not among them. Her brother Asa, a slave preacher, pronounced that "she was not under true conviction at all," and then a white overseer also "treated her with scorn and contempt." Dejected, Letty thought of suicide, but then threw herself on divine mercy and obtained saving faith. These three women came to identify themselves as Christians and two joined churches, but all of them, secure in their virtuosity, found its imprimatur in personal experience rather than clerical approval.[21]

Yet there were other women for whom the clergy's efforts at fostering spiritual virtuosity were neither liberating nor incidental. These women were by turns beckoned and frightened by the prospect of leading more independent religious lives—and their sentiments may have been more nearly typical, at least among southern whites. Among them were many women in John Taylor's Baptist churches who spurned his invitations for them to pray and testify publicly. "But few of the brethren are backward to do their part in those prayer meetings," Taylor noted. "I wish the sisters would be more ready to pray with us also, as I have said, by covering their head they may make free." Yet most remained wary of their husbands' reaction to any sudden display of wifely spiritual virtuosity. They worried, for good reason, about becoming estranged from spouses who might resent their wives embracing religious views at variance with their own, or experiencing conversion first, or enjoying greater public distinction as virtuosos.[22]

While white southern women experienced a range of misgivings about the evangelical movement and its clergy, the attitudes of Baptist and Methodist preachers toward women—especially their devout followers— also betrayed ambivalence. Indeed, what may have aroused some women's reluctance to assert themselves spiritually were the mixed signals sent by ministers, whose public encouragement increasingly became mixed with private reservations. As early as the 1790s some were confiding to their journals the suspicion that evangelical teachings promoted too much self-assurance among female adherents. Perhaps the testiest when confronted with formidable women was Jeremiah Norman, who got rattled while preaching at a Virginia gathering in 1793 by the mere notice of a woman who "brought forth her Bible . . . to see if I coted [quoted] Scripture right." The future only brought stiffer challenges, and Norman seems to have omitted none of them from his diary. In 1797, he grumbled over "one or two Buxome Women" with whom "it is allmost impossible to hold a conversation and not fall into disputes," and two years later, he vowed to purge from membership "an Evil Woman" who had stubbornly "imposed herself" on a church by cowing a less stalwart itinerant.

Much as he disliked having his authority contested by women, Norman truly loathed those wives who dared to dominate their husbands in religious matters. When one Mr. Johnson confirmed for Norman the rumor that another church member, John Foxe, had "Gotten a bastard child," "Mrs. J. looked vengeance itself saying what if he did get a Bastard—why need any one care." Having handily dispatched the Methodists' discipline and her spouse's indiscretion, the lady took aim at the hypocrisy of all men, sneering that Foxe's misconduct "was no more than What the generality of them would do if they had the chance." At this, her husband "seemed much afflicted and Blushed in confusion on her account," while the vexed preacher allowed that "I do not know how a Man that had such a wife could be otherwise." Norman felt an even greater "want of patience and fortitude" at the sorry spectacle of Colonel Wingate, a Methodist who not only refused to contradict his Baptist wife's views on doctrine but seemed himself "not perfectly free" of her misguided opinions.[23]

Norman's sensitivity to strong women was more extreme than that of his colleagues, but his concerns were not entirely singular. Even John Taylor, who unstintingly praised the women in his Baptist congregations, judged that some were too outspoken. He had in mind Hannah Graves, a pious matron who showed an uncanny ability to predict the onset of revivals as well as "a considerable understanding in the Scriptures," accomplishments that made her both "a good judge of christian experience," and, as Taylor may have known to his cost, "a nice critic on preaching." Apparently Mrs. Graves's gifts had sharpened her tongue as well as her wits: "Her blunt dealings with preachers at times," he recalled, "seemed as if she ran some hazzard of violating a saying of God himself, 'touch not mine annointed, and do my prophets no harm.' "[24]

Other preachers also confessed to fears of being upstaged by rival female virtuosos. Hints of clerical resentment surface with particular frequency in portrayals of their early relationships with young brides or future wives. Decades later, Wilson Thompson still stewed over his future wife's having preceded him into the Baptist Church. Etched in his memory was the scene of her baptism, a "small, slender girl" being led into the water by a preacher, and his own roiling emotions as "the whole scene seemed changed to me; a dark, heavy, angry, threatening gloom hung over all within my view." What weighed on the youthful Thompson was not only anxiety about his eternal fate but also his humiliation, as the scion of a prominent local Baptist family, at being bested spiritually by "a small, slender girl." His colleague William Hickman admitted even more openly to being galled by the piety of his wife, who found faith in the 1770s and "offered" herself for membership in a Baptist church before he did. "I kept her from being baptized for months," he confessed, "but went with a guilty conscience." Irritated by his wife's newfound peace, Hickman also resented her independence in doctrinal matters. When he urged her to speak with an Anglican minister, who he hoped would convince her that "infant baptism was the right mode," his wife "replied she was fond to hear him preach, but she could not pin her faith to his sleeve."[25]

Close inspection, then, reveals the complexity of relationships between southern women and evangelical ministers during the decades following the Revolution. While clerical support drew some women to both the Baptist and Methodist Churches, others proved more resistant to both the disciplines demanded and the freedoms conferred. As for the preachers, even as they cultivated female religious talent, they sometimes feared succeeding too well. They wished women to be forthcoming about their religious ideas, but bristled when the sisters came forth too often or too forcefully. Preachers admired women who could move audiences, but felt unnerved when they outshone the brethren. In other words, early Baptist and Methodist preachers knew that they depended on women a great deal, but perhaps wished that they needed them a good deal less.

THOSE SECOND thoughts and bruised feelings made it easy for preachers to empathize with the many other white southern men for whom godly women threatened self-regard. Not least among them were the godly lay brethren. While male church members sometimes acknowledged to being inspired by the prayers and exhortations of female relatives and neighbors, just as often those same men responded to women's public performances with confusion, resentment, and even alarm. Most stopped short of the draconian solution adopted in 1804, by the Baptist brethren of one South Carolina church, who deprived female members of the liberty to pray in public. But the sentiments prompting that instance of backlash were widespread among evangelical laymen. As far west as Kentucky they soured some of the members of John Taylor's church on female members testifying publicly to their conversions. Taylor duly lectured his flock on the proper understanding of St. Paul's admonition, insisting that the apostle had not objected to a woman speaking in church, as long as she covered her head with a cap or veil, thereby showing that she "manifested due respect to her husband" and acknowledged that "the government of the church, mainly lay with the male members." "It is a pity," Taylor chided, that "a church should lose any gift that is among them, merely because it is found in a female." Even so, he acknowledged that women's virtuosity presented a real problem, especially in those churches, as he wryly added, where "the greatest strength of intellect and counsel is in the females."[26]

Scrupulous as the Baptists and Methodists had been in enshrining as a male prerogative the powers to preach and rule, they had not gone far enough to satisfy most southern men by the turn of the century. The spiritual and moral authority exerted by devout women through public prophecy, prayer, and exhortation still taxed the patience of the brethren—to say nothing of the feelings that such practices inspired among unchurched men. Indeed, during the same post-Revolutionary decades in which evangelical leaders discovered that spiritually empowering young men could prove a mixed blessing, they also learned that encouraging female adepts could create similar dilemmas. On the one hand, touting the religious gifts of both groups as extraordinary providences lent support to the claim that evangelical churches enjoyed divine favor. On the other hand, allowing those charismatic displays to become the basis for endowing the young or the female with authority of any kind diminished the churches' ability to attract mature white men.

It was troubling, then, when the clergy observed that even those men inclined toward evangelical views fell prey to warring emotions when their spouses won acclaim for their spiritual talents. That problem preoccupied, among other preachers, John Taylor, who noticed that even men who, although not church members, came regularly to his sermons balked when their wives' religious seriousness deepened. Some objected on the purely practical grounds that holy women made bad housekeepers, so consumed by spiritual concerns that they let the dust gather, the spindle stop, the weeds wave, and the children cry while supper burned on the hearth. The Kentuckian William Raymey, for example, sulked and cursed when his wife fell under conviction and lapsed into a distracted state for two weeks, "laid aside all her family business, even to that of cooking for her husband and little children." Knowing the couple as "a very pushing, industrious people," Taylor nipped Raymey's resentment in the bud by consoling his wife and then promptly urging her, "go to your spinning . . . as your family has suffered some time through your neglect." As Taylor's urgency suggests, southern husbands counted as a real cost the loss of their wives' labor, but this was not the only reason men resented their spouses' religious engagement. Even after Mrs. Raymey recovered the composure required to keep house, her subsequent baptism "became as a dagger to his [her husband's] heart," and his repertoire of curses came to "condemn all religion that was brought men in the bible."[27]

What may have bothered William Raymey, whose anger abated only when he, too, found saving faith, is suggested by the experience of another Kentucky couple in Taylor's circle. While both Thomas Reese and his wife came under conviction at the same time, she found assurance first and gave her public testimony, an eloquent performance that created a sensation among local Baptists. But while his wife basked in the church's approving notice, Thomas Reese still despaired over his sinfulness. Sensitive to his feelings, Mrs. Reese at first "meekly" told the church "that her companion had been long under distress, she hoped for his relief, and therefore she was inclined to wait and be baptized with him." But when some church members clamored for her to be dipped at once and she relented, an even greater darkness closed upon her husband. On the day of her baptism, as the Reeses rode home from the river across a muddy path, the two astride a single horse and she holding their infant child, his anger mounted. He "being naturally a rugged man . . . concluded his wife disregarded him, and therefore had left him and joined the Baptists, and they were all hypocrites together." When his wife dismounted to tend her child, "he broke out and declared for the offence she had committed in leaving him, he would never live with her another day . . . and off he went as fast [as] his horse would go." He got half a mile away, "when he was so struck with a fresh sense of his guilt," that he began to roar out with all his might like a mad man." By the time Mrs. Reese struggled up the miry road to her spouse, his anger was spent; he "dropped on his knees in the mud, and entreated his wife to pray to the Lord for him." A few days later he, too, found saving faith, and appeared to Taylor "as the man did, out of whom a legion of devils had been cast."[28]

Many devils, indeed, tormented Thomas Reese. Already unstrung by weeks of anxiety about his soul, he suffered a blow to both his spiritual hopes and his male pride when grace came first to his wife. Then he experienced the added humiliation of having his wife elevated over him in the esteem of their Baptist neighbors. When she acceded to the wishes of the church and accepted baptism before him, he exploded. It was not because his wife had directly defied his authority—the church had asked and he had granted permission for her baptism. Reese sensed instead a deeper and subtler betrayal: His wife had "disregarded" him—had placed obedience to the church above respect for his feelings. By that act, she had "left him and joined the Baptists," and by that alienation of spousal loyalty she and they became "all hypocrites together." In choosing the church over her husband, she had shamed him, withheld the deference that he viewed as the rightful tribute owed a "naturally rugged man."[29]

There were other white men who sat under Taylor's preaching who suffered, if not Thomas Reese's agony, a palpable discomfort when their wives preceded them into membership. For many husbands, it came as a shock to find their spouses, like Mrs. Raymey, suddenly taking the initiative in religious matters or, like Mrs. Reese, shedding their timidity long enough to exhibit spiritual gifts that commanded general attention. And some husbands, like Reese and Raymey, could not rest easy until they had equaled their wives' attainments. Indeed, what preachers took to be gratifying instances of wives exerting spiritual influence on husbands might more accurately be understood as face-saving gestures on the part of husbands fearful of being shown up by their wives. Possibly, too, their wives' conversions left those men who were still seeking religious assurance feeling uncomfortably dependent. Husbands seemed to find it easier to confide their struggles to wives who were also striving for saving faith than they were to those who had already obtained it. Before their conversions, both James Finley, a future Methodist itinerant, and Daniel Trabue, a Baptist layman, freely shared their religious anxieties with unawakened spouses. Not so Obadiah Echols, a Georgia planter who refused to reveal his distress to his devout wife, Lizzie, even though she was "the best friend I have got in the world . . . yet I will not let her in, but try to keep her from my secret."[30]

Whether well or ill disposed toward evangelicals, the unconverted husbands of believing wives commonly expressed a sense of vulnerability—a fear of losing control over themselves, their spouses, or their households. That anxiety told in the sharp conflicts sparked when wives tried to dictate their husbands' religious loyalties. To hear the rumble of one gathering storm, return to the Echols' home in 1809 when the newly converted Obadiah announced his decision to join the Baptists. Lizzie, a Methodist fixed in the opinion that all Baptists were habitual drunkards, reacted to the news like a "hard clap of thunder on a clear day." First she tried pleading with her husband that if he turned Baptist they would be parted "at the Lord's Supper, [for] the Baptists would not have my [Lizzie's] baptism and then we would be separated." Then a hard rain fell, Lizzie sobbing so hysterically that he could hardly get to the river in time to be dipped, "having my hands full at home." Obadiah insisted that he loved his wife's "integrity," but later events revealed otherwise. Her temerity in trying to make him a Methodist stuck deep in his craw; determined that his religious preferences would prevail, Obadiah ghoulishly assured the readers of his memoir that Lizzie had vowed to switch her loyalties to the Baptists just before succumbing to yellow fever in 1812.[31]

Assertive women like Lizzie Echols aroused their husbands' deepest anxieties about the loss of masculine independence and honor. And those fears, like the serpent's tooth, bit all the more sharply into some southern white men because of long-standing suspicions linking spiritually proficient women with sexual license. The association of female adepts with carnal abandon had served as a staple of religious polemic on both sides of the Atlantic long before it seeped into southern nightmares. Throughout the early modern period, the image of the whore posing as holy woman was invoked to discredit the most radical heirs of the Reformation, usually Baptists and Quakers, who accorded female members the greatest influence in their churches. Even in the late eighteenth century, critics alleged that Ann Lee, the founder of the Shakers, had been a camp follower of the British army, and that Jemima Wilkinson, the charismatic leader of another, more short-lived celibate sect, was a prostitute.[32]

The first southerner known to resort to similar slurs was the Anglican Charles Woodmason, who freely deployed them against Presbyterians and Separate Baptists in the Carolinas during the decades before the Revolution. He ridiculed one Baptist woman, "highly celebrated for her extraordinary Illuminations, Visions, and Communications," as a lying slut whose testimony of being visited at night by an angel concealed her dalliance with a preacher:

> It was very true that she was visited in the Night, and that the Apparation [apparition] did jump down upon her Bed . . . and that it came to her all on Fire. Yes! But it was in the Fire of Lust; And this Angel was no other than her Ghostly Teacher. . . . He afterward had a Revelation That it was the Will of God such a Man was to take her to Wife Which the Poor unthinking Booby did. . . . Little dreaming that He was to Father the Prophets Bastard.[33]

Decades later, southerners were still recycling Woodmason's libels of female religious virtuosos, bandying charges that evangelical zeal would spell the ruin of female chastity and male honor. In 1804, the Anglican Ebenezer Pettigrew facetiously informed James Iredell that some young Baptist women in his North Carolina neighborhood "have found a way to propagate without husband. . . . And what may appear still more wonderful, two of father Big[g]'s [a Baptist minister] spiritual children, whom he had washed from all their pollutions[?] in the Scuppernong River, made out some time ago to fabricate a natural production. . . . with such natural curioseities our Counties abound." Nor was it only the Anglicans who gossiped that giving greater scope to female religious talents would bring their modesty into reproach. Everywhere in the new republic, tongues wagged about Dorothy Ripley, an English woman who styled herself an independent preacher. As she itinerated throughout America during the first two decades of the nineteenth century, Ripley was constantly obliged to defend her chastity—from both sexually aggressive men and talebearers of both sexes. Her preaching against slavery won Ripley many enemies eager to discredit her, and she handed them a ready pretext by traveling everywhere alone—an independence of movement typically associated with women of easy virtue. Even American Quakers who shared her opposition to slavery and upheld the right of women to speak publicly were troubled by her traveling unaccompanied. One Maryland Quaker in 1802 thus concluded that Ripley had left England because she was "a lewd woman," and female Friends shared his disdain. A Quaker woman in Richmond refused Ripley her hospitality, while another told her bluntly that "I was a discredit to women, and had come there for none of my good deeds."[34]

Competing for salacious notice with Dorothy Ripley's rumored liaisons were reports whispered even in southern evangelical circles during the turn of the century about the sexual freedom of some women being converted at revivals in the western Carolinas and Tennessee. What drew particular concern was a ritual that most contemporaries called the "marrying exercise." As one evangelical layman, David Gray, described it, "A young man would go to a young lady and tell her that the Lord had given her to him for a wife, and they must get married or be lost; and sometimes the young lady would have the same kind of impression. Three couples were married this way at one prayer-meeting, and many were so married on other occasions." Joseph Moore, a western Methodist preacher, observed the same phenomenon in 1806: "Sometimes they would be exercised about getting married, and one would tell another he or she had a particular revelation that they must be married, and if the one thus addressed did not consent, he or she must expect to be damned." And a year earlier, Samuel Poole, a Baptist layman, described to his brother a spicier version of the same practice among his neighbors in Tennessee: "the girls will ask the young men to ly with them as good creaditable girls as any that can be. . . . Their was one young woman in good Credit that at a meeting askt a worthless Drinking fellow and he a married man to Come and lye with her Just in Publick Company he Damnd her and said he would not She Damned him and said if he would not then when he wanted to he Should not."

These accounts do not allow for fine discriminations between gossip and fact. It is possible that Gray and Moore were bowdlerizing, that Poole was sensationalizing, or that all three were exaggerating. Yet it is most likely that all three were telling something close to the truth, for many radical revival converts held that they were bound to act on any thought that entered their minds, believing that such "impressions" came directly from God. Prompt compliance with all such impulses, no matter how impractical or unconventional, supposedly attested to converts' "holy shamelessness," a conviction producing other forms of behavior as odd as the "marrying exercise." Following the dictates of their "impressions," some men and women deliberately spoiled their crops, and others engaged in what Samuel Poole described as "all manner of baudy [bawdy] talk as can be thought of they will cuss and sweir [swear] and every thing that is bad."[35]

Whatever actually went on at gatherings of radical evangelicals, many southern husbands and fathers suspected that something foul was afoot. And their suspicions often fastened not only on the fringes far gone in enthusiasm but on the evangelical movement as a whole. As early as the 1760s, Charles Woodmason linked the appearance of Presbyterians and Baptists in the Carolinas to a purported decline in virginity and a rise in illegitimacy and adultery, charging that their rituals abounded in opportunities for sexual indiscretion. Evening meetings for preaching and singing hymns invited later "assignations" under cover of darkness. The physical intimacy of rituals like the "kiss of charity," love feasts, or mass baptisms also stirred concupiscence—as Woodmason guessed from his own reactions. He shuddered in delicious horror at the spectacle of Bap-

tist women swooning in ecstasy at revival gatherings or emerging from
river baptisms with wet clothing clinging to their limbs. It was Woodmason, too, who did much to elaborate the image of evangelical preachers
as sexual Svengalis. He alleged that the South Carolina Baptist preacher
Joseph Reese made all of his female followers "strip in the Public Meeting
House, quite to their Shifts," in order to "make display of their Veneration
for Him, and shew the Power He had over them."[36]

For decades after the Revolution, fears persisted that the path to easy
virtue intersected with the way of the cross. Young, single itinerants
turned up ever more regularly in neighborhoods, lodging in homes where
they cultivated intimacies with women of all ages. Camp meetings, a
newly popular device for recruiting converts, also aroused male apprehensions. "There were a great many who thought it would have disgraced
their wife or daughter forever," the Methodist preacher John Brooks
reported, "if they had stayed on the camp-ground all night." Even the
emotional sharing of Methodist class meetings occasioned alarm among
some, including Virginia's David Campbell, who scolded his wife, Maria,
demanding, "Have you not often seen my anxiety about you at those
places, and why would you be willing to go to them and run the hazard of
being jostled about in a crowd of fanatics without my protecting arm?"
Those disturbing images linking spiritual engagement to sexual abandon
betray the deepest concerns of the men conjuring them. They were preoccupied by the virtue of southern white women because it bore so directly
on the honor of southern white men. In throwing off restraint, women
put the reputations of men—and the purity of family lineage—at their
mercy; rapacious female lust could dishonor a man by depriving him of
either mastery over himself or control over his wife's body and the legitimacy of her offspring. To be sure, not all southern men may have credited
the scandals swirling around female virtuosos, but even those who dismissed the gossip still wondered and worried how much dominion they
would surrender over themselves and their descendants by allowing wives
and daughters liberty in religious matters.[37]

WHITE MEN in the South responded in a variety of ways when their
wives and other female kin embraced evangelicalism. Some of the same
men who railed against being upstaged, overwhelmed, or undermined by
their spouses resolved their anger by following their wives into the same
church. Others, while they came to accept evangelical beliefs, asserted

independence from their wives by joining a rival church, like Obadiah Echols, who, being resolved "to think for myself now," chose the Baptists over Lizzie's Methodists. There appear to have been many such couples, among them a North Carolina pair who more amicably split their religious difference: the Methodist wife christened one son "John Wesley," while her husband named another boy for his favorite Baptist preacher.[38]

Not all men, however, proved so amenable to compromise or so susceptible to evangelicalism. Indeed, some white husbands and fathers sensed in those faiths a challenge too extreme to be tolerated, and imposed their will on wives and other dependents by force or fiat. Stith Mead reported that one western Virginian of this stripe appeared at a revival in 1795 armed with "a long Hickery switch . . . threatening his wife and servants," while his colleague, James Meacham, was awakened one night by a "furious [man] in pursuit of his poor Wife, that came to prayers, but who was gone home . . . before he came." That irate husband, a backslider whom Meacham had expelled from society a few months earlier, "went off in a rage," incensed by his wife's continuing connection with the Methodists. Still another Methodist itinerant, the infelicitously named William Gassaway, had the good fortune to convert one Mrs. Fisher during a revival in Camden, South Carolina; less fortunately, Mr. Fisher, away on business at the time, returned home shortly thereafter, "became furious, ordered his wife to take her name off the Church-book, and swore he would cowhide the preacher on sight." John Brooks painted an equally damning portrait of the "worldlians" in Tennessee, who, when their "wives and daughters would be so convicted [at camp meetings] that they would go up to be prayed for; they would come into the altar in great haste to take them out. . . . Then in great rage cursing the 'straw pen,' as they called the altar; and off home they would take them." The Baptist clergy recorded the same complaints, among them Henry Toler, who in 1783 consoled "a certain Woman in much distress" who had run away from her husband "by whom her Cloth[e]s were torn off for coming [to meeting] the Day before." Another woman in the Virginia Piedmont told William Hickman that since her baptism she "never dared to put her foot in her father's house" because "He cursed and swore and wished her in hell," while one Mr. Dawson of North Carolina carried out his threat of retribution by emptying a load of buckshot into Hickman's contemporary John Tanner, who had baptized Dawson's wife without his permission.[39]

In short, some of the South's masters took their prerogatives to include dictating the religious loyalties of their spouses, as well as other dependents, white and black. But if the South had its share of bullying patriarchs, such men were, in fact, far less common than the clergy's published recollections would suggest. Their memoirs, in this particular and many others, were modeled on those of late-eighteenth-century British evangelicals, in which are prominently featured the originals of those blustering white men whom southern clergymen would style as "furious opposers." Brought across the Atlantic and put through a quick change of costume, props, and dialect, that typecast male became an equally popular figure in the southern evangelical repertoire of stock villains. Thus scripted, they stalk the pages of devotional literature, dragging wives and daughters from camp meetings, threatening sons with disinheritance, and, with predictably less frequency, abusing slaves.[40]

Like all narrative conventions, this one discloses a great deal through its distortions. That the evangelical clergy on both sides of the Atlantic so often recounted such stories bespeaks their hope of fortifying the least powerful members of households to withstand family opposition. And that the plot of outraged patriarchy so compelled the imaginations of southern preachers reflects the psychic stresses of a religious movement led mainly by young bachelors trying to gain ascendancy in a culture dominated by older married men. But the formulaic regularity with which "furious opposers" turn up in published memoirs cannot be accounted as either a reliable index of their actual representation among white southern males or as a faithful reflection of how most nonevangelical husbands treated their pious wives.

Far more common were men who, while neither welcoming the conversion of their wives nor following them into evangelical churches, treated their spouses' piety with a combination of masterful indulgence and bemused condescension. Men of this sort are met with infrequently in published memoirs, but in the private journals of itinerants they considerably outnumber the "furious opposers." Such men usually kept themselves clear of membership in any church, let alone Baptist or Methodist, but allowed wives to worship as they chose and even tried to please them by providing the clergy with the occasional evening's worth of lodging, supper, and, perhaps, the freedom of the parlor to address a gathering of neighbors or to convene the family for prayer. Itinerants' diary entries often capture such men, in all their discomfort, trying to accommodate spouses while maintaining what they took to be a dignified distance from their religion. Jeremiah Norman detected that one Mr. Carr did not normally observe the evangelical ritual of gathering families for nightly prayer, but "made out to ask me to perform it for him before he Lay Down." Like Carr, most men impressed into the role of host mustered polite efforts to engage itinerants in conversation and submitted to a round of prayers and homilies. But the endurance of some did not outlast an evening of religious edification. While traveling with her husband, a Methodist itinerant, Susannah Johnson recalled lodging with the "deistical" Colonel Stump. When his wife urged the preacher to hold family worship, "The old Colonel was writing very busily, and still wrote on while Mr. Johnson read a chapter and sung a hymn, as if it were no concern of his; but I believe, though he stiffly kept his seat, he did lay down his pen when we knelt for prayer."[41]

For such men, humoring—if not quite respecting—their wives' religious sensibilities seemed a reasonable price to pay for peace in the household. But they had no intention of being dragooned into evangelical churches. Although no less disdainful of their wives' spirituality than were "furious opposers," they relied on a different strategy to protect themselves. Upholding male honor, to their way of thinking, did not require that wives share their husbands' religious views. But preserving manly independence did mean that husbands would keep their own counsel on religious matters, and that wives would refrain from challenging those views too often or too forthrightly.

Perhaps the closest approach to comprehending this outlook comes from viewing the world according to James Potter Collins, who, during the decades around 1800, earned a modest livelihood as a tailor and horse trader in Tennessee. A man with no formal church affiliation but many strong religious convictions, he also held fixed opinions about the nature of women: Eve's daughters all, they were inconstant and devious, ever scheming to bend men to their wills. In this perpetual war between the sexes, religion figured as no insignificant theater of battle, and Collins devoted many pages of his memoir to recounting the salvos exchanged with his second wife, a strong-minded Baptist. There was, for instance, the morning that he tried to do business over breakfast with a Methodist, only to find Mrs. Collins detouring the conversation into a debate over doctrine. To Collins's satisfaction, his wife soon "found herself rather headed," their Methodist guest being in his estimate "by far her superior." Having thus dispatched his wife's skills as a casuist, he went on to expose her credulity. Before tucking into the meal, the Methodist offered "a grace as long as a Scotchman would over a haggis," but later that day, after much haggling, Collins began to compare the man's "religion with the price of his horse," and concluded that he meant to cheat him. Collins bought the horse anyway, and upon informing his wife that the Methodist had gotten the better of their bargain, she shot back, "I am surprised at you; it seems like you are an enemy to religious people; you are always persecuting them." But as he had feared, the Methodist's horse proved a plug, and his trusting wife the dupe of evangelical double-dealers. Collins trained the same sly humor on recounting their later move to Louisiana. Knowing that his wife would object, because her aged parents would not pull up stakes again, he claimed, in good evangelical fashion, to have been inspired by a dream in which "a stranger . . . urged the propriety of my moving" by directing him to a passage of Scripture. When told of this purported dream, Mrs. Collins, a woman of many resources, declared that "she could easily interpret it: It is a warning for you to try and get religion, and you had better set about it." Her mother agreed, but the couple moved to Louisiana anyway.[42]

In short, Collins cast his recollections of sparring over religion with his wife as a series of jokes at her expense. His stories conveyed the message that women did not rank as worthy opponents in religious debate, being easily "headed" even by male evangelicals, and that husbands engaged their spouses in such talk merely as a diversion, perhaps to arouse the sort of wifely reproofs that showed how much they cared for a fellow after all. Note, too, that Collins, at least by his account, initiated all their exchanges about religion; their tacit etiquette evidently allowed his wife to defend herself when goaded but not to pester him about his soul in the absence of such provocations. So the pose of not taking his wife seriously served Collins well, buttressing his lavish self-regard, and it also allowed her to worship among the Baptists without having to weather his opposition. Beyond that, it permitted Collins to continue esteeming himself a good republican who upheld liberty of conscience for all whites, even women. The same logic seems to have shaped interactions in most other southern households divided over evangelicalism: Unawakened men permitted their wives—and, indeed, all their white dependents—to worship as they saw fit and even extended hospitality to evangelical preachers. They did not always like doing it, but they liked still less the sense of playing the tyrant, which was not, in their view, one and the same with exercising their rights as patriarchs.

Even so, the reactions of such men to the godly women in their midst always betray some uneasiness. Take the case of Collins, whose breezy dismissal of his wife's religious views is belied by how often he alluded to their disagreements. His belittling humor masked a discomfort that he could not openly acknowledge. Why such sentiments were so common can be no mystery: white southern men of every class regarded mastery over the members of their households as the essence of their masculinity. But before the Revolution, in a society lent greater religious unity by Anglican establishments, most men had not been obliged to consider whether extending those dependents liberty in spiritual matters might compromise their authority as patriarchs. Only in the new religious free market of the postwar decades did the aggressive proselytizing of Baptists and Methodists press most white southerners of both sexes, many for the first time, to make individual religious choices. And only then were most of the South's masters forced to confront the consequences of such decisions. Their response to that reckoning points up that patriarchy, in the early South and elsewhere, has a history. Although the domination of wives and offspring by husbands and fathers stands as a constant in most of human history, what they have deemed worthy of dominating has varied over time and place. Patriarchy could wear many faces, its particular features recast as changing circumstances prompted men to claim certain prerogatives as essential or to surrender others as indifferent to the exercise of their mastery.

So it was in the post-Revolutionary South, where the spread of evangelical influences made some men "furious opposers," husbands and fathers who would more sharply etch the physiognomy of patriarchy's visage by demanding absolute authority over the religious loyalties of wives, children, and slaves. Most did not go so far, but none could avoid coming to terms with a competitive, pluralistic religious climate that, among its other novelties, made spiritual matters central rather than incidental to all family relations. Gauging how to respond to their dependents' religious inclinations now entered into every man's private calculus of how to maintain authority within his household. Deciding how or even whether to monitor the evangelical affinities of their wives, children, and slaves came down to a matter of individual temperament, and nothing suggests that gentry husbands and fathers were any more or less inclined toward strictness or liberality than yeoman farmers or tenants. But on another point where evangelical religious culture impinged on their prerogatives within the household, there did exist a broad consensus among all southern masters, and one with which the evangelical clergy proved eager to comply.

. . .

By 1800, the sufferance of men like James Potter Collins stood as southern evangelicals' greatest accomplishment. It was no mean victory that
evangelicals enjoyed at least the grudging tolerance of most of their contemporaries, men who, born around the Revolution, headed most southern households in the early republic. The early teachings and practices of
Baptists and Methodists, some of which challenged the authority of those
masters, had not aroused among most an animus so great that they barred
evangelicals from their households altogether. True, they were determined not to be ruled by boy preachers who presumed to dictate to their
elders in religion while flattering their wives, flirting with their daughters,
emboldening their sons, stirring up their slaves, and generally meddling in
every intimate matter of their households. Yet for all those provocations,
what had won them a civil reception among most of the South's masters
by 1800 was the punctilious deference paid by Baptist and Methodist
preachers to what every white male regarded as the most essential article
of his prerogative: controlling access to the household over which he
reigned as lord and master. Respectfully as the clergy attended to white
southern women, it did not approach the deference with which they
solicited menfolk for approval to preach and lodge within their private
domains. For even if most southern men did not expect to dictate the religious views of their dependents, the head of every white family demanded
the right to govern entry to his home and behavior within it. That expectation effectively determined the religious influences to which their wives,
children, and slaves would be exposed. Masters decided which ministers
might receive their hospitality, whether they might be permitted to preach
or only to pray, and how other family members should govern their conduct during worship.

The power of that prerogative appears in offhand comments, snatches
of conversation, and brief encounters recorded by the clergy from the
beginnings of the evangelical movement in the South. It was an authority
recognized by itinerants in need of shelter at short notice, who made their
requests only to white men heading even the humblest household. It was
admitted by the many preachers who praised godly wives for prevailing
upon husbands to open their homes. It was honored by a young South
Carolina merchant, newly converted to Methodism, who "asked permission of his landlord to pray with the servants." Withheld, it soured
William Ormond on "one Besile, a Church-man [Anglican], flat and
formal, not willing to have the gosple preached . . . in his house," but,

when granted, softened him toward another Anglican, "Mr. Hooks . . . very Morral, and seem'd willing to open his doors." It was, to Jeremiah Norman's delight, exercised by his once wary brother-in-law, who "now submitted to my praying in his family nights and morn, nay once insisted me to do." It was asserted by Captain Bowie of Natchez, Louisiana, who, after years of humoring his Methodist wife, finally declared that he had heard enough of one itinerant who "had preached so much about hell, that his chimney had fallen down, and he would have him there no longer." It was invoked by Virginia's fabulously rich Robert Carter, who could never hear enough of John Taylor, thus distressing his lady, who fretted whenever the young Baptist preached at the mansion "because she must remove her great candle glass, lest the sound should break it to shivers." It resounded in Nicholas Mead's angry resolve that his wife had heard enough of his brother Stith's praying to "fall," and in Colonel Gordon's grumbling that his slaves had heard enough for his brother-in-law to cease speaking altogether.[43]

The authority of southern husbands and fathers to decide when enough was enough made them a power—indeed, the main power—for preachers to reckon with. And their scrupulous observance of that prerogative betokens a crucial truth about the conditions of Baptist and Methodist expansion in the South: In order to reach most southerners, white and black, evangelicals needed access to the home itself, which in most cases lay solely in the control of masters. Because of rapid westward expansion and dispersed settlement, most southern households lay at long distances from an often small number of local churches. Under those circumstances, the clergy commonly conducted worship within private dwellings or outdoors on privately owned land. Many white women and children, as well as slaves, whose lives were physically confined to far-flung plantations, could hear preaching only in such settings—and only when the South's masters permitted ministers to speak in their own or neighboring households. Isolation also retarded the development of female religious and benevolent associations, which, outside of the South's few urban centers, remained scarce throughout the early national period. This situation contrasts strikingly with that in the North during the same decades. There, especially in the Northeast, greater population density afforded many more women easy access to a variety of churches and fostered the development of voluntary organizations as important centers of autonomous female worship, philanthropy, and sociability. In other words, southern men held more power to shape the spiritual lives of their wives and other dependents because the southern household still commanded the center of most religious activity.[44]

It is likely, too, that by the beginning of the nineteenth century, northern and southern men held diverging views about their religious prerogatives within the households. As commercial and industrial development in the early republic transformed northern middle-class households into a private sphere overseen by women, their socially accepted role came to include setting the tone of family spirituality. Northern men, drawn daily out of their homes, increasingly allowed their wives to take the lead in religious matters. Yet during the same period in the South, the household remained the workplace of most white men—the family farm or plantation—enabling them to continue exercising a far greater degree of oversight over all domestic matters, including religious observance. Also reinforcing the rule of white males over spiritual life in some southern homes was the exigency of controlling slaves; indeed, the recurring role of evangelicalism in inspiring slave conspiracies and insurrections heightened the importance of masters' monitoring African-American access to worship.[45]

The deference of southern preachers thus acknowledged the pivotal position of southern masters. So, too, did the clergy's close scrutiny of individual southern men, a habit revealed in countless journal entries that noted the names of those hosts who welcomed them as guests or permitted preaching in their households and sometimes even the names of men who lent their land for camp meetings. Preachers well understood that to win any claim on hospitality of white male heads of households was also to gain potential influence among all of his dependents. Hence John Early's precise report on one North Carolina Anglican, Mr. Tatum, who "would not let [his family] join the Methodists," but still tolerated the evangelical inclinations of his wife and children and entertained preachers. And hence Jeremiah Norman's gloating over his first invitation to lodge with Mr. McJunkin, a "rigid" Presbyterian pillar of the local squirearchy in one upcountry South Carolina settlement. "He treated me with all possible kindness," Norman effused. "I have since been told that there never has been a Methodist minister that tarryed a night with him before."[46]

Indeed, it is telling to watch preachers as they watched the South's masters—and to imagine how often, when talking to wives, they stole glances at their husbands. Look on then, and catch two ministers, as their calling often required, trying to detect the precise point at which each individual layman drew the line between the permissible and the intolerable, judging the exact distance to the end of his patience. During a western Virginia revival in 1795, Stith Mead knew that he had overstepped the bounds with one "old man [who] got offended and drew out his wife and Children saying this was too much noise for him." But the Baptist William Hickman proved a more practiced judge of his quarry. Weighing whether to take up a new pastorate, he shrewdly sized up the neighborhood's leading settler, a man "very thoughtless about his soul," who nevertheless tried to lure the preacher by promising him a tract of land on his property. "I said to him," Hickman recalled, "Sir, you don't care about religion; I want to know why you wish me to come," to which the promising reply came, "If it never is any advantage to me, it may be to my family."[47]

Yet if some of the South's masters seemed heroically resigned to their eternal fate, the clergy could not be so complacent. They aimed at winning more than a master's hospitality—they wanted his soul. And, to put the matter bluntly, evangelicals could not rest content with a religion that was the faith of women, children, and slaves. For that reason, the polite reserve, sometimes tinged by tacit disdain, with which many southern men rebuffed their overtures loomed as the greatest challenge facing Baptist and Methodist preachers after the turn of the century. Indeed, the desire to win something warmer from white husbands and fathers drove evangelicals' efforts during the early decades of the nineteenth century to alter the character of their ministry and their teachings on the family in ways that upheld every man's mastery over his household. During the same period, it also reshaped the Baptist and Methodist clergy's vision of the role of women in the lives of their churches.

IT HAD BECOME apparent by the turn of the century that even some laymen within evangelical circles wondered whether it was wise to take godly women quite so seriously. It had become clear, too, that some men outside those circles, who scorned to take any woman seriously, would bar their wives and daughters from joining Baptist and Methodist churches. It was also plain that many more unawakened men, while allowing their female kin to worship however they chose, would refuse to take seriously any church that took women seriously. Yet it had become equally evident that while some southern women longed for the reprieve of being taken less seriously by evangelicals, many others had come to enjoy and even to expect it and now exerted real influence within their churches. And so a dilemma confronted the southern clergy at the opening of the nineteenth century. If they tried to conciliate men by retreating from the teachings and practices that endorsed the spiritual authority of women, they might affront their female constituency. But if they conceded no more to masters than bowing to their authority as hosts, most white laymen would continue to hold their churches at arm's length.

Here, then, was a matter fraught with difficulty on all sides. It was not a problem peculiar to southern evangelicals; northern ministers in the new republic also recognized that women were the mainstays of church membership, but worried that encouraging female adepts would undermine gender hierarchies and permanently estrange laymen. Even so, for southern clergymen the stakes were higher, for they had more to lose by alienating those husbands and fathers who, far more effectively than their northern counterparts, controlled the access of preachers to their dependents. In the South, too, male anxieties ran higher because of the earlier and relatively greater prominence enjoyed by female virtuosos in their churches. Indeed, decades before most of their northern sisters, southern evangelical women figured as forceful presences in sexually mixed religious gatherings, exerting influence in those public settings that southern men could not ignore.[48]

Women were more visible as religious virtuosos in the South because the forms of evangelicalism predominant in that region differed from those in the North. Among northerners, evangelicals remained overwhelmingly Congregationalist and Presbyterian until the 1830s. In those churches, the clergy encouraged women to develop outlets for their religious energies by forming single-sex voluntary associations to promote personal spiritual growth and moral reform. Although women sometimes testified to their experiences in those churches, they did not pray or exhort in sexually mixed settings until the 1830s, which meant that for many decades after the Revolution, most northern men did not routinely witness public displays of female religious virtuosity. By contrast, Baptists and Methodists quickly emerged after the Revolution as the majority of evangelicals in the South. Both churches permitted women to prophesy, pray, and exhort at mixed gatherings, thus creating many opportunities for southern men to observe the talents of spiritually proficient women.[49]

Most did not look on easily. They did not fail to notice that women's public exercise of their charisma often accorded them a spiritual stature in the churches rivaling that of men, nor could they have missed being yet again reminded of the affinities between Baptists and Methodists and the Quakers. And by the first decade of the nineteenth century, as the Shakers began filtering into the western country, neither did it escape the notice of southern laymen that some evangelicals shared with that sect an uncommon regard for female adepts. True, the Shakers went well beyond Baptists or Methodists by endowing their female members with governing authority over their fellowships, but that policy had won acceptance only at the beginning of the nineteenth century. Despite the early prominence of Ann Lee, Shaker men, many of whom did not endorse the right of women to rule, had dominated the sect's governance for most of the eighteenth century. Only after Lucy Wright took control of the movement in 1796 did the Shaker brethren finally affirm women's equal powers to govern their societies, whether as the head of their church or as "mothers" and eldresses in their villages. "Mother Lucy" made it known there was no place among her followers for men like Angell Mathewson, who was expelled in 1799 for declaring that "wimmin are fools and that men that are willin[g] to have a woman rule over them are fools also." And only in 1808, when Benjamin Youngs wrote the sect's first official history, was the doctrine first officially set forth that Jesus Christ had chosen a woman, Ann Lee, as the vessel for his second incarnation.[50]

Evangelicals, of course, had a horror of being confused with the Shakers. And that dread, as Shaker villages sprang up in the midst of southern settlements in the western country, only added to the urgency of resolving the dilemma posed by female virtuosos in Baptist and Methodist churches. Now southerners could witness firsthand women wielding both spiritual and temporal power over such Shaker "families," claiming superior religious charisma as the basis of that authority. Here, indeed, was a caution to Baptists and Methodists, whose own ranks harbored clergymen urging, on the same grounds, that godly women might hold church office and preach. Accordingly, evangelicals took steps to distinguish their views on women from those of the Shakers. One of their shrewdest polemicists was Abram Van Vleet, a Presbyterian printer in Lebanon, Ohio, who acquainted southerners with Mary Dyer and Eunice Chapman, two northern women who sought divorces and custody of their children after their husbands joined the Shakers. In 1818, Van Vleet's press put out a new edition of their lurid revelations—updated with the latest gossip from the western country—including allegations that the Shakers regarded wedlock as "a contract with hell" and motherhood as a defilement of the female body. Dyer and Chapman also disclosed that many Shaker women, bearing the shame of scarlet pasts replete with adulterous affairs and illegitimate pregnancies, eagerly embraced that sect's practice of "spiritual wifery," which allowed members to change sexual partners annually. Finally, there were the Shaker eldresses, to whom believers confessed their sins and "reverenced . . . even to peeling off their shoes and walking softly in their presence." In short, the strategy pursued by evangelicals like Van Vleet aimed at transforming a potential disaster into a godsend by shifting onto the Shakers the onus of tempting women from the path of purity and submission. Even Baptists and Methodists might now appear moderate by contrast, accruing respectability by the sheer vitriol of their attacks on the Shakers.[51]

It was a clever tack, but it backfired. Unforeseen was that western Shakerism would find so resourceful a defender as Richard McNemar, a former Presbyterian minister in Kentucky, who counterattacked with weapons that he knew well. Hoisting his former evangelical colleagues on their own petard, McNemar published a pamphlet in 1819 that depicted Dyer and Chapman as fearsome specimens of *evangelical* womanhood, equal parts siren and virago, who pursued carnal pleasure and dominion over men. He "exposed" Eunice Chapman as a woman whose lewd, contentious behavior had finally forced even the Presbyterians to expel her from fellowship. As for Dyer, who had had ties to both the Baptists and the Methodists before briefly joining the Shakers, he confided that for her husband "to live with her in peace, he must consent to be ruled by her; that it was her disposition to lead rather than to be led." And what she tried to lead him toward was "spiritual marriage," by taking as lovers two evangelical preachers and later attempting to seduce a young male Shaker. McNemar also alleged that Dyer had schemed to abandon her domestic duties altogether and become a Baptist preacher, and then joined the Shakers hoping to become "a leader in their society." Not surprisingly, McNemar observed a discreet silence about governing powers open to women in Shaker villages, insisting instead that his sect impressed on wives the duty of obeying their husbands and refused to admit married women without the consent of their spouses.[52]

Dyer and Chapman were northern women, but that made them even more perfectly suited to McNemar's purposes in addressing his largely southern audience. He intimated that not Shakerism but evangelicalism turned women into whores and harridans, and that southern women who

joined those churches risked becoming thus debased and altogether indis-
tinguishable from the dread Yankees. He implied, too, that Van Vleet was
the sorry dupe of two harpies, a man so easily misled that he defended the
rights of sluttish scolds who set their husbands at nought while hankering
after supremacy in both the household and the church. Overall, McNemar
managed to create the impression that the Shakers' soberly conventional
views of wifely submission set them apart from evangelicals intent on subverting domesticity. It was a masterful, if utterly disingenuous, performance, McNemar spouting the rhetoric of misogyny even as his own sect
was steadily ceding ruling power to women. Indeed, his most amazing
grace was subterfuge, a talent not entirely unexpected, perhaps, in one
prizing the gift of simplicity.

Yet McNemar's talent for turning the tables only confirmed for evangelicals that Shaker-bashing alone would not suffice as a strategy for dispelling lay doubts about the suspect ways of their own godly women. Well
before being bested in this encounter, the Baptist and Methodist clergy
had calculated the costs to their churches of the squeamishness inspired in
southern men by female virtuosos; that the Shakers and their eldresses
had now come too close for comfort merely added to the toll. And the
preachers had decided that their difficulties admitted of no other resolution than to reconsider what was proper religious conduct for women
adhering to their faiths.

THE RESULTS of that reassessment were not manifested by sweeping
revisions in official church policy or practice concerning female members.
Instead, they appear in telling, if sometimes subtle, changes in the clergy's
response to both godly women and their husbands and fathers. They are
registered by shifts of emphasis in the entries of preachers' journals, as
well as in stories enjoying a long circulation in their sermons before being
set down in their published memoirs. And, taken together, they reveal a
new concern to impress upon southern women what southern men—the
clergy included—regarded as acceptable female religious behavior: modes
of spiritual expression less assertive and more private than those exhibited
by many women before 1800.

Southern preachers in the early nineteenth century did not stint in
praising godly women. But many, especially those men who entered the
ministry after 1800, now balanced those admiring reports with self-
congratulatory accounts of how they extracted submission from other

women, either by enforcing conformity to doctrinal orthodoxy or by curbing ecstatic forms of spiritual expression. The Methodist John Early, for example, applauded public prayer and exhortation by gifted women, but asserted that they overstepped their bounds by disputing openly with any preacher. In 1811, when one North Carolina Baptist woman "blazed out at me in the congregation and said . . . I must explain my preaching," he retorted that "I did not quarrel with women." And when another Baptist woman scoffed at his counsel, he proudly noted in his journal that afterward she "cried powerfully and told somebody she was sorry for what she had said about me . . . for now she like[d] me very well." Meanwhile, his contemporaries in the western country also lingered over stories of vanquishing independent-minded females. At a camp meeting in the 1820s, Peter Cartwright met a rarity among southern white women, "a very confirmed Arian lady," meaning one "who denied the supreme divinity of Jesus." When the woman "desired some one to go and bring me to her, for she wanted to show that . . . I was in error," he first refused to come at her beckoning, but then hit upon a better strategy: He surrounded her with a group of Methodists who prayed "to dislodge the . . . Arian devil" from her heart. A few weeks later, Cartwright's views on the divinity of Jesus were borne out by no less an authority than Christ himself, who humbled the lady with "a vision or dream" in which "she saw her Savior . . . and he told her she was wrong, but he frankly forgave her; and when she came to herself or awake, she was unspeakably happy." Preachers also crowed over their success at squelching dramatic forms of ecstatic response among women. In 1811, John Early upbraided one Methodist woman by declaring that "I disliked the young women rolling and shouting on the floor and would oppose it again if I saw it among my flock." Similarly, Joseph Travis boasted in his memoir of taking "summary process" with the African-American woman known as Aunt Katy, who claimed "that she was 'young King Jesus.' " With typical satisfaction, he reported Aunt Katy's subsequent submission, which rendered her "a rational and consistent member of the church."[53]

In short, preachers now took pains to assure both themselves and the readers of their memoirs that they brooked no nonsense from either disputatious or charismatic females. Such behavior on the part of women had aroused resentment among some clergymen in the late eighteenth century as well, but they had been less open and emphatic in their opposition. By contrast, their successors styled themselves as the sort of men who were willing and able to bring women to heel by public censure, and increasingly styled outspoken sisters as insubordinate rather than inspired. Not surprisingly, the women most likely to draw the clergy's disapproval were those whose behavior suggested affinities with that of the Shakers, in the form of either theological heterodoxy or ecstatic displays.

In other ways, too, early-nineteenth-century clergymen asserted their claim to prerogatives within the churches as absolute as the authority of southern masters over their households. Women continued to exhort, pray, and testify at public gatherings of both sexes, but there emerged a new sensitivity on the part of many clergymen that such activities would not stray into the realm of preaching. While southern Baptists had never approved of women preachers, their advocates among the Methodists now met with stiffer resistance from within their own ranks. John Early numbered among those opponents, and he took on Dorothy Ripley during her last American tour in 1812 when the two converged on the same tent at a Virginia camp meeting. Early, who dismissed her as "an English woman who passed for a preacher," was taken aback when Ripley threw down the gauntlet, and "asked me if I had not evil in my heart against her." He rebuffed her request for them to pray together, relenting only when the tent's proprietor insisted. On the following day, he rallied, telling her that "I did not believe it was practicable for a woman to preach the Gospel," and that she "lacked several qualifications to prepare for preaching and she should behave herself better than she had done." Ripley stalked off.[54]

While Early never enumerated the "several qualifications" that might have made it "practicable" for Ripley to preach, his contemporary, James Finley, candidly declared that their gender alone disqualified all women. Like other southern preachers in the western country after 1800, Finley encountered many emigrant Yankee women, and first impressions, on both sides, were not favorable. For his part, Finley was unsettled by their aggressive behavior in the churches, typified by one "female prophet" who, feeling "inspired" to deliver her "impressions," interrupted him in mid-sermon. He commanded her to sit down until he had finished, after which she might exhort the gathering. There was a time for women to speak in the churches, in Finley's view, and it did not fall during that bastion of male and clerical prerogative, the sermon: "I thought the practice a wrong one, and contrary to that decency and order which should characterize the worship of God, and quoted the language of St. Paul in regard to women teaching in the Church, and expressed a hope that the Spirit would not move any more to speak on such occasions."[55]

For the same reason, both Finley and his fellow itinerant in the West,

Peter Cartwright, "gave battle" to a tiny group known as the Halcyon Church. That sect arose from the inspiration of Abel Sargent, a former Universalist preacher turned "millennial messenger," who professed to see visions and converse with angels. During the first decade of the nineteenth century, he gathered a group of twelve "Apostles," composed mainly or perhaps entirely of women drawn from the ranks of New England migrants. The little band preached throughout southeastern Ohio and adjacent western Virginia and western Pennsylvania, spreading the reassuring message that hell and the devil did not exist. They also spread the less reassuring message that "a Woman has a right to leave her husband and wed in a spiritual manner to whom she pleases." It was with considerable relief, then, that Peter Cartwright reported the extinction of this sect, which came about shortly after a male Halcyon, believing that personal holiness had rendered his "animal nature" immortal, stopped eating, died sixteen days later, and defied Sargent's efforts to effect his resurrection. Here was a cautionary tale, and Cartwright relished it, warning that no good could result from the religious empowerment of women, particularly of the Yankee variety, whom he gleefully lampooned as "thin-faced, Roman-nosed, loquacious . . . glib on the tongue."[56]

Besides closing ranks against women who aspired to preach, the clergy now put forward as paragons those women who confined the exercise of their spiritual talents to the household. From the first, Baptists and Methodists had linked the perfection of women's godliness to the fulfillment of their duties as wives and mothers, daughters and sisters. But by the opening of the nineteenth century, the identity between female piety and domesticity came to dominate evangelical devotional writings published throughout the Anglo-American world. Most energetic in disseminating that notion in the American South were Methodist itinerants, who stuffed their saddlebags with writings by and about Hester Ann Rowe Rogers for distribution among the faithful. Casting Rogers as the embodiment of domesticated female religiosity was a delicious irony. A prolific writer, her meditations, memoirs, and religious poetry went through countless English and several American editions during the decades around 1800, and in midlife, her husband, an English Methodist minister, had to fend for himself while she served as housekeeper to an aging John Wesley. Even so, the posthumous editions of her work included fulsome assurances from her neglected spouse that Rogers's voluminous literary output never interfered with her wifely duties, while in her funeral sermon, Thomas Coke pointedly remarked that "she never assumed the authority of teaching in the church," but confined her activities to consoling the troubled, the sick, and the dying.[57]

In keeping with the new insistence that a woman's way to eternal bliss lay in devotion to her family and the nearly deceased, southern Baptist clergymen came forward with hints on how wives might appease un-awakened husbands. Going, if not gone altogether, were the days when preachers like William Hickman had boasted of secretly baptizing wives in defiance of their spouses; his junior colleague Wilson Thompson shunned such deception when approached by an elderly Missouri woman whose husband refused to let her join the church. Thompson admitted that a knotty problem arose when a wife's duty to her husband conflicted with her duty to God, but he cut through it by inveigling the woman's husband, a staunch Jeffersonian Democrat, into a discussion of liberty of conscience. When the husband declared his hearty support for that freedom, Thompson sprang to his wife's desire for baptism: "It is always pleasant in such cases, to have the free consent and cordial approbation of the husband, so that no disturbance or reflections should be made after-ward." The preacher continued, "[A]nd as our conversation has led to this point, I will ask your consent." John Taylor likewise learned from his long experience to summon equal finesse in soothing resentful spouses. When one woman presented herself to the church for baptism, "I reminded the church of her husband who sat near the door, the utility of his approba-tion, in her joining the church, he rose up before the question was asked of him, and gave his consent."[58]

Although Thompson and Taylor preferred to characterize the assent of husbands—especially those sitting "near the door"—as "pleasant" and "useful," some Baptist associations now deemed it essential. In 1809, one in North Carolina recommended that any woman whose desire for bap-tism met with opposition from her spouse "wait patiently, hoping that God in his providence may make a way for her to come into the church by the husband's consent." The message was unmistakable: Baptist churches would go to almost any length to uphold the authority of men married to female believers. Indeed, Taylor even argued that the churches showed misguided zeal in urging wives to proceed to baptism before their hus-bands if those men had come under conviction. Thus were godly women given to understand just who was their lord and master—and that spiri-tual virtuosity allowed them no license to defy or even upstage those husbands.[59]

They learned, too, from evangelical memoirs, that a woman most adorned her spouse by following his lead in religious matters. After the death of the staunchly Methodist Lizzie, an older and shrewder Obadiah Echols sought a mate who would not challenge his Baptist convictions. He found her in Bettie Dismukes Jones, a young widow who bewailed the inequality of their match only because she was not a Christian, although she wanted to become one "the worst of all things in the world." Her want of any fixed religious opinions, particularly those that might impugn the temperance of Baptists, bedazzled Obadiah. He magnanimously expressed confidence in her eventual conversion, before which time "the risk would be with me only." Thus were they wed, with her new lord boasting that "both myself and my brother were proud of our new trophy." More pliant than her predecessor, the bride joined the Baptists within a year of marrying. Into this chorus of endorsements for the authority of men over their female dependents, the Methodist clergy added their voices. When one young man tried to remove his sister from a camp meeting in 1825, Alfred Brunson voiced what had become the conventional wisdom among his colleagues by replying that "you can't be allowed to take her away by force" because "You are not her father or husband." And by the middle decades of the nineteenth century, Methodist preachers observed that most southern women followed the course of trophy wives: They either postponed joining a church until they married or switched to the church of their newly wed husbands.[60]

Nineteenth-century preachers also took new care to depict godly women in ways that would stanch the swirl of rumor associating them with sexual abandon. Some of these new images conjured by the clergy aimed at easing male anxieties by implying a connection between female religious charisma and reproductive prowess. For example, the Methodist Alfred Brunson recalled at one western camp meeting during the 1820s that Sister Chamberlain "exhorted and talked of religion for three hours, in one incessant flow of the most powerful and convincing eloquence. . . . While thus talking, some one brought her babe to her . . . and she sat in a chair and nursed it, continuing her talk as before." Equally striking is John Taylor's description of one Mrs. Price, a virtuoso of renown not only for her success at converting her kinfolk and neighbors but also for her "gift in poetry, as some of the hymn books will show some of her poems in print." But Taylor found it prudent to mention that this paragon could also boast being the "mother of many children," and having an impeccable pedigree: As the daughter of the celebrated Baptist preacher John Gano, "She is, by way of compliment, among us at times called the seed of

Abraham." Taylor thus tamed Mrs. Price's extraordinary religious talents by linking them to both her male ancestry and her fecundity. Surely it had not escaped his notice that southern men set great store on the continuity of their lineage, and if they could be encouraged to believe that their wives' piety assisted that outcome, so much the better for the Baptists.[61]

More commonly, however, preachers opted for the strategy of desexing spiritually dynamic women. Perhaps not surprisingly, the most radical denial of female sexuality appears in John Taylor's depiction of the remarkable slave convert Letty. Validating the religious virtuosity of an African-American woman plainly proved harder for Taylor than bestowing the same accolade on a white woman—or, for that matter, an African-American man like her brother Asa. That ambivalence Taylor at once revealed and tried to resolve by denying Letty's womanhood, explaining at some length that "Her masculine strength made her equal to any black man on the plantation, her high spirit and violent temper, often brought her in contact with them in bloody blows; as her body was strong so was her mind; nature had done more for her than common." Already endowed by southern whites with a mystique of sensuality, black women who could also claim charisma represented a female potency too threatening for men of either race even to acknowledge.[62]

Evangelicals showed more reluctance about depriving godly white women of their female identity, but strove to neutralize their sexuality in other ways. Grandmothers and prepubescent "virgins" increasingly commended themselves to preachers as sexually "safe" exemplars of female spiritual prowess, while even wives, mothers, and married sisters emerge in preachers' memoirs as figures of ethereal purity whose lives' purpose centered on assisting the salvation of male kin. Indeed, among the more arresting conventions of clerical autobiographies published throughout the first half of the nineteenth century are the recurring episodes of women sacrificing conjugal intimacy to solace spiritually beleaguered young men. Thus Peter Cartwright's mother "sprang from her bed" to console her despairing son; John Brooks's sister deserted her husband's side to pray for her brother after a troubling dream; and Wilson Thompson took to sleeping in his parents' room during a crisis of faith.[63]

Important as they were in shaping the southern evangelical strategy for expansion, clerical efforts to accommodate southern patriarchs should not obscure how much remained the same in the daily practices of ministers and churches. Preachers still cultivated close relations with godly women who continued to exert a vital influence in the churches. True, the prospects that a few ministers had earlier entertained for enhancing the official power of women in the churches had been foreclosed. But if that door had been slammed shut by the beginning of the nineteenth century, it had never been open more than a crack. It was also true that ministers became ever more likely to express unqualified praise for women who trained their religious energies on the private sphere of the household rather than exercising their gifts in public settings. But women still received unwavering clerical support for exercising certain gifts at sexually mixed religious gatherings—testifying, praying, and exhorting. By preserving a substantial public role for women in Baptist and Methodist churches, the clergy stopped short of fully capitulating to the anxieties of southern laymen. Even the impetus provided by the proximity of Shaker eldresses, while dampening ministerial enthusiasm for female visionaries and ecstatics and all but demolishing support for female preachers, did not snuff out all opportunities for women's public religious performances.

Those continuities betoken the formidable, albeit informal, authority that many women had attained within southern Baptist and Methodist churches by the turn of the nineteenth century. Their influence persisted throughout the century and, indeed, has continued to the present day. Eloquent testimony to their power appears in records such as the book kept by the male clerk of the Methodist church in Edenton, North Carolina. Female voices are nowhere heard in his chronicle of the church's temporal and secular business, which rested entirely in the hands of the brethren. But in the pages of obituaries eulogizing the pillars of that little society, women appear as often as men—although the latter, of course, head the list. The largely unrecorded but palpable presence of women like Edenton's Methodist sisters thus circumscribed the choices available to a clergy who, by the turn of the century, had targeted husbands and fathers as *the* force to be reckoned with in their campaign to evangelize the South. In their efforts to conciliate southern men, the clergy dared not infringe too far upon the freedom to speak at religious gatherings which many southern women had grown accustomed to exercising. And by continuing to endorse that liberty, even as they urged female submission to the authority of preachers and husbands, the clergy hoped to hold the loyalties of those women who discerned in evangelicalism a rare opportunity to exert power and find fulfillment outside of their households.[64]

For all of that, southern women still figured less prominently in the strategy for regional expansion being formulated by evangelical clergymen after the turn of the century. Their determination to cultivate the South's masters is registered not only in the subtle ways that preachers signaled their altered stance toward women but in every significant revision of earlier evangelical teaching and practice after 1800—the shifts in the character and authority of their ministry, their discipline and ritual practice, and their views on the family. What set and sustained that new course was the changing character of the South's evangelical clergy, a group that by the 1820s was no longer dominated by young, single men. As southern Methodist and Baptist preachers collectively acquired greater maturity and self-confidence, as they gained in authority and professional status, they grew all the more inclined to identify with other southern masters, and became even more intent on securing full acceptance among those white men. The mounting force of those affinities was to find fullest expression in ministerial efforts to meld the South's regional mores of masculinity and martial honor with the evangelical ethos. While showing that they could stand up to southern women, Baptist and Methodist preachers also set about proving that they could also stand up to southern men.[65]

5

MASTERY

But Jacob said to Rebekah his mother, Behold, my brother
Esau is a hairy man, and I am a smooth man. Perhaps my
father will feel me, and I shall seem to be mocking him,
and bring a curse upon myself and not a blessing. . . .

Then Rebekah took the best garments of Esau her
older son, which were in her house, and put them on
Jacob her younger son; and the skins of the kids she put
upon his hands and the smooth part of his neck. . . .

So he went into his father, and said "My father"; and
he said, "Here I am; who are you my son?" Jacob said to
his father, "I am Esau your first-born. I have done as
you told me; now sit up and eat of my game that you
may bless me. . . ."

So Jacob went near Isaac his father, who felt him and
said "The voice is Jacob's voice, but the hands are the
hands of Esau."

—GENESIS, 27:11–22

J EREMIAH NORMAN was not the sort of man southerners would
later hail as "a good old boy" or "one helluva fella." Yet he came
closer than most early evangelical preachers to meeting the standards
for manhood current among whites in the 1790s and for generations
thereafter. Unlike many of his colleagues, Norman cast a cold eye on
women who spoke their minds on religious matters; unlike some, he
refrained from criticizing slaveholders, once even helping to track down a
runaway. His pleasures, too, were peculiar for a Methodist preacher: He
joined hunting parties whenever opportunity offered and bragged of his
skills as a marksman. And, just possibly, he indulged in convivial drinking
with the same company, for he objected with the shrill righteousness that
fingers an uneasy conscience when one Methodist—a woman, as it happened—declared drunkenness to be the worst of sins.

For all of those reasons, white men of every class might have regarded young Norman as, if not exactly a boon companion, one more agreeable than the usual run of Methodist itinerants. Even gentlemen may have taken a fancy to the fastidious preacher who, styling himself their social equal, did not account it a snare of Satan to sport a watch fob or carry an umbrella. Set next to most of his colleagues, whose indifference to dress beggared them even before the scarecrows, Norman appeared almost natty. Perhaps, too, the better sort took pleasure in the company of a young man so well spoken and widely read, who often waxed earnest to his journal about the importance of polished manners in a minister. And surely they noted that this self-proclaimed gentleman did not lightly bear any slight to his honor. After one disagreeable encounter with a scruffy blasphemer, Norman first went to the law and "had [him] prosecuted for his wickedness"; when his enemy threatened retaliation in the form of tar and feathers, the preacher "kept myself prepared for defense, but none mistreated me."[1]

In short, if the South's masters, great and small, had cause to feel well disposed toward any evangelical clergyman, it was Jeremiah Norman. Preacher though he was, the young man shared many of their pastimes and passions, values and vanities. And for precisely that reason, men of his stripe—not only cultivated and learned but, more important, self-proclaimed as masculine in recognizably southern ways—became more common within the clergy's ranks after the turn of the century. By then, many of the South's earliest evangelical preachers, men whose deportment flouted that region's reigning mores of mastery, had passed from the scene. Now a rising generation of preachers, often in league with their remaining elders, aimed at showing the godly brethren how admirably they upheld the customary ideals of southern manhood. That entailed not only endorsing the authority of masters over their dependents, white and black, but also affirming the importance of men commanding respect in the company of their peers. In many ways, then, Norman's ministerial persona, still somewhat novel in the 1790s, foreshadowed the image that early-nineteenth-century clergymen would strive, by force of their own imitation, to impress upon the laity: that men of God were men of honor, initiates into the mysteries of competition, combat, and mastery.

Creating that impression would not come easily. As Norman's colleagues and successors knew by long experience, no matter how congenial a preacher might make himself to white laymen, he remained a preacher nonetheless, bound by that office to impress upon their minds the truth of his creed and to submit their hearts to his understanding of the divine will. Such interventions, no matter how deftly executed by the most agreeable of preachers, did not often produce the desired result. As all Baptists and Methodists whose ministries straddled the turn of the century came to realize, the South's masters knew how to resist being thus mastered.

The problem facing southern preachers was not that southern men were disengaged from religious concerns. On the contrary, most of the white men whom Norman met on his travels—whether encountering them by chance or being invited into their homes—were willing, even eager, to favor him with their religious views. Typical was one man who relished the evening he spent regaling the young preacher with arguments in support of the Universalist doctrine of "Hell Redemption"—the belief that a merciful God would not consign sinners to eternal punishment in the hereafter. On an even more dismal night, when Norman took refuge from a storm at the first available home, his accidental host seized the chance to air still more eccentric notions. "He views the Kingdom of God in a military light believing . . . that no other people but the Jews will have any share in the Blessing," the mystified preacher reported, and thus "he would be sure of Salvation if he knew himself to have descended from Jacob." "I think in fine he may be said to be a mongrel," Norman sniffed, little imagining that one person's mixed breed may be another's pedigree, among the latter being his host, who boasted that "he could find no man of the same tenets" and "neither could he find any an equal antagonist."[2]

Such exchanges confirmed for Norman that getting southern men to talk about their religious views was not the problem. Unfortunately, their private creeds made it hard to imagine many men as part of any evangelical solution. Everywhere in the South, white men cherished idiosyncratic, often wildly heterodox, religious opinions, disgorged by some with cheerful insouciance and by others spat out in sullen challenge. To be sure, not every southern master was his own theologian, and the many nonevangelicals in their ranks sometimes identified themselves as Universalists or deists. But more men seem to have taken pride in elaborating highly individualized theologies, usually a pastiche of Christian doctrines, natural religion, personal interpretations of the Bible, and popular supernaturalism.[3]

True to that type was Norman's contemporary James Potter Collins, who retained from his Presbyterian upbringing a Calvinist conviction of the deity's inscrutability but mixed it with a decidedly liberal confidence in mankind's innate moral sense. A strict observer of the Sabbath and a devotee of sacred music, Collins read the Bible nightly and described himself as having "a strongly moral bent." Yet with those Christian tenets and tastes, he combined a firm belief in both the magical prowess of German immigrants and the conjuring skills of African Americans, resorting to slave practitioners on several occasions to cure his chronic insomnia. He held in much lower regard the powers of the Christian clergy, particularly evangelicals, whom he disdained as intolerant hypocrites intent on thrusting their hands into a man's pocket while cramming their religious opinions down his throat.[4]

Collins's religious beliefs were of his own devising, but many of his white male contemporaries shared in the spirit, if not the letter, of his thinking. Kindred spirits included one of Jeremiah Norman's hosts, who announced that he "neither respected Preaching or Praying but utterly detested all things of that nature," and entertained Methodist itinerants only to please his wife. Yet even this churlish fellow eagerly set forth his personal theology, the specifics of which Norman dismissed as "too many and absurd for me to take notice of them now, seeing they are not Christian or pure heathen." Other white men exhibited the same prickly independence—and the same aversion to any clergyman who threatened to compromise their intellectual autonomy by authoritative pronouncements either from the pulpit or around the hearth. While ready to voice and sometimes even to debate their doctrinal opinions, many either resisted or simply shrugged off the clergy's effort to enforce conformity to evangelical doctrines.

In their stubbornness lay one challenge for evangelical preachers. For Jeremiah Norman it was embodied in Judge Smith, who, upon being quizzed by him, "denys being a Deist which many have branded him with," and "professes to have a high regard for the Bible," but stopped far short of upholding Methodist orthodoxy, being "very tenacious of his own opinions." Similar responses frustrated many other preachers, like Jacob Young, who spent long evenings trying to reduce a Kentucky man, "sometimes a Deist, and sometimes a Universalist," from his religious errors. "Frequently I left him at eleven o'clock at night, nearly right, but next day found him an infidel." Even more obdurate was another man who, in response to James Meacham's prayers for a deathbed repentance, rallied long enough to object to being described as a "miserable sinner." Finally, there was one Mr. Maculler, a North Carolinian "fill'd with strange notions," who argued for three hours with William Ormond about vegetarianism, Unitarianism, "and I know not what beside." These laymen, like many others, equated accepting formal systems of religious orthodoxy with surrendering the habits of independence essential to self-mastery. That sentiment sharpened their suspicion that the clergy were a pack of confidence men bent on bilking laymen of both their money and the harder currency of their skepticism. In fact, the fear of being snook-ered gave some white men misgivings about the very core of Christian teaching—the redemptive sacrifice of Jesus. Obadiah Echols recalled struggling for years with his "discomfort" at "the doctrine of one man's being saved by another, and that eternally, and upon such cheap terms too to the party saved."[5]

The South's masters were more reluctant still about disclosing their religious feelings. Even those diverted by a night spent sparring over theo-logical abstractions shied away when preachers tried to steer conversa-tions toward the state of their souls. Yet sooner or later, matters came to that pass, for Baptist and Methodist ministers saw it as their pastoral duty not merely to debate doctrine with the laity but to probe the extent to which the conviction of sinfulness had "disturbed their carnal repose." They exulted over the likes of Jesse Lister, who, to Jeremiah Norman's sat-isfaction, suddenly "seem[ed] engaged to save his soul" and had begun to conduct family prayer. They even took heart, as Norman did, from troubled but confiding souls like Byrd Bowker, who "Tho he has for a long time sought the Lord, he has never professed to have found him yet." But most southern white men were inclined neither to bare their souls nor to express their feelings. Thus Norman described one of his hosts as showing kindness toward preachers, "but I fear not to his own soul"; another "treats me with utmost Hospitality, but it is to be feared he has not that peace that those possess who love God." So unfolds the litany of discouragement, varying little as Norman traveled from Virginia to South Carolina, always taking the measure of his male hosts' spiritual progress and almost always meeting with disappointment. From such experiences he learned that "Close preaching and Enquiry into men's states do not suit some." The same hard lesson was brought home to James Jenkins in the 1790s when he led family prayer at the South Carolina home of a widow whose son-in-law "was so afraid lest the power of God should take hold of him, he kept stirring the fire all the time." Trying a more direct approach at another stop, Jenkins asked his host "if he did not wish to serve God," to which the man retorted that "he did not wish to be questioned on that subject."

Most of those unyielding laymen were not agnostics, let alone atheists. But they were uncomfortable with evangelicals' insistence on introspection and their fervid style of expression. For a homely evocation of their uneasiness, move west to middle Tennessee just after the turn of the century and squeeze into the rude cabin where John Brooks was examining a Methodist class—the "worst scared set of men, you never saw." Turning to one Catron, a German immigrant, he asked, "Well, brother, do you think the Lord for Christ's sake has ever pardoned your sins?" The man replied, in Brooks's rendering of a German accent, "Sometimes I toes [do], and sometimes I toesn't [don't]." Brooks persisted: "Do you ever pray?" And the answer came: "Sometimes I toes, and den [then] I shovels him [Jesus] off again." While this interrogation went forward, another man awaiting his turn shifted in his seat by the fireplace and cast longing glances "towards the door and up the chimney." As Brooks came closer, "examining one or two next to him," the man could bear the agony of impending scrutiny no longer and took the quickest escape: "[H]e sprang to his feet, took up the cabin chimney, mounted his horse bareheaded, and rode five miles home."[6]

Not only the emotional but also the physical intimacy entailed in evangelical fellowship deepened the apprehension of many masters. Touching among male evangelicals took many forms, but all of them departed from the ways in which southern white men usually made bodily contact—shaking hands, slapping backs, and engaging in the bare-fisted, eye-gouging, nose-biting, dirk-wielding brawls that settled scores among plain folk. Gentlemen touched even less: They avenged insults from their inferiors at arm's length by drubbings with canes or whips and resolved affairs of honor among themselves at several paces by dueling with pistols or rifles. By contrast, Baptists and Methodists urged other ways that men might come close. When William Watters came under conviction, his brother knelt beside him, wept, and prayed in "a low, soft voice"; upon hearing of his conversion, "two good friends . . . caught me in their arms." Spiritual catharsis also banished the reserve of Obadiah Echols, who sought out a pious male neighbor and "without ceremony, told him all the truth; he . . . hugged me and spoke many words of comfort." After joining the Baptists, Echols felt "so afresh enamored with the Bible that . . . I actually would hug it to my bosom, and would more willingly have done so to the God of the Bible, if I could have approached Him as a man." But most white southern men did not take readily to such close encounters with other men, their savior not excluded. James Ireland balked when his spiritual mentor, "as we were singing together [at a Baptist gathering] . . . kept his left arm around my waist, and feeling affected at some passages as he sung them, he would hug and press me up to him." Voicing an aversion common among those who held the Baptists at greater distance, Ireland admitted that "I felt ashamed at such effeminancy, as that of one man to be hugging another; and I confess, it stretched my modesty to bear with it."[7]

Wary of the intimacy demanded by evangelical fellowship, many southern men dreaded even more the rigors of conversion, identifying the wrenching experience of repentance with the loss of self-mastery. Hence, one "fine, strong, good-looking young man" who felt the stirrings of remorse at a camp meeting "found no relief until he drew a large pistole out of his pocket, with which he intended to defend himself if any one should offer to speak to him on the subject of religion." Even those men who joined evangelical churches recalled that the onset of conviction filled them with panic over losing self-control. Overcome by emotion at a Kentucky camp meeting, James Finley fled into the woods, where "I strove to rally and man up my courage," but when he returned "a sense of suffocation and blindness seemed to come over me, and I thought I was going to die." Finley refused to give way to his distress, which the preachers present would promptly have identified as a spiritual awakening and some hierophants of a later faith might diagnose as an anxiety attack. The price was too high: "I felt that such an event would have been an everlasting disgrace, and put a final quietus on my boasted manhood and courage."[8]

To be sure, some of Finley's contemporaries found in religious awakenings a reprieve from their culture's rigidly defined gender roles. Those men also found greater satisfaction in church fellowship than in swaggering male camaraderie. That may have been the lure of evangelicalism for Thomas Cleland, whose Kentucky boyhood devoted to hunting, horseracing, and logrolling earned him so formidable a reputation for "hardy endurance and well-known strength," that "I carried the soubriquet of 'Pine Knot' and 'Jackscrew.'" But sustaining that bravado burdened the sensitive young man, always "shy and reserved" with an emotionally remote father, and he finally confided his religious feelings to his mother. Perhaps because he associated spirituality with the feminine side of his nature, Cleland, when describing his conversion, reached for a venerable Christian metaphor, casting himself as the bride of Christ: "I thought, indeed, it was the heavenly bridegroom calling and inviting his poor, feeble and falling one to rise from my low condition, and come away and follow him more entirely." Swooning at the prospect of union with Jesus, Cleland celebrated his outpouring of tender feelings: "My heart was melted! my bosom heaved! my eyes, for the first time, were a fountain of tears. . . . I felt like giving away." Nor did he feel any embarrassment when "my position was discovered by a friend standing near me," a young man who then "took hold on me, and gently drew me beside him, with my head in his lap," where Cleland "continued, weeping, talking, praying."[9]

But many of Cleland's contemporaries could accept neither feelings that they identified as "womanish" nor churches that "unmanned" their members. It hobbled their cause, too, that some early evangelical leaders were notably feminine in their appearance. Thomas Ware admitted that his heart sank at first glimpsing the Methodist bishop Thomas Coke, for "his stature, complexion, and voice, resembled those of a woman rather than those of a man." Some, too, remarked on the "uncommonly long" eyelashes and delicate health of another bishop, Francis Asbury. Indeed, the early Methodist itinerancy seems to have drawn a disproportionate number of consumptives, including the frail George Dougherty, who had also lost an eye to smallpox. That disfigurement, in the view of his colleague James Jenkins, "added interest to all of his public exhibitions," as perhaps did Dougherty's "somewhat effeminate" voice. But most itinerants shunned that sort of notice, some fretting that the rigors of travel and preaching left them so wasted and sickly that they cut a poor figure as men. Beverly Allen, for one, lamented that "my Strength is well near exha[u]sted—my Constitution is very much shat[t]ered. . . . [N]ow I am something like Samson when his hair was lost." Well may the clergy have worried about the impression that effeminate features or shrunken physiques made on the laity, for most southern men were consumed by matters of appearance. So it was all the worse for evangelicals that what most forcibly struck nonbelievers when male friends converted was their outward transformation. "In the name of God, what has happened to you?" exclaimed one of James Ireland's cronies at his first meeting with that new Baptist convert. Another Virginian, Joseph Carson, was just as stunned when his brother, a newly minted Methodist, cropped his long hair. Whether shorn of flowing locks or otherwise stripped of pride's presence, God-humbled converts struck many nonevangelical men as shamefully denuded of masculine dignity.[10]

Small wonder, then, that even the lay brethren feared that showing piety would cause them to lose face among their unchurched fellows. Their horror of appearing supplicant in public settings surfaces in southern men's habitual efforts to conceal—especially from other males—their religious feelings. After Joshua Thomas, a fisherman on Maryland's Eastern Shore, fell under the influence of Methodism, he often felt moved to offer thanks for a good catch, but "I was ashamed to pull off my hat and kneel in the presence of others." He hoped for conversion, yet "I was opposed to having this done . . . at the mourners' bench or altar, in public, where the eyes of so many people would be fixed on me." When repentance overtook the Kentuckian Moses Scott, he "strove to laugh" off attending Baptist gatherings "by saying he came to see what sort of a thing a night meeting was, as he had never yet seen one of them." Even the throes of religious despair did not dispel James Finley's terror of rejoining the young men who had accompanied him to a camp meeting; so he "cautiously avoided them, fearing lest they should discover something the matter with me." Such efforts to hide displays of religious emotion, rare among white southern women, came to men as second nature, arising as their first impulse when swept up by strong feelings. And many men who lost their self-possession by weeping or "falling" at evangelical gatherings made sure never again to so disgrace themselves. That came as a bitter disappointment to the Methodist preacher Jacob Young after an Ohio camp meeting in 1805 at which some men "acted nearly as though the great deep of their hearts was broken up." Young "thought the victory was won," only to discover that most regained their composure and "few of them ever were converted."[11]

The association of evangelical loyalties with unmanly dependence drew added force from the ways that church discipline compromised the authority of male heads of household over their dependents. Every man who joined a Baptist or Methodist fellowship implicitly agreed to curb his authority within the home by submitting to the rule of the church, a court in which his wife, children, and slaves might appeal any master's dictates. Even devout laymen chafed under such constraints, among them a Methodist who, exasperated by his wife's repeated disruption of family prayer, threatened to beat her. When "she dared him to do that, telling him he would be put out of society," he quit the church and carried out his threat, whereupon his wife implored the class leader, "For the Lord's sake take him in again or he will kill me."[12]

To the injury of second-guessing patriarchal authority, evangelical churches added the insult of overseeing the brethren's business dealings and, worse still, barring them from cherished leisure pursuits. Many milieux in which southern masters gathered to haggle and socialize—court and election days, militia training fields and taverns, horse races and cockfights—became uncomfortable settings for the brethren because of their obligation to shun sharp dealing, drinking, fighting, and gambling. Meeting those standards posed more a challenge to men than it did to women, because of the greater frequency with which males did business and found pleasure in the world beyond the household. Itinerants often complained of preaching to audiences of women whenever their appointments coincided with militia musters, court days, or auctions. When those diversions beckoned, even the brethren deserted worship in droves, and many succumbed to the forbidden pastimes in which southerners proved their manliness. Some who strayed got caught and were called before their churches to answer for this misconduct.[13]

White men were not only more likely to be cited for breaches of discipline than any other group of church members, they were also less likely to submit to the public repentance that might restore them to church fellowship. Once "backslidden," they proved hard to reclaim because reinstatement to the church extracted too high a cost in personal honor. For a closer look at manly dignity being upheld in the face of churchly disapproval, meet some of Jeremiah Norman's other hosts, like Mr. Bees, who "altho he has been expelled [from] the society yet he is very kind and perhaps desirous to save his own soul," and Mr. Webster, "tho he is excluded . . . still appears to have great love for us." Although ousted from fellowship, both men admired Methodist teachings and treated Norman, who hoped to restore their membership, with the utmost regard. Yet what loomed as an insurmountable obstacle was their reluctance to humble themselves before the brethren and condemn the pastimes that unchurched men enjoyed with impunity. Another backslider who parried Norman's overtures, one Mr. Wooten, believed that church membership "would make him a happier man," but chafed under "Subordination" to church discipline. Then there was Squire Old, who had cooled toward the Methodists as some had warmed to denouncing "his favorite practice, the

excessive use of spiritous liquors." As Norman's colleague Freeborn Garrettson summed up the case of a similar character, "Surely this man wants
to go to heaven, but in his own way."[14]

What can be deciphered from preachers' inability to reclaim such men
is the reason why many male church members preferred expulsion to
repentance. By bowing to the discipline of the brethren, wayward males
allowed other men to become the masters of their conduct. But by
accepting expulsion, they asserted their independence—and found support from the many men who took pride in having steered clear of evangelicals altogether. Such was the reasoning of a sheriff in one Kentucky
neighborhood, a lapsed Methodist who, as Jacob Young recalled, "would
weep when I preached, treat me kindly when I tarried with him, and
always gave a hearty shake of the hand when I left." But like Norman's lost
souls, the sheriff stoutly refused to renew his membership, because, in
Young's view, "his worldly prospects were good, and he would not give up
all for Christ." Plainly, the "worldly prospects" at stake here meant the
respect of other masters in Wayne County, which, in the sheriff's view,
would have been diminished by his groveling before the Methodist
brethren. Saving face also stoked the feistiness of one John Stevens when
he was hauled before a Baptist church in 1791 for helping his brother to
elope with the preacher's underage daughter; he withdrew from membership, declaring that he would not "hang on" the brethren's judgment of
his conduct.[15]

Taken together, these tableaux of male resistance array the difficulties
that faced the evangelical clergy during the decades surrounding 1800.
Many masters were willing to discuss, some even to debate, theology, but
when preachers tried to probe their souls or to insist on the truth of evangelical creeds, most drew back. Even those who did not recoil from searching inquiries or dogmatic assertions resented the churches' infringements
on their freedom of conduct, both within their households and among
their male peers. At stake for all masters was maintaining their independence, the essence of masculine honor, and when they felt it had been violated, the carapace of their seeming civility toward the clergy cracked. For
the same reason, the humbling regimen of repentance aroused intense
anxieties among white laymen. Even those who converted first experienced conviction as an "unmanning" rite of passage. And those who fell
short of success—or were not even inclined to try—regarded it as a
debasing, if fitting, entry to faiths that demanded submission from mas-

ters. In their view, becoming an evangelical meant being stripped of dignified restraint along with the liberty to think and act for oneself. It was to
embrace the postures of powerlessness appropriate only to women, children, and slaves. For men of honor, this was unthinkable.[16]

For men of God, then, there could be only one course: persuading
other southern white men that becoming evangelical would leave them no
less masculine and masterful. But that was no mean task, and one made
even harder by early Baptist and Methodist practices that compromised
patriarchal authority within the household and endowed women and
young men with spiritual authority in the churches. And what made the
obstacles before preachers even more daunting were two other inconve-
nient legacies from the eighteenth century, both of which had etched in
the minds of many southern masters that real men, men of honor, could
hold no communion with evangelicals.

IT WAS AFFRONT enough that Baptists and Methodists called upon
southern patriarchs to forswear the self-control and liberty that made
every free white man the master of himself and his household. But the
whiff of sheer insolence—and, as time passed, the stench of racial
betrayal—hung over church practices that obliged white men to compete
for spiritual recognition with blacks. That resentment, which mounted
even as the churches strove to beckon slaveholders into fellowship at the
end of the eighteenth century, confirmed many southern laymen in their
opposition to evangelicalism. No matter that most of the clergy were
abandoning their testimony against slavery; many masters still felt threatened by the growing prominence of African-American virtuosos in Baptist and Methodist churches, especially black men.

Like white converts, early black Baptists and Methodists were drawn
disproportionately from the ranks of women, who typically outnumbered
African-American male members by about three to two. But the black
brethren were eligible to hold church offices forbidden to women of both
races—to serve as preachers, deacons, and exhorters. Attaining those
positions conferred on African-American men no rule over white members: Black preachers and deacons were strictly limited to overseeing discipline among other black members. Still, these distinctions betokened the
spiritual and moral authority that some of the black brethren won within
the churches through the exercise of their religious charisma. Then, too,
even though most evangelical worship services were racially segregated,

southern whites still had many opportunities to witness public displays of African-American virtuosity. The entire membership of biracial churches assembled to hear blacks as well as whites recount their experience of conversion, and in the more informal milieux of camp meetings, segregationist etiquette was sometimes honored only in the breach, especially when emotions ran high. In both settings, black men often held the center of attention. At one North Carolina camp meeting in 1802, James Jenkins reported that a male slave electrified both whites and blacks with the power of his extemporaneous prayer. Meanwhile in southern Ohio, Philip Gatch detected the makings of a future preacher in a black youngster whose sudden conviction sparked a revival among Methodists of both races. And in early-nineteenth-century Kentucky, a mulatto Baptist brother broke his habitual silence at church meetings to pour out his distress at a division among white members, who then agreed that they had behaved in a "disorderly" fashion.[17]

Most prominent among African-American adepts were male preachers, both slave and free, who appeared in increasing numbers after the Revolution. While some restricted their ministries to separate black churches or the slave quarters, others spoke before racially mixed gatherings. Like many of his Virginia neighbors in the 1780s, Richard Dozier, a white Baptist blacksmith, regularly attended the sermons of a renowned local slave preacher named Lewis. So "unboundedly popular" was Harry Hosier, known as "Black Harry," who often accompanied Francis Asbury on his travels, that many white Methodists "would rather hear him than the bishops." Indeed, more than one of his darker brethren upstaged the bishop: At a preaching stop in South Carolina in 1789, Asbury admitted that he found "few hearers," because of "a black man's preaching not far distant." And Henry Evans, a free black shoemaker and Methodist preacher, drew so many white listeners to his meetings in Fayetteville, North Carolina, that they crowded African-American congregants out of their church. In a few upper South Baptist churches before 1800, blacks even served as pastors to largely white congregations.[18]

White evangelicals invariably described black preaching as evoking awe and surprise in white audiences. Thus Thomas Haskins dubbed Harry Hosier "a wonder of grace," and James Smith observed a black Baptist preaching "to the wonder and astonishment of whites" in Kentucky. Some African-American preachers claimed the added curiosity of being literate, among them the Virginia slave Lewis, who read part of a chapter from Scripture "to the astonishment of the auditory." Such responses at once bespoke white esteem for individual blacks and disdain for the race as a whole. White clergymen touted black spirituality as a marvel for the same reason that they celebrated the virtuosity of white women and children: the conviction that their natural capacities were so limited that supernatural intervention alone could account for such piety and eloquence.[19]

But that way of explaining away black virtuosity did not instantly commend itself to all whites, even evangelicals. On the contrary, the sheer spiritual force of some African Americans stymied such smooth evasions. Entertain the doubts rising in the mind of Richard Dozier as he listened over the years to the slave preacher Lewis. In 1782, when Lewis exhorted a crowd of four hundred Virginians, Dozier was impressed by "the greatest sen[sibil]ity I ever expected to hear from an E[thiopia]n." It set Dozier to wondering from whence had arisen the power of this particular black man—and questioning, perhaps, whether he might have underestimated the "Eithiopians" as a group. By 1787, he had decided that Lewis's "gift exceeded [that of] many white preachers." With that judgment, by his very willingness to venture such a comparison, Dozier teetered on the brink of the most radical of conclusions, for he now regarded Lewis as a man not merely remarkable among his race but superior to some white men. Yet Dozier subsequently retreated from the trajectory plotted by his own reasoning: Two years later, he duly invoked the standard evangelical formula to account for the extraordinary talent of the black clergy. It surfaced first after he attended the sermon of one Jacob, another "most wonderful" slave preacher, and reflected, "Oh, see God choosing the weak things of this world to confound the things that are mighty." By 1794, when Lewis himself preached at a funeral, Dozier saw only "the power of God" behind the eloquence of "a poor Eithiopian."[20]

If such explanations finally answered at the bar of reason for some white men, they did not offer as much satisfaction within the court of feeling. As much is manifested by the ways that awe alloyed with darker emotions in white men's reactions to black men's virtuosity. Even the saintliest, like Asbury, were troubled to find that their own talents as preachers sometimes came up short compared with those of African Americans. Catch the note of wistful envy struck by one of his novice itinerants, who poured his heart into exhorting a Maryland congregation but then confessed to his diary that "Black Harry [Hosier] who spoke after excited and won the attention and admiration of the audience." For those less than saintly, the burden was heavier still. Hear the false bravado in the mocking laugh of "a poor young backslider" at a class meeting who resented a "black Man [who] began to get happy with Shouting." James Meacham, the preacher in attendance, asked the white youth "if he was not ashamed and told him if it was me I would go out at the dore [door] if I could not behave no better—he gave me a silly look grited and gnashed his Teeth and out he went." Such jealousies also made white men more likely than white women to withhold approval from African-American preachers. When Henry Evans first drew whites to his Methodist church, it was the mistresses of Fayetteville, not the masters, who led the way.[21]

While some of the white brethren gritted their teeth at black virtuosos, a proverbial gnashing resounded from the ranks of nonevangelical masters. At a Tennessee camp meeting in 1816, John Brooks recalled looking on as a "large healthy looking young negro man," stricken by conviction, fell "screaming and wallowing on the ground," whereupon his skeptical master, "a large well dressed and good looking man . . . swore he could raise him, and started toward him with a drawn loaded whip." But when the slave uttered a triumphant shout signaling conversion, his master "seemed unmanned, became very pale and turned away and walked off." True, this encounter could have been either embellished by Brooks, a Methodist preacher, or stage-managed by a resourceful slave trying to ward off a beating. Yet even allowing for white fictions and black feints, it suggests that African-American adepts were even more intimidating to nonevangelical whites precisely because such doubters rejected the view that the deity wrought wonders among Baptists and Methodists. Unlike Richard Dozier, they did not come to accept the reassuring explanation that divine power alone enabled black virtuosos to transcend their "natural inferiority." More readily than white evangelicals, they saw in black religious performances evidence of innate talents all too disturbing in a race that was supposed to be subordinate. It was disturbing to such masters when African Americans, especially their own slaves, suddenly shed poses of submission to reveal potent selves compelling to people of both races. Disturbing, too, were the conclusions that other African Americans might draw from such performances. Surely it did not serve the ends of mastery when blacks, like those in John Taylor's Kentucky neighborhood, "sometimes debate[d] among themselves, which is the greatest preacher, uncle Jack or Vard[i]man [a white Baptist]: they mostly say that uncle Jack is the greatest." And perhaps most disturbing to the South's masters of first rank, the great planters, was that the doubts about racial supremacy to which such contests gave rise might trouble the minds of middling whites, yeoman farmers or artisans like Richard Dozier. It would not do at all, as that elite well knew, if they could no longer enlist the hatreds of race to offset the hatreds of class.[22]

Ironically, what encouraged those subversive comparisons were the very practices among evangelicals that recalled the competitive rituals of the South's secular culture. This point of symmetry is unexpected, because evangelicals touted their churches as havens from the vying for recognition, especially among men, which dominated virtually every other social gathering. They taught that the self was something to be anni-hilated, and pride a sin to be overcome through surrender to the divine will and subordination to church discipline. Of course, in a world where families living on dispersed plantations met infrequently with their neigh-bors, many attended church mainly to see and be seen. On those occa-sions, more than one woman found herself embarrassed by a Methodist preacher who frowned at the gold ring on her finger, and more than one man writhed as the eyes of a Baptist elder froze on his ruffled shirtfront. Such petty contests for notice the churches duly chastised with a rigor dis-proportionate to their innocence—even as they provided plenty of other ways for individuals to jockey for acclaim.[23]

Those subtler forms of competition, all the more intense because they were unacknowledged, involved displays of spiritual virtuosity. As laymen and -women—of both races—prayed and testified, exhorted and sang at evangelical gatherings, onlookers meticulously measured those perform-ances by the criteria of emotive power, scriptural knowledge, and popular response. How ably individuals, black or white, acquitted themselves, determined their standing in local spiritual hierarchies, based not on for-mal authority but on charismatic power, yielding an elusive, ever-shifting pecking order reflecting the collective esteem of the congregation. Even sharper lay eyes and ears were trained on preachers, and sermonizing stood as the real test of a man's mettle, for it required not only the famil-iarity to command the Bible and the eloquence to hold the audience but also, because homilies were always extemporaneous and services stretched on for hours, sheer nerve and physical stamina. What added to the inten-sity of such occasions was that the laity could compare a variety of speakers who took the preaching stand on the same or different occasions.

John Williams captured the edge of competition animating one Virginia Baptist gathering in 1771 as a series of ministers held forth: "Brother Burrus got up immediately and preached . . . set the Christians all afire," followed by "Brother Waller exhorting till he got spent; then Brethren Marshall and E[lijah] Craig both broke loose together, the Christians shouting, and they speaking for the space of half an hour or more." Taxing performances, these—and performances they were—a point that neither eluded nor impressed the New Englander Christiana Holmes Tillson, who concluded, after watching two Methodist preachers in southern Illinois, that their "whole manner evinced . . . arrogance and self-display."

Southerners proved just as unsparing, but they were more likely to complain about the want of pulpit drama than its excess. Among the many lay critics who ranked preachers with the keen interest otherwise reserved for racehorses and hunting dogs was one Benjamin Snelling, a Kentuckian. He dismissed the Baptists outright, for they "knew not how to preach." Somewhat better were the Presbyterians, even though their ablest orator, David Rice, "Chewed tobacco and preached at the same time," a dexterity so suspect that Snelling questioned how "a man could think of two things at once." As for the Methodists, he rated Francis Poythress, a "domineering man" who "Prayed with his eyes open, looking around to keep order," well below Wilson Lee, one of whose sermons Snelling experienced as "so weighty, it fell on my right thigh, and I could scarcely walk for five days." (Whatever Snelling meant by that remark, it surely redounded to the credit of the Methodists.) With a laity so alert, men who faltered in the pulpit paid a terrible price. After one Baptist novice bungled a sermon, "his Brethren were highly and generally wounded—Several attacked him as soon as Meeting was concluded, Some said they wished they had not been there and others wished he never wou'd preach again."[24]

So it was that within every evangelical fellowship of spiritual equals, tacit church consensus made some more equal than others. At the top of those elusive rankings based on the intangible qualities of charisma and godliness were the most renowned virtuosos among the clergy and laity. But unlike every other hierarchy in the early South, this elite of adepts was not restricted to mature white males: It was instead a mixture of old and young, men and women—and blacks and whites. And that peculiarity made Baptist and Methodist churches the only settings in the South in which white men were required to compete for standing not only with white women but also with African Americans. Most directly, of course, the white brethren contended for spiritual stature, if not formal governing authority, with black men. That was not a prospect beguiling to many masters, who recognized that seeking preference within the churches would oblige them to prove, against all comers, a superiority they had until then taken to be, by virtue of age, gender, and race, uncontested.

There was something else, too, that made the competition for spiritual influence within evangelical churches still more disconcerting for the South's masters. It was that early Baptists and Methodists occasionally bestowed on the most gifted black brethren the greatest of all accolades— liberty. In a few late-eighteenth-century churches, white Baptists purchased the freedom of slave preachers, perhaps reasoning that individuals so favored by God should be treated at least as handsomely by their fellow Christians. More commonly, both Baptists and Methodists accorded slave adepts the license to travel as companions to white itinerants. In short, evangelicals rewarded blacks for displaying those attributes which their race was not supposed, by most whites, to possess. Manumitted black preachers and slave itinerants thus embodied the connection between African-American virtuosity and their desire for freedom, one that would find harrowing confirmation when black adepts led slave insurrections during the early nineteenth century.[25]

Here, then, was a dilemma for Baptists and Methodists similar to that presented by charismatic white women. In both instances, masters felt threatened by being placed in direct competition with social subordinates who might prove their spiritual superiors. Yet to deny either white women or blacks the public exercise of their religious talents would sharply diminish the churches' appeal to both groups. Besides, evangelicals would appear ridiculous if they banned displays of charisma among the very groups whose spiritual gifts they had celebrated as proofs of the deity's presence in their midst. So it is not surprising that nineteenth-century clerics pursued much the same strategy to blunt white male resentment of black virtuosos that they had deployed to dispel anxieties aroused by white female adepts: They confirmed southern masters' control over charismatic dependents by sustaining their authority as heads of households, governors of churches, and members of the ruling race.

How evangelicals executed that strategy, as it applied to African Americans, can be traced in several shifts in church practice dating from about

1800. Symptomatic is the increasing severity with which the white Baptist brethren judged the skills of African-American men as preachers. Those who dared to preach or even exhort without leave from white church officers were duly censured, and even those who won official approval were often saddled with exacting restrictions about where they might speak and even which biblical texts they might use. Typical is the watchfulness of the white brethren at North Carolina's Flat River Baptist Church who, following a revival in 1823, scolded three black exhorters for having "taken more liberties than the church allowed them," and summoned them to receive some "instructions." Similar changes took place among the Methodists, who quietly deleted from the editions of their *Discipline* that circulated in the South any mention of rules allowing African-American men to receive ordination as preachers or deacons. That sleight-of-hand did not discourage every aspiring black preacher, including, as James Jenkins recalled, one "influential coloured man, who desired further promotion" among South Carolina Methodists and grew "quite impatient and troublesome." "I have generally found that these people cannot bear promotion," the sympathetic Jenkins jibed, "like too many white people, they become proud." But most of his white colleagues did not relish the joke, and their resistance proved so effective that it was not until 1824 that the Virginian David Payne was ordained as the South's first black Methodist deacon. Increasingly, too, both Methodists and Baptists restricted the ministries of black preachers to the slave community.[26]

White clergymen also sought in their published memoirs to "rehabilitate" some of the earliest African-American preachers by stripping away every vestige of their stubborn dignity. Hence Methodist chroniclers posthumously endowed Henry Evans with a most punctilious deference, "never speaking to a white man but with his hat under his arm; never allowing himself to be seated in their houses; and even confining himself to the kind and manner of dress proper for negroes in general, except his plain black coat in the pulpit." In fact, it was Evans's defiant courage that had first won adherents to Methodism among Fayetteville's slaves; when the town council outlawed his evangelism, he moved his preaching to the surrounding sand hills. Also lauded for his subservience was John Charleson, a "stout, athletic" preacher who aimed to gain freedom by itinerating with his master, Stith Mead. But what white memoirists chose to celebrate was Charleson's deference to Jesse Lee, whom he met by chance at a miry crossroads in Lynchburg, Virginia. Seeing the white preacher's reluctance to muddy his boots, Charleson offered to carry him across the street—no small favor, since Lee tipped the scales at something in excess of 250 pounds. This tale may touch closest to the truth at the point when, in the middle of the street, Charleson is said to have groaned, " 'O wretched man that I am, who shall deliver me from this body of death!' "—that being a common Methodist metaphor for the weight of sin. Although useless for recovering the lives of black preachers, such stories exemplify white clergymen's attempts after 1800 to dispel lay fears of African-American virtuosos. So, too, did their ploy of reaching for familial language to cast spellbinding black preachers as so many "good old uncles." That avuncular persona was a telling choice, because it at once domesticated black male adepts but stopped short of conceding them the closer spiritual consanguinity denoted by the terms "Father" and "Daddy," titles that white preachers reserved for themselves.[27]

Those steps taken to ease the fears aroused by African-American preachers dovetailed with other changes being adopted by white Baptists and Methodists after about 1800. At the same time, the churches were relinquishing their claims to primacy over the natural family, trying to contain the charisma of white women, and curtailing the authority of youthful clergymen. The sum of those efforts affirmed that the evangelical commitment to spiritual equality would not diminish the sway of masters over dependents, churches, and society as a whole. But, as early-nineteenth-century preachers were well aware, witnessing their churches' first decades in the South had left many men dubious about more than the matter of whether evangelicalism would uphold their prerogatives as patriarchs and whites. That history had also imbued masters with a profound mistrust of the Baptist and Methodist stance toward physical aggression—the willingness to meet challenge with force—which figured as both the ultimate guarantee of mastery over subordinates of both races and the essential insignia of masculine identity. Those suspicions first struck root in the period before and during the American Revolution.

THE EARLIEST MODEL of evangelical manhood came to occupy that not insignificant part of their past that later Baptists and Methodists tried to live down. Those embodying that ideal, their first preachers in the South, often departed from the code of conduct prevailing among other white men, differences manifested most dramatically in the clergy's response to persecution. Whether initiated by gentlemen and Anglican parsons or by crowds drawn from the middling and lower ranks of society, such efforts at repression were neither constant nor systematic. Both official and popular harassment of the Baptists was largely confined to the Northern Neck of Virginia during the 1760s and early 1770s, while the Methodists met with the greatest opposition during the Revolution, mainly in Maryland and Delaware. Thereafter, civil persecution ceased. But well into the nineteenth century, both outraged individuals and angry mobs occasionally beset preachers or disrupted worship services. Such attacks occurred throughout the South and its western country, and everywhere, at least until the turn of the century, no matter how great the provocation or how lowly the provocateur, ministers submitted to whatever their tormentors meted out—taunts, threats, and insults, as well as whippings, drenchings, and beatings. While some preachers evaded abuse by talking their way out of trouble or outrunning their pursuers, all took pride in refusing to fight back, even in self-defense.[28]

That took great physical courage, but it was the stoic's ability to endure without yielding to fear or weakness. Among some lay people—women, in particular, because they often commanded the same fortitude—such displays enhanced the clergy's stature by authenticating their apostolic qualities. Daniel Trabue recounted that in 1772 one beleaguered Virginia Baptist preacher, "Mr. Eastern [Augustine Eastin] spoak [spoke] so earnestly and feelingly that this was the persecution that the saviour had foretold of that he got the people . . . to Crying, and some women crying aloud. . . . The people Did cry and pray to the Lord to forgive them as they did not know what they weare [were] a Doing." Yet many white southern men were at once mystified and affronted when preachers refused to display courage in more conventional forms—to return force with force. It was an enigma—and to some, a visceral challenge—that evangelical men fell back on words, or worse, wordless endurance, when subjected to insults for which manly dignity demanded the answer of fists, an aggressive vindication of personal honor.[29]

The very symbolism of attacks on early evangelicals expressed disdain for their unmanliness. Striking a familiar posture of mastery, men mounted on horseback galloped into the midst of assembled worshippers and cantered into rivers where mass baptisms were taking place. Of more obvious significance were other weapons of choice: One Anglican parson kept "running the end of his horse whip in his mouth" throughout one Baptist sermon, a gesture that preceded the preacher being dragged from the pulpit and lashed by another gentleman. And one group of Virginians, dispensing with subtlety altogether, stood on benches outside a jail and urinated into the faces of imprisoned ministers when they attempted to preach. In short, by flaunting the crudest emblems of mastery, all classes of white men sent the message that evangelicals had offended by rejecting the canons of manhood. Indeed, what prompted some physical attacks on both preachers and male converts was the hope of shaming or shocking them into fighting back—a culturally familiar response that might restore them to their right senses and reassure their adversaries. Recall that what William Mead hoped to achieve by inducing his Methodist sons to dance, their brother Mahlon tried to accomplish by provoking a brawl.[30]

Anxieties about the manliness of some evangelicals were mitigated by their participation in the Revolution. Presbyterian virility, never questioned by southerners, was only confirmed by their valor in battle, and for the Baptists, the war came as a godsend. Most proved willing rebels, mainly because they hoped that independence would mean the dismantling of Anglican religious establishments. In more settled parts of the South as well as along the frontier, the Baptists proved their fighting mettle. Men like the preacher James Smith, as one of his neighbors recalled, "Stood up like a brave soldier and encouraged the men well. Would have made a good officer." Even so, there were some Baptists, primarily those among the pacifist Separates, who remained neutral. Perhaps for that reason, the Baptists' ministry to rebel troops was not always welcomed. John Taylor noted that "some of the poor soldiers became much affected under preaching, and were despised by their officers, declaring that my preaching disqualified them from fighting," while "their fellow-soldiers also derided their tears and sorrows."[31]

Methodists aroused far graver misgivings among southerners. An official connection to the Church of England alone weighed against them; as the partisans of the resistance denounced the corruption of all British institutions, Anglican and Methodist clergymen alike came under a cloud of suspicion. That was a stroke of bad luck for John Wesley, the English founder of Methodism, whose tactlessness compounded the misfortune of bad timing. In a pamphlet of 1775, he scolded colonials for resisting Parliament's authority—just as a growing number were coming to regard English rule as tyranny. Not surprisingly, doubts arose about his sincerity when, a year later, he advised American Methodists to embrace neutrality and refuse "from a principle of conscience alone" to fight for either side.

Indeed, southern rebels set down Methodists, both preachers and lay people, as rank "tories" who, while pretending to neutrality, conspired to assist the effete British. Such suspicions were not entirely unfounded. Many itinerants were recent arrivals from England and shared Wesley's partisan views, the most notorious being Martin Rodda, who openly encouraged loyalists in Delaware and Pennsylvania before escaping to England with the aid of slaves. That made America an untenable mission field for most English preachers, all but two of whom had returned to England by 1776. Francis Asbury remained, but prudently went into "retirement" for two years in 1778; left to shift for themselves were a handful of young, mostly American-born preachers and a few thousand lay faithful, white and black, concentrated mainly in Maryland and Delaware.[32]

That tiny, embattled group of believers bore the brunt of partisan backlash. As the fighting dragged on, the rebel gentry of the upper Chesapeake discovered to their chagrin that wartime hardships undermined their authority over small planters and tenant farmers, men whose slim resources made them reluctant to meet mounting demands for manpower and logistical support. Many masters also worried that slaves would seize upon the crisis to escape bondage or foment rebellions. Under those circumstances, rebel partisans came to regard the Methodists, who preached against both fighting and slaveholding, as a lightning rod for the disaffected of both races. From their fears issued a campaign of repression, both civil and popular: rebel magistrates punished lay Methodists who refused conscription with fines and imprisonment; rebel crowds subjected their preachers to curses, beatings, and tar and feathers; rebel militias monitored their religious gatherings.[33]

Like the earlier harassment of the Baptists, opposition to the Methodists often targeted their unmanliness. Accompany the young itinerant Nelson Reed on his circuits in Virginia and Maryland between 1780 and 1781—fat years for the rebels beating back the British offensive in the South, but lean ones for the Methodists. The summer of 1780 brought Reed's first brush with trouble when a group of Continental soldiers impressed his horse. By May of 1781, Reed discovered that many homes at which he had once preached were now closed to him, and when he sought other places to hold worship, one man "fell into a passion and order'd me off his plantation and then swore hard calling me a sorry villain." Reed fell back on the hospitality of Quakers, neutrals and pacifists like himself, but met with deepening hostility from other southern whites. By June, rumors swirled of his impending arrest for refusing to take an oath of loyalty to the state. Mobs stoned the buildings in which he preached, and at one outdoor meeting, some shouted, "I would make a good soldier and that my horse would do to put in the wagon." As the Fourth of July approached, Reed wisely chose to observe that anniversary from his father's farm. While Methodist neutrality grew ever more unpopular as a rebel victory seemed ever more likely, Reed's adversaries also disdained his pacifism, which they regarded as the cowardice of "a sorry villain." That contempt sounded not only in the jeers that he "would make a good soldier" but also in the attempts to impress his horse. By rebel lights, depriving the preacher of his mount served up both practical and poetic retribution, for the horse was his only valuable piece of property, his only means of spreading the Methodist message, and his only emblem of male mastery.[34]

The clergy's image also suffered when women rose to their defense with a fighting spirit singularly lacking among the objects of their solicitude. When a Maryland mob armed with tar and feathers seized Philip Gatch, his supporters were "anxious to fight my way through"; the sisters being "especially resolute . . . dealt out their denunciations against the mob in unmeasured terms." And when a Delaware rebel leader waving a pistol waylaid Freeborn Garrettson, "Several of the women who were with us surprized me; they were in an instant off their horses, and seizing hold of his gun, held it until I passed by." Rebel partisans witnessing such episodes could only have felt confirmed in their contempt for men who let women fight their battles.[35]

In short, the reputation of Methodism took a battering during the war years, and not only because its adherents lacked the foresight to cast their fortunes with the victors. While it was bad enough that the Methodists withheld the fealty to the new republic that came to be called patriotism, it was devastating that their men refused to fight on either side. The refuge of pacifism seemed to most other southern whites either a hypocritical ruse that cloaked pro-British sympathies or, even worse, a warning that the Methodists could not be counted on to defend community and country. Such negative impressions weighed heavily against a group seeking acceptance in a society composed of anxious masters and restive slaves expanding into a frontier filled with scheming Spaniards and nervous Indians within a republic that had barely won its independence from an empire unaccustomed to defeat. Threatened by so many enemies at home and abroad, many southern masters winced at the prospect of living amid more men like the Quakers—passive in their own defense and proud of it.

So it was that, long after the Revolution, many southern whites expected the Methodists to drop their mask, revealing their true character as traitors and cowards. In South Carolina, suspicions of Methodist disloyalty to slaveholding republicanism triggered sporadic mob assaults on itinerants that lasted into the nineteenth century. Meanwhile, in the upper South, mistrust of Methodist allegiances was renewed in the 1790s when the schismatic James O'Kelly charged that the English-born Francis Asbury had betrayed the Revolution by establishing an "unrepublican" form of church government. The slur found a receptive audience among many southern men: One Capt. Anthony Goodwin told James Meacham that "it was fully believed by many (from the conduct and conversation of Mr. O'K[elly]) that the original Methodists could not be any thing else but (in fact) Enemies to the Constitution of the States—." Despite Methodist efforts to dispel those fears by granting the lay brethren a greater role in church discipline, doubts about their political sympathies lingered into the early nineteenth century. During the War of 1812, one Chesapeake neighborhood swarmed with rumors that the itinerant John Early "and a Scotchman (with whom I was not acquainted) had private communication with the British and that I was acting in the capacity of a British agent."[36]

Such suspicions merged with broader misgivings about the manliness of both Methodists and Baptists that persisted into the early nineteenth century. Much of that mistrust focused on their opposition to the leisure pursuits favored by most southern men and often found release in the ridicule of preachers. John Early complained that some North Carolina wags planted a deck of playing cards in the meetinghouse and then spread the word that he "had them in his pocket and had dropped them about the house." On another occasion, as he rode past a group of men preparing for a horse race, "one ludicrous fellow cried out, 'Get Brother Early to ride.' " As common and infinitely more various were jibes aimed at the evangelical disdain for intemperance. The patrons of one South Carolina grog shop took revenge on James Jenkins by chopping his pulpit into splinters while other revelers dubbed whiskey "Jenkins' devil." But by far the most ingenious baiters were those Kentuckians who belonged to Lexington's Free and Easy Club. Writing to his wife in 1808, the local Presbyterian minister, Joshua Lacy Wilson, sputtered with indignation as he described their nightly meetings "to drink and sing songs," and, worse still, "once a week an infamous scoundrel preaches them a sermon or makes a talk that is so termed." But worst of all, the clubmen had listed on their roll as honorary members, "all the respectable religious characters in Lexington," which left Wilson wringing his hands that "a future historian may hand it down to posterity that such and such characters were members of the Free and Easy Club."[37]

Postwar hazing of preachers also reprised the phallic tropes of earlier attacks on the Baptists. Itinerants' horses endured the indignity of having their tails sheared off by mischievous boys; rougher men goaded preachers by flicking whips and flashing knives. One irate fellow, "who supposed that special reference had been made to him in a very severe part" of a sermon, avenged that insult by approaching the offending preacher "and seizing his nose wrung it violently." And when an "infidel" lit up, a cigar may have been more than just a cigar. Jacob Gruber recalled one convivial band of skeptics headed by a "little French doctor" who regularly attended Methodist gatherings "to annoy the people by engaging in controversy with any they could find willing to enter into a discussion." "To show his contempt," the doctor, "with a cigar in his mouth, crowded up close to the altar, near the pulpit . . . and puffed away much to the annoyance of all."[38]

It was at camp meetings, however, that southern white men most dramatically vented their contempt for evangelical manliness. More than any other southern church, the Methodists relied on these large outdoor gatherings, often lasting several days, to attract a mixed multitude. They frequently succeeded all too well: while the pious and the hopeful would turn out in force, many of less conspicuous sanctity showed up too. Prostitutes trolled the outskirts of encampments, soliciting business from both the backslid and the devotedly heathen, who conducted their own sacraments over kegs of whiskey in the surrounding woods. For many, such diversions sufficed, but not those men whom the evangelicals termed "rowdies"—usually young and armed, often drunk, and always spoiling for a fight. Sometimes such fellows were content with a harmless show of irreverence; as John Brooks recalled, when preaching ended at night, "they would get to the altar and one of them would preach and the rest would cry Amen!" But at other times, surging testosterone would be satisfied only by verbal or physical violence—most often directed at preachers. Like all of his colleagues, John Early recorded several episodes similar to this encounter at a North Carolina camp meeting in 1811: "I reproved two young men for some imprudence and one of them drew a knife and a pistol at me and threatened my life."[39]

To be sure, evangelicals in the early national South were not subject to constant harassment. Most white men did not bully and beat preachers; those who did often targeted the Methodists, who were vulnerable because of their reliance on both a youthful clergy and camp meetings. But if evangelicals—and none more adroitly than the Methodist clergy—exaggerated the incidence of their sufferings at the hands of southern men, they did not misjudge the extent of their opposition. Village infidels baited preachers with impunity because of their confidence that men more circumspect shared in the spirit of their challenges, if not the depth of their skepticism. Young rowdies felt free to raise hell at camp meetings because of the contempt for the clergy that their fathers voiced in private. Even children echoed paternal disdain, among them a boy who, as he rode past John Early, shouted, "I'll be damned if you are not a preacher and I never saw a preacher but what was a God damned RASCAL." As Early later learned, this forthcoming lad was the son of one "Col. B.," the likely source of his scion's views. In other words, from the mouths of babes—and a minority of rowdies and freethinkers—issued the misgivings of the more outwardly civil majority. And unmistakably, much of that opposition drew its force from widespread suspicions that many men of God were less than men of honor.[40]

TO DISPEL that devastating impression, early-nineteenth-century clergy, none more energetically than the Methodists, marshaled more than their usual ingenuity. While never ceasing to celebrate their earliest preachers as spiritual kin to the long-suffering apostles, the next generation of ministers left no doubt that they were men cast in another mold. As much is evident from the striking repertoire of their personal narratives—stories first rehearsed from pulpits and at informal religious gatherings around the turn of the century—that later became codified in published memoirs. That devotional lore announces the appearance of a new breed of male evangelical: Its unvarying plot dramatizes the distinctively southern manliness of the ministry, and its insistent theme is that real men could embrace that faith without sacrificing their masculinity. It takes a tough man to make a tender Christian, these stories aver, with preachers' lives exemplifying that novel truth.[41]

And what an astonishing lot they are. For starters, every man among them has sprung from the loins of heroes—some noble sires having soldiered in the Revolution, others against the Indians in the western country, still others crowned by both distinctions. In fact, most clergymen opened their memoirs with detailed accounts of the fierce courage, martial ardor, and fervid patriotism of their fathers and other male relatives. William Capers described his father as "a chivalrous soldier of the Revolution . . . whose ardent patriotism cooled not to the last year of his life. . . . [T]o muster a brigade seemed his highest recreation." Peter Cartwright recalled that his father, freshly mustered out of service in the rebel army and bound for Kentucky, had defended an encampment "with a rifle in one hand and a tomahawk in the other." Not to be outdone, James Finley boasted that all of his maternal uncles fell martyrs to the fight for independence, while his father became a fearless Indian fighter and explorer of the Ohio Valley, "personally acquainted with Col. [Daniel] Boone." Some clergymen even used their memoirs to redress slights to their fathers' reputations. Among them, amazingly, was the pacifist Stith Mead who, obsessed with a slur against his father's military leadership dating back to the Seven Years' War, went to the length of producing testimonials from his father's former subordinates. Setting the record straight affirmed the clergy's loyalty to clan, while rehearsing tales of family valor established their bona fides as men bred to the ways of battle. "So," James Finley nudged his "gentle reader," "you see that I took my birth in the storm of war, and my nursery tales and songs were all of war."[42]

Setting forth their warrior lineage as prologue, preachers went on to claim boyhoods which confirmed that legacy, proof that the same red-blooded impulses surged within them. The youthful dissipations to which the clergy confessed ran the predictable gamut of male passions—swearing and gambling, dancing and drinking, fighting and hunting. But they served up those memories in a spirit suggesting that pride in their skill offset remorse for their misdeeds. The clerical biographer of Benjamin Abbott confided that his subject in youth "was particularly noted for a great fighter; and but few excelled him in divers[e] kinds of vice," while Peter Cartwright disclosed owning a racehorse and a deck of cards. True, squandered youth has been a staple of spiritual autobiography since Augustine, but southern preachers half-boastfully recounted their roistering boyhoods to make a particular point to a specific audience. Tales of youthful hell-raising attested that they had not been puny, sickly, bookish sissies who fled into the church because they could not pass muster in the rough-and-tumble masculine world. No, they had ranked among the best of the good old boys—the wiliest of hunters, the stoutest of fighters, the most agile of dancers and profane of swearers—who, upon conversion, had willingly forsworn their proven skill at such sports to pursue stiffer challenges and higher glory in God's service.[43]

Indeed, the new evangelical man, even while shunning many customary forms of combat and competition, surrendered none of his will to prevail. On the contrary, the early-nineteenth-century clergy identified spreading the gospel as a spiritualized form of aggression, one requiring not only a gambler's nerves and a dancer's endurance but also the cunning of a hunter and the courage of a soldier. Metaphors of the chase came easily to preachers, among them John Taylor, who compared converting one Kentuckian to shooting a buck: "tears began to trickle from [his] eyes, but being willing to hide, as buck generally do, when they received the deadly ball; sitting down he concealed himself." Thomas Cleland also believed that the preacher who triggered his repentance " 'struck the trail' of my experience" and "at length he came right up with me." But more prevalent still—a veritable mantra of evangelical metaphor—were the array of martial images that dominated Baptist and Methodist discourse in the South during the first half of the nineteenth century. Clergymen styled the quest for souls as a military campaign commanded by warrior preachers: The newly repentant had received their "death wounds" and fell "like men slain in battle," while older church members served as "old regulars in the army of Jesus."[44]

Southern evangelicals did not invent the rhetoric of spiritual warfare, even if they ranked among its most lavish borrowers. Such imagery abounded in the books that they read many times over during their lives—both the Old and New Testaments and the writings of John Bunyan—as well as in the hymns they knew by heart. Accordingly, the language of martial combat suffused both their private and public forms of expression. Read over the shoulder of Edward Dromgoole a letter from James Jennings, a Virginia Methodist preacher: "I intend now to fire my Cannon," and with Dromgoole's help, "I really think we would take possession of these lowlands." Eavesdrop as James Finley urges a younger itinerant to preach: "you are a minute man; whet up your old Jerusalem blade and go at it." Listen as John Brooks sulks after preaching to a camp meeting without making a single convert: "I hated to be whipped that way." Finally, regret hearing only James Finley's rendition of his exchange in 1816 with a bemused British army officer who kept a journal describing camp meetings. As the officer understood such gatherings, the pious viewed "the Church [as] an army making an attack on the army of the world. . . . Every meeting was regarded as an engagement with the enemy, and the number of converts were reported as the loss in Diabolus's army." Earnestness having long since estranged him from irony, Finley rejoiced when the officer promised that "he would carry the report which he had written to England, and show his countrymen how Americans conducted a holy war." Alas, no record survives of how he actually reprised camp meetings for an English audience, but his astonishment suggests that a military ethos infused southern evangelical culture to a degree that struck outsiders as extraordinary.[45]

It followed that the prize quarry of preacher-hunters and the prime objectives of preacher-soldiers were those laymen who were elusive, formidable, or both. They were the South's strapping libertines, sneering deists, and strutting soldiers—whose conversions were chronicled in every clergyman's recollections. One of John Taylor's choicer triumphs with Kentuckians of this stripe was "a tall, raw boned giant-looking man" who the preacher at first believed "hated me more than any man of earth." Back in Virginia, Jeremiah Jeter preened himself on overcoming another lord of misrule with the build of an ox and a mind only slightly more elevated. No less keen than the Baptists to recount their humbling of hulking white males, Methodist preachers took special glee in reducing the South's vaunted men of battle to tearful trembling over salvation. Among the most paraded of these trophy-souls who had dodged British bayonets or Indian scalping knives only to be singed by hellfire sermons were a former army general—and brother-in-law of Patrick Henry—and Simon Kenton, second only to Daniel Boone among the heroes of the western country. Although preachers crowed loudest over conquering former officers in the rebel forces, converts of any rank from any army would do. Possibly the ordinary recruit who did best was one of James Finley's reclamations, a veteran of the Napoleonic wars hailing from France, that fabled land of infidelity.[46]

Spiritual talent played a part—but only a part—in preachers' accounts of their triumphs over the flower of southern manhood. Most often it came into play when their sermons brought battle-scarred veterans, scoffing he-men, and smug infidels to quake in fear of the Lord. Such capitulations became staples of southern evangelical lore, retold in scores of recollections like those of Henry Smith, who bragged that some of the roughest drunks on his western Virginia circuit "were absolutely afraid of me, and said 'He has been to the West, where he learned the art of knocking them down.' " Yet preachers sought respect among masters less by calling on religious charisma—which was, after all, the sole resort of white women, youths, and blacks—than by claiming the combative skills prized by most southern men. Indeed, their narratives transformed the model man of God from a willing martyr into a formidable fighter who, when the situation required, fended off opposition with superior physical strength. While the clergy described even their ability to evoke remorse as an act of violent domination—"the art of knocking them down"—more often they boasted of powers that went well beyond forceful eloquence. Alfred Brunson recalled that his imposing physique alone discouraged troublemakers at religious gatherings, while James Finley bragged that when some rowdies menaced a camp meeting in 1816, one of the company reported that, as I was a Kentuckian, I carried a long dirk in my waistcoat, and that I would as soon stab a man as not."[47]

When dangerous reputations did not prove deterrent enough, preachers—at least in the afterglow of memory—commanded no shortage of threats. Joseph Carson recalled warning one obstreperous fellow who refused to leave a class meeting that "if he did not go out, it would be because he was a stronger man than I." Even preacher's wives professed to have heard a lion's heart pounding beneath the frock coats of their spouses, among them John Johnson, memorialized by his loyal Susannah as a man who "I suppose, never felt fear in his life." Taunted by drunken ruffians in southern Illinois who, among other indignities, overturned the family privy, Johnson loaded his musket against future invasions and announced to his wife and children, "I'll defend you." Even some eighteenth-century clergymen, as polished up by later hagiographers, emerge as a fearsome lot. John Travis celebrated his predecessor, Joseph Everett, as a Methodist preacher of "plethoric frame" who once routed a bully by "rolling up his shirt sleeve, and exclaiming at the top of his voice, 'Do you think that God ever made this arm to be whipped by a sinner? No, no!' "[48]

Baptists and Methodists, of course, frowned on fighting. But lest that teaching tempt any to dismiss their threats as empty, southern preachers devised various ways to exempt themselves and the lay brethren from its strictures. Among the more inventive was the Methodist chronicler, Ezekiel Cooper, who recounted a scuffle at Annapolis in which one young layman beat off a preacher's assailants, and then "told them to come again if they chose; that he was not angry, but he fought for God." "What shall we think of this?" Cooper asked, with the air of a man ready with the answer, which was that fighting for God "in good humor" was "an uncommon principle." Many of his colleagues, no less resourceful, extended the same license to come out swinging to those brethren who had not experienced the "second blessing" that made for perfect sinlessness. A popular tale circulated about—of all people—the feeble Francis Asbury threatening rowdies at a camp meeting: "You must remember that all our brothers in the Church are not yet sanctified, and . . . if you get them angry . . . they are the strongest and hardest men to fight and conquer in the world."[49]

If that was so, preachers either abounding in "good humor" or lacking "sanctification" lay heavy on southern soil. The clergy's memoirs overflow with tales of their tangling with the godless, even spoiling for bold challengers to make their day. The Tennessean John Brooks, overhearing one "noted infidel . . . disparage Jesus Christ as a d——d bastard . . . threw him into a large fire and put my right foot on him to hold him there." Elsewhere in the western country, Alfred Brunson displayed his "combative powers" when "a young man went over to the women's side [of a camp meeting] and made a very indecent assault upon a girl," whereupon the preacher "stepped upon the bench between two of the mourners and with one leap cleared them, and at the next step I had the rowdy by the breast, and was running him backwards toward the door." Recalled just as fondly by Peter Cartwright was a camp meeting in the 1820s, at which the assembled rowdies planned an elaborate assault, even electing a "captain" who "called his name Cartwright," and other "subordinate officers" who also "assumed the name of some preacher." After fortifying themselves with drink and clubs, this legion "of the Philistines" mounted their horses and charged the meeting, whereupon Cartwright, the self-styled "captain of the interior," "sprang into the breach; he raised his club, bidding me stand by, or he would knock me down. I cried, 'Crack away!' "[50]

True, Cartwright—or, more likely, the persona he conjured for public consumption—ranked as the most trigger-fisted of his clerical colleagues. Most others, restrained either by their churches' ban on fighting or a greater regard for the truth, found satisfaction enough in recalling their chest-thumping threats. No matter: the point is that all early-nineteenth-century preachers styled themselves as men who would defend both their personal honor and the security of their households and congregations against all comers. It was the Methodists who labored hardest to cast themselves in this image, but the value of such posturing was not lost on the Baptists. Wilson Thompson, for one, spent several pages of his memoir relating how he single-handedly saved his wife and child from a gang of robbers. Beyond that, such devotional literature explicitly positioned the clergy in the company of the most celebrated heroes of the early republic. James Finley's autobiography opens with a rehearsal of his family's record of heroism in the Revolution, followed by a history of Kentucky's earliest explorers, hunters, and Indian fighters, before finally detailing his own exploits as an itinerant. Pious editors took the same tack, one prefacing the memoirs of Jacob Young by declaring: "Biographical sketches have been written of very many of our Revolutionary patriots; and yet, who feels that they are too many? . . . So with regard to those old veterans of the cross. . . . Let their heroism, their devotion, toils, and triumphs be placed on record."[51]

Designed to beguile the male laity, those publications—and the oral tradition from which they were drawn—asserted the congruence between preachers' lives and the prevailing ideals of white southern manhood. True, their narratives admitted of some divergences from worldly norms of masculinity: memoirists described the harrowing of their pride by repentance, the conforming of their intellects to creedal orthodoxies and their conduct to church discipline; they confessed to bouts of weeping, periods of morose introspection, and fondness for sentimental religious poetry and hymns. Even so, preachers insisted that they, too, were masters, men who had lost neither the will nor the skill to dominate and, when necessary, by violent means.

This lore of evangelical manliness seems so patently concocted, so transparently a matter of myth posing as fact. Nor is it hard to imagine that some devout contemporaries, people at least as shrewd as moderns in detecting the subterfuges of oration and print, suppressed knowing smiles when regaled with preachers' yarns of how, with chest hair sprouting and fists swinging, they made swaggering rowdies beg for quarter. After all, most had heard and many uttered the common sally that preachers were "a sort of people between men and women." Such skepticism about the clergy's recollections of their manly prowess was not—and is not—

misplaced. To still the ridicule that they were hormonally challenged, preachers embroidered their pasts into a tapestry of heroic lineages, knockabout youths, and militant ministries. Even so, it would be a mistake to dismiss their tales as sheer fictions. Although the gaudiness of their embellishments beggars belief in the clergy's claims, it was not only the gauzy stuff of wishful thinking but also a skein of lived experience from which preachers spun idealized masculine selves. Those images, for all their exaggeration, reflect actual changes in the ways that Baptist and Methodist clergymen were refashioning their behavior, particularly their conduct among worldlier men.[52]

EVANGELICALS, as pragmatic as they were imaginative, knew that it would take more than telling stories to win over the South's masters. So, during the opening decades of the nineteenth century, preachers reinvented themselves in life as well as in literature. And in the lives of southerners, knowing how to handle oneself as a man and a master was something displayed mainly within the public realm—an individual's esteem among his peers rose and fell by engaging in legal disputes, political contests, military matters, and affairs of honor. To be sure, church sanctions against drink and dueling limited in some measure the clergy's ability to compete, but whenever the chance beckoned, they shaped their behavior to the reigning norms of white southern manhood and showed their skill in wielding the masculine weapons of the lawsuit and the partisan pen, the threat, and even the fist.

Follow preachers into the male-dominated world of the southern courthouse. Before the Revolution, they had appeared most memorably in that setting as defendants charged with unlicensed preaching, breaches of the peace, or even vagrancy. But thereafter, especially in newly settled regions with few churches, courthouses often served as places of preaching open to all religious groups because of their size and central location. And everywhere in the postwar South, law now bound magistrates such as sheriffs and justices of the peace to protect the same preachers they had once prosecuted, most often by keeping order at public religious gatherings. Under those circumstances, former adversaries sometimes became allies, with preachers pointing out troublemakers to civil authorities and even assisting in making arrests.[53]

Beyond enlisting the law on their side, the clergy advertised their expertise in applying its full force. While both Baptists and Methodists still prohibited their members from taking one another to court, they now routinely pressed charges against those who disrupted their worship. Such small victories were sweet, and perhaps sweeter still when they prevailed against adversaries who initiated legal action. After a fracas at a western Virginia camp meeting conducted by Joseph Carson in 1808, one Shon Myers charged him with breach of the Sabbath, alleging that the preacher "collared him and called him a d——d black candidate for Hell." The ensuing trial opened inauspiciously, with the presiding judge delivering "a long tirade against Methodist preachers," but Carson's skill as his own attorney, recounted at immodest length in his journal, won an acquittal, whereupon he threatened to countersue for perjury. And who could now doubt Carson's instinct for the jugular, "for I knew where to find the grand jury, and I had the requisite number of witnesses to prove it [perjury]." Not the hapless Myers, now "scared . . . so bad that he soon left for parts unknown."[54]

As Carson's account suggests, some southern magistrates still regarded preachers as a threat to local peace, mainly because the clergy's highhanded behavior antagonized so many manly fellows like Shon Myers. But the clergy took pains to disabuse civil authorities of their suspicions. To close in on that strategy of conciliation, enter the Virginia camp meeting at which Joseph Carson proved himself as adept at diplomacy as at advocacy. The man seething at his side, a local magistrate, was mortally offended because Carson shot him a stern look for breaching decorum by standing on a bench. "How came you to insult me in the public congregation?" he fumed. Carson tactfully replied that "he [the magistrate] was the one to whom I was looking for protection, that I feared the effect of his example." Then, even more tactfully, Carson hit upon a clever response that would preserve honor on both sides: " 'I ask your pardon, sir,' " he continued, " 'for all I have *said* against you'; thus we parted friends." In every particular, Carson's dealings with the courthouse and its officers epitomizes the style of the new breed of Baptist and Methodist preachers. These were men of God who cultivated cordial relationships with men of law and strove to appear in courthouse settings either as honored speakers addressing worshippers or as litigants smooth-talking their way into favor with judges and juries. Innocent as doves yet wise as serpents, they styled themselves a match for the worldlier men who went to law to defend their rights and liberties.[55]

The political arena, another realm where southern men contended for mastery, also beckoned preachers after the turn of the century. Despite both public sentiment that the clergy ought not to hold public office and constitutional prohibitions in many southern states, some did. Despite the consensus that ministers ought not to declare their political loyalties either in private conversations or from the pulpit, a growing number did. The ideal of preachers remaining aloof from the partisan fray was already being honored in the breach by 1800, when Jeremiah Norman regretted being drawn into a discussion of elections, because "my heart does not feel as solemn as I wish it to do [but] when I am among political men I am apt to dip into politics." Little more than a decade later, John Early suffered from no scruples about either airing his own views or using his influence to sway local elections. Those outspoken ways earned him the enmity of one former North Carolina state senator, who charged that he "had been recently shut out [not returned to office] and said I had been the cause of it by directing my brethren not to vote for him." Unchastened, Early justified his behavior by claiming that the fellow "had not acted with decorum, though a magistrate at a camp meeting in his city." Fears of dividing congregations, alienating members, and distracting attention from religion made other ministers wary, if not disdainful, of dabbling in politics. But in political as in legal circles, many clergymen of Early's generation and the next were moving from the sidelines and contending as more prominent players, ultimately helping to fashion the defenses of both slavery and secession.[56]

No matter what their involvement in partisan contests, all early-nineteenth-century preachers boasted elaborately and often of their loyalty to the new republic. Not unexpectedly, it was the Methodists who outstripped every other church in wrapping themselves in the flag, and never more fulsomely than when challenged by rowdies. At one western camp meeting in 1824, Alfred Brunson reminded one gang of his own service in the War of 1812, defending "this very ground on which we have met, and the homes of some of you, from being overrun by the merciless savages of the forests, and to secure and perpetuate the liberties secured to us by our forefathers." Preachers also hugged the high ground of patriotism to confound their religious competitors—few more deftly, by his own account, than Peter Cartwright. Warned off by a Presbyterian minister from organizing a Methodist church in one neighborhood, the itinerant retorted that "the people were a free people and lived in a free country . . . [and] that my father had fought in the Revolution to gain our

freedom and liberty of conscience." Irked by a Baptist preacher who sermonized against the Methodists, Cartwright threatened to "shoot him
in the back for a tory." And when a Methodist tried to keep Wilson
Thompson from preaching at an old blockhouse in Missouri, he staked
his claim by pointedly rejoining that "The Baptist people have always
proved to be good soldiers in the Revolutionary war; and in all other
wars for independence and liberty, they have proved to be valiant and
trustworthy."[57]

Asserting their fervid nationalism also led preachers to ingratiate themselves with those southern masters to whom the new republic owed its
existence and expansion—the military. At a camp meeting in southern
Illinois, William McKendree, one of the few Methodist itinerants who had
served in the Continental Army, flattered a major in the local militia by
announcing that "We are Americans, and some of us have fought for
our liberty, and have come here to teach men the way to heaven." That
statement "seemed to strike the Major, and he afterward became friendly,
and has remained so ever since." Such tales of wooing militia officers, like
those of joining forces with magistrates, expressed as much about what
the clergy hoped to gain as about what they had actually won. Well into
the nineteenth century, young warrior lords fired up for a fight by guz-
zling whiskey after militia musters often went looking for one at camp
meetings. For their part, Baptists and Methodists still harbored ambivalent feelings toward men of battle, which surfaced both in barbs linking
army life with dissipation and deism and in laments that religious enthusiasm waned whenever the *rage militaire* waxed.[58]

But whatever reservations lingered on both sides, there can be no
mistaking the earnestness with which men of God tried to identify themselves with men of war. Soldiers were everything that many evangelicals,
weighed in the court of popular opinion, were not: men of unimpeachable
repute for action, honor, and patriotism who were pledged to defend
family, neighborhood, and country against the threats embodied by
British soldiers, hostile Indians, and rebellious slaves. No wonder, then,
that southern evangelicals were fixed on aligning their churches with the
male warrior culture. That they did most inventively at camp meetings,
fashioning them into settings where men of martial bent might feel comfortable. Not only were sermons on those occasions redolent of martial
images, but many rituals recalled the regimen of army life. The blowing of
trumpets roused participants at daybreak, often followed by another blast

a few minutes later to signal the beginning of private devotions, sometimes still another to announce the morning meeting for prayer and
preaching, and then a final one at sunset. But darkness did not mark the
end of worship, nor, in some cases, the sounding of the last trumpet. At
one Virginia night meeting in 1818, as Joseph Carson recalled, he stirred a
"spiritless" audience by rekindling the campfires, launching into a hymn
called "Blow ye the trumpet blow," and then leading the congregation "in
a slow march for the altar [by] encircling the camp ground; at intervals
the trumpet was blown, while the chorus of the hymn swelled out in full
power." Carson knew his audience: People rushed from their tents to join
the march, and by the time the procession halted, "the ground was literally strewn with penitents from the starting place to the altar."[59]

Enhancing the martial atmosphere was the strict decorum expected of
all in attendance. Trees ringing encampments bore lists of rules governing
behavior, including the strict separation of the sexes during public worship. To enforce those regulations, preachers did not rely on magistrates
alone but also appointed a "guard" of between five and twenty-five men—
devout, of course, young and beefy besides. Headed by a "chief" or "captain," they patrolled the grounds day and night to prevent mischief and
remand obstinate offenders to civil authorities. Known also as "managers"
or, less grandly, "dog-whippers," these guards wore an insignia in the
form of a printed label attached to their hats or coats identifying their elevated rank. Often, that was, as John Thomas recalled, "the first office
[that] many who are now the oldest and most honored men in the
Church would ever remember to have received . . . [and] in their young
days was regarded as a badge of great distinction." Small wonder, then,
that when George Brown, newly mustered out of the army, attended
his first camp meeting in 1813, he enjoyed "an agreeable survey of the
encampment—so large, regular, and military in its appearance."[60]

If imitating the military was not the sincerest form of evangelicalism
in the early-nineteenth-century South, it was an inspired device for recruiting male converts. Here was a strategy calculated to counter lay suspicions lingering since the Revolution, as well as one admirably designed
to capture the loyalties of two generations of southern white men. Many
among the elder generation were, in fact, men of battle, veterans of either
the Continental Army or local militias, some having fought against the
British in Virginia and the Carolinas, others against Indians on the frontiers of Georgia and Kentucky. Covered with gathering glory as time

passed and each retelling enlarged their exploits, this cohort of veterans and pioneers may have found in camp meetings a spur to memory—a setting recalling their youthful military service with some of the excitement, none of the risk, and a heady dose of filiopietistic plaudits doled out from every preaching stand. But it is likely that evangelicals beamed their militant rhetoric and ritual even more directly at the sons of such men, a generation coming of age during the decades on either side of 1800. Its most senior members had been infants when their fathers rallied against the British, mere children when they routed Indians in the western country. Some of its more junior members had reached fighting age in time to serve in the War of 1812, but only to discover that conflict less gloriously embalmed in living memory than the earlier struggles of their heroic fathers. Among them were men like John Brooks, who joined the army under Andrew Jackson's command in 1812 but fell ill before seeing any action. Even more ignominiously, he was retrieved from camp by his father, first a soldier in the Revolution, later a skirmisher against the Georgia tribes, who now "looked like an old veteran returning home from a heavy battle with his prize." George Brown also came away from the War of 1812 with no tales to match the earlier martial exploits of his male relatives; as an orderly sergeant, he spent several miserable months keeping account books and meeting no peril more life-threatening than army food.

It was for this younger generation, men overawed by paternal heroism but bereft of the same chances to prove themselves, that preachers, often their contemporaries, equated religious struggle with military conflict. George Brown, for one, hoped to see some real action after his conversion to Methodism in 1813, which he described as "entering the service of Christ . . . just one year after I entered the service of my country under General Harrison." John Brooks also fulfilled the thwarted martial ambitions of his youth in his subsequent career as a Methodist preacher, which he summed up at the end of his memoir by proclaiming:

> I have given you the character of the officers and troops of the old army in this country, who broke and carried the enemy's lines. . . . I was in those battles. . . . I saw the treaty and the terms of peace acknowledged and ratified. . . . [A]nd when the war is over and we all meet in the war department to render a just account, you will not be ashamed to hear the commander-in-chief say to the old army officers and troops, you have fought a good fight, you have kept the faith. . . .

The Baptists, too, touted spiritual warfare as a substitute for martial glory. A lifelong civilian, Obadiah Echols still described conquering his fear of the devil by opining that "General Jackson when he left New Orleans, in 1815, never felt more a victor than I did."[61]

It was an ingenious appeal, this message that men might win immortality by something akin to but other than force of arms. It met the conflicting inner needs of an entire generation by paradoxically casting evangelical commitment as a way for young men both to identify with and separate from their fathers. On the one hand, youthful converts marked their new life courses by spurning their birthrights in the form of presents endowed or pursuits prized by their worldly fathers. Like Stith Mead, they renounced balls and gay society or, like Peter Cartwright, sold racehorses and burned playing cards or, like James Finley, put aside hunting rifles and knives. What such gestures symbolized, Jacob Young, the son of a Revolutionary veteran, stated directly after delivering his first sermon: "I thought I was delivered from the snare of the fowler—that I should learn war no more." On the other hand, these same preachers depicted their religious careers as waging war by other means, yielding victories that equaled if not exceeded the triumphs of their fathers. Typically, Young felt himself "pretty well harnessed for battle" after a year of itinerating and shortly thereafter honored his father's Indian-fighting past by naming one of his circuits for "Mad Anthony" Wayne, the hero of the Battle of Fallen Timbers.[62]

This strategy for exploiting the filial anxieties of younger white men decisively shaped the future character of southern evangelicalism. Above all, it lent religious culture in that region a newly pugnacious character, an ethos not only expressed in militant rhetoric and ritual but exemplified in the conduct of the clergy. Even though evangelical lore bloated the clergy's reputation as fighters, the core of truth in those tales is that many sprung to their own defense with physical force. Private diaries dating from the early nineteenth century confirm that preachers sought recognition among the South's masters not only by making themselves over as men to be reckoned with by magistrates, politicians, and militia officers but also by fighting back to maintain their honor.

Join young John Early on his North Carolina circuit in 1808, where he met with trouble from a "great BULLY," one Duke Jeffreys. Understandably, that young gentleman nursed a grudge against the preacher for declaring publicly that his sister, "who was thrown out of a chair in going from a dance not long before that and killed, was gone directly to hell."

Upon learning that Jeffreys meant to settle the score with a "loaded whip" and the aid of a few close friends, Early assured his journal, "I felt unmoved in my mind, knowing no weapon used against me should or would prosper." Once cornered, he coolly informed Jeffreys that if he did not reform, "God would kill him" too. At that, Jeffreys sprang, swinging his whip, which "struck me on the side of the head but did not knock me down." Then Early "caught the whip and pulled it out of his [Jeffreys's] hand and was powerfully tempted to strike him but I thought vengeance belonged to God and perhaps as I had him in my power I might get angry and kill him with the whip." Before his assailant's friends could converge, Early beat a prudent retreat, congratulating himself that God "gave me grace to bear patiently the insults of the devil's gang." But in fact, Early had not submitted passively to attack, and by disarming his adversary, to say nothing of boasting that he could have finished him off, he set himself apart from earlier preachers.[63]

Upholding personal honor was no indifferent matter to Early or to many of his colleagues. Indeed, beyond wishing to be respected as equals among the South's masters, evangelical preachers now aspired to be treated as gentlemen. By 1792, official Methodism endorsed that desire by substituting the *Discipline*'s earlier order to preachers, "Do not affect the gentleman," with a vaguer admonition to "Avoid all affectation." But recognizing the Baptist and Methodist clergy as social equals was not a courtesy that came easily to some elite southern men, Duke Jeffreys among them. When he raised his whip to Early, that gesture conveyed not only outrage but also his considered judgment that the preacher was no gentleman. Had he regarded Early as his peer, he would have challenged him to a duel. For their part, the clergy found defending their status as gentlemen a tricky business. Had Jeffreys challenged him to a duel, Early would have been bound by his faith to refuse, for even though evangelical churches now allowed preachers to strike back in self-defense and even winked at their picking fights with the irreverent, they did not countenance settling affairs of honor in cold blood. It was a taboo that left many feeling marginalized as men of honor, a discomfort betrayed by Peter Cartwright who, when challenged to a duel by one "Major L.," sheepishly joked that his preferred weapon was "cornstalks."[64]

It is tempting to suspect that such uneasiness prodded southern preachers to style their theological debates as dueling by other means. Public disputations on doctrinal points waged by Presbyterians, Baptists, and Methodists became a fixture of religious life everywhere in the new republic, despite complaints that open squabbling demeaned the clergy, confused or angered the laity, and divided neighborhoods. Nevertheless, salvos traded in print won a wide readership, and hours-long exchanges between preachers of rival churches drew large crowds. Doubtless this peculiar taste was fostered by the pious persuasion that it was more blessed to engage in the sober fanaticism of hair-splitting religious contro-versy than the godless lunacy of partisan politics. But southern appetites may also have been whetted by the ritual affinity of contests between preachers and duels between gentlemen.[65]

Note the elaborate protocol of public debates held in 1819 between the Methodist John Johnson and his Baptist adversary, one Vardiman. Famed as a controversialist, Vardiman was traveling throughout Tennessee, declaring his readiness to "sponge out any [Methodist] preacher"; John-son took up the gauntlet. He confronted the Baptist in public meet-ings, proclaimed him a liar, offered to meet him in open debate; the challenge accepted, both men then decided the rules and questions for their encounter. All of these elements—the slight to honor, the charge and countercharge of lying, the challenge to settle scores at a future date ac-cording to mutually agreed forms—were drawn from the etiquette of the duel. The source of these revelations, Susannah Johnson, also helpfully added that on several occasions the cowardly Vardiman, after consenting to parry words with her husband, sneaked out of town before the debate could take place. Certain that honor was at stake in such exchanges, the Methodists were not about to be found wanting; as for the Baptists, they had triumphs of their own to relate.[66]

Such were the strategies by which preachers pursued respect for them-selves and acceptance of their faiths among the South's masters. In their public dealings with magistrates, politicians, and soldiers, the clergy strove to assert their manliness in ways that all southern men could recognize. Beyond that, they fashioned evangelical rituals like debates and camp meetings into occasions for displaying and paying homage to widely cher-ished ideals of masculinity. Baptists and Methodists recognized that their churches could not prevail by rejecting entrenched notions of what made men manly, but hoped that they might succeed by acknowledging the imperative of upholding honor and then providing other means and set-tings for its expression.[67]

That the clergy's efforts met with some success is borne out by the many ways in which southern masters came to return the flattery of imitation. Indeed, one of the more striking features of white southern culture during the middle decades of the nineteenth century is the infusing of some elements of evangelical ritual and rhetoric into secular forms of male sociability. The changing pageantry of southern Freemasonry provides one case in point. That popular fraternal order held evangelicals in hearty contempt during the eighteenth century, while early Baptists and Methodists, knowing the competition when they saw it, despised the Masons as libertines and wastrels and deplored their "clandestine" rites. Yet within a few decades after 1800, southern Masons were routinely inviting Baptist and Methodist clergymen (who now bragged of that distinction) to inaugurate their grandest celebrations with sermons and to preach at the funerals of deceased members. Even more unmistakably, partisan politics came to bear the impress of evangelical rhetoric and ceremony: By the 1840s, if not earlier, campaign rhetoric heralded favored candidates as "redeemers" and "saviours" whose election would ensure the country's "salvation" from rival contenders enthralled to the devil. Political rallies that often lasted for several days not only mimicked camp meetings but were sometimes convened in the same places, and "converts" who pledged their fealty to the party were initiated by mock baptisms and communion services (in which only one of the elements was represented). As for the military, that ultimate embodiment of southern honor, the Confederate Army, saw its encampments become the scenes of mass revivals, often presided over by Methodist preachers who, in a fine irony, outnumbered all other Protestant clergymen among the ranks of military chaplains.[68]

So it came to pass that the world of southern evangelicals converged with that of southern masters. As Baptists and Methodists alike found common ground with worldlier men, the cultures of primal honor and evangelical Christianity interpenetrated, and their distinctiveness, once sharply etched, began to blur. From that meeting there issued a new ideal of evangelical manhood, one distinctly southern at its inception but foreshadowing the "muscular Christianity" later elaborated throughout the United States by Protestant ministers who came to share the conviction that Jesus Christ, for all his charity, held no communion with sissies. Beyond that, the merging of evangelicalism and honor in the South colluded with other circumstances to call forth an unintended consequence. Although meant to spiritualize the culture of honor, the strategy of making evangelicalism appear aggressive and militant lent itself in the wake of a deepening sectional crisis to the spiritualizing of all assertions of southern manliness, militancy, and masterly prerogative. Primed by decades of proving themselves men of honor in recognizably southern ways, Baptists and Methodists rose readily to defend slavery in the 1830s, secession in the 1850s, and the holy cause of upholding both with force of arms in 1861.[69]

EVEN AS THE WAY of the cross intersected with many of the avenues of southern honor, their paths did not join so completely as to become one and the same. Nineteenth-century Baptists and Methodists, although endorsing the view that the will to prevail defined masculinity, still insisted upon the sinfulness of some customary forms for its assertion. Specifically, they hewed to the conviction that drunkenness, brawling, swearing, and gambling—activities long regarded by southern men as conferring respect—were not, in fact, respectable. Indeed, strictures against those male pastimes not only remained in force after 1800 but dominated church disciplinary proceedings.

White men were even more disproportionately represented among those cited for misconduct in the decades after 1800, despite the continuing preponderance of female members. But a steadily decreasing number of the brethren stood accused of doing wrong against household members or kin. Crimes like adultery, bigamy, and desertion, along with the verbal or physical abuse of wives, children, siblings, and slaves—all common male misdeeds often spelled out in humiliating detail by church clerks in the eighteenth century—recede from their records after 1800. Instead, church discipline came to focus, even more intensely than in previous decades, on public misdeeds committed by the brethren while in the company of other men. No doubt many men got drunk and dangerous at home, but most masters who were called upon to answer for tippling, swearing, and fighting had attracted notoriety while indulging in such pleasures in public settings where other men were similarly occupied—in country towns on market and court days, at barbecues during political campaigns, at horse races and shooting contests and militia musters. They were men like the hapless William Morrow, hauled before his church for "acting very much out of character at muster quarrelling with James Commons, giving him the lie, strip[p]ing to fight and it is said using very ill words." It was in such convivial settings that the male church members ran the greatest risk of being detected in their backsliding by their scandalized brethren, who risked less by reporting such misdeeds than did the offenders' wives and other dependents.[70]

Early-nineteenth-century evangelicals thus signaled that their main goal was no longer to dominate the private realm of the household. Now they aimed to reform the public spheres of male camaraderie, even if that goal had to be accomplished one man at a time. The warier churches became of infringing the discretion of patriarchs in ruling their dependents, the more staunchly did they enforce the right to dictate how the same men conducted themselves with other masters. Those shifts in discipline suggest an emerging evangelical consensus that what distinguished the expression of masculinity by the godly brethren from that of men of the world was less their gentle and forbearing behavior as husbands, fathers, and masters than their self-contained deportment among their peers. The willingness of the churches to relax their monitoring of the brethren's private behavior sent the message that evangelical men might rule their households pretty much as they saw fit, running little risk of interference or censure. But it was another matter entirely when those same men entered the society of other, more worldly masters; then, church disciplinary committees exerted their authority as courts of accountability and enforced a code of self-restraint.[71]

Nineteenth-century churches were not so rigid as to mete out summary expulsion to every man who got drunk, profane, and rowdy at male conclaves. In many cases, the churches pronounced themselves "satisfied" either that the charges were false or the transgressors were repentant; in other instances, those who strayed received only a few months' suspension from fellowship. Even among the minority expelled for their misdeeds, some were restored to membership after a decent interval produced a show of contrition. Those outcomes notwithstanding, evangelicals remained unsparing in calling the white brethren to account for their public behavior whenever any report, no matter how vague, impugned their religious profession. There could be no mistaking that the churches had drawn a line defining what they would tolerate from the brethren, and it could be crossed whenever they came into the company of worldlier men. Showing self-mastery in those settings—holding in check the impulses that betrayed other men into excess and violence—had become the litmus test of male evangelical commitment by the early nineteenth century.

In some sense, then, Baptists and Methodists continued to expect that all their male members would conform their behavior to the model of self-restraint embodied by earlier preachers in the South. To be sure, neither preachers nor laymen were bound to endure public abuse from male antagonists: Churches exacted no penalties from a man like Elias Fort, who, when he came upon his brother staring down the barrel of a gun pointed by one Jacob Ison, wrestled the weapon away. If attacked physically or obliged to defend family and church—or, for that matter, race and region—godly men now had license to fight back. But the brethren, in good conscience, could not give way to other forms of anger or aggression; they could not start a fight or join in any other shows of prowess—competitive drinking, shooting, racing, or swearing—calculated to display their conformity to traditionally masculine forms of self-assertion.[72]

What sustained the churches' determination to control how their male members behaved in the company of other masters? Why did evangelicals remain so consistent—indeed, increasingly intransigent—on this particular issue, even as they accommodated the prerogatives of patriarchy on matters of seemingly greater significance? Their long history of swallowing camels—changing their ways to accommodate southern hierarchies of race, age, and gender makes it a matter of wonder that evangelicals should have strained at the seeming gnat of overlooking the brethren's indulgence in convivial pastimes. Surely that strictness hobbled their efforts to attract converts, and just as surely Baptist and Methodist leaders knew as much, since for decades such restraints had inspired lay resentment and ridicule. Even so, on this point the churches stood their ground, leaving historians to wonder why.[73]

Perhaps that enduring vigilance arose, at least in part, from the recognition that the brethren were the most visible representatives of evangelical faiths to the wider world. For that very reason, the churches also feared that their hold on the loyalties of many such men was tenuous. While most white southern women ventured beyond their homes only for occasional church services, quilting bees, or neighborly visits, their menfolk, who traveled more widely and frequently, relied far less on evangelical churches for companionship and diversion. Acutely sensitive to the formidable competition of worldly distractions, the churches responded swiftly with disciplinary actions against carousing brethren, as well as with citations for "nonattendance" even after men missed a few meetings. In other words, nineteenth-century discipline was aimed at tying male converts securely to their religious fellowships by insulating them as much as possible from secular male pastimes.

Yet it is even more likely that the deeper source of their desire to exact a particular kind of conformity from masters was that evangelicals had come to accept the most basic assumption of the code of honor. This is the axiom that the measure of a man is his reputation—the public judgment of his outward performance, particularly his behavior in the company of other masters. Evangelicals, of course, esteemed men who held back from surrendering to impulse in secular public settings, while the ethic of honor elevated those men whose very inability to maintain restraint in the face of open challenge expressed "high-mindedness." That difference about what made for manly dignity was not insignificant. But it should not obscure the truth that what had come to matter most to men of God was what had always mattered most to men of honor: vindicating their mastery within the public sphere.[74]

Epilogue

EVANGELICALS, southern and otherwise, the quick and the dead, have attracted uncommon attention from scholars and journalists in recent decades. Much of that fascination is owing to the resurgence of their churches in the latter half of the twentieth century, a movement of such scope and force that even the most secular of humanists have taken to reckoning with evangelicals to understand American culture, past and present.

Within academic circles, many of those most intrigued are not historians of particular churches or even, strictly speaking, specialists in American religion, but rather students of society and politics in the early national period. What spurs their curiosity is a growing appreciation of how profoundly the new American republic was being transformed as a burgeoning national market economy and a widening gulf between rich and poor, the surge of white settlement westward and the democratization of politics, swelled into a veritable tsunami of social change. In the midst of these upheavals, Baptists and Methodists drew converts in growing numbers everywhere in the new republic, so it is reasonable to suspect that what happened within those churches might provide some clues about how many Americans were responding to the other forces reshaping their lives.

But little agreement has emerged among scholars about either how best to characterize the Baptists and Methodists or how to explain what drew men and women to their ranks. Some historians portray these evangelicals (along with other groups like the Mormons) as liberating insurgents who democratized Christianity by imbuing Protestantism with a populist ethos. The religious culture that they created—described as liberal, individualistic, and optimistic—is said to have embodied the values of ordinary citizens and meshed perfectly with a newly mobile, competitive, market-oriented society. But other historians offer an entirely different perspective. While acknowledging that the Baptists and Methodists excelled at making Christian teachings and ritual more accessible to ordinary people, they contend that both groups otherwise preached and practiced the most limited kind of democracy, one that affirmed the equality of white men while demanding the subordination of African Americans and white women and children. These churches, in their view, reflected the ideals and anxieties of those who ruled them—male heads of modest households who, far from meeting the future with hope, feared the advance of a liberal, capitalist social order which they saw as undermining economic equality and so threatening their independence and authority as patriarchs. In short, probing the past has yielded sharply divergent conclusions about the character of both "popular evangelicalism" and "the people" in the early republic.[1]

When historical inquiries approach this point of sharp polarization, they usually generate more heat than light. So the moment may have arrived to emphasize that evangelicalism has never been a static, monolithic structure of belief and that its adherents have never been an undifferentiated mass. As much is borne out by the experience of Baptists and Methodists in the early South and its western country, which also happen to have been the regions where most members of those churches lived until as late as the 1830s. In that place and time, change was the only constant in the experience of both churches, which substantially altered both their teachings and their ritual practice to cultivate support among the widest possible constituency. In their late-eighteenth-century incarnation, such evangelical fellowships indeed did hold forth to southern society's most subordinated groups—the poor, the young, the female, the black—the prospect of greater freedom and fulfillment. On the other hand, during the early nineteenth century the same churches retreated from those promises of liberation and invested their energies in upholding the equality and honor of all white men. Then, too, the member-ship of evangelical churches defies any easy classification. Women usually predominated, but after about 1800 they were an increasingly silent majority. African Americans began to join biracial churches in larger numbers in the wake of the Revolution, but as whites pushed them to the margins of fellowship, black members organized to conduct their worship apart. And among white patriarchs, men of more than modest means were seeking communion with the Baptists and Methodists in ever-growing numbers by the 1790s.

The very diversity of this body of believers makes it difficult to gen-eralize about their attitudes and values, let alone to categorize them as either uniformly liberal and individualistic or conservative and nostalgic. And the range of concerns and objections that kept many men and women outside of those churches only reinforces the conclusion that a richly varied popular culture flourished in the early South. Both within and without the evangelical fold were some so steeped in nearly medieval convictions about the supernatural that they feared a literal devil who preyed upon human beings, while others relegated Satan to the realm of allegory. Some were so beguiled by the prospect of spiritual self-expression that they sought out evangelical fellowships to free themselves from the pressure of family obligations, while others resented any loyalty that claimed priority over the traditional bonds of blood. Some celebrated "boy preachers" as young gifts while others, more insistent on the time-honored prerogatives of age, thought them downright impudent. Some women embraced, even insisted on, a public role in religious life, while others held back. Some husbands and fathers anxiously asserted the most rigid patriarchal prerogatives, taking it upon themselves to dictate even the religious loyalties of their dependents, while others strove to assert their mastery more subtly.

It fell to the lot of leading Baptists and Methodists in the early-nineteenth-century South to reckon with the disparate beliefs and ideals, the hopes and fears, of both the souls they had claimed and hoped to hold and those they still strove to win. But those who chiefly set the future direction of their churches were not a cross-section of members; on the contrary, they were a minority composed of clergy and laity who claimed that privilege by virtue of being white male heads of household. They were the ones who decided that the ultimate success of evangelicalism in the South lay in appealing to those who confined the devil to hell, esteemed maturity more than youth, put family before religious fellowship, upheld the superiority of white over black and of men over women, and prized their honor above all else. Even so, the extent to which they could recast evangelicalism in their own image was limited by the many ways in which it had earlier, for a time at least, empowered the most dependent members of society by taking their religious views seriously and allowing their voices to be heard in the churches. Both groups—church leaders and ordinary laypeople—left their impress upon evangelicalism, and that influence endures still, in the South and elsewhere.

EVANGELICALISM'S COMPLEX beginnings in the early South would probably claim the curiosity of only a small circle of historians were it not for the fact that this legacy now shapes the character of conservative Protestant churches in every region of the United States. Its influence is evident among large denominations like the Baptists, smaller Pentecostal groups like the Assembly of God, and a rapidly growing number of "independent" congregations. So the chroniclers of contemporary American religious life—scholars and journalists whose close observations have yielded telling political commentary and cultural criticism—may find that even more might be told by recognizing the many ways that evangelicalism's distant southern past persists into the present everywhere in America.[2]

Perhaps the most direct approach to appreciating the power of this southern heritage is to look in on one community of the faithful—a suburban Baptist church located between Philadelphia and Baltimore that pretty much typifies today's evangelical mainstream. Every Sunday morning two worship services draw big audiences composed largely of middle-class families; whites predominate, but there is a sprinkling of African Americans and Asian-Americans. The lay people contribute handsomely to the maintenance of an impressive church edifice and to the construction of an ever-expanding number of smaller buildings for offices and classrooms. They also support a pastor and three other full-time ministers, all male, white, middle-aged, and married, whose sermons start from the assumption that the Bible is the revealed word of God and end by urging sinners to accept Jesus Christ as their savior. Aside from unbelief, the sins most commonly condemned from the pulpit are adultery, drunkenness, and neglect of family and church. Preachers also routinely allude to the evils of abortion and homosexuality, but forbear elaborating their objections to such practices. What prompts such reticence is both the desire to shield young children in the congregation and to avoid offending those adults who hold differing views on these controversial matters or who oppose any mixing of religion and politics.

No mention is made of a Christian's responsibility to seek social justice for the less fortunate, except on those rare Sundays when local African-American clergymen are invited to deliver the sermon. Even on these occasions, black preachers raise the issue of racism mainly to reassure whites in the congregation that all has been forgiven and forgotten in the name of their common Christianity, at which the collective sense of relief is almost palpable—though short-lived. For black ministers immediately turn to calling upon the guilty to repent of the more familiar litany of moral lapses with a driving eloquence and stark emotional force to which their white colleagues never resort. Such verbal pyrotechnics probably lie outside the scope of some white preachers, but all, in any event, studiously disdain such tactics, favoring instead low-key, genial homilies that interlace biblical references with humorous anecdotes and moral bromides. At the root of their resistance is less that they regard this tradition of fiery oratory as alien, a performance art peculiar to African Americans, but that it is all too familiar a fixture from the white evangelical past to have fallen from memory: they associate that pulpit style with darker days in the 1920s when all evangelicals had sunk so low in public esteem that H. L. Mencken could, with gleeful impunity, lampoon the entire South as "a cesspool of Baptists, a miasma of Methodism, snake charmers . . . and syphilitic evangelists." Nor is the caution of white preachers on this score misplaced, for African-American preachers elicit enthusiastic responses mainly from other black members of the congregation, while many whites register a mixture of confusion, amusement, and, above all, discomfort.

To observe these reactions among whites is to recall the dynamics of biracial gatherings of southerners being sermonized by black preachers two centuries earlier, and the same holds true in other matters as well. The devil is still raised both to awaken lay interest and to compel lay wariness: in a recent sermon blasting adultery, the pastor informed the congregation that Satan was "present" at every wedding ceremony, lying in wait to tempt the new husband and wife to betray their vows. A compelling image of a stalking Lucifer, to be sure, but still a demon many shades removed from the horrific Prince of Darkness of the contemporary evangelical fringe, who demands that his followers pay homage by molesting their own children. Indeed, the preferred demon of most conservative Protestants today—an active yet comfortably vague presence—is the same sort of Satan settled on by nineteenth-century southern evangelical preachers.

Those departed clerical spirits would take equal satisfaction from the ways in which this church, like many other evangelical congregations, cultivates the spiritual talents of the young. Every week features a variety of activities ranging from Sunday school classes and missionary societies to volleyball games and slumber parties. That mixture of what preachers dub "fun and discipleship" at once heightens the intensity of adolescent piety and contains its force: young people are encouraged to regard themselves as a vital constituency within the church, but their influence is restricted to a sphere set apart from that of adult believers. No matter how zealous or eloquent, even older adolescents are schooled to regard themselves as fledgling Christians; they may jockey for spiritual leadership among their peers, but only after entering adulthood—and serving an apprenticeship in their twenties and thirties as "youth ministers"—will they assume any authority within the church as a whole.

Attainment of the highest positions of spiritual leadership requires not only being mature—nearly middle-aged—but also being male and married with children. Women, no matter how gifted or devout, are barred from entering the clergy; neither are they permitted to preach, to pray, or to read from the Bible during Sunday worship, nor even to serve as ushers. Yet laywomen do enjoy some public presence in the church—spheres of activity in which their participation is not only accepted but applauded. They are featured soloists in the choir, leaders of youth groups and Sunday school classes, organizers of campaigns to ban abortion and allow prayer into the public schools, and, perhaps most remarkably, members of missionary teams dispatched abroad.

In all these ways, evangelicalism in contemporary America hews to the shape it had assumed in the South by the mid-nineteenth century. But even more striking are the ways in which social changes unfolding over the latter half of the twentieth century have encouraged evangelicals to reclaim territory they were long ago obliged to cede. Particularly notable in this regard is the oddly ambiguous relationship between the church and the family. For all the vigor with which conservative Protestant congregations assert their aim of defending "the family," many encourage their members to participate in a consuming regimen of activities that draw them away from the domestic circle and into the church, where they culti-

vate intimacies mainly with fellow believers of the same age, and sometimes the same gender and marital status. For example, the suburban
Baptist church's Sunday bulletins boast schedules packed with church-
sponsored doings on every weeknight and throughout the weekend: a bat-
tery of choir rehearsals, prayer meetings, Bible study groups, home and
foreign missionary endeavors, and social events for single adults and adolescents. Since the number of such gatherings has multiplied largely at the
behest of adult church members, evangelical leaders can justly claim that
their purpose is not to supplant the family but to save it. Such functions
are said to sustain pressured two-career couples and beleaguered single
parents by creating opportunities for all adults to grow spiritually, by
affording occasions for single, divorced, and widowed people to meet new
partners, and by offering parents both support in the moral nurture of
children and many chances simply to get them out of the house in order
to enjoy some peace and privacy. But it can as justly be said that the family
members caught up in this swirl of activities see a good deal less of one
another as a result. Beyond that, it restores to the church an extraordinary
influence over the upbringing of children, as well as over the friendships,
romantic partnerships, and spousal relationships of adults. And it does so
far more subtly and effectively than the earlier evangelical expedients of an
intrusive church discipline and strict prohibitions against marrying outside of the faith.

Equally intriguing is the rising national prominence of "Promise
Keepers," an organization that encourages husbands and fathers to re-
assert moral authority and spiritual leadership in their families. When the
aforementioned suburban Baptist church founded a chapter, the pastor
took pains to deny that Promise Keepers endorsed, as he put it, a "me
Tarzan, you Jane" model of marriage. Even so, the group's guiding
assumption is that Christianity calls upon men to be patriarchs and that
dominance of the household is their natural prerogative. At one level,
Promise Keepers is only the latest in a long series of evangelical efforts
since the early nineteenth century to position their churches as mainstays
of patriarchal authority. But in fact, this group has a considerably broader
cultural agenda and one that, oddly enough, harkens back to the goals of
the first southern evangelicals. Indeed, it aims at nothing less than restoring to the churches a role in regulating the behavior of men within
their own households: the purpose of the round of prayer breakfasts and
other private meetings run by individual chapters is to monitor and guide

men's conduct toward their wives and children. Even more ambitiously, the national organization strives to remodel the ideal of masculinity itself. According to its teachings, not only do real men assume an authoritative religious presence in the home, but they also express their tender feelings freely—most freely, it would appear, toward their fellow Promise Keepers. Tens of thousands have been openly weeping and embracing at mass rallies throughout the United States, duly assured that such displays will in no way endanger their manliness. Those assurances come from the group's founder, a former collegiate football coach as renowned for his opposition to homosexuality as for his mastery of the gridiron, and from a regional leadership whose ranks include a number of military officers.[3]

If the shades of Peter Cartwright and his colleagues hover over such spectacles, they are doubtless murmuring "Amen"—but must also be agog with wonder at what their descendants now dare. Indeed, there can be no more eloquent testimony to the confidence of contemporary evangelicals than their recolonizing of cultural terrain so long ago relinquished. Both in their readiness for the church to subsume the family and in their efforts to remodel masculinity, those now shaping the evangelical future are less the heirs of accommodating nineteenth-century preachers like Cartwright than of earlier, more uncompromising figures like Stith Mead. Like all their predecessors, evangelical leaders in the late twentieth century seek acceptance and power by insisting that the authentic voice of "the people" finds utterance in the language of Canaan—as spoken in their accent—articulating their deepest desires, values, and aspirations. But, in many respects, today's evangelicals strive to keep the faith especially with those who first introduced southerners to the way of the cross, their common ground being the resolve to recast the very cultures that they claim to represent. And they do so, as the next millennium approaches, with more imposing resources and even greater ingenuity than in any other period of American history.

Appendix

My aim in counting southern church members and churchgoers, white and black, is to offer something a shade more precise than mere impression in answer to some important questions. What was the relative success of different churches in that region over time, measured strictly in terms of acquiring members? What proportion of the South's total population, both white and black, was drawn toward evangelical Christianity between 1750 and the 1830s? How rapidly did the three leading evangelical churches claim converts, or at least an attentive audience, among white and black southerners?

Answering those questions is difficult, in part, because evangelical affinities were not neatly circumscribed by denominational boundaries. While all Methodists and nearly all Baptists were evangelicals, some southern Presbyterians—a minority, but there is no way of knowing how small—were not. The larger obstacle is the nature of the evidence on church membership in the eighteenth and early nineteenth centuries. It is often fragmentary, especially for the Presbyterians and small sectarian groups like the Moravians and other German pietists. When it is fuller, as in the case of the Baptists and Methodists, numbers were often padded by clergymen eager to claim success for their ministries and churches. Trying to determine the representation, to say nothing of its significance, of African Americans among the membership of Protestant churches affords even more exquisite frustrations.[1]

ESTIMATING CHURCH MEMBERSHIP, 1750–76

Table I: Southern Congregations at 1750 and 1776

	1750		1776	
	N	% of total	% of total	N
Anglican	188	54.8	27.3	304
Baptist	27	7.9	22.0	244
Methodist	0		3.4	38
Presbyterian*	76	22.2	24.0	268
Quaker	**		10.0	111
German Reformed	15	4.4	3.7	40
Lutheran	19	5.5	4.3	48
Roman Catholic	16	4.7	3.5	39
Dunker	*		0.7	8
Moravian	*		0.6	7
Dutch Reformed	0		0.2	3
Mennonite	*		0.2	3
French Reformed	2	0.5	0.1	2
TOTAL	343	100.0	100.0	1,118

*Includes Congregationalist
**No data available

SOURCES: Edwin S. Gaustad, *Historical Atlas of Religion in America* (New York, 1962), 157; Roger Finke and Rodney Starke, "American Religion in 1776: A Statistical Portrait," *Sociological Analysis* 49 (1988): 47.

Throughout the period before 1790, figures for church membership exist only for the Congregationalists and Methodists, and the Methodists alone distinguished between white and black members, but only beginning in the 1780s. The best sources to gain some sense of the relative strength of other denominations are estimates of the total number of congregations claimed by each religious group in the colonies for 1750 and 1776.[2]

To convert the total number of congregations into an estimate of white church members for the Baptists, Presbyterians, and Methodists, the South's major evangelical denominations on the eve of the American Revolution, I first assumed that African Americans constituted a statistically insignificant percentage of those total memberships, an assumption borne out by the tiny number of black members listed in the records of individual congregations. Then I used the following formula to arrive at estimates of church membership for the Presbyterians and Baptists in 1776: Patricia Bonomi and Peter Eisenstadt suggest that the average eighteenth-century congregation included 80 families; using a multiplier of 6—the median size of white southern households in the late eighteenth century—yields an average total of 480 men, women, and children in each congregation. Multiplying 480 by the total number of congregations for each denomination yields, in turn, the total number of men, women, and children under sixteen who worshipped regularly in all congregations of each religious group. To arrive at an estimate of church members, I used the statistics of a Baptist historian writing in the eighteenth century, Morgan Edwards, whose work on North Carolina Baptist congregations in 1772 indicates that 12.8 percent of all regular worshippers (men, women, and children under sixteen) were church members—or an average of 61 members in a congregation of 480.[3]

Table II: White Membership in Major Southern
Evangelical Churches, 1776

Methodists	4,921*
Baptists	14,991
Presbyterians	16,466

*Information from Minutes of the Annual Conferences of the Methodist Episcopal Church, 1773–1839, 2 vols. (New York, 1840).

ESTIMATING EVANGELICAL CHURCH MEMBERSHIP IN 1790

In 1790, the Baptist historian John Asplund traveled throughout the United States taking a census of membership in all Baptist churches. The Methodists continued to publish a precise annual accounting of their membership, both white and black. Assessing the strength of Presbyterianism in the South is more difficult; Edwin Gaustad estimates a total membership for the entire United States in 1789 at something in excess of 20,000—well in excess of that figure, in my judgment. I have estimated about 20,000 in the South alone, virtually all of whom were white.[4]

It should be emphasized here that African-American membership in evangelical churches in 1790 is especially difficult to gauge. While the annual reports of the Methodists listed white and black members separately, Asplund was less obliging, providing only a figure combining both. Some sense of the proportion of black members within Baptist congregations in different parts of the South can be extrapolated from the records of local congregations, and based on such evidence I estimate that about 10 percent of all southern Baptists in 1790 were black. What this statistical sleight-of-hand does not assess is the extent to which Christianity genuinely appealed to African Americans. There is considerable evidence in literary sources to suggest that many slaves applied for church membership solely at the behest of newly pious masters and mistresses, but other evidence suggests that some slaves were prevented from applying for church membership by pressure from their owners.

Table III: White and Black Membership in the Major Southern* Evangelical Churches, 1790

	White	Black
Methodists	31,817	8,640
Baptists	36,480	4,012
Presbyterians	20,000	–

*The South includes Delaware, Maryland, Virginia, North and South Carolina, Georgia, Kentucky, and Tennessee.

SOURCES: John Asplund, *The Annual Register of the Baptist Denomination in North America; to the First of November 1790* (Richmond, 1792); *Minutes of the Annual Conferences of the Methodist Episcopal Church, 1773–1839.*

ESTIMATING EVANGELICAL CHURCH MEMBERSHIP, 1813

The enumeration of Baptists in Table IV, drawn from the work of David Benedict, an early church historian, seems reliable, but the total number of Methodists may fall short by several thousand, mainly because of a schism in the 1790s that formed the Republican Methodist Church, virtually all of whose members lived in the South and its western country. The figures for the Presbyterians, again a conjecture, are based on considerable literary evidence attesting that they grew at a far slower rate over this period than either Baptists or Methodists. In part, their declining presence among southerners can be attributed to church schisms that drew off members into other religious groups like the Methodists, the Shakers, and even smaller splinter groups. My figure for black southern Baptists is also an estimate, based on an extrapolation from records of individual congregations, that the Baptists, like the Methodists in 1813, drew about 20 percent of their members from among African Americans.

Table IV: White and Black Membership in the Major Southern* Churches, 1813

	White	Black
Methodists	107,411	30,223
Baptists	90,844	22,710
Presbyterians	40,000	–

*The South includes Delaware, Virginia, District of Columbia, Maryland, North and South Carolina, Georgia, Kentucky, Tennessee, and Mississippi, as well as Ohio and Indiana because of the large number of southerners settled there.

SOURCES: David Benedict, *A General History of the Baptist Denomination in America and Other Parts of the World,* 2 vols. (Boston, 1813); *Minutes of the Annual Conferences of the Methodist Episcopal Church, 1773–1839.*

ESTIMATING EVANGELICAL CHURCH MEMBERSHIP, 1834–36

These years mark the first time that counts of members exist for all three of the leading evangelical churches in the South. I relied on records from the three different denominations compiled by John Hayward in 1836. The figures for the Methodists may underrepresent their strength somewhat, for in the 1820s they suffered a second schism that formed the "Methodist Protestants," who lived mainly in the Mid-Atlantic and the South. The Baptist figure could be slightly larger as well, since Hayward did not include some of the smaller Baptist sects in his count. On the other hand, the figures for the Presbyterians are for once fairly complete, including both members in the main body of the Presbyterian Church and splinter groups existing mainly in the South (i.e., the Covenanters, Associate Reformed, and Cumberland Presbyterians). My guess is that the higher growth rates registered by Presbyterians between 1790 and 1813 reflect the highly successful evangelizing in the western country conducted by the splinter church known as the Cumberland Presbyterians; these churches closely resembled those of the Methodists, and their proselytizing ranged beyond Scots-Irish settlements. My figure for the total number of southern black Baptists is an estimate, based on the assumption that African Americans made up about one-fifth of the Baptists' total membership, as they did for the Methodists (18 percent) in this period.

Table V: White and Black Membership in the Major Southern* Evangelical Churches, 1834–36

	White	Black
Methodists	329,177	72,898
Baptists	232,113	58,028
Presbyterians	160,784	–

*The South includes Delaware, Maryland, District of Columbia, Virginia, North and South Carolina, Georgia, Kentucky, Tennessee, Alabama, Mississippi, and Missouri, as well as the western country settled principally by southerners—Ohio, Indiana, and Illinois.

SOURCES: John Hayward, *The Religious Creeds and Statistics . . .* (Boston, 1836); *Minutes of the Annual Conferences of the Methodist Episcopal Church, 1773-1839.*

MEMBERSHIP IN EVANGELICAL CHURCHES PROPORTIONATE TO TOTAL WHITE AND BLACK POPULATION IN THE SOUTH, 1776–1835

To understand the progress of evangelicalism in the South, it must be ascertained not only how successfully the major churches competed among themselves, but how they fared within the population at large. In other words, it is necessary to arrive at some estimate of membership in the major evangelical Protestant denominations among the entire adult population, both white and black. To calculate the percentage of evangelical church members within the white population, I divided the total number of white and black members in the three major evangelical denominations by the total white and black population sixteen and over. (My assumption, based on literary evidence, is that few children under the age of sixteen either applied for or were admitted to church membership.) This approach excludes smaller evangelical groups, mainly German pietist sects like the Moravians, but their numbers were not statistically significant in the period under study.

Table VI: Percentage of White and Black Southern Population, 16 and Over, Who Held Membership in the Methodist, Baptist, or Presbyterian Church

	White	Black
1776	9.0	–
1790	14.4	3.7
1813	17.0	8.3
1835	25.6	11.4

THE PROBLEMS AND POSSIBILITIES OF "ADHERENCE"

Church membership provides only the narrowest measure of evangelical influence in the South. There were some men and women who worshipped in a particular church all of their lives but never sought membership, either because they felt unworthy of such a distinction, unequal to that obligation, or unwilling to accept all of the teachings of a particular fellowship. Others shifted their attendance from one church to another over the course of weeks, months, even years, decisions usually based on how easily they could reach places of worship or how well they liked different preachers. For all of those reasons, public worship in most churches always drew many more congregants than church members, a group that historians refer to as "adherents."[5]

According to contemporary accounts, Baptist adult adherents outnumbered members by about three to one. The ratio may have been the same or lower for the Presbyterians: Like the Baptists, most of their churches restricted membership to those who could give an account of their conversion, but with the exception of the Cumberland Presbyterians, they did not proselytize as widely as the Baptists. Most likely, the Methodists had a lower ratio of adherents to members because those seeking admission to their churches were not obliged to meet standards as stringent as those of the Baptists. So my ballpark guess would be two adherents for every member among the Methodists. Based on those calculations and hunches, the percentages in Table VII may provide some measure of how many southerners had regular contact with evangelical preaching.[6]

Table VII: Percentage of White and Black Adult Adherents to Southern Evangelical Churches

	White	Black
1776	25.8	–
1790	38.0	8.6
1813	43.3	20.3
1835	65.8	28.0

BAPTIST AND METHODIST STRENGTH IN THE SOUTH, 1790–1835

Despite the difficulties of estimating church membership and adherence, it is clear that Baptists and Methodists both drew a majority of their following from the South and those parts of the western country settled mainly by southerners. Between 1790 and 1835, about 48 percent of the total population of the United States resided in those regions, but nearly two-thirds of all Baptist and Methodist church members. That preponderance of southerners underscores their key role in shaping the early character of both churches.

Table VIII: Percentage of Baptists and Methodists Living in the South and Its Western Country

	1790	1813	1835
Baptists	61.5	64.9	64.1
Methodists	70.6	64.2	61.6

A final caveat: It should not be assumed that the number of church members, congregations, or adherents can confirm either the religious intensity and seriousness, or lack thereof, on the part of southerners, white or black. What the numbers indicate is only the most general estimate of the formal or informal affiliation of southerners with evangelical churches.

Notes

ABBREVIATIONS

CHDC, RLUC	Church History Documents Collection, Regenstein Library, University of Chicago
DC, RLUC	Durrett Collection, Regenstein Library, University of Chicago
PLDU	Perkins Library, Duke University, Durham
SCL	South Caroliniana Library, University of South Carolina, Columbia
SHC	Southern Historical Collection, University of North Carolina, Chapel Hill
VHS	Virginia Historical Society, Richmond, Virginia
WMQ	*William and Mary Quarterly*

PROLOGUE: CANAAN'S LANGUAGE

1. Mary MacDonald to Catherine MacDonald, 31 July 1814, Elizabeth Furman Talley Papers, SHC.
2. For this phrase and similar evangelical references to "speaking the same language," see Henry Boehm, *Reminiscences, Historical and Biographical, of Sixty-four Years in the Ministry*, ed. Joseph B. Wakeley (New York, 1865), 9–10; John Taylor, *A History of Ten Baptist Churches* (1823; 2nd ed., Bloomfield, 1826), 38; John Rankin, Sr., Autobiography [written at South Union Kentucky, 1845; copied by H. L. Eads, August 1870], 21, DC, RLUC; John Early, An Account of the Experiences and Travels of John Early, 7 September 1807, 9 November 1807, SHC (cited hereafter as Account).
3. For examples of this sacralization of the landscape, see Adam Wallace, *The Parson of the Islands* (Philadelphia, 1861), 130; Taylor, *History*, 16–17, 58; Christian Newcomer, *Life and Journal of the Reverend Christian Newcomer . . .* , ed. John Hildt (Hagerstown, 1834), 187; William Woodward, *Surprising Accounts of the Revival of Religion in the United States* (Philadelphia, 1802), 109.

The differences among various evangelical churches unfold in what follows, but they can be briefly summarized here. With regard to their theological outlook, all Presbyterians and some Baptists were Calvinists and held that God had predestined some people, and only those people, for salvation before the beginning of human history, and that individuals could do nothing to alter that divine decree. Other Baptists and all Methodists took the Arminian or Wesleyan theological position, rejecting predestination, holding that men and women could freely decide to accept or reject divine grace, and that, once converted, individuals could "backslide" and lose their hope of salvation. All evangelicals, however, shared the view that human beings were utterly sinful and could be saved by faith alone. In terms of church polity, Methodists and Presbyterians organized their churches hierarchically, while the Baptists favored a decentralized system in which each congregation was self-governing and autonomous.

4. Jesse Lee, *Memoir of the Reverend Jesse Lee*, ed. Minton Thrift (New York, 1823), 65; James Finley, *Autobiography of the Reverend James B. Finley; or Pioneer Life in the West*, ed. W. P. Strickland (Cincinnati, 1853), 169. See also, Jeremiah Norman, Diary [1793–1800], 406, SHC. When citing entries from Norman's diary, I use either page numbers or dates, whichever is easiest for any reader of that text to identify.

5. Mary MacDonald to Maria MacDonald, 21 September 1816, Elizabeth Furman Talley Papers, SHC. For a fuller and highly suggestive discussion of the evangelical temperament and relations between parents and children, see Philip Greven, *The Protestant Temperament: Patterns of Child-Rearing, Religious Experience, and the Self in Early America* (New York, 1977), 21–148.

6. The best summary of Jefferson's religious views is Edwin S. Gaustad, "Religion," in *Thomas Jefferson: A Reference Biography*, ed. Merrill D. Peterson (New York, 1986), 277–93; for a more detailed discussion, see Charles B. Sanford, *The Religious Life of Thomas Jefferson* (Charlottesville, 1984), passim.

7. Devereux Jarratt, *The Life of the Reverend Devereux Jarratt . . . Written by Himself* (Baltimore, 1806; reprint, New York, 1969), 43; William Ormond, Journal [1791–1800], I:15, PLDU. See also Stith Mead, *A Short Account of the Experience and Labours of the Reverend Stith Mead* (Lynchburg, Va., 1829), 48.

8. Wilson Thompson, *The Autobiography of Elder Wilson Thompson* (Cincinnati, 1867), 131; Elias Pym Fordham, *Personal Narrative of Travels in Virginia, Maryland, Pennsylvania, Ohio, Indiana, Kentucky; and of a Residence in the Illinois Territory: 1817–1818*, ed. Frederic Austin Ogg (Cleveland, 1906), 147. See also Richard R. Beeman, *The Evolution of the Southern Backcountry: A Case Study of Lunenberg County, Virginia, 1746–1832* (Philadelphia, 1984), 99–101.

   Such unchurched people comprised the largest single group of whites in the pre-Revolutionary South, more numerous than either Anglicans or dissenters. Only about half of all white southerners regularly attended public worship and regarded themselves as adhering to one of the major Protestant churches. Those conclusions are drawn from Patricia Bonomi and Peter Eisenstadt, who have done the most thorough and imaginative study to date. ("Church Adherence in the Eighteenth-Century British American Colonies," WMQ, ser. 3, 39 [1982]: 274.)

9. His exact words are: "I trust there is not a *young man* now living in the United States who will not die an Unitarian" (Thomas Jefferson to Dr. Benjamin Waterhouse, 26 July 1822, in Paul Leicester Ford, ed., *The Writings of Thomas Jefferson* [New York and London, 1899], 12:219–20).

10. On the transatlantic character of evangelical revivalism in the mid-eighteenth century, see Michael J. Crawford, *Seasons of Grace: Colonial New England's Revival Tradition in Its British Context* (New York, 1991), 1–86; Susan O'Brien, "A Transatlantic Community of Saints: The Great Awakening and the First Evangelical Network, 1735–1755," *American Historical Review* 91 (1986): 811–32; W. Reginald Ward, *The Protestant Evangelical Awakening* (Cambridge, England, 1992), 2. See also, John Walsh, " 'Methodism' and the Origins of English-Speaking Evangelicalism," in *Evangelicalism: Comparative*

Studies of Popular Protestantism in North America, the British Isles, and Beyond, 1700–1900, ed. Mark A. Noll, David W. Bebbington, and George A. Rawlyk (New York, 1994), 19–34.

11. The best recent account of Anglican institutional development in colonial America is Jon Butler, *Awash in a Sea of Faith: Christianizing the American People* (Cambridge, Mass., 1990), 99–116.

   An uncommonly rich scholarship chronicles the early history of evangelicals in the South; cited here are the sources I found most lucid and detailed. Donald Mathews, *Religion in the Old South* (Chicago, 1977), remains the most thoughtful introduction to this topic; a more recent and equally elegant synthesis is Robert M. Calhoon, *Evangelicals and Conservatives in the Early South, 1740–1861* (Columbia, S.C., 1988). The most detailed overview of early evangelical progress in each of the southern states is Samuel Hill, ed., *Religion in the Southern States: A Historical Survey* (Macon, Ga., 1983); for the western country, see especially, John B. Boles, *The Great Revival, 1787–1805: The Origins of the Southern Evangelical Mind* (Lexington, Ky., 1972). An earlier but still useful work, Wesley M. Gewehr, *The Great Awakening in Virginia, 1740–1790* (Durham, 1930), sets forth the beginnings of evangelical influence in that important colony.

   There is also a body of excellent work on specific denominations. For an exhaustive study of Presbyterians in the region, see Ernest Trice Thompson, *Presbyterians in the South,* 3 vols. (Richmond, 1963–73); the best recent work is Marilyn Westerkamp, *The Triumph of the Laity: Scots-Irish Piety and the Great Awakening, 1625–1760* (New York, 1988); Paul Conkin, *Cane Ridge: America's Pentecost* (Madison, 1990); and Leigh Eric Schmidt, *Holy Fairs: Scottish Communions and American Revivals in the Early Modern Period* (Princeton, 1989). For the Baptists, two early histories are worth consulting: David Benedict, *A General History of the Baptist Denomination* (Boston, 1813); and Robert Baylor Semple, *A History of the Rise and Progress of the Baptists in Virginia* (Richmond, 1810). Probably the best recent overview is William Lumpkin, *Baptist Foundations in the South: Tracing Through the Separates the Influence of the Great Awakening, 1754–1787* (Nashville, 1961); helpful, too, are two state-based studies, George W. Paschal, *History of North Carolina Baptists,* 2 vols. (Raleigh, 1930–55); and Leah Townsend, *South Carolina Baptists, 1670–1805* (Florence, S.C., 1935). For the Methodists, the best contemporary account is Jesse Lee, *A Short History of the Methodists, in the United States of America; Beginning in 1766 and Continued till 1809* (Baltimore, 1810), while the most thoughtful modern works are Emory Stevens Bucke et al., *The History of American Methodism,* 3 vols. (New York, 1964); Russell Richey, *Early American Methodism* (Bloomington, 1991); William H. Williams, *The Garden of American Methodism: The Delmarva Peninsula, 1769–1820* (Wilmington, 1984). The most useful statewide studies are William W. Bennet, *Memorials of Methodism in Virginia* (Richmond, 1871), and Albert M. Shipp, *The History of Methodism in South Carolina* (Nashville, 1883).

12. The best evocation of the texture and significance of Anglican worship in the South is Rhys Isaac, *The Transformation of Virginia, 1740–1790* (Chapel Hill, 1982), esp. 58–651. See also, S. Charles Bolton, *Southern Anglicanism: The Church of England in Colonial South Carolina* (Westport, Conn., 1982), esp. 140–57. On Anglican theology, see John Walsh, "The Church and Anglicanism in the 'Long Eighteenth Century'" in *The Church of England, c.1689–c.1833: From Toleration to Tractarianism,* ed. John Walsh and Stephen Taylor (Cambridge, England, 1993), 36–37; Carol Van Voorst, *The Anglican Clergy in Maryland, 1692–1776* (New York, 1989), 279–81.

13. Richard Hooker, ed., *The Carolina Backcountry on the Eve of the Revolution: The Journal and Writings of Charles Woodmason, Anglican Itinerant* (Chapel Hill, 1953), 11,

14, 20, 30–31, 45–46 n.40; William Watters, *A Short Account of the Christian Experience, and Ministerial Labours, of William Watters* (Alexandria, 1806), 3; "Richard Dozier's Historical Notes, 1771–1818," ed. John S. Moore, *Virginia Baptist Register*, 1398. See also "The Journal of Colonel James Gordon, of Lancaster County, Virginia," WMQ, ser. 1, 11 (April 1903): 108–109; Norman, Diary, 3 January 1796, SHC. These negative images of the Anglican clergy were reinforced by later evangelical chroniclers; see Semple, *History*, 39, 43–44; Bennet, *Memorials of Methodism*, 105–106.

Many twentieth-century historians have appropriated the view of Anglicans set forth in early-nineteenth-century evangelical histories. Wesley Gewehr, for example, characterizes Anglicanism as a "spiritual failure in Virginia," "too closely identified with aristocratic society to be a factor in its uplift" and meaning "next to nothing in the lives of the common folk." He depicts the Anglican clergy as "incompetent castoffs," lacking both the talent and the moral stature to succeed as ministers in England and who bcame, once in Virginia, "mere parasites of the rich and the great" (*Great Awakening in Virginia*, 32–34, 36–37, 71; see also Isaac, *Transformation of Virginia*, 189–92). They seem untroubled that most of the evidence to support such conclusions is drawn from eighteenth-century evangelicals, who were hardly disinterested observers. Thus the criticisms of the Virginia Presbyterian merchant James Gordon, who deemed his local parson's discourses a waste of time, are adduced to show that no Anglican clergyman could deliver a decent sermon. And then there is the image commonly evoked of Sabbath observance among lay Anglicans—gentlemen planters boasting about the quality of their tobacco and their decadent sons bragging about the speed of their racehorses, both groups lingering outside the chapel until the last possible moment, when the clerk called them inside to hear "cool, spiritless harangues from the pulpit"—drawn directly from the journal of Philip Fithian, a schoolmaster from New Jersey who became a Presbyterian minister. ("Journal of Colonel James Gordon, of Lancaster County, Virginia," WMQ, ser. 1, 11 [April 1903]: 223.)

Fortunately, the most recent scholarship on Anglicanism in the colonial South has yielded a far more balanced and persuasive picture of both the clergy and the laity; see especially, Patricia Bonomi, *Under the Cope of Heaven: Religion, Society, and Politics in Colonial America* (New York, 1986), 42–48; Carol Van Voorst, *The Anglican Clergy in Maryland*, 204–18; and Joan R. Gunderson, *The Anglican Ministry in Virginia, 1723–1766: A Study of a Social Class* (New York, 1989), 119–42.

14. For Woodmason's criticism of the Anglican clergy, see Hooker, *Carolina Backcountry*, 44. In a similar vein, Devereux Jarratt took pride in pointing out that he was the only Anglican minister who rode circuit in Virginia—until he recruited Archibald McRoberts, one of the few parsons who shared Jarratt's evangelical sympathies, to join him. (Jarratt, *Life*, 101.)

15. Of new congregations formed in the South between 1750 and 1776, only 20 percent were Anglican—compared to 37 percent for Baptists, 29 for Presbyterians, 8 for Lutherans and German Reformed, and 6 for Methodists; see also Appendix.

16. Jarratt, *Life*, 28–29, 38. Joan Gunderson has aptly observed that "The evangelicals (excluding Methodists) pierced few Anglican strongholds [before 1776], but rather had the most success in areas where the Scots, Germans, and Quakers had settled. The areas of Baptist and Presbyterian strength correspond closely to areas of non-Anglican settlement" (Gunderson, *Anglican Ministry in Virginia*, 198).

There has also been a new appreciation among scholars of Anglicanism's hold on popular loyalties in England during the same period; see Walsh, "The Church and Anglicanism in the 'Long Eighteenth Century,' " 27.

17. George A. Phoebus, comp., *Beams of Light on Early Methodism in America: Chiefly Drawn from the Diary . . . of Rev. Ezekiel Cooper* (New York and Cincinnati, 1887),

12–13; Watters, *Short Account*, 1–2; Philip Gatch, *A Sketch of the Reverend Philip Gatch*, ed. John M'Lean (Cincinnati, 1854), 7; Lee, *Memoir*, 3; Chester Raymond Young, ed., *Westward into Kentucky: The Narrative of Daniel Trabue* (Lexington, Ky., 1981), 128; Mead, *Short Account*, 31; John F. Wright, *Sketches of the Life and Labors of James Quinn . . .* (Cincinnati, 1851), 16–17.

18. Early Presbyterians permitted their members to indulge in drinking, dancing, competitive games, and even the occasional brawl, but they were death on Sabbath-breakers; as James Potter Collins, reared in one Carolina Presbyterian church late in the eighteenth century, recalled, "There was no fishing, shooting, hunting, or visiting permitted on that day, or trading or dealing of any kind whatever, nor was it fashionable in the neighborhood" (James Potter Collins, *Autobiography of a Revolutionary Soldier* [1859; reprint, New York, 1979], 15, 21). For the greater acceptance that early Presbyterians won even among the southern gentry, see also, Beeman, *Evolution of the Southern Backcountry*, 102–104; and Rodger M. Payne, "New Light in Hanover County: Evangelical Dissent in Piedmont Virginia, 1740–1755," *Journal of Southern History* 61 (1995): 665–94. As Payne points out, the influence of the Scots-Irish played a decisive role even in Presbyterian successes in the Piedmont.

19. Young, *Westward into Kentucky*, 128–29. The early Baptist historian Robert Semple shrewdly drew attention to the power of civil persecution to draw adherents to the early Separates; see *History*, 42.

20. John Leland, *Virginia Chronicle*, in *The Writings of John Leland*, ed. L. F. Greene (1845; reprint, New York, 1969), 21; Isaac, *Transformation of Virginia*, esp. 161–77. See also, Semple, *History*, 38–39.

21. Young, *Westward into Kentucky*, 129; James Ireland, *The Life of the Reverend James Ireland* (Winchester, Va., 1819), 160, 165–66, 181; Jarratt, *Life*, 59. Sandra Rennie finds that seventy-eight Baptists were persecuted in Virginia between 1765 and 1778, with most assaults and imprisonments taking place in the Northern Neck of Virginia. ("Virginia's Baptist Persecution, 1765–1778," *Journal of Religious History* 12 [1982]: 48–61.)

22. Young, *Westward into Kentucky*, 128; Ireland, *Life*, 133. Robert Williams, a Virginia Methodist itinerant, also tried to provoke parsons to debate: After attending Anglican worship, "he went out of the Church, and standing on a stump, block, or log, began to sing, pray and then preach" (Lee, *Short History of the Methodists*, 43).

23. John Brooks, *The Life and Times of the Reverend John Brooks* (Nashville, 1848), 22; Ireland, *Life*, 110–11; Phoebus, *Beams of Light*, 15, 19. See also W. P. Strickland, *The Life of Jacob Gruber* (New York, 1860), 77, 86; and James B. Walker, *Experiences of Pioneer Life in the Early Settlements and Cities of the West* (Chicago, 1881), 51.

24. Mary Avery Browder to Edward Dromgoole, November 1777, Edward Dromgoole Papers, SHC; Brooks, *Life and Times*, 23; Taylor, *History*, 37. See also John Williams, Journal [1771], 8, CHDC, RLUC; and Robert Paine, *The Life and Times of William McKendree* (Nashville, 1880), 160.

25. No historian has evoked the ideals to which evangelical churches aspired more eloquently than Rhys Isaac; see his *Transformation of Virginia*, esp. 153–72.

26. William Hickman, Autobiography, 4–5, 8, 27, DC, RLUC; Taylor, *History*, 10, 19–20. See also, Thompson, *Autobiography*, 271–72.

27. Hooker, *Carolina Backcountry*, 102–103; see also, Williams, Journal, II, 15–16, 19, CHDC, RLUC; Taylor, *History*, 29, 57; B. C. Holtzclaw, "The Nine Christian Rites in the Early Baptist Churches of Virginia," *Virginia Baptist Register*, 243–60.

28. Lee, *History*, 46; Brooks, *Life and Times*, 118; Joseph Pilmore, Journal [1769–74], copied by Rev. Cornelius Hudson and Mahlon G. Moyer, 9 July 1772, CHDC, RLUC. See also, Bennet, *Memorials of Methodism*, 484; Shipp, *History*, 178–79; Gatch, *Sketch*, 110.

29. Sydney E. Ahlstrom, *A Religious History of the American People* (New Haven, 1972),

368–69, 371–72; Bolton, *Southern Anglicanism*, 63. See also, Appendix. Ahlstrom notes that two-thirds of all Anglican rectors in Virginia left their parishes. Outside of the Chesapeake, most Anglican clergymen were provided and paid by the Society for the Propagation of the Gospel; when the war erupted most of these missionaries, loyalists almost to a man, withdrew to areas held by the British army.

30. Methodist strength in the South swelled more than sixfold between 1776 and 1790, yielding a total membership approaching that of the Baptists, who built on their prewar gains more modestly, and well exceeding that of the Presbyterians. Baptists in the South added about 13,000 new white members between 1750 and 1776, growing by ninefold; between 1776 and 1790, they did slightly better than double their white membership, adding about 21,000 white members. The Presbyterians, who nearly quadrupled their membership between 1750 and 1776, adding about 12,000, appear to have gained no more than 5,000 new members between 1776 and 1790. See Appendix for additional data on church membership.

Historians of the South have been more inclined than most historians of religion to emphasize the slow pace of evangelical expansion in the region. The exception is Donald Mathews, who was the first scholar to note that "Evangelizing the South took a long time" (*Religion in the Old South*, 81). That insight has been most successfully pursued by scholars interested mainly in the broader contours of southern social and political evolution; see especially, Beeman, *Evolution of the Southern Backcountry*, 59; Lacy K. Ford, *The Origins of Southern Radicalism: The South Carolina Upcountry, 1800–1860* (New York, 1988), 19–37; Bertram Wyatt-Brown, "God and Honor in the Old South," *Southern Review* 25 (1989): 283–96.

31. John Dabney Shane Interview with Samuel Gibson, in Kentucky Papers, 12:121, Draper Manuscripts, State Historical Society of Wisconsin (microfilm); James Jenkins, *Experience, Labours, and Sufferings of Reverend James Jenkins* (Columbia, S.C., 1842), 102; Hooker, *Carolina Backcountry*, 13, 15, 26.

Many historians have called attention to the influence of migration in enhancing the appeal of church membership, and some have argued that it was instrumental in bringing about the so-called Great Revival, a religious awakening that began in Kentucky and Tennessee before spreading to many portions of the Southeast in the years around 1800; for the most recent example, see Ford, *Origins of Southern Radicalism*, 31–32. My own earlier research also suggests a connection between family participation in the American Revolution and later patterns of evangelical conversion; see Chapter Five, note 61, below.

32. For postwar evangelical efforts to win over the gentry, see Francis Asbury, *The Journal and Letters of Francis Asbury*, ed. Elmer C. Clark, J. Manning Potts, and Jacob S. Payton, 3 vols. (Nashville, 1858), 3 April 1773, 16 January 1774, 8 August 1789 (cited hereafter as Clark et al., eds., *Journal and Letters of Asbury*); John Early, Experiences and Travels and Labors of John Early, III:38, VHS (cited hereafter as Early, *Experiences*); Jacob Young, *Autobiography of a Pioneer* (Cincinnati, 1857), 157; Taylor, *History*, 40–41; Phoebus, *Beams of Light*, 116; Norman, Diary, 1 June 1794, 1011.

The evangelical clergy's views of the gentry are complex and intriguing. While preachers sought recognition from the elite to lend greater respectability to both themselves and their churches, they also took satisfaction from gaining spiritual sway over gentry converts and often construed their effecting repentance among the "better sort" as a kind of social leveling. Since most Baptist and Methodist ministers came from the yeomanry, smaller planters below the ranks of the gentry, that mingling of resentment and aspiration is not surprising. For anecdotes of postwar preachers humbling elite converts, see Thomas Rankin, Diary [1773–1777], 175, DC, RLUC; James

Meacham, Journal [1788–1797], 31 January 1792, PLDU; Peter Cartwright, *Autobiography of Peter Cartwright, the Backwoods Preacher* (Cincinnati, 1856), 48–49; Young, *Autobiography*, 115, 185; Taylor, *History*, 150.

33. There are several excellent treatments of the policies pertaining to slavery as they evolved among white evangelicals; see especially, James D. Essig, *The Bonds of Wickedness: American Evangelicals and Slavery, 1770–1808* (Philadelphia, 1980), esp. 115–34; Anne C. Loveland, *Southern Evangelicals and the Social Order, 1800–1860* (Baton Rouge, 1980), 186–218; Donald G. Mathews, *Slavery and Methodism: A Chapter in American Morality, 1780–1845* (Princeton, 1965), 3–61; David T. Bailey, *Shadow on the Church: Southwestern Evangelical Religion and the Issue of Slavery, 1783–1860* (Ithaca, 1985), passim; H. Shelton Smith, *In His Image, But . . . Racism in Southern Religion, 1780–1910* (Durham, 1972), 38–39, 45; Beeman, *Evolution of the Southern Backcountry*, 190–91; Ford, *Origins of Southern Radicalism*, 22–24.

    The best recent studies emphasizing the social conservatism of southern Baptists on slavery and other issues are Rachel Klein, *Unification of a Slave State: The Rise of the Planter Class in the South Carolina Backcountry, 1760–1808* (Chapel Hill, 1990), esp. 271–74, 278–82; Stephanie McCurry, *Masters of Small Worlds: Yeoman Households, Gender Relations, and the Political Culture of the Antebellum South Carolina Low Country* (New York, 1995), esp. 142–47; Catherine Grior O'Brien, "Evangelical Planters in Tidewater, Virginia, 1770–1845," a paper delivered at the annual meeting of the Southern Historical Association, 1994; and Jewel Spangler, "Salvation Was Not Liberty: Baptists and Slavery in Revolutionary Virginia," *American Baptist Quarterly* 13 (1994): 223–30.

    For contemporary testimony on the struggles over slavery among the Methodists in 1784, see Lee, *Short History*, 102. In 1800, the General Conference, which formulated policy for the Methodist Church, again voted down motions that would have barred slaveholders from church membership, but they endorsed a rule forcing itinerants to free their slaves where state law allowed. After 1800, antislavery Methodists focused their energies on persuading the laity of the evil of slavery and petitioning state legislatures for gradual abolition, but southern members refused to draw up such petitions. Southern Baptists also concluded that slavery should be dealt with through political institutions rather than in the churches.

34. Beeman, *Evolution of the Southern Backcountry*, 188; Ford, *Origins of Southern Radicalism*, 32–33; Klein, *Unification of a Slave State*, 276–77; Mathews, *Religion in the Old South*, xiii; McCurry, *Masters of Small Worlds*, 158–69; Mechal Sobel, *The World They Made Together: Black and White Values in Eighteenth-Century Virginia* (Princeton, 1987), 39.

35. See Appendix. The significance of evangelical gains over this period cannot be emphasized enough, because, for the first time, growth rates provide clear evidence that the major churches were gathering in unchurched men and women. No other circumstances can account for the substantial rise in church membership between 1813 and 1835.

1: RAISING THE DEVIL

1. The account of Glendinning's background and long bout of religious despair is drawn from his published narrative, *The Life of William Glendinning, Preacher of the Gospel* (Philadelphia, 1795), esp. 1–42; see also, Clark et al., eds., *Journal and Letters of Asbury*, 6 November 1780. Glendinning was exposed to evangelical influences from the Presbyterians during his youth in Scotland and England, and his susceptibility to extraordi-

nary spiritual manifestations predated his adult encounters with the devil. Twice in adolescence he recalled walking in a field when "the earth and all the elements appeared to me to be in a flame of fire" (p. 7).

The distinction between obsession and possession is set forth by Keith Thomas in *Religion and the Decline of Magic* (New York, 1971), 478, which remains the fullest and most lucid overview of this subject and diabolism generally for the early modern period. Thomas's discussion suggests that Glendinning's narrative was informed by a variety of seventeenth-century evangelicals whose writings remained popular among the devout on both sides of the Atlantic well into the nineteenth century. John Bunyan, for example, went through a period of spiritual struggle in which he believed himself possessed by the devil, while some of his contemporaries claimed that Satan appeared to them, as he had to Glendinning, in animal shape and tempted them to suicide. (*Religion and the Decline of Magic*, 474.) From these same sources, Glendinning could also have come across the story of Francis Spira, to whom he compared himself. After abjuring his Protestant beliefs, Spira suffered from despair, terrible dreams, and the conviction that he was possessed. (*Life of Glendinning*, 14; David Hall, *Worlds of Wonder, Days of Judgment* [New York, 1989], 132–34.)

There is a fascinating literature offering a range of psychological, anthropological, and theological explorations of possession in early modern settings; see especially, Fernando Cervantes, *The Devil in the New World: The Impact of Diabolism in New Spain* (New Haven, 1994); John Putnam Demos, *Entertaining Satan: Witchcraft and the Culture of Early New England* (New York, 1982), 97–131; Richard Godbeer, *The Devil's Dominion: Magic and Religion in Early New England* (Cambridge, England, and New York, 1992), 106–21; Carol Karlsen, *The Devil in the Shape of a Woman: Witchcraft in Colonial New England* (New York, 1987), 222–52.

2. James Meacham, Journal, 24 April 1790, 15 January 1797, PLDU; Francis Asbury to Edward Dromgoole, 24 December 1791, Edward Dromgoole Papers, SHC.

3. Glendinning, *Life of Glendinning*, 31–37, 42; Clark et al., *Journal and Letters of Asbury*, 25 December 1790. Glendinning's implication that his afflictions honed his spiritual virtuosity echoes the view of many earlier Catholic hagiographers who, as Fernando Cervantes observes, often interpreted diabolical possession as the "purging of a favored soul prior to mystical union" (*Devil in the New World*, 101–102, 105–106).

4. This tradition of Anglo-American wonder lore is superbly evoked in Hall, *World of Wonders*, 71–116.

5. Mary Avery Browder to Edward Dromgoole, November 1777, Edward Dromgoole Papers, SHC.

6. Benjamin Abbott, *The Experience and Gospel Labours of the Reverend Benjamin Abbott . . .*, ed. John Ffirth (New York, 1805), 72.

7. Stith Mead, *A Short Account of the Experience and Labours of the Reverend Stith Mead* (Lynchburg, Va., 1829), 14; Peter Cartwright, *Autobiography of Peter Cartwright, the Backwoods Preacher* (Cincinnati, 1856), 233–34; Edward P. Humphrey and Thomas H. Cleland, *Memoirs of the Reverend Thomas Cleland, D.D.* (Cincinnati, 1859), 59; John Taylor, *A History of Ten Baptist Churches* (1823; 2nd ed., Bloomfield, 1826), 17. See also, William W. Bennet, *Memorials of Methodism in Virginia* (Richmond, 1871), 53; Moses Hoge to Ashbel Green, 10 September 1801, extracted in William Woodward, *Surprising Accounts of the Revival of Religion in the United States* (Philadelphia, 1802), 53.

8. George A. Phoebus, comp., *Beams of Light on Early Methodism in America: Chiefly Drawn from the Diary . . . of Rev. Ezekiel Cooper* (New York and Cincinnati, 1887), 117; Hickman, Autobiography, 24, DC, RLUC; John Hagerty to Edward Dromgoole, 19 January 1788, Edward Dromgoole Papers, SHC. See also Mead, *Short Account*, 48;

Philip Gatch, *A Sketch of the Reverend Philip Gatch*, ed. John M'Lean (Cincinnati, 1854), 8–12.

To be sure, some converts embellished the reactions of their relatives and friends. That temptation beckoned because evangelicals, while condemning worldly pride, were not past preening themselves on having attained the humility to seem fools for the sake of righteousness. Hence the boastful note struck by James Ireland, a roistering Virginia schoolmaster subdued to sobriety by the Baptists, as he recounted one of his "old companions in vanity" lamenting, "Jemmy, you have turned a fool, you are certainly distracted and raving in despair." James Ireland, *The Life of the Reverend James Ireland* (Winchester, Va., 1819), 110–11; see also, Cartwright, *Autobiography*, 35; Taylor, *History*, 38; Mead, *Short Account*, 48; Obadiah Echols, *The Autobiography of Obadiah Echols* (Memphis, 1870), 88–89; Jacob Young, *Autobiography of a Pioneer* (Cincinnati, 1857), 46; Abbott, *Experience*, 10. But if evangelicals sometimes indulged and exaggerated, they did not invent the alarm felt by their intimates at the physical and emotional toll often taken by conviction.

9. Williams, Journal, 13, CHDC, RLUC; Ormond, Journal, III:17, PLDU; Meacham, Journal, 6 February 1793; see also 4 June 1795, PLDU.

10. Meacham, Journal, 8 August 1790, 14 March 1795, PLDU; Early, Account, 22 July 1807, SHC. See also, Robert Simpson, ed., *American Methodist Pioneer: The Life and Journals of the Reverend Freeborn Garrettson, 1752–1827* (Rutland, Vt., 1984), 192 (entry for 24 August 1781), and 198 (entry for 8 December 1781); Robert Paine, *Life and Times of William McKendree* (Nashville, 1880), 159; Dr. John Goodlet to Joshua Lacy Wilson, ca. 1810–11, Joshua Lacy Wilson Papers, DC, RLUC.

So accustomed were the evangelical clergy to link psychological ailments with spiritual causes that they tended to assume that any symptoms of emotional agitation required a spiritual remedy. Christian Newcomer, a Methodist preacher, recalled being summoned to the farm of a man who "told me that he felt himself in a very miserable condition; that a fear had seized on him which drove him almost to distraction; in restlessness he walked about not knowing what to do." Without hesitation, Newcomer diagnosed religious anxiety as the source of the man's troubles, and told him "the best and only means which I knew to get rid of this fear, was to humble himself before his God . . . and his fear would be removed" (Christian Newcomer, *Life and Journal of the Reverend Christian Newcomer . . .* , ed. John Hildt (Hagerstown, 1834), 37–38.

11. Taylor, *History*, 60, 75; Haskins, Journal, 3 March 1785, CHDC, RLUC; Newcomer, *Life and Journal*, 47; Hickman, Autobiography, 35–36, DC, RLUC. See also Taylor, *History*, 153. Such cases were not, of course, restricted to the South; as Julius Rubin observes, "Anyone living in early nineteenth-century New England could not fail to encounter common incidents of melancholy and debilitating religious crises among their acquaintances, and the same could be said of that region for the earlier period. (*Religious Melancholy and Protestant Experience in America* [New York, 1994], 158.) What should be underscored, however, is the novelty of that phenomenon among southerners.

12. Joseph Gregg, Journal (1796), 30 June 1796, DC, RLUC; Young, *Autobiography*, 131, see also 101–102, 141.

13. Abbott, *Experience*, 90–91.

14. Freeborn Garrettson, *The Experience and Travels of Freeborn Garrettson* (1790; 2nd ed., Philadelphia, 1791), 194–96; Cartwright, *Autobiography*, 87.

15. Wilson Thompson, *The Autobiography of Elder Wilson Thompson* (Cincinnati, 1867), 9–11, 51–57, 89, 156–63, 202–204.

16. Ibid., 206–207.

17. James Potter Collins, *Autobiography of a Revolutionary Soldier* (1859; reprint, New York, 1979), 20, 68, 113.

18. Louisa Maxwell Holmes Cocke, Diary, 11–12, in American Women's Diaries: Southern Women (microfilm collection). A number of scholars have drawn attention to the freer expression of emotion, as well as the new emphasis upon companionate marriage and more indulgent modes of child-rearing among elite southern whites by the late eighteenth century; see Jan Lewis, *The Pursuit of Happiness: Family and Values in Jefferson's Virginia* (Cambridge, Mass., 1983), passim; Daniel Blake Smith, *Inside the Great House: Planter Family Life in the Eighteenth-Century Chesapeake* (Ithaca, 1980), chapters 1–4; Allan Kulikoff, *Tobacco and Slaves: The Development of Southern Cultures in the Chesapeake, 1680–1800* (Chapel Hill, 1986), 183.

19. This overview of the basic conditions of life among the South's yeoman and tenant farmers does scant justice to the rich scholarship on this subject that has appeared in the last twenty years; see especially, Gavin Wright, *The Political Economy of the Cotton South: Households, Markets, and Wealth in the Nineteenth Century* (New York, 1978), 55–88; Steven Hahn, *The Roots of Southern Populism: Yeoman Farmers and the Transformation of the Georgia Upcountry, 1850–1890* (New York, 1983), 29–33, 50–58, 64–69; Lacy K. Ford, *Origins of Southern Radicalism: The South Carolina Upcountry, 1800–1860* (New York, 1988), esp. 71–88; Stephanie McCurry, *Masters of Small Worlds: Yeoman Households, Gender Relations, and the Political Culture of the Antebellum South Carolina Low Country* (New York, 1995), 47–91; Kulikoff, *Tobacco and Slaves*, 59–62, 205–31, 240–60; on the western country, see John Mack Faragher, *Sugar Creek: Life on the Illinois Prairie* (New Haven, 1986), esp. 87–89. My indebtedness to these works is evident throughout this study, but their authors should not be held responsible for any inferences about the inner lives of ordinary southerners that I have drawn from their findings.

20. Scholars of this subject will recognize that the preceding discussion diverges sharply from many previous interpretations that have emphasized the popular appeal of evangelical emotionalism, the most recent being Nathan O. Hatch, *The Democratization of American Christianity* (New Haven, 1989), passim. While it is indisputable that evangelical gatherings often encouraged dramatic displays of feeling, it is quite another matter to conclude that most men and women who attended those gatherings did so because they sought and prized such emotional release. On the contrary, virtually all contemporary accounts emphasize the opposite—that nonbelievers scorned and resisted such freedom of expression.

21. Gordon, Journal of Col. James Gordon, WMQ, ser. 1, 11 (1903): 227; Reed, Diary, 23 July 1778, 31 May 1780, 26 August 1781, CHDC, RLUC; Norman, Diary, 874, SHC; Henry Toler, "The Journal of Henry Toler," ed. William S. Simpson, Jr., *Virginia Baptist Register*, 1580. See also, Pilmore, Journal, 2 August 1772, CHDC, RLUC; Meacham, Journal, 12 January 1789, PLDU; Norman, Diary, 20 November 1796, 24 December 1797, SHC; Mechal Sobel, *The World They Made Together: Black and White Values in Eighteenth-Century Virginia* (Princeton, 1987), 183–87, 204–206.

   On the percentage of black membership in evangelical churches, see Appendix; see also, Albert J. Raboteau, *Slave Religion: The "Invisible Institution" in the Antebellum South* (New York, 1978), 131; Donald Mathews, *Religion in the Old South* (Chicago, 1977), 137; and Sylvia R. Frey, *Water from the Rock: Black Resistance in a Revolutionary Age* (Princeton, 1991), 296–97; on the biracial character of early churches, see Sobel, *World They Made Together*, 180, 189, 191–97, 204–206.

22. Reed, Diary [1778–1781], ed. Frank G. Porter, 15 June 1781, CHDC, RLUC; Meacham,

Journal, 4 March 1790, 9 February 1793, 9 March 1790, PLDU; see also, Norman, Diary, 238, SHC.

23. Ireland, *Life*, 135; James Jenkins, *Experience, Labours, and Sufferings of Reverend James Jenkins* (Columbia, S.C., 1842), 86, 96–97, 102–103, 154–55; Meacham, Journal, 30 August 1789, PLDU; Flat River Baptist Church Records [1786–1979], June 1790, SHC; Norman, Diary, 30 October 1793, SHC.

24. Phoebus, *Beams of Light*, 116; Meacham, Journal, 16 August 1790, 27 July 1794, 9 September 1790, PLDU; see also entry for 10 September 1791.

25. Phoebus, *Beams of Light*, 14; "The Journal of Benjamin Lakin," in *Religion on the American Frontier, 1783–1840: The Methodists*, vol. 4, ed. William Warren Sweet (Chicago, 1946), 14 November 1795 [cited hereafter as "Journal of Lakin"]; Meacham, Journal, 20 April 1790, PLDU; see also, Jesse Lee, *A Short History of the Methodists, in the United States of America; Beginning in 1766 and Continued Till 1809* (Baltimore, 1810), 134; Bennet, *Memorials of Methodism*, 274.

26. Norman, Diary, 317–18, 889, SHC; Meacham, Journal, 23 July 1789, PLDU; John Leland, *The Virginia Chronicle*, in *The Writings of John Leland*, ed. L. F. Greene (1845; reprint New York, 1969), 98; Jenkins, *Experience*, 50; W. P. Strickland, *The Life of Jacob Gruber* (New York, 1860), 120–22; Newcomer, *Life and Journal*, 195; Simpson, ed., *American Methodist Pioneer*, 187, entry for 3 July 1781. See also, Taylor, *History*, 94.

Nearly any contemporary account of revival gatherings and camp meetings betrays the clergy's discomfort in the face of unrestrained lay enthusiasm; for some examples, see ministerial accounts collected in Woodward, *Surprising Accounts*, passim. Some scholars have suggested that southern whites learned patterns of ecstatic response from blacks, but this seems unlikely given European precedents for such enthusiastic behavior, especially in places like mid-eighteenth-century Scotland, a society not conspicuous for the density of its black population. (Leigh Eric Schmidt, *Holy Fairs: Scottish Communions and American Revivals in the Early Modern Period* [Princeton, 1989], 145–53.)

27. Norman, Diary, 237–38, SHC; Mead, *Short Account*, 48; Meacham, Journal, 4 May 1790, PLDU. For traditional West African religions, see Raboteau, *Slave Religion*, 5–16; John Thornton, *Africa and Africans in the Making of the Atlantic World, 1400–1680* (Cambridge, England, and New York, 1992), 239–43, 251; on the syncretism of West African and European beliefs about the sacred among African Americans, see Raboteau, *Slave Religion*, 44–86, 212–88; Thornton, *Africa and Africans*, 254–71; Mechal Sobel, *Trabelin' On: The Slave Journey to an Afro-Baptist Faith* (Princeton, 1988), passim; Lawrence W. Levine, *Black Culture and Black Consciousness: Afro-American Folk Thought from Slavery to Freedom* (New York, 1977), 3–80; Eugene D. Genovese, *Roll, Jordan, Roll: The World the Slaves Made* (New York, 1972), 209–32.

28. Simpson, ed., *American Methodist Pioneer*, 231, entry for 3 November 1783; John Travis, *The Autobiography of John Travis, A.M.*, ed. Thomas Summers, D.D. (Nashville, 1856), 71–72. On slave funerary rituals, see also, Jenkins, *Experience*, 31–32. A number of scholars have pointed up the pivotal role played by beliefs in spirit possession in the merging of African and Christian religious traditions, see Thornton, *Africa and Africans*, 243, 270–71; Raboteau, *Slave Religion*, 58–75; Sobel, *World They Made Together*, 181.

29. For the tradition of associating blackness with the devil and identifying West African religion as heathen "devil worship," see Winthrop D. Jordan, *White Over Black: American Attitudes Toward the Negro, 1550–1812* (1968; reprint, Baltimore, 1969), 7, 24, 39n, 41, 258–59.

30. "Letters of Patrick Henry Sr., Samuel Davies, James Maury, Edwin Conway and

George Trask," WMQ, ser. 2, 1 (October 1921): 265; Lee, *Short History*, 40–41; for the Baptists, see Williams, Journal, 3, CHDC, RLUC.

31. Sarah Jones to Edward Dromgoole, 4 September 1788, Sally Eastland to Edward Dromgoole, 21 February 1789, and Mary Avery Browder to Edward Dromgoole, November 1777 in Edward Dromgoole Papers, SHC; Myles Greene, Journal [1789], 40, PLDU; Garrettson, *Experience*, 198–99; Simpson, ed., *American Methodist Pioneer*, 162 (entry for 8 December 1779); John Craig, Autobiography, 25, VHS; see also, "Journal of Lakin," 9 May 1795; Meacham, Journal, 4 June 1789 and 21 November 1789, PLDU; Phoebus, *Beams of Light*, 18; Thomas Haskins, Journal [1783–85], 2 January 1792, CHDC, RLUC; Williams, Journal, 3, 5, 11, CHDC, RLUC; Daniel Grant to John Owen, 4 October 1788, Campbell Family Papers, SHC; Reed, Journal, 26 December 1778 and 21 July 1778, CHDC, RLUC; Agnes Templin to Joshua Lacy Wilson, 18 July 1799, Joshua Lacy Wilson Papers, DC, RLUC. See also, Early, Account, 4 August 1807, SHC; Clark et al., eds., *Journal and Letters of Asbury*, 9 August 1778.

   Elaine Pagels has argued that early Christians made reference to the devil mainly to stigmatize their religious rivals—a strategy far from foreign to southern evangelicals. More commonly, however, evangelicals focused on Satan as a source of spiritual and moral danger, leading astray individual Christians and congregations. As Brent D. Shaw points up, it is this latter role that has "kept Satan central in Christianity" (Elaine Pagels, *The Origin of Satan* [New York, 1995], passim; Brent D. Shaw, "The Devil in the Details," *The New Republic*, 10 July 1995, pp. 30–36).

32. Reed, Diary, 19 April 1781. Adult believers also reported seeing angels and benign spirits. Wilson Thompson saw a "shadowy form" bending over his bedside which assured him that reading certain biblical passages would resolve his anxieties about becoming a Baptist preacher, while Obadiah Echols "espied" an angel at the moment of his conversion. (Thompson, *Autobiography*, 75–76; Echols, *Autobiography*, 119–20.)

33. Collins, *Autobiography*, 152–53; James Taylor, Autobiography of General James Taylor, 3, DC, RLUC. In such disarming allusions to the devil's antiquity, there is a resonant, and maybe more than a coincidental, resemblance to the ways that masters might designate their eldest slaves.

34. Simpson, ed., *American Methodist Pioneer*, 170 [entry for 15 February 1780]; John Barr, *History of John Barr* (Philadelphia, 1833), 16–19.

35. George W. Paschal, *History of North Carolina Baptists*, 2 vols. (Raleigh, 1930–55), vol. 1, 293n; Ormond, Journal, III: 26–27, PLDU.

36. Early, Account, 6 October 1807 SHC; Stith Mead to John Kobler, 15 June 1795, Stith Mead Letterbook [1792–95], VHS; Echols, *Autobiography*, 119, 120; *Georgia Analytical Repository* (September and October 1802), 128–29. See also, Abbott, *Experience*, 12; George Brown, *Recollections of an Itinerant Life: Including Early Reminiscences* (Cincinnati, 1866), 40–41; Garrettson, *Experience*, 201; Cartwright, *Autobiography*, 36. Other lay people feared that the devil lay in wait for them to die under the rigors of conviction; thus William Mead's brother-in-law, worn down by his struggle for assurance, "informed me not to make any more trouble about him, for the Devil stood ready as soon as his breath was gone, to take him to hell" (Mead, *Short Account*, 14–15).

37. Simpson, ed., *American Methodist Pioneer*, 238 [entry for 12 March 1784]; Adam Wallace, *The Parson of the Islands* (Philadelphia, 1861), 180. See also, Smith, Journal, III, dated Sunday the 8th, CHDC, RLUC. Southerners also held certain places to be haunted by visible spirits of the dead, among them any crossroads in which suicides and hanged horse-thieves had been buried; see Collins, *Autobiography*, 116.

38. For his failure to reenter the Methodist ministry in the 1790s, see Glendinning, *Life of Glendinning*, 49–55; Clark et al., eds., *Journal and Letters of Asbury*, III: 105–106, 111–12.

Most of his clerical colleagues believed that Glendinning remained deranged, but there were some among both the clergy and the laity who supported his bid for restoration; see Clark et al., eds., *Journal and Letters of Asbury*, 4 July 1794; Lee, *Short History*, 122; Edward Dromgoole to Francis Asbury, 12 December 1805, Edward Dromgoole Papers, SHC; Phoebus, *Beams of Light*, 131; Glendinning, *Life of Glendinning*, 47–48.

Most Methodist clergymen also resisted restoring Glendinning to their ministry because of his objections to the increasingly hierarchical character of the American church, reservations that he voiced as early as the mid-1780s. By the mid-1790s, he had become even more outspoken on that subject, and argued that his unique spiritual experiences had endowed him with "an extraordinary mission" that warranted his being freed from the direction of the bishops. In other words, Glendinning hoped to use his claims to virtuosity as a leverage against Asbury's growing authority. After leaving the Methodist Church, he may have briefly joined the schismatic Republican Methodists, headed by James O'Kelly, who shared his criticisms of hierarchical church government. For a fuller description of that movement, see Chapter Two. (Glendinning, *Life of Glendinning*, 72, 79, 83, 99, 106.)

39. It is, of course, also possible that Glendinning subconsciously used Satan as a "scapegoat" to explain and excuse his madness; other scholars have construed the behavior of early modern demoniacs in that manner. See Thomas, *Religion and the Decline of Magic*, 481; Cervantes, *Devil in the New World*, 101–102. On Glendinning's conversion to Unitarianism, see Clark et al., eds., *Journal and Letters of Asbury*, II: 663n.

    Asbury may also have been speaking figuratively when he referred to the devil as being "in Glendinning." That interpretation is suggested by Asbury's response to visiting "the calvary of the witches" at Salem, Massachusetts, in the summer of 1791, where he deplored the execution of "many innocent, good people." On the other hand, other entries in his journal indicate that Asbury was willing to entertain the notion of spirits, good or evil, taking visible form. He noted, for example, the "strange relation" of one Methodist layman that "A person in the form of a man came to the house of another in the night," predicting that "This will be the bloodiest year that ever was known." When his host inquired "how he knew," the stranger replied, "It is as true as your wife is now dead in bed," a statement that proved accurate. Similarly, Asbury reported that at a meeting of the Methodist clergy near Baltimore in 1776, "One of the preachers brought an account of an apparition that appeared to a lad, and gave a particular account of being murdered by his fellow-soldier, requesting that the lad's father might lodge an information against the murderer: which was done" (Clark et al., eds., *Journal and Letters of Asbury*, 7 November 1776, 16 June 1777, 29 June 1791; see also, entries for 4 February 1778, 1 February 1782).

40. Red River Baptist Church Records [1791–1826], 16 August 1800, SHC; Bush River Baptist Church Records [1793–1840], 12 November 1803, 7 January 1804, SCL. Such notions, of course, began circulating decades earlier: In 1779, the Methodist preacher Nelson Reed went to the length of burning a sermon which argued "that the torments of hell were not endless but that the devil himself would either be redeemed or destroyed so as to cease to be" (Reed, Journal, 10 March 1779, CHDC, RLUC). Nor was the western country immune to such views; see George Johnston to Joshua Lacy Wilson, 20 May 1803, Joshua Lacy Wilson Papers, DC, RLUC.

41. Glendinning, *Life of Glendinning*, 19–21, 23, 25–26, 33–34. The John Hargrove of Glendinning's memoirs is almost certainly the same head of household who is listed as residing in Granville County, North Carolina, in the U.S. census of 1790; the name of his son-in-law, Argil Hanks, also appears in the same county. Unfortunately, the existing census information for Granville County in 1790 does not include an enu-

meration of other household members, white or black. Fuller information is supplied
by the U.S. Census for 1800, which shows a John Hargrove in Granville County, North
Carolina, who owned eleven slaves; he is more likely to have been Glendinning's host
than another Granville resident, identified as John S. Hargrove, who had no slave-
holdings. According to Glendinning's account, the Hargroves owned slaves numerous
enough to occupy a separate quarter on his plantation; he also complained that their
noise kept him awake at night.

Census records for 1800 also show a Leonard Sims, the husband of Glendinning's
visitor, heading a household in adjacent Warren County. The Sims family was considerably more affluent than their Hargrove neighbors, that household including thirty-
six slaves in 1800. Historians of the South define the planter class as those households
that included more than twenty slaves; by that standard, the Sims family ranked
among the gentry, but the Hargroves were a substantial yeoman household. (U.S.
Census for 1790, p. 90; U.S. Census for 1800, Granville County, North Carolina, 515,
534; Warren County, 830.)

Like the Hargroves, those men and women disinclined to believe in devils who
walked among mortals might have been equally disconcerted by Glendinning's reliance on exorcism. Most southern churchgoers in the 1790s, mainly Anglican in their
religious training, would have known that the Church of England had dismissed as a
vulgar superstition this device for staving off the devil since early in the seventeenth
century. Worse still, the resort of exorcism enjoyed continuing favor only among the
adherents of Roman Catholicism. Here, indeed, was a popish trick unbecoming in a
proudly republican country.

42. For this discussion and my understanding of early American religious history in general, I am indebted to Jon Butler's provocative *Awash in a Sea of Faith: Christianizing
the American People* (Cambridge, Mass., 1990); on this point see esp. 228–36. For contemporary references to African-American beliefs in the afterlife, good and evil spirits,
apparitions, and dream interpretation, see Mead, *Short Account*, 33, and Strickland,
Life of Gruber, 120–22; see also, note 27 in this chapter; on Native American sacred
belief systems, see Richard White, *The Middle Ground: Indians, Empires, and Republics
in the Great Lakes Region, 1650–1815* (Cambridge, Mass., 1991), 329–32; Joel W. Martin,
Sacred Revolt: The Muskogees' Struggle for a New World (Boston, 1991), 26.

43. Craig, Autobiography, 11, VHS; Wallace, *Parson of the Islands*, 189; Jenkins, *Experience*,
9, 11, 34, 97, 120; Young, *Autobiography*, 47; Taylor, *History*, 35, 36–37, 66; Thompson,
Autobiography, 324; John Brooks, *The Life and Times of the Reverend John Brooks*
(Nashville, 1848), 12, 14; "Journal of Lakin," 14 December 1795, 24 May 1809; Meacham,
Journal, 13 February 1797, PLDU; Barr, *History*, 19–20; Gatch, *Sketch*, 20; Early, Ac-
count, 6 March 1811, SHC; Abbott, *Experience*, 100; Hickman, Autobiography, 32, DC,
RLUC. For the related belief in presentiments, often of the approach of death, see
Jenkins, *Experience*, 174–75.

44. See especially, Clark et al., eds., *Journal and Letters of Asbury*, 2 June 1783; Brantley
York, *Autobiography of Brantley York* (Durham, 1910), 40; Cartwright, Autobiography,
185; Gatch, *Sketch*, 61; James Finley, *Autobiography of the Reverend James B. Finley; Or
Pioneer Life in the West*, ed. W. P. Strickland (Cincinnati, 1853), 414; "Journal of Lakin,"
undated entry for early May 1799, 30 April 1810, and 29 June 1810; Jenkins, *Experience*,
32, 37; Simpson, ed., *American Methodist Pioneer*, 218 [entry for 5 April 1783].

45. York, *Autobiography*, 8–10; Jenkins, *Experience*, 32; Collins, *Autobiography*, 77, 90,
142–47; Chester Raymond Young, ed., *Westward into Kentucky: The Narrative of Daniel
Trabue* (Lexington, Ky., 1981), 48–49; Craig, Autobiography, 26–27, VHS; Ormond,
Journal, III:33, PLDU. See also, William M. Wightman, *The Life of William Capers*, D. D.
(Nashville, 1858), 116–18; Paschal, *History of North Carolina Baptists*, II: 236. Most con-

temporary accounts reputed German immigrants to be most adept at working simple and curious "tricks"; see also Butler, *Awash in a Sea of Faith*, 87.

46. Morgan Edwards, "Materials towards a History of the Baptists in the Province of North Carolina," ed. George W. Paschal, *North Carolina Historical Review* 7, no. 3 (1930): 386–87; Albert M. Shipp, *The History of Methodism in South Carolina* (Nashville, 1883), 348, 585; Bennet, *Memorials of Methodism*, 365; Newcomer, *Life*, 83, 117; Wallace, *Parson of the Islands*, 86; Abbott, *Experience*, 59, 93; see also, Mead, *Short Account*, 44. Minter repeated those charges in his memoir, *A Brief Account of the Religious Experience, Travels, Preaching, Persecutions from Evil Men, and God's Special Helps in the Faith and Life, Etc. of Jeremiah Minter* (Washington, D.C., 1817), 70–71, claiming to have aired them twice "in the public news" earlier in the century. I have been unable to track down the periodicals in which those accusations initially appeared.

47. Clark et al., eds., *Journal and Letters of Asbury*, 28 September 1779.

48. Thus ran the preface to Wesley's account of one Elizabeth Hobson, an English Methodist, who professed to have routinely since childhood seen and conversed with ghosts of the dead and dying (*The Journal of John Wesley*, ed. Nehemiah Curnock, 8 vols. [London, 1909–16], V: 265–75).

49. Garrettson, *Experience*, 72; Pilmore, Journal, 9 August 1772, CHDC, RLUC; Rankin, Diary, 17 November 1779, CHDC, RLUC; Meacham, Journal, 23 July 1789, 7 November 1789, 15 August 1789, 15 June 1792, 10 May 1789, PLDU; Haskins, Journal, 9 April 1783, CHDC, RLUC; Jesse Lee, *Memoir of the Reverend Jesse Lee*, ed. Minton Thrift (New York, 1823), 82; Abbott, *Experience*, 102; Phoebus, *Beams of Light*, 137, 140–41; Early, Experiences, III:26, VI:50, VHS; Woodward, *Surprising Accounts*, 57; Henry Boehm, *Reminiscences, Historical and Biographical, of Sixty-four Years in the Ministry*, ed. Joseph B. Wakeley (New York, 1865), 63. For a superb account of how rapidly white southern Baptists reduced blacks to "second-class members," see Jewel Spangler, "Salvation Was Not Liberty: Baptists and Slavery in Revolutionary Virginia," *American Baptist Quarterly* 13 (1994): 223–30; see also, Sobel, *World They Made Together*, 180, 207–208, 213.

    As racial separation became more pronounced at southern religious gatherings, many ministers regarded evangelizing blacks as subordinate in importance to converting whites. For example, at a camp meeting in Middle Tennessee in the 1820s, John Brooks found that every white person attending professed religion; "Brother Harris asked me what they should do, for, said he, we have no timber to work upon. I told him to call up the negroes" (*Life and Times*, 70).

50. Red River Baptist Church Records, 2 August, 19 August, 20 August 1820 and 13 and 14 April 1821, SHC.

51. Leland, *Virginia Chronicle*, 98; for discussions of separate black churches, see Frey, *Water from the Rock*, 289–90, 294–97; Raboteau, *Slave Religion*, 137; Mathews, *Religion in the Old South*, 137, 197, 204. In some Baptist churches left without a white clergyman, unordained black preachers continued to baptize and admit African Americans to the membership; when such churches were again supplied with a white preacher, "Many [black] members refused to give up their independent state" (Robert Baylor Semple, *A History of the Rise and Progress of the Baptists in Virginia* [Richmond, 1810], 290–91).

52. Flat River Baptist Church Records, 1804, June and July 1805, SHC. The church had attracted seven black members in just four years after 1796, but between 1800 and 1815 drew only four new members, only one of them male. Black membership rebounded in the period between 1816 and 1830 when twenty-one new converts joined, twelve of them men.

53. Semple, *History*, 130; *Minutes of the Ketocton Baptist Association* (Baltimore, 1810), n.p.; *Minutes of the Dover Baptist Association* (Richmond, 1803), 25–26; *Minutes of the Long*

Run Baptist Association, September 1810 (Lexington, 1810). For the most thoughtful recent work on the role of African Americans in church governance, see Frey, *Water from the Rock*, 270–71; Spangler, "Salvation Was Not Liberty: Baptists and Slavery in Revolutionary Virginia," 223–29; and Janet Moore Lindman, "A World of Baptists: Gender, Race, and Religious Community in Pennsylvania and Virginia, 1689–1825" (Ph.D. dissertation, University of Minnesota, 1994), 135–36, 138, 155–58; Sobel, *World They Made Together*, 208–209; Richard R. Beeman, *The Evolution of the Southern Back-country: A Case Study of Lunenberg County, Virginia, 1746–1832* (Philadelphia, 1984), 190.

54. Taylor, *History*, 212–19, passim; consulting any of the published clerical memoirs cited herein will provide similar examples. Sectarian animosity sometimes inspired lapses from the rule of happy endings. For example, Methodists often claimed that lay people who accepted the Calvinist doctrines of the Baptists later despaired of their "election," ran berserk, and committed murder or suicide. Conversely, the Baptists were given to suggesting that those who embraced Methodism came to equally bad ends because, rejecting the Calvinist notion of the "perseverance of the saints," they lost their assurance of salvation.

55. Garrettson, *Experience*, "author's copy," Morris Library, University of Delaware, 78–79, 128–29, 159–60, 171–73. For a good biographical sketch of Garrettson, see Simpson, ed., *American Methodist Pioneer*, 1–33.

56. Of course, the Methodists found it easier to salvage Garrettson, since he had not run raving mad; then, too, being the son of a slaveholding Maryland Anglican family rather than a poor Scottish tailor weighed in his favor. Glendinning, however, exacted some revenge: His own narrative recapitulated Garrettson's excised accounts of seeing a "ghostly appearance" and Satan in the form of a cat, "to show the great partiality of those who condemn me for the same things, which in another, they so far applaud, as to *publish* and *sell* them." Glendinning also justified his views by alluding to Wesley's belief in witchcraft, as well as Martin Luther's claim that the devil appeared to him in the shape of a black boar. (Glendinning, *Life of Glendinning*, 56–59.)

The periodical that serialized Garrettson's extensively revised memoir as well as parts of his private journal was the *Arminian Magazine*, later issued under the name *Methodist Magazine*. Although published in London, its readership included a wide American audience. (See the issues from January 1794 through September 1794.) I discovered Garrettson's intention to revise the earlier American editions of his memoirs in the Special Collections Department at the University of Delaware's Morris Library, which holds a copy of the 1791 memoirs inscribed on the flyleaf "author's copy" and is marked with handwritten deletions of certain passages. I am indebted to Nancy Packer for identifying the *Arminian Magazine* as the periodical for which Garrettson intended these revisions, as well as for pointing out to me that he took pains to exclude from his memoirs as serialized therein any invidious references to the British role in the American war for independence.

While excluding any references to Satan assuming visible form, Garrettson retained references to disembodied voices, dreams, and visions that he attributed to angelic origin; on this point, see the issues for 1794, pp. 8, 62, 174, 239.

57. Abbott, *Experience*, 10–12, 42; Cartwright, *Autobiography*, 36. See also, Echols, *Autobiography*, 120.

58. Wallace, *Parson of the Islands*, 92; Edward Stevenson, *A Biographical Sketch of the Reverend Valentine Cook, A.M.* (Nashville, 1858), 65–66.

59. Red River Baptist Church Records, 14 February 1812, SHC; Early, Account, 22 May 1811, SHC; Abbott, *Experience*, 58; Alfred Brunson, *A Western Pioneer: or, Incidents of the Life and Times of Rev. Alfred Brunson* (Cincinnati, 1872), 218; Caleb Jarvis Taylor, *News*

from the Infernal Regions, or, a Conference of the Black Brotherhood (Fredericktown, Md., 1806; 2nd ed., Philadelphia, 1809; 3rd ed., New York, 1812).

60. Flat River Baptist Church Records, July, 1823, SHC; Charles Colcock Jones, *The Religious Instruction of the Negroes in the United States* (1842; reprint, New York, 1969), 127–28. For examples of the more guarded approach to dreams and visions, see Barr, *History*, 20; Thompson, *Autobiography*, 86; for their rejection of beliefs in witchcraft, see Wightman, *Life of Capers*, 171–73. The churches' determination to root out witchcraft beliefs is vividly illustrated in the Welsh Neck Baptists' discipline of a black male slave accused of murdering a black woman whom he believed to be a witch; see Welsh Neck Baptist Church Records [1737–1935], entries for 21 May, 3 June, 4 June 1826, SCL. Similarly, a Kentucky Baptist association in 1823 advised churches to bar from membership anyone "who believes in what is generally called *witchcraft*, or practices any so-called charm, or any other idle means to remove what they call witchcraft" (John R. Logan, *Sketches, Historical and Biographical of the Broad River and King's Mountain Baptist Associations from 1800 to 1882* [Shelby, N.C., 1887], 40). Jon Butler offers an illuminating discussion of the evangelical retreat from supernaturalism during this period in *Awash in a Sea of Faith*, 90, 236–41.

61. Cartwright, *Autobiography*, 49.

62. Travis, *Autobiography*, 36–37; Early, Experiences, III:24, VHS; Henry Smith, *Recollections and Reflections of an Old Itinerant* (New York, 1848), 335–36; Stevenson, *Life of Cook*, 57. See also, Brooks, *Life and Times*, 9; Early, Account, 22 September 1807, SHC; Jeremiah Jeter, *The Recollections of a Long Life* (1891; reprint, New York, 1980), 25; Bennet, *Memorials of Methodism*, 172–73.

63. Asbury's remark is cited in Jenkins, *Experience*, 142.

2: THE SEASON OF YOUTH

1. *The Georgia Analytical Repository* (Savannah, 1802–1803); *The Western Missionary Magazine* (1803–1805); *The New York Missionary Magazine* (New York, 1800–1803); *The Connecticut Evangelical Magazine* (Hartford, 1808–15); Theophilus Armenius [pseud.], "Account of the Rise and Progress of the Work of God in the Western Country," *Methodist Magazine* 2 (1819): 184–87, 221–24, 272–74, 304–308, 349–53, 393–96, 434–38; William Woodward, *Surprising Accounts of the Revival of Religion in the United States* (Philadelphia, 1802), passim. Many of the memoirs of clergymen noted below include similar accounts; for evangelical criticisms of lay enthusiasm, see John B. Boles, *The Great Revival 1787–1805: The Origins of the Southern Evangelical Mind* (Lexington, Ky., 1972), 90–110.

2. David Hall, *Worlds of Wonder, Days of Judgment* (New York, 1989), 71–116. The influence of earlier evangelicals on southern chroniclers appears most clearly in Jonathan Edwards, *A Faithful Narrative*, vol. 4 of *The Works of Jonathan Edwards: The Great Awakening*, ed. C. C. Goen (New Haven, 1972), 144–211; see 199–205 for Edwards's account of Phebe Bartlet; see also, Leigh Eric Schmidt, *Holy Fairs: Scottish Communions and American Revivals in the Early Modern Period* (Princeton, 1989), 63–65. Southern preachers and lay people alike also came into contact, closer to home, with Quakers who produced their own child virtuosos who, like Phebe Bartlet, rebuked adults for their moral lapses; see Stith Mead, *A Short Account of the Experience and Labours of the Reverend Stith Mead* (Lynchburg, Va., 1829), 61, and David Hackett Fischer, *Albion's Seed: Four British Folkways in America* (New York, 1989), 512.

3. Edward P. Humphrey and Thomas H. Cleland, *Memoirs of the Reverend Thomas Cleland, D.D.* (Cincinnati, 1859), 27; John Taylor, *A History of Ten Baptist Churches* (1823;

2nd ed., Bloomfield, 1826), 105; Philip Gatch, *A Sketch of the Reverend Philip Gatch*, ed. John M'Lean (Cincinnati, 1854), 130–31; James Finley, *Autobiography of the Reverend James B. Finley; Or Pioneer Life in the West*, ed. W. P. Strickland (Cincinnati, 1853), 367; Jeremiah Jeter, *The Recollections of a Long Life* (1891; reprint, New York, 1980), 57; Armenius, "Account of the Rise and Progress of the Work of God in the Western Country," 224, 305; see also, Christian Newcomer, *Life and Journal of the Reverend Christian Newcomer . . .* , ed. John Hildt (Hagerstown, 1834), 117.

4. Taylor, *History*, 107–108; Reed, *Diary*, 21 October 1778, CHDC, RLUC; James Jenkins, *Experience, Labours, and Sufferings of Reverend James Jenkins* (Columbia, S.C., 1842), 90–91; Wilson Thompson, *The Autobiography of Elder Wilson Thompson* (Cincinnati, 1867), 28; Charles R. Elliott, *The Life of Bishop Robert R. Roberts* (Cincinnati, 1854), 25. Among southern whites, the clergy tended to be less skeptical than the laity about the piety of young blacks: John Taylor, for one, credited the conversions of the same black children that white church members doubted, while Freeborn Garrettson lauded one young black Virginian who "exceeded all the youths ever I saw for a gift and power in prayer" (Freeborn Garrettson, *The Experience and Travels of Freeborn Garrettson* [1790; 2nd ed., Philadelphia, 1791], 69).

5. Jenkins, *Experience*, 86–87; Jeter, *Recollections*, 48, 50; Jacob Young, *Autobiography of a Pioneer* (Cincinnati, 1857), 23. On children's classes, see Norman, *Diary*, 24 September 1793, SHC.

6. Chester Raymond Young, ed., *Westward into Kentucky: The Narrative of Daniel Trabue* (Lexington, Ky., 1981), 76; Jeter, *Recollections*, 44, 50; Brantley York, *Autobiography of Brantley York* (Durham, 1910), 22–23. For the role of peer influence, especially among young men, see also Thompson, *Autobiography*, 20–51; Mead, *Short Account*, 35, 38–39; Henry Smith, *Recollections and Reflections of an Old Itinerant* (New York, 1848), 239–40; Gatch, *Sketch*, 12, 15; Taylor, *History*, 15–16, 19, 27; William Watters, *A Short Account of the Christian Experience, and Ministerial Labours, of William Watters* (Alexandria, 1806), 16; Finley, *Autobiography*, 170; Young, *Autobiography*, 52; Peter Cartwright, *Autobiography of Peter Cartwright, the Backwoods Preacher* (Cincinnati, 1856), 56–57.

7. Ernest Trice Thompson, *Presbyterians in the South*, 3 vols. (Richmond, 1963–73), III: 144–55; Wesley M. Gewehr, *The Great Awakening in Virginia, 1740–1790* (Durham, 1930), 101; Anne C. Loveland, *Southern Evangelicals and the Social Order, 1800–1860* (Baton Rouge, 1980), 47–48, 55; Finley, *Autobiography*, 172. The Cumberland Presbyterians split from the main body of Presbyterianism in 1810 primarily because of their objections to the parent church's strict standards for ministerial education, which they believed impeded the progress of revivalism.

8. William Warren Sweet, *Religion on the American Frontier: The Baptists, 1783–1830*, vol. 1 (New York, 1931), 39–40; Emory Stevens Bucke et al., *The History of American Methodism*, 3 vols. (New York, 1964), I: 467–68; David Sherman, *A History of the Revisions of the Discipline of the Methodist Episcopal Church*, 3rd ed. (New York and Cincinnati, 1890), 422 [cited hereafter as *Revisions*]. For firsthand accounts of the apprenticeship of the Baptist clergy, see Thompson, *Autobiography*, 63–64, 72–74, 95, and Norvell Robertson, Sr., *Autobiography*, 32, 34, VHS; for Methodist apprenticeships, see William M. Wightman, *The Life of William Capers, D.D.* (Nashville, 1858), 76–79; Jenkins, *Experience*, 36, 48.

Each Methodist church, usually called a "society," contained a number of "classes," each consisting of about a dozen members who met regularly to confide their spiritual trials and triumphs. Class meetings were segregated by sex, race, and marital status and limited to members belonging to a Methodist society or those intending to join who had received "tickets" to gain admission from itinerant preachers. Lay "class leaders" conducted meetings when itinerants were not on hand. Class meetings also served as occasions for training aspiring itinerants; as James Jenkins recalled, "here I was drilled and instructed, warned and comforted" by more experienced church members (*Experience*, 37).

9. Cartwright, *Autobiography*, 49, 64; Young, *Autobiography*, 97, 186; Thompson, *Autobiography*, 112; Norman, Diary, 439, SHC; Jeter, *Recollections*, 63.

10. Watters, *Short Account*, 18; Martha Bonner Pelham to Sarah Pelham Dromgoole, 30 August 1810, Edward Dromgoole Papers, SHC; Young, *Autobiography*, 52; Humphrey and Cleland, *Memoirs*, 60–62.

11. Clark et al., eds., *Journal and Letters of Asbury*, 25 August 1773; Thompson, *Autobiography*, 100–101, 105; Gatch, *Sketch*, 20. A man's local connections sometimes made his ministry less credible, as Christian Newcomer reflected when he returned to his boyhood home on a preaching tour: "some of them [his former neighbors] may have said or at least thought, who is he that take upon himself to teach us; do we not know him? is he not the carpenter and carpenter's son, Christian Newcomer? Are not his brothers and sisters still with us?" (*Life and Journal*, 39–40).

12. Williams, Journal, 3, CHDC, RLUC; Robert and Hannah Chambers to Stith Mead, 20 July 1794; Stith Mead to John Kobler, 12 March 1795 in Mead Letterbook, VHS; Early, Experiences, III:38, VI:54, VHS.

13. The difficulties arising from their reliance on a youthful clergy were not the only source of friction within early Baptist and Methodist churches. The Baptists had sharp differences over theology and church organization, while the Methodists battled over the power of their bishops. In general, however, those issues were contested among the clergy more than they engaged the laity.

14. For itinerants' salaries, see notes 52 and 53 in this chapter (and note 55 in Chapter 3). On the relationship between marriage and location of itinerants, see Edward Dromgoole to Francis Asbury, 20 December 1805, Edward Dromgoole Papers, SHC; Thomas Ware, *Sketches of the Life and Travels of Thomas Ware* (New York, 1839), 94, 107. Nathan Hatch estimates that during Francis Asbury's tenure as bishop (1784–1815), "probably not more than a quarter of the . . . itinerants were married." By contrast, among Britain's better-paid Methodist ministers, only one-fourth remained single. (*The Democratization of American Christianity* [New Haven, 1989], 88.)

My sample of men who entered the itinerancy prior to 1800 indicates that twenty-four was the median age for joining the traveling connection. Most Methodist itinerants in the South and its western country began their careers at younger ages than Presbyterian and Congregationalist ministers in New England, who typically received ordination in their late twenties or early thirties. (Joseph Kett, *Rites of Passage: Adolescence in America, 1790 to the Present* [New York, 1977], 32–33.)

The high rate of turnover within the itinerancy can be traced by taking samples from the *Minutes of the General Conferences of the Methodist Church, 1773–1813* (New York, 1813): In 1785, nineteen men from the South and the western country were admitted on trial and eleven finally admitted in full connection; by 1793, only two of the original nineteen remained in the itinerancy, or about 10 percent. In 1800, the story was about the same: of twenty-two admitted on trial, nineteen were received in full connection, but only three were still itinerants in 1809, or about 14 percent of the probationers. When itinerants' annual salaries were raised from $64 to $100 in 1800, the itinerancy attracted more probationers and rates of retention improved slightly: of fifty-two men admitted on trial in 1805, forty-four were received in full connection and fourteen were still in the traveling connection by 1813, or about 27 percent.

The *Minutes* also provide a picture of how little supervision young preachers received. In 1802, of the nineteen men who entered on trial in 1800, nine were either the only preachers on their circuit or sharing a circuit with another probationer from 1800; another three shared circuits with men who were still probationers; only five shared circuits with preachers of greater, but not much greater, experience. (Two of the nineteen I was unable to trace in the *Minutes*.) For example, of the twenty-four men itinerating in North Carolina during 1800 only one, the presiding elder, dated his ministry from the 1780s; eighteen of the twenty-four had five or fewer years of experience since being admitted on trial, and the rest had between six and nine years. In Kentucky and Tennessee, six of eleven itinerants had five or fewer years of experience, and five between six and nine. In other words, the majority of itinerants on most circuits probably had been traveling for no more than five years, and only presiding elders could claim ministries of longer than ten years. Typically, Methodist itinerants in the South during the 1790s were visited only twice a year by their supervisors, the presiding elders. (Jenkins, *Experience*, 58, 60.)

15. In the 1770s and 1780s, some preachers changed circuits as often as every three or six months; by the 1790s, annual relocations appear to have become the rule. In 1801, the General Conference resolved that no itinerant could be appointed to the same circuit for more than two consecutive years. (Jesse Lee, *A Short History of the Methodists, in the United States of America; Beginning in 1766 and Continued Till 1809* (Baltimore, 1810), 52, 298.) Methodist concerns about imposters posing as itinerants first appear in 1782 and continued into the 1790s; see Lee, *Short History*, 80, 100, 169, 197; Beverly Allen to Charles Pettigrew, 11 June 1785, *The Pettigrew Papers*, ed. Sarah McCulloch Lemmon (Raleigh, 1971); Early, Experience, VI:52, VHS; Smith, *Recollections*, 51; James Potter Collins, *Autobiography of a Revolutionary Soldier* (1859; reprint, New York, 1979), 103–104, 155. For similar worries among the Baptists, see Robert Baylor Semple, *A History of the Rise and Progress of the Baptists in Virginia* (Richmond, 1810), 196.

16. Norman, Diary, 878; SHC; Meacham, Journal, 23 March 1790, 6 September 1794, PLDU; see also Ormond, Journal, III: 9–10, PLDU; J. Gregg, Journal, 16 May–1 June, 1796, DC, RLUC. Riding circuit broke the health of many itinerants; after less than two years of traveling, James Meacham complained that "if I never was to preach again while I live, I never should be the Man in Constitution as I have formily [formerly] been" (Journal, 5 July 1789, PLDU). Itinerants commonly reported spitting up blood, some because they were consumptive, but most from the strain of frequent preaching. (Early, Experiences, VI:55, VHS.) William Boyd's analysis of Meacham's journal indicates that he typically preached at least seven times a week. ("Methodist Expansion in North Carolina After the Revolution," *Trinity College Historical Papers*, ser. 12 [1916], 41.) Other itinerants added to their rigors by fasting once a week. ("Journal of Lakin," 8 December 1809.) All of these hardships resulted in mortality rates among young itinerants that probably exceeded those for their age cohort within the southern white population. My sampling of the *Minutes* suggests that at least one man in each group of entering probationers died while still within the traveling connection. See also, Abel Stevens, *A Compendious History of Methodism* (New York and Cincinnati, 1867), 267; Hatch, *Democratization of American Christianity*, 88.

17. Haskins, Journal, 19 January 1783, CHDC, RLUC. To be precise, the Methodist *Discipline* until 1800 accorded the "preacher in charge of the circuit" with absolute powers over admission and expulsion of members. Generally, the preacher in charge was not an itinerant on trial but one who had been received in full connection. However, most preachers in charge assumed that responsibility during their first year in full connection. Before the Revolution, the preacher in charge was known as an "assistant," and the younger preachers were styled "helpers" (Lee, *Short History*, 41).

18. Norman, Diary, 547, SHC; Haskins, Journal, 18 January 1785, 12 July 1783, CHDC, RLUC; Early, Experiences, III:54, VHS; Jenkins, *Experience*, 89–90; see also, Ormond, Journal, I:4, PLDU; Reed, Diary, 8 December 1779, CHDC, RLUC. Experience could make a difference in the way itinerants handled cases of discipline, and Meacham's journal provides the best example. In 1797, after about a decade of riding circuit, he expelled two members for attending local balls and barbecues. The following day, one of the excommunicants, a woman, applied for readmission, which Meacham refused to consider until his next visit, "as I could wish to know, whether the Society could fellowship her or not." In other words, Meacham had learned to rely on support from other members for his decisions in such cases. (Journal, 6 and 7 February 1797, PLDU.)

    The lay resistance encountered by itinerants intent on discipline also made the position of class leader a thankless assignment for many laymen. As James Finley observed, many class leaders so feared alienating their neighbors by exercising strict discipline that "Classes too frequently lead the leader" (Finley, *Autobiography*, 259, 268–69; see also, Norman, Diary, 560, SHC).

19. Sherman, *Revisions*, 451, 456; Lee, *Short History*, 143. Beginning in 1788, the *Discipline* provided expelled members with a process of appeal by bringing their case to the Quarterly Conference before a tribunal consisting of the circuit's presiding elder, itinerant and local preachers, class leaders, and stewards.

20. Jenkins, *Experience*, 68; Early, Experiences, VI:49, 56, VHS; Ormond, Journal, III:27, PLDU; Wightman, *Life of Capers*, 103. See also, Norman, Diary, 23 March 1794, SHC.

21. Jenkins, *Experience*, 116–18.

22. Norman, Diary, 831, SHC; Meacham, Journal, 27 and 28 February 1790, PLDU. Similarly, James Finley offended the lay members of one society in the western country when he insisted on expelling a Lutheran couple from class meeting because they refused to renounce their membership in that church and join the Methodists. (Finley, *Autobiography*, 203.)

23. Ormond, Journal, II:56, PLDU; Norman, Diary, 968, SHC.

24. Meacham, Journal, 1 August 1790, 4 July 1790, 9 March 1790, 17 April 1790, 25 December 1791, 16 March 1790, 3 October 1791, 29 May 1790, 1 February 1792, PLDU; Ormond, Journal, II: 22, 30, PLDU. See also, Early, Experiences, III:26, VI:55, VHS. Several years later, in 1800, Jeremiah Norman was frustrated to find that the Methodist stance on slavery still angered one Colonel Wingate. No antislavery advocate himself, Norman was the right man to persuade Wingate that the Methodists' position "could do him no harm, for it only desired liberty for those who desired to manumate [manumit] their Servants." Despite his efforts, the Colonel only managed "to cool a bit but was not satisfyed" (Norman, Diary, 1103, SHC).

25. George A. Phoebus, comp., *Beams of Light on Early Methodism in America: Chiefly Drawn from the Diary . . . of Rev. Ezekiel Cooper* (New York and Cincinnati, 1887), 108; Devereux Jarratt to Edward Dromgoole, 31 May 1785, 22 March 1788, Edward Dromgoole Papers, SHC; Meacham, Journal, 6 May 1792, 27 February 1790, 25 February 1797, PLDU; Norman, Diary, 1 and 8 November 1795, SHC. Norman also assisted Methodists on his circuit in tracking down and returning runaway slaves. (Diary, 935.)

26. Meacham, Journal, 11 March 1792, 4 August 1790, PLDU; Ormond, Journal, III:51, PLDU. Itinerants traveling the same circuit together might also differ on disciplinary matters; when John Early criticized the members of one society on their fancy dress, "they said they had dressed no more superfluously than my colleague, the other preacher" (Experiences, III:26, VHS).

27. Reed, Diary, 5 September 1781, 30 December 1779, CHDC, RLUC; Garrettson, *Experience*, 72–73. See also, Jenkins, *Experience*, 61–62; Meacham, Journal, 25 April 1790, PLDU.

28. Young, *Autobiography*, 97; Cartwright, *Autobiography*, 78; Meacham, Journal, 20 May 1789, PLDU.

    Jesse Lee read more quickly than most itinerants, but most shared his literary tastes. During one year, he made his way through long-standing evangelical best-sellers like Baxter's *Saints Everlasting Rest*, Doddridge's *Rise and Progress*, the journals of White-field and Brainerd, various writings of Wesley, and the New Testament, which he read twice. (Leroy M. Lee, *The Life and Times of the Reverend Jesse Lee* [Richmond, 1848], 63.) Thomas Haskins's list included a book on the "art of preaching" and one Dr. DuPin's history of the Christian church, which he judged "pretty well so far as it goes . . . if we keep in our minds that he was a rigid Roman Catholic" (Journal, 22 and 24 January 1783, CHDC, RLUC). Jeremiah Norman was equally curious about non-Protestant groups, attending worship at Charleston's Jewish synagogue in 1797, where he was fascinated by their chanting and menorah, after tackling all of Josephus two years earlier. Some itinerants set themselves even more ambitious intellectual goals— John Kobler, for example, taught himself Greek. (John Kobler to Stith Mead, 5 September 1793, Stith Mead Letterbook, VHS; Norman, Diary, 97, 544, SHC.) The clergy also enjoyed poetry, particularly the works of Milton, Young, Cowper, and Pope. Novels, predictably, were less popular, although Norman admitted to reading *The Vicar of Wakefield* in 1798. (Norman, Diary, 62, 618, SHC.) For lists of readings by other itinerants, see Young, *Autobiography*, 51; Cartwright, *Autobiography*, 279; Finley, *Autobiography*, 196; Jenkins, *Experience*, 52; George Brown, *Recollections of an Itinerant Life: Including Early Reminiscences* (Cincinnati, 1866), 98. For a typical Methodist preacher's library in the early nineteenth century, see Susannah Johnson, *Recollections of the Rev. John Johnson and His Home* (Nashville, 1869), 90; for the regimen of study prescribed by the Methodist *Discipline*, see Sherman, *Revisions*, 170–71. Preachers' journals reveal that their efforts at self-education effected steady improvement over the years, at least in their spelling and vocabulary.

    Most members of the early southern Baptist clergy appear to have read less extensively than most Methodist itinerants, probably because the Baptists were obliged to work at secular occupations as well as preach. Wilson Thompson admitted that "a small Bible, Rippon's Hymn-Book, and Bunyan's *Pilgrim's Progress* constituted my library, and, up to the time I was thirty years old, I had never read any other books, notes, or comments on the Scripture. My reading was always very slow. I had to stop frequently, to read it over and over again, so as to be sure I understood the writers meaning" (Thompson, *Autobiography*, 189).

29. Reed, Diary, 13 November 1778, 9 March 1779, 20 August 1780, 29 March 1779, 22 December 1778, CHDC, RLUC; Norman, Diary, 21 March 1793, 415–16, SHC; Haskins, Journal, 8 January 1783, CHDC, RLUC; "Journal of Lakin," 27 July 1795, 5 January 1803; Early, Experiences, III: 25, VHS, and Early, Account, 29 September 1807, SHC; Wightman, *Life of Capers*, 109–110.

30. Meacham, Journal, 3 March 1797, PLDU.

31. Haskins, Journal, 4 and 5 August 1783, CHDC, RLUC; Early, Experiences, III:25, VI:57, VHS. See also, Jenkins, *Experience*, 85. The uneven talents of young American-born clergymen also tried the patience of Francis Asbury, who often complained in his journal about their "coarse" delivery and lack of "depth." Clark et al., eds., *Journal and Letters of Asbury*, 22 and 27 December 1772, 1 September 1773, 1 December 1773.

32. Norman, Diary, 394–95, 575, SHC; Wightman, *Life of Capers*, 118. Baptist preachers endured a similar scrutiny from the laity. In 1785, one layman objected to young John Taylor assuming the pastorate of a Kentucky Baptist church because he thought "my coat was too fine" (Taylor, *History*, 56).

33. Early, Experiences, III:24, VHS; Chappel Bonner and "JB" to Sarah Pelham Drom-goole, 2 September 1810, Edward Dromgoole Papers, SHC; Meacham, Journal, 28 July 1789, 22 June 1795, 19 December 1796, 8 March 1797, 16 March 1797, PLDU; anonymous woman to Stith Mead, 23 May 1793, 12 February 1794, Mead Letterbook, VHS; Johnson, *Recollections*, 92–93. See also, Norman, Diary, 20 July 1794, 488, 998–99, SHC. For the details of Josiah Cole's trial, see Norman, Diary, 965–66, 983, SHC.

    Concern about protecting his reputation also prompted James Jenkins to clear him-self of gossip on his South Carolina circuit in 1796 that he had "frightened" the daugh-ters of his host one evening. Taking two other Methodists with him, Jenkins satisfied the old man of his innocence, noting that "a young Irishman, who at that time was making shoes on the plantation, acknowledged, several years after, that it was he who occasioned the alarm of the old man's daughters" (*Experience*, 80).

    I wish to thank Peter Brown and Sean Wilentz, whose comments on an earlier version of this chapter helped to clarify my thinking about the romantic appeal of itinerants.

34. Norman, Diary, 28 September 1793, 17 October 1793, 433–34, 939, SHC.

35. Nicholas Snethen, *Reply to an Apology for Protesting Against the Methodist Episcopal Government* (Philadelphia, 1800), 57; Daniel Grant to John Owen, 28 July 1791, Camp-bell Family Papers, PLDU; William Watters to Edward Dromgoole, 16 May 1795, Edward Dromgoole Papers, SHC.

36. Sherman, *Revisions*, 455–56; see also, 403–405, 415–16. The concern for preserving the "impartiality" of itinerants also prompted Asbury to examine men in the traveling connection regularly and publicly to ensure that they were clear of all debts. (Albert M. Shipp, *The History of Methodism in South Carolina* [Nashville, 1883], 178.)

37. Lee, *Short History*, 255.

38. John F. Wright, *Sketches of the Life and Labors of James Quinn . . .* (Cincinnati, 1851), 25; Meacham, Journal, 26 June 1789, 26 February 1790, 9 November 1795, 14 April 1797, PLDU; Young, *Autobiography*, 87; Gatch, *Sketch*, 108–109; Wightman, *Life of Capers*, 94; Shipp, *History*, 234–35, and Jenkins, *Experience*, 153–54, 195, 198. Their admiration even persuaded some itinerants to press for according local preachers greater recogni-tion. In 1792, for example, William Ormond proposed to his fellow itinerants at the General Conference that local preachers be made eligible for ordination as elders. But more typical attitudes were expressed by the large majority at the General Conference who defeated Ormond's suggestion by arguing that the honor of eldership would encourage local preachers to "draw the Peoples Money and Power from Itinerant min-isters" (Ormond, Journal, 36, PLDU).

39. William W. Bennet, *Memorials of Methodism in Virginia* (Richmond, 1871), 324–25. In his letter of 1795 in which William Watters warned Edward Dromgoole about the high-handed behavior of itinerants, he added that disaffected Virginians had sent for O'Kelly, "who is now preaching through the neighbourhood while multitudes flock to hear him." Henry Smith attested that O'Kelly's appeal reached as far west as Kentucky, where many local preachers supported his schism and drew a popular following because "These men, it was said, are with us and we know them; as for these traveling preachers, we know them not or from whence they came" (*Recollections*, 51). For treat-ments of the O'Kelly schism and its support among some local preachers, see Bucke et al., *History of American Methodism*, I: 443–51; Lee, *Short History*, 180, 196, 202–205. O'Kelly's influence faded after 1795, mainly because his adherents could not agree upon a form of church organization. Originally known as the Republican Methodists, O'Kelly's followers took the name of "Christians" in 1801 and later merged with the Disciples of Christ.

40. The General Conference agreed in 1796 to limit its membership to those itinerants in full connection, and another decision in 1800 restricted attendance to itinerants in full connection who had traveled for four years. In 1808, when the Methodists adopted a new system of "delegated conferences," it was agreed that delegates would be selected from among the entire body of itinerants on the basis of seniority. (Lee, *Short History*, 231, 270.)

    With regard to local preachers, the reforms of 1796 provided for those accused of misdeeds to be tried first before a committee of three or more local preachers. If a majority agreed upon his guilt, he was suspended until the next quarterly conference of his circuit, when a tribunal consisting of the circuit's presiding elder, traveling preachers, local preachers, class leaders and stewards would decide his fate. Decisions of the quarterly conference could be appealed to the annual conference. (*Journals of the General Conference of the Methodist Episcopal Church*, 3 vols. [New York, 1855], vol. 1, 26–27.)

    The General Conference of 1796 granted local preachers other concessions as well. It allowed them payment for taking over the duties of sick or absent itinerants and stipulated that they were eligible for ordination as deacons four years after being licensed as local preachers. (Robert Emory, *History of the Discipline of the Methodist Episcopal Church* [New York, 1856], 179, 183–84.)

    For the reform of lay discipline in 1800, see *Journals of the General Conference*, vol. 1, 39; Lee, *Short History*, 269.

41. Thomas S. Chew to Edward Dromgoole, 20 August 1804, Edward Dromgoole Papers, SHC; Early, Experiences, VI:49, 56, 57, 65, VHS; Early, Account, 21 February 1814, SHC; Daniel Grant to John Owen, 28 July 1791, Campbell Family Papers, SHC; William Watters to Edward Dromgoole, 16 May 1795, Thomas Sheradine Chew to Edward Dromgoole, 20 August 1804, James Keys to Edward Dromgoole, 3 August 1810, all in Edward Dromgoole Papers, SHC; *Journals of the General Conference*, vol. 1, 101, 104, 125, 179.

    The authority of itinerants remained considerable, despite the changes at the end of the eighteenth century. They still retained the exclusive right to attend General Conferences, held the sole power over admissions, examined candidates applying for licenses as local preachers, and endorsed those applying for ordination as deacons. They also continued to exert influence over the discipline of members by attending the trials of accused lay people and advising societies about individual cases. Some went further still: There were complaints as late as 1816 about preachers expelling members without trial. (*Journals of the General Conference*, I: 156–57.)

    The experience of the Methodists with their youthful itinerancy raises questions about David Hackett Fischer's thesis that a "deep change" took place in attitudes toward age everywhere in the new republic between 1770 and 1820—that egalitarian notions and ideals of liberty undermined the hierarchy setting age over youth. He draws evidence in support of that view almost entirely from the northern United States, mainly New England. (*Growing Old in America* [expanded ed., London and New York, 1978].)

42. Sweet, *Religion on the American Frontier*, I: 36, 40; Charles D. Mallary, *Memoirs of Elder Edmund Botsford* (Charleston, 1832), 45; William Hickman, Autobiography, 12, DC, RLUC; Taylor, *History*, 29.

43. Semple, *History*, 77, 351–52; Joseph Bishop, *The Life of Joseph Bishop*, ed. John W. Gray (Nashville, 1858), 48. Decisions concerning admission and expulsion required either unanimity or two-thirds vote. (Sweet, *Religion on the American Frontier*, I: 48.) An instructive example of the lengths to which Baptist churches went to avoid alienating powerful male members appears in the case of one "Brother Bell," whom Tennessee's Red River church refused to discipline until the county court convicted him of usury,

thus forcing their hand; see Red River Baptist Church Records, 20 December 1817, 15 January 1818, SHC.

44. Ironically, the years right after revivals, when Baptist churches gained the greatest number of new members, were also those periods most fraught with the potential for disputes or lasting divisions within congregations over doctrine, discipline, and leadership. Revivals did more than heighten lay concern with defining doctrinal orthodoxy and renew their commitment to enforcing rigorous discipline. They also introduced new converts—sometimes entire families—into membership, whose zeal and numbers could transform the character of congregations.

45. Taylor, *History*, 11–12.

46. Jeter, *Recollections*, 90.

47. Taylor, *History*, 54–56, 65–66, 80–81, 124. For examples of the sorts of disputes that raged both between Baptist preachers and among the laity, see also, Taylor, *History*, 173–77, 183–86; Thompson, *Autobiography*, 324ff; Williams, Journal, 5–7, CHDC, RLUC.

48. Hickman, Autobiography, 38–39, 46, DC, RLUC; Taylor, *History*, 200, 202.

49. All of these controversies between Baptist associations and their member churches can be traced in Lemuel Burkitt and Jesse Read, *A Concise History of the Kehukee Baptist Association* . . . (1850; reprint, New York, 1980), 70–73, 92–96, 106–107, 114, 119–21, 126, and Semple, *History*, 292; see also, George W. Paschal, *History of North Carolina Baptists*, 2 vols. (Raleigh, 1930–55), I: 505–11, II: 208–11; Flat River Baptist Church Records, July 1792, SHC.

    Associations were purely advisory bodies; they could, as a last resort, expel disorderly member churches, but they held no authority over the governance of individual congregations. (Sweet, *Religion on the American Frontier*, I: 54–55.)

50. It was Steve Aron who first dubbed the "season of youth" a "winter of discontent" when he commented on an earlier draft of this chapter in a session sponsored by the Davis Center at Princeton University. He kindly consented to my swiping this turn of phrase, and I assume he received similar permission from the minor English dramatist with whom it originated.

51. Robertson, Autobiography, 34, SHC. John Taylor urged that all Baptist churches adopt shared pastorates as an antidote to divisive wrangling; see Taylor, *History*, 65–66. For the mobility of preachers, see Thompson, *Autobiography*, 95, 113, 242–44, 257–58; Taylor, *History*, 77–80, 139, 159. These pressures contributed to the high rate of turnover in the pastorates of early Baptist churches that George W. Paschal detected in his study of North Carolina congregations. According to Paschal, few elders held the same pastorate throughout their careers; far more typically, pastorates lasted between five and ten years. (*History of North Carolina Baptists*, II: 202–203.)

52. Wightman, *Life of Capers*, 202. Lay resistance to supporting the families of married preachers first appears in 1783 when the General Conference required wealthier circuits to help support the wives of itinerants in less affluent regions. Many of the "leading men . . . did not approve of it; and thought it unreasonable that they should raise money for a woman they never saw; and whose husband had never preached among them." Desires to placate a cost-conscious laity probably prodded the Conference into its mean-spirited resolution of 1792 to grant allowances to itinerants' wives only "if they be in want of it." Not until 1796 were spouses acknowledged as having an equal claim to support. Allotments for the children of itinerants, first tried in 1784, also met with lay opposition—so much so that the General Conference revoked provisions for their support in 1787 and did not reinstate them until 1800. (Lee, *Short History*, 83, 100–101, 183; Shipp, *History*, 514–15.)

    Itinerants assembled in annual conferences throughout the South and its western country also tried to avoid admitting married men into the traveling connection, reasoning that they would either locate soon or alienate the laity with their greater financial needs. (Shipp, *History*, 342–43; Alfred Brunson, *A Western Pioneer: Or, Incidents of the Life and Times of the Reverend Alfred Brunson* (Cincinnati, 1872), 167, 169; "Journal of Lakin," 3 September 1816.)

53. *Journals of the General Conference*, I:35, 38; Clark et al., eds., *Journal and Letters of Asbury*, 8 June 1780, 1 February 1809; Phoebus, *Beams of Light*, 239–43; Bennet, *Memorials of Methodism*, 184, 534, 555; M. H. Moore, *Sketches of the Pioneers of Methodism in North Carolina and Virginia* (Nashville, 1884), 192–93; Lee, *Life*, 55–56, 97; Wightman, *Life of Capers*, 179. For Wesley's views, see Henry Abelove's superb biography, *The Evangelist of Desire: John Wesley and the Methodists* (Stanford, 1990), 49–72. E. P. Thompson has also emphasized the obsession with the sinfulness of sexuality among early English Methodists, see *The Making of the English Working Class* (New York, 1963), 370.

Asbury had long been aware that low pay sustained the perennial youthfulness of the itinerancy, and in the 1780s he had even entertained plans for raising salaries. But the first efforts in that direction came not from Asbury but his fellow bishop Thomas Coke, who, after years of lobbying, finally mustered a slim majority of the General Conference in 1800 to approve a princely increase of $16. Much more might have been done sooner if Coke's energies had not been drawn off into organizing foreign missions and the leadership of the church in America entrusted entirely to Asbury.

54. William McKendree, Diary, 18 September 1790, Vanderbilt Divinity School, Nashville, cited in James D. Essig, *Bonds of Wickedness: American Evangelicals and Slavery, 1770–1808* (Philadelphia, 1980), 58; Bucke et al., *History of American Methodism*, I: 48; *Journals of the General Conference*, I:128–29, 148–51, 155, 159–61. My conclusion about the improved rate of persistence within the traveling connection is based on tracing the careers of the fifty-six men who were admitted on trial in 1816, the year that the General Conference voted to improve support for married preachers. Of those fifty-six men, twenty-six were still itinerating in 1824, or about half (46 percent). The comparable percentages for men admitted on trial in 1785 (10 percent), in 1800 (14 percent), and in 1805 (27 percent) suggest the efficacy of the reforms. (*Minutes of the Annual Conferences of the Methodist Episcopal Church*, 1773–1839, 2 vols. [New York, 1840].)

3: FAMILY VALUES

1. All of the above is based on Stith Mead, *A Short Account of the Experiences and Labours of the Reverend Stith Mead* (Lynchburg, Va., 1829), 20–23, 34–42, 44, 48.
2. Stith Mead, Journal (original no longer extant), excerpted in William W. Bennet, *Memorials of Methodism in Virginia* (Richmond, 1871), 309–10.
3. Stith Mead to Samuel Mead, 24 September 1792, Mead Letterbook, VHS.
4. Stith Mead to William Mead, 12 June 1793, Mead Letterbook, VHS.
5. William Mead to Stith Mead, 20 October 1793, Cowles Mead to Stith Mead, 20 October 1793, Mead Letterbook, VHS.
6. Stith Mead to John Kobler, 16 August 1794, Stith Mead to Hope Hull, 7 July 1794, J. M. Simmons to Stith Mead, 19 October 1793, Stith Mead to William Mead, 1 September 1794, Mead Letterbook, VHS.
7. William Mead to Stith Mead, 7 September 1794, Mead Letterbook, VHS; Mead, *Short Account*, 17–18.
8. Virtually all clerical memoirs chronicle their quick and early success at converting parents, siblings, and in-laws. For examples, see Philip Gatch, *A Sketch of the Reverend*

Philip Gatch, ed. John M'Lean (Cincinnati, 1854), 16, 112; William M. Wightman, *The Life of Capers*, D.D. (Nashville, 1858), 86; James Jenkins, *Experience, Labours, and Sufferings of Reverend James Jenkins* (Columbia, S.C., 1842), 39–40; Jacob Young, *Autobiography of a Pioneer* (Cincinnati, 1857), 48–49; William Watters, *A Short Account of the Christian Experience, and Ministerial Labours, of William Watters* (Alexandria, 1806), 5, 7, 12.

9. The surviving evidence defies any attempt at drawing accurate generalizations about the dynamics of conversion within families—that is, the incidence of wives converting husbands, children converting parents, and so forth. Anecdotal evidence provides instances of every possible configuration, although mature women and young men and young women are most often identified as fostering the conversions of husbands and fathers. Church records, which exist in significant numbers only for the Baptists, indicate only the date of admission to membership, not the date of an individual's conversion. In addition, records of admission to church membership often list several members of the same family entering the church on the same date, which further complicates the problem of detecting whose conversion catalyzed the rest of the family. Even if none of those obstacles existed, ages of converts is difficult to trace because many families in the same church shared the same surname, and many of those the same first name, while the lack of marriage records obscures the maiden names of married women. On the centrality of family to evangelical recruitment strategies, see Donald Mathews, *Religion in the Old South* (Chicago, 1977), 98–99; A. Gregory Schneider, *The Way of the Cross Leads Home: The Domestication of American Methodism* (Bloomington and Indianapolis, 1994), passim.

   Richard Rankin's careful study of correspondence among elite Anglican families in early-nineteenth-century North Carolina reveals the frequency of family strife over religious loyalties, confirming the typicality of the Meads' troubles. (*Ambivalent Churchmen and Evangelical Women: The Religion of the Episcopal Elite in North Carolina, 1800–1860* [Columbia, S.C., 1993], 111–16.) Preachers' journals indicate that such conflicts were equally common and intense in the households of yeomen and tenants throughout the South.

10. *Western Missionary Magazine 1* (October 1803): 332; John Taylor, *A History of Ten Baptist Churches* (1823; 2nd ed., Bloomfield, 1826), 38; Meacham, Journal, 23 April 1789, 1 May 1789, 3 March 1790, 14 March 1790, 6 July 1790, PLDU; Norman, Diary, 5 and 7 January, 15 March 1794, SHC; Gatch, *Sketch*, 10, 14; Ebenezer Pettigrew to Ann S. Pettigrew, 2 December 1815, *Pettigrew Papers*, ed. Sarah McCulloch Lemmon (Raleigh, 1971). Gail Malmgreen makes a similar point about English Methodism during the same period, arguing that when younger people took the initiative in joining evangelical churches, generational struggles within families often resulted; see her thoughtful essay, "Domestic Discords: Women and the Family in East Cheshire Methodism, 1750–1830," in *Disciplines of Faith: Studies in Religion, Politics and Patriarchy*, ed. Jim Obelkevich, Lyndal Roper, and Raphael Samuel (London and New York, 1987), 64.

11. These themes emerge in all collections of family correspondence dating from the Revolutionary and early national periods; for examples, see Edward Dromgoole Papers, SHC; Campbell Family Papers, PLDU; William Southerland Hamilton Papers, SHC; see also Joan Cashin, *A Family Venture: Men and Women on the Southern Frontier* (New York, 1991), passim. For other overviews of westward migration among southerners in the period covered by this study, see Allan Kulikoff, *Tobacco and Slaves: The Development of Southern Cultures in the Chesapeake, 1680–1800* (Chapel Hill, 1986), 77; and Frank L. Owsley, "Pattern of Migration and Settlement on the Southern Frontier," in *The South: Old and New Frontiers*, ed. Harriet Chappell Owsley (Athens, Ga., 1969), 3–29.

12. For discussions of evangelical descriptions of heaven, see Jan Lewis, *The Pursuit of Happiness: Family and Values in Jefferson's Virginia* (Cambridge, Mass., 1983), 81; Mathews, *Religion in the Old South*, 101; Schneider, *Way of the Cross*, 46–47, 60, 74.

13. This family correspondence can be traced in numerous letters of Frances Goodwin, Isabel, Mary, and Mildred Owen to Dr. John Owen and Mary Owen; John Owen, Sr., to Dr. John Owen, 22 December 1808; Elizabeth Anderson to Dr. John Owen, 21 October 1810, 8 August 1814; Thomas Anderson to Dr. John Owen, 2 November 1814; John Owen, Sr., to Dr. John Owen, 12 September 1814; Frances Goodwin Smith to John Owen, 31 August 1814, all in Campbell Family Papers, PLDU; see also, Early, Experiences, VI:50, SHC.

14. Wilson Thompson, *The Autobiography of Elder Wilson Thompson* (Cincinnati, 1867), 41, 43.

15. Robert Simpson, ed., *American Methodist Pioneer: The Life and Journals of the Reverend Freeborn Garrettson, 1752–1827* (Rutland, Vt., 1984), 222 (entry for 19 May 1783); Meacham, Journal, 22 November 1789, 3 September 1791, 24 October 1794, PLDU; Watters, *Short Account*, 109; Rankin, Diary, 19 February 1775, CHDC, RLUC. In devaluing marriage, the early Methodist clergy were hardly singular figures within the western Christian tradition. As John Boswell points out, Christianity "remained overwhelmingly ambivalent about most forms of heterosexual marriage during the first millennium of its existence," and only thereafter elevated "the biological family as the central unit of Christian society" (*Same-Sex Unions in Premodern Europe* [New York, 1994], 110–11). Indeed, these beliefs respecting marriage may have enhanced the Methodists' identification of their movement with the primitive Christian church.

16. Meacham, Journal, 25 April 1790, PLDU; Early, Account, 18 March 1814, SHC; Norman, Diary, 3 November 1793, SHC; Susannah Johnson, *Recollections of the Rev. John Johnson and His Home* (Nashville, 1869), 91.

17. Thomas Ware, *Sketches of the Life and Travels of Thomas Ware* (New York, 1839), 144–46; Peter Cartwright, *Autobiography of Peter Cartwright, the Backwoods Preacher* (Cincinnati, 1856), 144; Norman, Diary, 223–24, SHC. See also, Simpson, ed., *American Methodist Pioneer*, 227 (entry for 19 July 1783).

18. Meacham, Journal, 5 July 1790, 2 February 1789, 18 February 1790, 25 June 1791, 11 April 1792, PLDU; Haskins, Journal, 19 January 1783, 2 May 1783, CHDC, RLUC; Simpson, ed., *American Methodist Pioneer*, 219 (entry for 16 April 1783); Ormond, Journal, II: 22, III: 50–51, PLDU. See also Myles Greene, Journal, 71, PLDU, and "Journal of Lakin," 4 February 1796. Meacham, already obsessed with sexual purity, found even more to worry about on a trip to Baltimore where he "met with a Treatise which I never saw before the Sin Onania" (Journal, 14 November 1792).

19. Sarah Jones to Jeremiah Minter, 28 January 1790, in Sarah Jones, *Devout Letters*, ed. Jeremiah Minter (Alexandria, Va., 1804); Jeremiah Minter, *A Brief Account of the Religious Experience, Travels, Preaching, Persecutions from Evil Men, and God's Special Helps in the Faith and Life Etc. of Jeremiah Minter* (Washington, D.C., 1817), 13–15, 21, 24; Clark et al., *Journal and Letters of Asbury*, 8 April 1791. Minter sought to still lingering public curiosity about his relationship with Sarah Jones by editing and publishing her letters to him and other clergymen after her death. But that correspondence only confirmed the very impression he wanted to dispel by revealing how much more frequently and ardently she addressed her attentions to him. It seems improbable, however, that they ever acknowledged, let alone consummated, their attraction. In the aftermath of the scandal that led to his expulsion from the itinerancy, she informed him that "God knew our integrity and simplicity in heart, but his jealous eye saw danger of idolatry in setting each other up, which by many was censoriously

deemed carnal" (Sarah Jones to Jeremiah Minter, 22 December 1792, in Jones, *Devout Letters*).

For years after this episode, Methodist leaders regarded Minter as an embarrassment—and one that would not go away, because he continued to seek reentry to the itinerancy until the turn of the century. In 1792, the General Conference dispatched him as a missionary to the West Indies, which, like Nova Scotia, was one of the church's dumping-grounds for failed itinerants, and when he returned to the United States six months later, he was made a local preacher because of his refusal to admit the sinfulness of self-castration. Resentful of this demotion, Minter became an independent preacher and part-time schoolmaster, a career that he pursued to the end of his life, punctuated by several months when his father, believing that his son had run mad, chained him up at the family's home in western Virginia. (Minter, *Brief Account*, 19–20, 27ff.)

20. Cartwright, *Autobiography*, 62; Early, Account, 25 May 1807, SHC; Watters, *Short Account*, 24, quoting Matthew 8:21; Reed, Diary, 18 October 1780, CHDC, RLUC; Young, *Autobiography*, 68; Meacham, Journal, 13 February 1797, PLDU. Even preachers who did not travel experienced conflicts between duty to God and family. After both of his parents died around 1800, the Kentuckian Thomas Cleland was torn between his responsibilities to rear his siblings and his desire to enter the Presbyterian ministry. (Edward P. Humphrey and Thomas H. Cleland, *Memoirs of the Reverend Thomas Cleland, D.D.* [Cincinnati, 1859], 59–68.) Again, Francis Asbury was the prototype: The only surviving child of aging parents, he left England in 1771 and never returned to visit them.

21. Jesse Lee, *A Short History of the Methodists, in the United States of America; Beginning in 1766 and Continued Till 1809* (Baltimore, 1810), 235–37; Alfred Brunson, *A Western Pioneer: Or, Incidents of the Life and Times of the Reverend Alfred Brunson* (Cincinnati, 1872), 174; Edward Dromgoole to Thomas Sheradine Chew, 1784, Edward Dromgoole Papers, SHC; Jenkins, *Experience*, 164–65, 167–68; "Journal of Lakin," 13 April and 8 May 1810; Johnson, *Recollections*, 193–94; Thompson, *Autobiography*, 238, 240; William S. Simpson, ed., "The Journal of Henry Toler: Part I, 1782–1783," *Virginia Baptist Register*, 1586; for a detailed account of the hardships endured by one Methodist itinerant's wife, see Johnson, *Recollections*, 96–99, 101–103, 109, 112–13, 124–25.

22. "Journal of Lakin," 23 June 1809; Gatch, *Sketch*, 53; Johnson, *Recollections*, 200–201; Cartwright, *Autobiography*, 184.

23. Bertram Wyatt-Brown has written eloquently of the importance of lineage in the Old South; see his *Southern Honor: Ethics and Behavior in the Old South* (New York, 1982), 119–25.

24. Cashin, *Family Venture*, passim. Cashin associates this new set of social values emphasizing personal fulfillment over family welfare with the sons of the seaboard planter elite who moved to the western country during the early decades of the nineteenth century. As Steve Hahn and Lacy Ford have shown, the southern yeomanry of the Georgia and South Carolina up-country resisted competition and risk-taking, practicing "safety-first" agriculture and limiting their dependence on the market economy, but many of their counterparts in the Southwest had uncertainty thrust upon them because of the insecurity of land titles. (Steven Hahn, *Roots of Southern Populism: Yeoman Farmers and the Transformation of the Georgia Upcountry, 1850–1890* [New York, 1983], 15–85; Lacy K. Ford, *Origins of Southern Radicalism: The South Carolina Upcountry, 1800–1860* [New York, 1988], 44–95. See also, John Mack Faragher, *Daniel Boone: The Life and Legend of an American Pioneer* [New York, 1992], 241–45; Fredrika A. Teute, "Land, Liberty and Labor in the Post-Revolutionary Era: Kentucky as the Promised Land" [Ph.D. dissertation, Johns Hopkins, 1988], passim.)

25. John Bunyan, *The Pilgrim's Progress* (New York, 1949), 11; Will of Edward Dromgoole, 2 November 1833, Edward Dromgoole Papers, SHC; Hester Ann (Rowe) Rogers, *A Short Account of the Experience of Mrs. Hester Ann Rogers* (New York, 1806), passim; on the popularity of Bunyan, see "Journal of Lakin," 10 February 1796. The importance of devotional imagery cannot be overstated; even in the 1850s, between one-fifth and one-quarter of adult southern whites were illiterate. (Wyatt-Brown, *Southern Honor*, 193–94.)

26. Benjamin Abbott, *The Experience and Gospel Labours of the Reverend Benjamin Abbott . . .* , ed. John F. Ffirth (New York, 1805), 93.

27. Flat River Baptist Church Records, March 1786, November 1786, June 1790, August 1790, 1 October 1791, SHC. The matter of how openly to discipline wayward members evidently bedeviled many early Baptist churches: South Carolina's Cashaway Baptist Church decided in 1767 that "if a member falls publickly . . . he shall be sensured [*sic*] publickly." Just what the church understood by transgressing "publickly" is not entirely clear, but their intent appears to have been disciplining those convicted of such offenses before the entire congregation, not merely the church. (Cashaway Baptist Church Record Book, 20 June 1767, SCL.)

It is unusual to find instances of church discipline from this era involving homosexual acts. Besides the case at Flat River cited above, the only other possible reference that has come to my notice appears in the minutes of a South Carolina church where, in 1811, one Noel Johnson was summarily excluded for "being found to be a transgressor both of the laws of God and Nature." The deliberate vagueness of wording precludes any certainty about his offense, but the same reserve also suggests that the church expelled Johnson not for sexual misdeeds with a woman but rather with another man or an animal. (New Providence Baptist Church Records, 21 September 1811, SCL.)

28. Meacham, Journal, 30 May 1789, PLDU; Ormond, Journal, II: 30, PLDU. For instances of individual Methodists being disciplined or expelled for selling or buying slaves throughout the 1790s, see Norman, Diary, 722, 767, 868, 876, SHC.

29. Daniel Grant to John Owen, 3 September 1790, 15 September 1791, 8 September 1792, undated, ca. 1792, Campbell Family Papers, PLDU; for biographical information on the Grant family, see Clark et al., eds., *Journal and Letters of Asbury*, I:593, 25n.

30. Simpson, ed., "Journal of Henry Toler," 1582; Lemuel Read and Jesse Burkitt, *Concise History of the Kehukee Baptist Association . . .* (1850; reprint, New York, 1980), 73; David Sherman, *A History of the Revisions of the Discipline of the Methodist Episcopal Church*, 3rd ed. (New York and Cincinnati, 1890), 228–29; George A. Phoebus, comp., *Beams of Light on Early Methodism in America: Chiefly Drawn from the Diary . . . of Rev. Ezekiel Cooper* (New York and Cincinnati, 1887), 141; Simpson, ed., *American Methodist Pioneer*, 224 (entry for 16 June 1783); Meacham, Journal, 21 February 1790, 25 February 1792, PLDU; "Journal of Lakin," 25 December 1802; Lee, *Short History*, 105; Norman, Diary, 262–63, 774, 790, SHC. Daniel Blake Smith finds that, by the late eighteenth century, marriages among the gentry increasingly reflected children's romantic preferences rather than parental control; however, as the examples above suggest, such practices may not have spread below the level of the elite. (*Inside the Great House: Planter Family Life in the Eighteenth-Century Chesapeake* [Ithaca, 1980], 118–19.)

31. For the continuity of disciplinary practices, especially disownment, among westering Quakers, see Neva J. Specht, "Mixed Blessing: Trans-Appalachian Settlement and the Society of Friends" (dissertation in progress, University of Delaware). For instances of Methodist preachers praising Quaker religiosity see Meacham, Journal, 22 May 1791, PLDU; Haskins, Journal, 21 September 1783, CHDC, RLUC; Gatch, *Sketch*, 9. Wesley's

preference for celibacy among his clergy and lay followers may also reflect Quaker influence, for some radical Friends, in both the seventeenth and eighteenth centuries, embraced that practice—Ann Lee, the founder of Shakerism, being the best-known example. Even more orthodox early Quakers sought to "spiritualize" marriage by devaluing physical attraction as a basis for conjugal unions. (Barry Levy, *The Quakers and American Domesticity: British Settlement in the Delaware Valley* [New York, 1988], 72–73.)

32. Christiana Holmes Tillson, *A Woman's Story of Pioneer Illinois* (Chicago, 1919), 79–80.

33. Robert Paine, *Life and Times of William McKendree* (Nashville, 1880), 41–42; Mead, *Short Account*, 32; Cartwright, *Autobiography*, 27, 34. See also, Edward Stevenson, *A Biographical Sketch of the Reverend Valentine Cook, A.M.* (Nashville, 1858), 10–11, 16. The memoirs of British Methodists may well have served as models for these recollections of youthful religious precocity and ritualized condemnations of parents; see especially, Rogers, *Short Account*, 1–7.

34. "Journal of Lakin," 23 July 1795. Southerners who shifted their loyalties from one evangelical church to another also took part in public parent-bashing and the ritualized wringing of hands over their spiritually lax rearing of children. The Methodist preacher James Jenkins, after describing his deep religious impressions during boyhood, pilloried his parents, both members of the Baptist Church, for not cultivating his piety. Although they restrained him from "outward acts of vice," Jenkins "never heard my father pray in his family but once." Beyond that, "I imbibed the notion, that my parents were partial in their love to their children; and that I was least beloved of all. I seemed to be the butt for the whole family, even for the negroes" (Jenkins, *Experience*, 9–10, 13–14).

35. Phoebus, *Beams of Light*, 18; Bennet, *Memorials of Methodism*, 290; Charles D. Mallary, *Memoirs of Elder Edmund Botsford* (Charleston, 1832), 62; Taylor, *History*, 45; Thompson, *Autobiography*, 109; Jenkins, *Experience*, 39, 84, 92, 230; Sherman, *Revisions*, 417, 423; George Brown, *Recollections of an Itinerant Life: Including Early Reminiscences* (Cincinnati, 1866), 116; Wightman, *Life of Capers*, 56.

36. Taylor, *History*, 61; James Finley, *Autobiography of the Reverend James B. Finley; Or Pioneer Life in the West*, ed. W. P. Strickland (Cincinnati, 1853), 181; Thompson, *Autobiography*, 164. That usage is still current in many communities in the South, where joining a particular congregation is known as "finding a church-home."

  The first English Quakers in the seventeenth century appear to have coined the term *mother in Israel*, and I am indebted to Neva Specht for pointing out that eighteenth-century Quakers in the American South also used the term. It is likely, if not entirely certain, that southern Baptists and Methodists adopted it directly from their Quaker neighbors. According to Phyllis Mack, seventeenth-century English Quakers used the phrase to denote an image of female virtue combining traditional domestic responsibilities with religious roles endowing extraordinary spiritual authority and stature—visionary, public evangelist, adviser, and amanuensis to traveling male Friends. (Phyllis Mack, *Visionary Women: Ecstatic Prophecy in Seventeenth-Century England* [Berkeley, 1992], 215–18, 240, 246.)

37. Meacham, Journal, 2 June 1791, 20 September 1791, PLDU. Both A. Gregory Schneider and Gail Malmgreen have pointed up the role of Methodist churches as "surrogate families"; see Schneider, *Way of the Cross*, 60, 74, 124–28, and Malmgreen, "Domestic Discords," in *Disciplines of Faith*, 59.

38. There is some evidence to suggest that some Methodist laywomen—and possibly laymen as well—also adopted the practice of covenantal kinship. Sarah Jones, for example, wrote to Susanna Williams of "feeling" her prayers and those of other

women "at the appointed hours of covenant prayer" (Sarah Jones to Susanna Williams, n.d., in Jones, *Devout Letters*, 136).

39. Stith Mead to John Kobler, 25 November 1793, 18 December 1794, 1 March 1795, 1 April 1795, John Kobler to Stith Mead, 15 December 1794, all in Mead Letterbook, VHS.

40. For the literature on same-sex relationships, see Carroll Smith-Rosenberg, "The Female World of Love and Ritual: Relations Between Women in Nineteenth-Century America," in *Disorderly Conduct: Visions of Gender in Victorian America* (New York, 1985), 53–76; E. Anthony Rotundo, "Romantic Friendship: Male Intimacy and Middle-Class Youth in the Northern United States, 1800–1900," *Journal of Social History* 23 (1989): 1–25; Drew Gilpin Faust, *James Henry Hammond and the Old South: Design for Mastery* (Baton Rouge, 1982), 18n–19n; Steven Stowe, *Intimacy and Power in the Old South: Ritual in the Lives of the Planters* (Baltimore, 1987), 203–205; Donald Yacovone, "Abolitionists and the 'Language of Fraternal Love,' " in *Meanings for Manhood: Constructions of Masculinity in Victorian America*, ed. Mark Carnes and Clyde Griffen (Chicago, 1990), 85–95; and Laura McCall, " 'With all the Wild, Trembling, Rapturous Feelings of a Lover': Men, Women, and Sexuality in American Literature, 1820–1860," *Journal of the Early Republic* 14 (1994): 71–89.

Anthony Rotundo has found that "romantic friendships" were widely accepted among young, middle-class men in the antebellum North, and that such associations were marked by sharing intimate emotions, addressing one another in terms of endearment, applying marital imagery to describe their relationships, and, sometimes, exchanging physical affection such as kissing and embracing while sharing the same bed, but not engaging in genital sex. Set against that model, Mead's professions of attachment to Kobler are distinctive for a number of reasons. First, unlike young men in the North, who always strove for a joking tone when comparing their friendships to marriage, Mead was in earnest when he spoke of being "married" to Kobler. In addition, northern men reserved language implying same-sex erotic attraction for their journals, while Mead used that imagery in his letters. Perhaps most significant, all of the northern youths included in Rotundo's research combined romantic friendships with their male contemporaries with equally intense involvements with young women, while Mead and Kobler carefully avoided even flirting with members of the opposite sex.

41. Meacham, Journal, 2 November 1789, 4 November 1789, 23 and 24 November 1789, 28 March 1790, PLDU. Images of intimate encounters with Christ also appear in women's accounts of their spiritual experiences. In 1789, for example, Sally Eastland wrote to the Methodist preacher Edward Dromgoole that "when I hear from Him [Jesus], some times all my poor heart dessolves in love, in some of his love visits to my poor soul of late, He's left me as it were helpless on the ground, ah sweet momentes, how fain would I faint away in his arms, and never see a sinner more . . ." (21 February 1789, Edward Dromgoole Papers, SHC).

Thomas Cleland, a Presbyterian, invoked the more conventional image of Christ as a bridegroom to describe his conversion: "I thought, indeed, it was the heavenly bridegroom calling and inviting his poor, feeble and falling one to rise from my low condition, and come away and follow him more entirely." (Humphrey and Cleland, *Memoirs of Cleland*, 54). For a thoughtful analysis of the themes of homoeroticism and marital imagery in the religious literature of seventeenth-century New England, see Richard Godbeer, " 'Love Raptures': Marital, Romantic, and Erotic Images of Jesus Christ in Puritan New England, 1670–1730," *New England Quarterly* 68 (1995): 355–84.

42. John Kobler to Stith Mead, 27 November 1793, 15 January 1795, John Metcalf to Stith Mead, 17 November 1793, Horatio Burns to Stith Mead, 30 November 1793, Stith Mead to William Mead, 12 June 1793, Mead Letterbook, VHS; Freeborn Garrettson, *The*

Experience and Travels of Freeborn Garrettson (1790; 2nd ed., Philadelphia, 1791), 51; Wightman, *Life of Capers*, 90, 112–13.

The covenant brotherhood of early Methodist itinerants bears a close and intriguing resemblance to the bonding between the first Quaker male preachers in seventeenth-century England, who commonly traveled in pairs described as "knit together, in love that's everlasting, passing the love of women" (Mack, *Visionary Women*, 224–25). I have not been able to confirm whether that tradition continued among American Quaker missionaries during the early national period.

Some young Baptist preachers also developed intense friendships and spent their itinerant years traveling in pairs. Such was the case with John Taylor and Joseph Redding, who itinerated throughout western Virginia and Kentucky together during the 1770s. It was still a common practice in the 1820s, when young Jeremiah Jeter and his contemporary, Daniel Witt, spent several months preaching together in western Virginia. (Taylor, *History*, 19–37; Jeremiah Jeter, *The Recollections of a Long Life* (1891; reprint, New York, 1980), 62–64.)

Neither Baptist nor Methodist preachers expressed any uneasiness at the affectionate behavior of their colleagues, no matter how intensely those emotions were conveyed. Yet many were careful to qualify their written endearments by emphasizing the "pure" or spiritual character of their attachments. The intensity of these same-sex bonds was noticed by some contemporaries; on this point, see Philip Greven, *The Protestant Temperament: Patterns of Child-Rearing, Religious Experience, and the Self in Early America* (New York, 1977), 139.

43. Sherman, *Revisions*, 139–40, 448–50.
44. William Spencer to Mary Gordon, 22 May 1796, Gordon-Hackett Family Papers, SHC.
45. The most famous of those southern captives is Daniel Boone, who developed close ties to the Shawnee family who adopted him in 1778. Blackfish, the head of his adoptive household, referred to Boone as "my son," while Boone called his Indian mother his "old mamma." Boone escaped from the Shawnees, but his open and lasting regard for Blackfish's family caused many white Kentuckians to question his loyalties thereafter. (Faragher, *Daniel Boone*, 165, 170.) The best single source for the southern fascination with white Indians are the John Dabney Shane interviews in the Lyman Draper MS; see especially those with William Boyd, William Sudduth, Marcus Richardson, Jacob Stevens, and John Hanks, Kentucky Papers, Draper MS, State Historical Society of Wisconsin, XII: 59, 62–63, 90, 126, 136, 142.
46. For anti-Shaker literature written by southerners in the western country, see James Smith, *Remarkable Occurrences Lately Discovered Among the People Called Shakers . . .* (Paris, Ky., 1810); James Smith, *Shakerism Detected . . .* (Paris, Ky., 1810); John Woods, *Shakerism Unmasked . . .* (Paris, Ky., 1826). Anti-Shaker polemics on the same themes appeared first in New England in the 1790s; on that point and for the history of early Shakerism, see Steven Stein, *The Shaker Experience in America: A History of the United Society of Believers* (New Haven, 1992), esp. 57–66; Lawrence Foster, *Religion and Sexuality: Three American Communal Experiments of the Nineteenth Century* (New York, 1981), 27–39, 237. As many scholars of the early South have noted, African Americans also extended their understanding of family beyond the circle of kin defined by blood or marriage. Often they referred to other blacks, particularly older men and women on the same plantation, who were not relatives as "aunts" or "uncles," and encouraged their children to accord them the deference owed to family members. But unlike Native Americans, African Americans reserved such intimacies for members of their own race, and, unlike the Shakers, blacks did not subordinate natural bonds to communal loyalties.
47. Early, Account, 21 October 1811, SHC; Jeter, *Recollections*, 26.

48. John F. Wright, *Sketches of the Life and Labors of James Quinn . . .* (Cincinnati, 1851), 17; *Georgia Analytical Repository* (July/August 1802), 76–77; Thompson, *Autobiography*, 16.

49. Early, Account, 13 November 1807, SHC; Benjamin McReynolds, Diary [1783], 25 July and 27 October 1783, SHC. See also, Norman, Diary, 370, SHC.

    The Baptist belief in the "perseverance of the saints" also lent itself to Methodist efforts to discredit their rivals' fidelity to family security and the purity of the lineage. The doctrine of perseverance follows logically from the Calvinist belief in predestination: Since divine decrees of an individual's eternal fate are immutable, no action on the part of men and women can alter their celestial destination. In other words, those predestined for heaven cannot "fall from grace." The Methodists, among whom theological precision languished even as polemical talent flourished, distorted that teaching into the view, which they ascribed to all Baptists, that any person once stirred to repent might thereafter indulge any sinful impulse with impunity. Such charges were purveyed by Methodists like Thomas Ware, who, while itinerating in Tennessee, recorded local gossip concerning the disreputable behavior of two Baptist preachers. Deluded by their belief in the perseverance of their own saintliness, they "eloped under circumstances of great scandal, having ruined the domestic felicity of several families" (Ware, *Sketches*, 145–46).

50. On antislavery evangelical preachers in the Southwest, see David T. Bailey, *Shadow on the Church: Southwestern Evangelical Religion and the Issue of Slavery, 1783–1860* (Ithaca, 1985), passim.

51. Sherman, *Revisions*, 228–29. The changes of 1804 also reduced the penalty imposed on those consenting to such unions from expulsion to a probation of six months, during which it might be determined whether marriage was weakening the faith of the Methodist spouse. Methodists retained the earlier rule allowing women to marry without parental consent in certain circumstances, but by gradually widening the pool of acceptable spouses, they had eliminated a prospective partner's religious affinities as legitimate grounds on which women might reject the preferences of their parents.

52. Early, Experiences, VI: 68, VHS.

53. Smith, *Shakerism Detected*, 27–29; Woods, *Shakerism Unmasked*, 9, 19, 32.

54. For a typical example of this new quest for respectability, see Charles R. Elliott, *The Life of Bishop Robert R. Roberts* (Cincinnati, 1854), 132–33; see also, Wyatt-Brown, *Southern Honor*, 188–89.

55. At a somewhat later date—1869—Susanna Johnson directly assured the readers of her memoirs of her itinerant-husband's fondness for hearth and home: "He [the itinerant] sees other men at their own firesides, surrounded by their little dependent loved ones, and he cannot but contrast his lot with theirs. How gladly would he, too, join his little and desolate family circle at the close of day. . . . My husband, cold and passionless as he usually appeared, shed many a bitter tear as thoughts like these arose" (*Recollections*, 81).

    It is difficult to assess the relationship between salary and standard of living, but among the Methodists, Susanna Johnson accounted her itinerant husband's annual salary of $232 in 1818 as "an ample allowance" for supporting the couple and their two children in Nashville, Tennessee. However, Susanna also worked as a seamstress and milliner to supplement the family income, and the Johnsons received some support-in-kind, including food and the labor of slaves. A decade earlier, in 1808, the Presbyterian minister of Cincinnati, Joshua Lacy Wilson, was probably one of the best-paid clergymen in the western country with an annual salary of $350. (Johnson, *Recollections*, 144–45; Memoirs of Joshua Lacy Wilson, 31, Joshua Lacy Wilson Papers, DC, RLUC.)

    The general trend toward better maintenance did not elevate the South's evangelical clergy into the ranks of highly paid professionals. On the contrary, penury remained the plague of most ministerial families, especially Methodist itinerants and Baptist preachers in country churches, whose salaries typically amounted to no more than about $200 to $250 annually. Settled clergymen routinely supplemented those minimal allotments by farming, teaching, and trusting in Providence. Anne Loveland finds that as late as the 1850s the pay of rural southern clergymen, perhaps $500 annually, fell well below the salaries of physicians and lawyers, who averaged $10,000 annually. (Anne C. Loveland, *Southern Evangelicals and the Social Order, 1800–1860* [Baton Rouge, 1980], 57–62.)

56. Loveland, *Southern Evangelicals and the Social Order*, 95–96; Ted Ownby, *Subduing Satan: Religion, Recreation, and Manhood in the Rural South, 1865–1920* (Chapel Hill, 1990), 130–32.

57. Donald Mathews was the first scholar to note the decline of congregational discipline, which was borne out by my statistical sampling of citations of white members in three Baptist churches in different southern states. Between 1800 and 1814, the total number of citations for all three congregations is 109; between 1815 and 1830, the total drops to 67—despite white membership either increasing or holding constant. (Bush River Baptist Church Records [Newberry County, South Carolina], SCL; Red River Baptist Church Records [Robertsen County, Tennessee], SHC; and Flat River Baptist Church Records [Person, North Carolina], SHC. See also, Mathews, *Religion in the Old South*, 100–101, and Loveland, *Southern Evangelicals and the Social Order*, 97–98.)

As I explain below in Chapter Five, n. 70, churches did not relax their oversight of all categories of offenses; indeed, the overall decline of citations of white members reflects primarily the growing reluctance among evangelicals to discipline men for offenses committed within their own households. Black members, both male and female, did not enjoy a similar reprieve from church oversight—not only their public but their private conduct remained strictly monitored by the white brethren. For a particularly telling and typical instance of that determination, see Welsh Neck Baptist Church Records, December 1828–February 1829, SCL.

58. For examples, see Young, *Autobiography*, 39, 43; Cartwright, *Autobiography*, 35–37; Finley, *Autobiography*, 21, 26; John Brooks, *The Life and Times of the Reverend John Brooks* (Nashville, 1848), 11–14; Jeter, *Recollections*, 42–43; Phoebus, *Beams of Light*, 12; David Purviance, *A Biography of Elder David Purviance* (Dayton, 1848), 271; Gatch, *Sketch*, 7; Garrettson, *Experience*, 12. See also, Mathews, *Religion in the Old South*, 100–101, for the change overtaking treatises on family religion, which increasingly addressed mothers rather than fathers.

4: MOTHERS AND OTHERS IN ISRAEL

1. Meacham, Journal, 17 July 1790, 7 July 1790, 17 August 1792, 16 March 1790, 27 February 1793, PLDU. Written reports of Susanna Williams's "visions" also circulated among the Methodist laity: Sarah Jones informed her sometime in the 1790s that "I have just now finished reading your vision" (Sarah Jones to Susanna Williams, n.d., in Sarah Jones, *Devout Letters*, ed. Jeremiah Minter [Alexandria, Va., 1804], 87).

For much of the analysis in this chapter I am indebted to Linda Kerber's advice that historians take an "interactive view of social processes" by showing "how women's allegedly 'separate sphere' was affected by what men did, and how activities defined by women in their own sphere influenced and even set constraints and limitations on what men might choose to do. . . ." ("Separate Spheres, Female Worlds, Women's Place: The Rhetoric of Women's History," *Journal of American History* 75 [1988]: 18). A similar approach informs the scholarship of Caroline Walker Bynum, who argues for treating "women's piety not in isolation but in such a way as to reformulate also our understanding of men's religious beliefs and practices" (see especially, *Fragmentation and Redemption: Essays on Gender and the Human Body in Medieval Religion* [New York, 1992], passim).

2. James Jenkins, *Experience, Labours, and Sufferings of Reverend James Jenkins* (Columbia, S.C., 1842), 39; Reed, Diary, 3 August 1779, CHDC, RLUC; Norman, Diary, 875, SHC. See also the correspondence of Mary Avery Browder and Sally Eastland with the Methodist preacher Edward Dromgoole, dated November 1777 and 21 February 1789, Edward Dromgoole Papers, SHC.

   Clergymen took equal satisfaction in helping women to overcome their religious scruples, their fears of not being worthy to join a church or to attain the promise of salvation. The Baptist preacher John Taylor recalled one Kentucky woman, Mrs. William Raymey, whose feeling of being "base and vile" made her fear being baptized. Her "distraction" filled him, Taylor admitted, with "a secret pleasure, as her mistake could easily be removed" by pointing out that such "fiery trials" were "common to the people of God." Stith Mead noted with the same delight that his wife had finally gained the confidence to credit her sanctification once realizing that "her timidity thro' fear of being deceived has influenced her many years to her great disadvantage" (John Taylor, *A History of Ten Baptist Churches* [1823; 2nd ed., Bloomfield, 1826], 153–55; Stith Mead, *A Short Account of the Experiences and Labours of the Reverend Stith Mead* [Lynchburg, Va., 1829], 9).

3. Ormond, Journal, III:41, PLDU; Hickman, Autobiography, 11–12, DC, RLUC. See also, Jacob Young, *Autobiography of a Pioneer* (Cincinnati, 1857), 41; Mead, *Short Account*, 42.

4. James Smith, Journal, in "Third Journal," dated Sunday, the 8th, Richard H. Collins Papers, DC, RLUC; Haskins, Journal, 24 January 1783, CHDC, RLUC; Pilmore, Journal, 29 March 1772, CHDC, RLUC. For the clergy's skepticism concerning male visionaries, see Freeborn Garrettson, *The Experience and Travels of Freeborn Garrettson* (1790; 2nd ed., Philadelphia, 1791), 206–207, and Peter Cartwright, *Autobiography of Peter Cartwright, the Backwoods Preacher* (Cincinnati, 1856), 274–75, 283.

5. "Journal of Lakin," 14 March 1802, 22 March 1802; Ormond, Journal, III:54, PLDU; James Finley, *Autobiography of the Reverend James B. Finley; Or Pioneer Life in the West*, ed. W. P. Strickland (Cincinnati, 1853), 231.

6. Reed, Diary, 9 August 1778, CHDC, RLUC; Norman, Diary, 30 July 1793, SHC.

7. Hickman, Autobiography, 31–32, DC, RLUC.

8. Clark et al., eds., *Journal and Letters of Asbury*, 28 March and 10 November 1786; Rankin, Diary, 5 November 1773, CHDC, RLUC; Norman, Diary, 435, SHC; John Travis, *The Autobiography of John Travis, A.M.*, ed. Thomas Summers, D.D. (Nashville, 1856), 62; Henry Smith, *Recollections and Reflections of an Old Itinerant* (New York, 1848), 57. See also George Paschal, *History of North Carolina Baptists*, 2 vols. (Raleigh, 1930–55), I: 289; Christian Newcomer, *Life and Journal of the Reverend Christian Newcomer . . .* , ed. John Hildt (Hagerstown, 1834), 123; Charles R. Elliott, *The Life of Bishop Robert R. Roberts* (Cincinnati, 1854), 21; Orville Vernon Burton, *In My Father's House Are Many Mansions: Family and Community in Edgefield, South Carolina* (Chapel Hill, 1985), 132. Stephanie McCurry has eloquently evoked the significance that antebellum South Carolina women attached to giving testimonies of their conversion before the churches; see *Masters of Small Worlds: Yeoman Households, Gender Relations, and the Political Culture of the Antebellum South Carolina Low Country* (New York, 1995), 181.

While Methodist women continued to exhort public gatherings in the South into the nineteenth century, Baptist women may have lost that liberty by about 1800. The practice was occasioning some opposition by the 1780s, when one church in North Carolina felt it necessary to affirm that "it shall not be an offense if by the constraining power of God's spirit in time of public worship, they [female members] should pray or drop a word of ex[h]ortation" (Flat River Baptist Church Records, June 1786, SHC). And John Taylor, whose Kentucky churches generally pursued liberal policies with respect to the participation of both women and blacks in church governance, mentioned women engaging in public prayer but not exhorting during the opening decades of the nineteenth century. More conservative practices appear to have prevailed in New England Baptist churches by about 1800, and most prohibited women from any public speaking. (Susan Juster, *Disorderly Women: Sexual Politics and Evangelicalism in Revolutionary New England* [Ithaca, 1995], 130–31.)

9. Mead, *Short Account*, 16; see also, Newcomer, *Life and Journal*, 46, 223. Among English Methodists, John Wesley had, by 1761, accepted the practice of his female followers exhorting and praying in public, and in 1777, he endorsed the practice of women preaching locally although not itinerating. Female preaching, however, stirred opposition, both among the English laity and Methodist leaders. After 1800, English Methodist itinerants took steps to discourage women from preaching, arguing that the increasing number of men entering the clergy obviated the need for women to serve as local preachers. Although women were still permitted to preach, such liberty was granted only to those who felt "an extraordinary call" and restricted their ministry to other women within their own circuit—after receiving written permission from male clergy in charge of that circuit. Those discouragements deterred many women, but some continued to speak publicly under the guise of "teaching" or "praying." By the 1820s, Wesleyan Methodists in England had decisively rejected female preaching, although the practice continued longer among Primitive Methodists and other splinter groups. See D. Colin Dews, "Ann Carr and the Female Revivalists of Leeds," in *Religion in the Lives of English Women, 1760–1930*, ed. Gail Malmgreen (Bloomington, 1986), 68–87; Malmgreen, "Domestic Discords: Women and the Family in East Cheshire Methodism, 1750–1830," in *Disciplines of Faith: Studies in Religion, Politics, and Patriarchy*, ed. Jim Obelkevich, Lyndal Roper, and Raphael Samuel (London and New York, 1987), 66–67; Abel Stevens, *The Women of Methodism* (London, 1876); Earl Kent Brown, *Women of Mr. Wesley's Methodism* (New York, 1983); Deborah Valenze, *Prophetic Sons and Daughters: Female Preaching and Popular Religion in Industrial England* (Princeton, 1985). On female preaching among the English Quakers, see Leonore Davidoff and Catherine Hall, *Family Fortunes: Men and Women of the English Middle Class, 1780–1850* (Chicago, 1987), 138–39; and for the northern United States, see Louis Billington, "Female Laborers in the Church: Women Preachers in the Northern United States, 1790–1840," *Journal of American Studies* 19 (1985): 369–94; Stephen Marini, *Radical Sects of Revolutionary New England* (Cambridge, Mass., 1982), 117–19. On the more restricted role of southern Presbyterian women in worship, see James Potter Collins, *Autobiography of a Revolutionary Soldier* (1859; reprint, New York, 1979), 155.

10. For the debate over female deacons, see Morgan Edwards, "Materials towards a History of the Baptists in the Province of North Carolina," ed. George W. Paschal, *North Carolina Historical Review* 7, no. 3 (1930): 384, 388–89; Leah Townsend, *South Carolina Baptists, 1670–1805* (Florence, S.C., 1935), 123–25; Taylor, *History*, 204; Rachel Klein, *Unification of a Slave State: The Rise of the Planter Class in the South Carolina Backcountry 1760–1808* (Chapel Hill, 1990), 44, 279–80; some mid-eighteenth-century Sepa-

rate Baptists also appointed eldresses, but Taylor did not suggest restoring that office. The Separates retreated from appointing women to church offices after merging with the Regular Baptists, who objected to the practice, at the end of the eighteenth century.

For the struggle over women's voting rights among the Baptists, see Lemuel Read and Jesse Burkitt, *A Concise History of the Kehukee Baptist Association . . .* (1850; reprint, New York, 1980), 80; Red River Baptist Church Records, 5 August 1771 and 25 January 1794, SHC; Robert Baylor Semple, *A History of the Rise and Progress of the Baptists in Virginia* (Richmond, 1810), 130; *Minutes of the Dover Baptist Association*, 25–26; Taylor, *History*, 56; Jean Friedman, *The Enclosed Garden: Women and Community in the Evangelical South, 1830–1900* (Chapel Hill, 1985), 5, 11–13; Sylvia R. Frey, *Water from the Rock: Black Resistance in a Revolutionary Age* (Princeton, 1991), 268–69; Mechal Sobel, *The World They Made Together: Black and White Values in Eighteenth-Century Virginia* (Princeton, 1987), 190–91; McCurry, *Masters of Small Worlds*, 179–80; Randy Sparks, *On Jordan's Stormy Banks: Evangelicalism in Mississippi, 1773–1876* (Athens, Ga., 1994), 51; Janet Moore Lindman, "A World of Baptists: Gender, Race, and Religious Community in Pennsylvania and Virginia, 1689–1825," (Ph.D. diss. University of Minnesota, 1999), 135–36, 138, 155–58.

A determination to curtail women's participation in the governance of evangelical churches took place simultaneously in New England and Britain, both among the Congregationalists and the Baptists; for Britain, see Davidoff and Hall, *Family Fortunes*, 131–37; on New England, see Susan Juster, *Disorderly Women*, 41–43, 122–34. Juster has found that in New England, as in the South, some Baptist churches in the 1830s restored the right of women to speak publicly, but, as she suggests, "It may be that when women spoke it was with the subdued cadences of the disempowered, voices that no longer threatened because they no longer mattered" (178).

11. Elliott, *Life of Roberts*, 126–27; Robert Simpson, ed., *American Methodist Pioneer: The Life and Journals of the Reverend Freeborn Garretson, 1752–1827* (Portland, VT., 1984), 237 (entry for 28 February 1784); John Brooks, *The Life and Times of the Reverend John Brooks* (Nashville, 1848), 56; see also William Watters, *A Short Account of the Christian Experience, and Ministerial Labours, of William Watters* (Alexandria, Va., 1806), 112; Travis, *Autobiography*, 71–72. Leonore Davidoff and Catherine Hall have shrewdly observed, in the English context, that female power to snub ministers or extend hospitality offered them "one weapon in the passive armoury of women" (*Family Fortunes*, 142).

12. Henry Boehm, *Reminiscences, Historical and Biographical, of Sixty-four Years in the Ministry*, ed. Joseph B. Wakeley (New York, 1865), 60; Norman, Diary, 841, SHC; Philip Gatch, *A Sketch of the Reverend Philip Gatch*, ed. John M'Lean (Cincinnati, 1854), 124. See also, Wilson Thompson, *The Autobiography of Elder Wilson Thompson* (Cincinnati, 1867), 78–80.

13. Taylor, *History*, 36–37; Sally Eastland to Edward Dromgoole, 21 February 1789, Edward Dromgoole Papers, SHC.

14. Meacham, Journal, 8 July 1790, PLDU.

15. Norman, Diary, 3 January 1798, SHC; Taylor, *History*, 134–35; Freeborn Garrettson, *The Experience and Travels of Freeborn Garrettson* (1790; 2nd ed., Philadelphia, 1791), 112. See also, William S. Simpson, ed., "The Journal of Henry Toler: Part 1, 1782–1783," *Virginia Baptist Register*, 1586.

16. Norman, Diary, 550–52, SHC.

17. Norman, Diary, 926, SHC.

18. For the Johnston case, see Red River Baptist Church Records, 2 August 1820, 16 September 1820, 13 October 1820, 18 November 1826, SHC; for examples of other cases in which the brethren met separately, see entries for 18 July 1821 and 8 June 1826. A similar

practice may also have prevailed in other churches, among them, South Carolina's Bush River, where the charges against some male members were not set before the church in detail because they were "too immodest to relate in an assembly of women" (Bush River Baptist Church Records, 10 June 1819, SCL). Jean Friedman's study of church discipline among nineteenth-century southern evangelicals makes a similar point that religion often contributed to southern women's sense of living under male domination. (*Enclosed Garden*, 5–20.)

19. On southern male attitudes toward women, see Bertram Wyatt-Brown, *Southern Honor: Ethics and Behavior in the Old South* (New York, 1982), 226. There is much to commend Suzanne Lebsock's view that religion gave southern women "a psychological distance from male authority" and "a respectable space" to "indulge in new kinds of assertion" (*The Free Women of Petersburg: Status and Culture in a Southern Town, 1784–1860* [New York, 1984], 216). It should be emphasized, however, that not all southern women discerned that scope in evangelicalism and that others feared the consequences of self-assertion. Even so, her formulation is more accurate than Orville Vernon Burton's view that in the South's "patriarchal rural society conversion especially gave women an escape from male oppression" (*In My Father's House*, 23). Jean Friedman's findings alone, which point up the domination of evangelical discipline by male church members and clergymen, suggest the need for a refining of Burton's generalization.

20. Brantley York, *Autobiography of Brantley York* (Durham, 1910), 19–20.

21. Garrettson, *Experience*, 123–25; Taylor, *History*, 158–59.

22. Taylor, *History*, 208.

23. Norman, Diary, 23 June 1793, 374–75, 464, 478, 740, 978, SHC.

24. Taylor, *History*, 105–106.

25. Thompson, *Autobiography*, 35; Hickman, Autobiography, 5–9, DC, RLUC. Suzanne Lebsock offers an intriguing discussion of the embarrassment of clergymen and male members at the predominance of women in southern churches later in the nineteenth century; see *Free Women of Petersburg*, 225–34.

26. McCurry, *Masters of Small Worlds*, 141–42; Taylor, *History*, 204–205.

27. Taylor, *History*, 153–55.

28. Ibid., 73–75.

29. Such tensions between husband and wife persisted well into the antebellum period; see McCurry, *Masters of Small Worlds*, 184.

30. Finley, *Autobiography*, 179; Chester Raymond Young, ed., *Westward into Kentucky: The Narrative of Daniel Trabue* (Lexington, Ky., 1981), 131; Obadiah Echols, *The Autobiography of Obadiah Echols* (Memphis, 1870), 55–56, 59–60; Thompson, *Autobiography*, 199–201. Men seem to have been more inclined to share their religious struggles with pious laymen. On one occasion in 1809 when his agitated state overwhelmed Echols, he took to his bed but reassured his wife, "Don't be scared, I am not going to die," and then sought solace from a male neighbor, "an old saint . . . who had lived out his time and just lying by mellowing for Heaven." When the Baptist minister Wilson Thompson experienced a crisis of faith, he, too, found insufficient the comfort offered by his wife. Although he shared his doubts with her, and she encouraged him to write a poem expressing his feelings, Thompson ended up taking his problems to a neighboring male Baptist.

Historians continue to debate both the quality of marital relations among white southerners and the influence of religion in reshaping conjugal ideals. Both Jan Lewis and Daniel Blake Smith contend that gentry couples increasingly idealized companionate marriage by the latter half of the eighteenth century, although, as Smith shrewdly observes, "conjugal love did not imply a democratization of authority in the household." By contrast, Bertram Wyatt-Brown argues for a lack of intimacy between spouses of all classes, which he infers from the reluctance of most men to share their thoughts and feelings with their wives and a high incidence of domestic violence. (Jan Lewis, *The Pursuit of Happiness: Family and Values in Jefferson's Virginia* (Cambridge, Mass., 1983), 169–208; Daniel Blake Smith, *Inside the Great House: Planter Family Life in the Eighteenth-Century Chesapeake* (Ithaca, 1980), 160; Wyatt-Brown, *Southern Honor*, 273, 283.) His model of marital relations serves as a foil against which scholars like A. Gregory Schneider and Richard Rankin have juxtaposed the more affective evangelical ideals of domesticity, which, by emphasizing the importance of gentleness and emotional sharing among spouses, in their view, fundamentally challenged southern patriarchy. (A. Gregory Schneider, *The Way of the Cross Leads Home: The Domestication of American Methodism* [Bloomington and Indianapolis, 1994], passim; Richard Rankin, *Ambivalent Churchmen and Evangelical Women: The Religion of the Episcopal Elite in North Carolina, 1800–1860* [Columbia, S.C., 1993], 34, 100.)

Like most sharply delineated oppositions, this one risks caricaturing spousal relations among southern whites, no matter what the partners' religious persuasion, rather than capturing their complexity. While Wyatt-Brown is right in stressing that emotional reserve typified most southern men (as well as women), particularly non-evangelicals, any collection of family correspondence reveals that the majority, regardless of church affiliation or social standing, were neither remote authority figures nor unloving husbands and fathers. As Daniel Blake Smith suggests, affective bonds between spouses were not incompatible with patriarchal claims and existed long before evangelicals rose to prominence in the South; and as Jan Lewis argues, evangelical influence fostered only the freer and more effusive expression of tender sentiments among all family members. Yet even as they encouraged more expressive forms of intimacy between husbands and wives, evangelicals endorsed the authority of white male heads of household over all their dependents. For other discussions of the consonance between evangelical teachings and the claims of patriarchy, see Klein, *Unification of a Slave State*, 293–97; Elizabeth Fox-Genovese, *Within the Plantation Household: Black and White Women of the Old South* (Chapel Hill, 1988), 232; McCurry, *Masters of Small Worlds*, esp. 171–209.

31. Echols, *Autobiography*, 61–63. Susan Juster offers some astute observations on men's resentment of women's "indirect coercion" in *Disorderly Women*, 175–77.

32. For the sexual innuendo surrounding the early Quakers in both Old and New England, see Phyllis Mack, *Visionary Women: Ecstatic Prophecy in Seventeenth-Century England* (Berkeley, 1992), 56, 85–86; Barry Levy, *The Quakers and American Domesticity: British Settlement in the Delaware Valley* (New York, 1988), 82–84; and Christine Leigh Heyrman, *Commerce and Culture: The Maritime Communities of Colonial Massachusetts, 1690 to 1750* (New York, 1984), 101–104. For attacks on the chastity of Ann Lee, see *Testimonies Concerning the Character and Ministry of Mother Ann Lee* (Albany, 1827), 43, 74; on Jemima Wilkinson, see Herbert A. Wisbey, Jr., *Pioneer Prophetess: Jemima Wilkinson, the Publick Universal Friend* (New York, 1964), 54.

33. Richard Hooker, ed., *The Carolina Backcountry on the Eve of the Revolution: The Journal and Writings of Charles Woodmason, Anglican Itinerant* (Chapel Hill, 1953), 103–104.

34. Ebenezer Pettigrew to James Iredell, 1804, *Pettigrew Papers*; Dorothy Ripley, *The Extraordinary Conversion and Religious Experiences of Dorothy Ripley* (New York, 1810), 77, 78, 84, 113, 119, 133–34. Ripley received a warmer welcome in some Methodist circles, speaking to gatherings of their adherents and even dining with Bishop Asbury on one occasion. But when she attempted to address an African Methodist congregation in

Philadelphia, their black pastor, the celebrated Richard Allen, rebuffed her. Allen may have believed that black churches had trouble enough without inviting more in the form of the scandal-ridden Ripley, but his refusal suggests a thoroughgoing opposition to female preaching. Permitting Ripley his pulpit, he averred, was "diametrically opposite" to "the rule of society in particular and the discipline in general of the Methodist Episcopal Church." For southern attitudes toward women traveling alone, see Fox-Genovese, *Within the Plantation Household,* 195.

35. Albert M. Shipp, *The History of Methodism in South Carolina* (Nashville, 1883), 273–76; Samuel Poole to James Poole, 21 December 1805, William Southerland Hamilton Papers, SHC. James Potter Collins appears to have witnessed a similar practice at the same time and in the same place, which he called "the exercise of love" (*Autobiography,* 151–52). For conservative evangelicals' disdain of sexual disorder at camp meetings, see Klein, *Unification of a Slave State,* 283–84.

36. Hooker, *Carolina Backcountry,* 98, 100, 113.

37. Brooks, *Life and Times,* 40; see also Nathan Blount to Charles Pettigrew, 25 May 1805, *Pettigrew Papers*; David Campbell to Maria Campbell, 3 January 1823, Campbell Family Papers, PLDU. On the prominence of sexual misdeeds in the churches' discipline of women, see McCurry, *Masters of Small Worlds,* 182; for two fine discussions of the relationship between female chastity and male honor, see Catherine Clinton, *The Plantation Mistress: Woman's World in the Old South* (New York, 1982), 87–89, 94, and Wyatt-Brown, *Southern Honor,* 52–53, 227.

38. Echols, *Autobiography,* 62; York, *Autobiography,* x, 2–3. See also, Early, Account, 14 September 1807, SHC.

39. For the Methodists, see Stith Mead to John Kobler, 15 April 1795, Mead Letterbook, VHS; Meacham, Journal, 5 September 1792, 30 March 1792, PLDU; Gatch, *Sketch,* 10, 14, 40; William W. Bennet, *Memorials of Methodism in Virginia* (Richmond, 1871), 493; Young, *Autobiography,* 44; Smith, *Recollections,* 309; Shipp, *History,* 196; Brooks, *Life and Times,* 40–41. See also, Sparks, *On Jordan's Stormy Banks,* 50. For the Baptists, see Simpson, ed., "The Journal of Henry Toler," 1582; Hickman, Autobiography, 31–32, DC, RLUC; Thompson, *Autobiography,* 190–96; Read and Burkitt, *Concise History,* 58–60.

   It should also be noted that some evangelical men, as well as nonevangelicals, laid claim to that authority. In 1793, for example, one Virginia woman complained to James Meacham that her husband's support for James O'Kelly left her no choice but to join his schismatic movement and desert the Methodists. A quarter century later, another Virginia woman whom John Early converted to Methodism told him that her Baptist relatives forbade her defection from their church, while the Methodist John Brooks charged that not only "worldlians" but Baptists were among the men hustling their wives and children away from his Tennessee camp meetings. (Meacham, Journal, 25 April 1793, PLDU; Early, Account, 20 December 1807, SHC; Brooks, *Life and Times,* 41–42.)

40. The American clergy found many such anecdotes in Hester Ann Rowe Rogers's popular memoirs; see especially, her *A Short Account of the Experience of Mrs. Hester Ann Rogers* (New York, 1806), 144–45, 163.

41. Norman, Diary, 247–48, SHC; Susannah Johnson, *Recollections of the Rev. John Johnson and His Home* (Nashville, 1869), 191.

42. Collins, *Autobiography,* 130, 139–41, 170, 172.

43. Jenkins, *Experience,* 88; Young, *Autobiography,* 233; Taylor, *History,* 40; Ormond, Journal, 15, PLDU; Norman, Diary, 7 January 1794, 15 March 1794, SHC; Mead Letterbook, 15 April 1795, VHS. See also, Cartwright, *Autobiography,* 23; Young, *Westward into Kentucky,* 128–29.

44. A. Gregory Schneider's observations about Methodist evangelism in the Old North-

west applies to the South as well—that they strove to foster the recruitment of entire families by "making domestic space one of its chief ritual areas" (*Way of the Cross*, 72–73). Jean and John Comaroff point to a similar strategy deployed by evangelical missionaries in nineteenth-century South Africa, whom they characterize as contending with native tribes "not for sacred sites but for the mastery of the mundane areas of lived space" (*Of Revelation and Revolution: Christianity, Colonialism, and Consciousness in South Africa*, vol. I [Chicago, 1991], 200–51). On women's isolation and their difficulty attending church in the South, see Burton, *In My Father's House*, 22; Fox-Genovese, *Within the Plantation Household*, 45–46, 98; and McCurry, *Masters of Small Worlds*, 123.

On the dearth of women's voluntary associations in the rural South, see Friedman, *Enclosed Garden*, 19–20, and McCurry, *Masters of Small Wonders*, 189–90; for contrasting developments in the Northeast, see especially, Nancy F. Cott, *The Bonds of Womanhood: "Woman's Sphere" in New England, 1780–1835* (New Haven, 1977), 132–46, and Mary P. Ryan, *Cradle of the Middle Class: The Family in Oneida County, New York, 1790–1865* (New York, 1981), passim. Women residing in southern towns, of course, enjoyed easier access to churches and also formed voluntary associations. (Lebsock, *Free Women of Petersburg*, 195–236; Burton, *In My Father's House*, 132.) By contrast, Brantley York reported that even by the 1820s, Methodist band meetings were not available to women in the western North Carolina countryside: "It was impracticable for women in the country to meet separately, so band meetings of women were restricted to town dwellers." But Brantley's band of young Methodist men met weekly at night, "with members of the band taking turns acting as leader" (York, *Autobiography*, 26). Class may also have influenced the access of women to religious gatherings outside of their own households: Catherine Clinton's research suggests a refinement of Friedman's findings by noting many references in the letters of women from the planter class to meetings for prayer and Bible study. (*Plantation Mistress*, 161.)

45. On the continuing power of men over southern households, see Fox-Genovese, *Within the Plantation Household*, 38–39; McCurry, *Masters of Small Worlds*, 188–91; Wyatt-Brown, *Southern Honor*, 256. On religious life within early-nineteenth-century northern households, see Ann Douglas, *The Feminization of American Culture* (New York, 1977), 87–88, and Ryan, *Cradle of the Middle Class*, 102, 104, 159.

46. Early, Account, 11 January 1814 SHC; Norman, Diary, 776, SHC.

47. Stith Mead to John Kobler, 15 April 1795, Mead Letterbook, VHS; Hickman, Autobiography, 51, DC, RLUC.

48. For this parallel development in the North, see Cott, *Bonds of Womanhood*, esp. 157–59; Lebsock, *Free Women of Petersburg*, 195–236; Carroll Smith-Rosenberg, "Women and Religious Revivals: Anti-Ritualism, Liminality, and the Emergence of the American Bourgeoisie," in *The Evangelical Tradition in America*, ed. Leonard Sweet (Macon, Ga., 1984), 200–203, 214.

49. Cott, *Bonds of Womanhood*, 157; Ryan, *Cradle of the Middle Class*, 34, 71–74; Laurel Thatcher Ulrich, "Daughters of Liberty: Religious Women in Revolutionary New England," in *Women in the Age of the American Revolution*, ed. Ronald Hoffman and Peter J. Albert (Charlottesville, 1989), 223.

50. Benjamin Seth Youngs, *The Testimony of Christ's Second Appearing* (Lebanon, Ohio, 1808); Steven Stein, *The Shaker Experience in America: A History of the United Society of Believers* (New Haven, 1992), 52–53, 57, 63, 76–87. It was also during the two decades after 1800 that the Shakers' first historians enshrined Ann Lee as their acknowledged founder, affirming her special status as the second incarnation of Jesus Christ and celebrating the miracles and wonders accompanying her ministry.

By underscoring the new legitimacy of female leaders among the Shakers after 1800, I do not intend to diminish the role played by men, particularly that of David Darrow, who was largely responsible for the expansion of that sect into the western country and dominated its governance in that region.

51. For his edition of the anti-Shaker polemic of Eunice Chapman and Mary Dyer, see Mary Dyer, *An Account of the Conduct of the Shakers* (Lebanon, Ohio, 1818), 16–19, 61, 63–64; see also James Smith, *Remarkable Occurrences Lately Discovered Among the People Called Shakers . . .* (Paris, Ky., 1810), 21, for charges that the Shakers commonly practiced birth control and infanticide to conceal their members' liaisons.

52. Richard McNemar, *The Other Side of the Question* (Cincinnati, 1819), see esp. 55–57.

53. Early, Account, 16 August 1807, 18 November 1807, 4 September 1811, 15 November 1811, SHC; Travis, *Autobiography*, 71–72; Cartwright, *Autobiography*, 221–23. There is also some evidence of preachers drawing greater attention to their power to reclaim women from worldly diversions. The young Methodist itinerant Henry Smith, for example, recalled preaching one Sabbath at the turn of the century when "a blooming gay young lady came in, and took a seat near where I stood. Her smiling countenance seemed to say, I am proof against your art. I thought, Perhaps you may weep before I am done." And, of course, the woman succumbed during his sermon. (*Smith, Recollections,* 101; see also, Taylor, *History,* 134–35.)

54. Early, Account, 9 June 1812, SHC.

55. Finley, *Autobiography,* 286–87.

56. *The Western Star* [Lebanon, Ohio], 13 February 1807; Cartwright, *Autobiography,* 99–102; see also, Finley, *Autobiography,* 257, 373.

The loathing was mutual. Christiana Holmes Tillson, a New England migrant to the southern Illinois frontier, recalled her "intense disgust" with the Methodist preachers riding circuit there during the 1820s, dismissing them as ignorant ranters. Perhaps the low esteem of Yankee women for the speaking skills of southern preachers emboldened some of them to take up preaching, certain that they could do better. (Tillson, *A Woman's Story of Pioneer Illinois* [Chicago, 1919], 78–80.) Tillson left an equally acerbic portrait of southern husbands, depicting them as verbally and sometimes physically abusive of their wives, whom they treated like draft animals and prevented from acquiring even basic education. (*A Woman's Story,* 27, 63–65, 82.)

The Methodist hierarchy was just as averse to female preaching. In 1827, one Miss Miller, a northern woman, hoped to follow her triumphs in the Yankee-dominated Western Reserve by preaching in neighboring western Virginia. This was too much for Joshua Soule, a Methodist bishop who should have been christened by Dickens: "I will not hear that girl," he thundered. "She has no authority to preach." Then Soule advised the northern itinerant who sponsored Miss Miller that he "had better have stayed at home, minding his work, than to be accompanying that strolling girl about the country" (George Brown, *Recollections of an Itinerant Life: Including Early Reminiscences* (Cincinnati, 1866), 183–88).

57. Rogers, *Short Account,* 122–23, 127; for English ideals of evangelical womanhood in the early nineteenth century, see Davidoff and Hall, *Family Fortunes,* 114.

58. Taylor, *History,* 134–35, 148; Thompson, *Autobiography,* 223–30.

59. Paschal, *History of North Carolina Baptists,* II: 466; John Logan, *Sketches, Historical and Biographical, of the Broad River and King's Mountain Baptist Associations from 1800 to 1882* (Shelby, N.C., 1887), 25.

60. Echols, *Autobiography,* 78–83; Alfred Brunson, *A Western Pioneer: Or, Incidents of the Life and Times of the Reverend Alfred Brunson* (Cincinnati, 1872), 305; Jenkins, *Experience,* 144; Finley, *Autobiography,* 245. Steven Stein has found that, as early as 1802, the

first Shaker missionaries in the western country aimed at converting men, confident that wives would follow the religious lead set by their husbands. (Stein, *Shaker Experience in America*, 56.) Stephanie McCurry's work on the Carolina low country also demonstrates how deeply entrenched evangelical support for husbands' authority over the spiritual choices of wives had become by the antebellum period; see *Masters of Small Worlds*, 194–95.

McCurry and other historians have observed that the proslavery argument, elaborated first in the 1830s, with its emphatic analogizing of marriage and slavery that linked the subordination of women and slaves, reflects white southern male anxieties about delineating the proper social role of women. (*Masters of Small Worlds*, 215–17.) My findings suggest that these anxieties surrounding male authority and gender roles surfaced among some men even earlier in the nineteenth century, fueled both by their concerns about charismatic evangelical women and the sudden appearance in the South of even more radical groups like the Shakers. I am indebted to my colleague, Anne Boylan, for drawing my attention to this point. On the new evangelical emphasis on wifely submission, see Donald Mathews, *Religion in the Old South* (Chicago, 1977), 112–13.

61. Brunson, *Western Pioneer*, 219; Taylor, *History*, 204. The diarist Mary Chesnut remarked that "these people [southern whites] take the old Hebrew pride in the number of children they have" (cited in Wyatt-Brown, *Southern Honor*, 236–37). Connections between female religiosity and fecundity were also reflected by evangelicals' habit of referring to their churches with the feminine pronoun as "she." Baptists also denoted the first congregation established on any spiritual frontier as the "mother" and its offshoots formed when membership expanded as "daughters."

62. Taylor, *History*, 157.

63. Ibid., 105; Finley, *Autobiography*, 21, 26; Brooks, *Life and Times*, 12; Cartwright, *Autobiography*, 34; Thompson, *Autobiography*, 75.

64. Church Book, Edenton Methodist Church, Edenton, North Carolina, SHC.

65. In this respect, the experience of southern evangelical clergy conforms closely to that of their counterparts in Britain, who also augmented their authority and professional status during the same period, becoming, in the phrase of Leonore Davidoff and Catherine Hall, "public somebodies" as spokesmen for a respectable middle-class culture and leaders of educational and philanthropic institutions. (*Family Fortunes*, 126.) By contrast, Ann Douglas argues that liberal clergymen in the northeastern United States declined in public stature and sought to restore their cultural dominance by allying with white, middle-class women. (*Feminization of American Culture*, passim.)

5: MASTERY

1. Norman, Diary, 106, 621, 4 June and 15 July 1794, SHC; for the disapproval of many of Norman's pastimes among stricter Methodists, see W. P. Strickland, *The Life of Gruber* (New York, 1860), 86.

2. Norman, Diary, 23 June 1794, 12 December 1795, 11 January 1796, SHC.

3. Norman, Diary, 798, 872, SHC.

4. James Peter Collins, *Autobiography of a Revolutionary Soldier* (1859; reprint, New York, 1979), 91–92, 94, 130; see also Thomas Ware, *Sketches of the Life and Travels of Thomas Ware* (New York, 1839), 146.

5. Norman, Diary, 23 June 1793, 798, SHC; Jacob Young, *Autobiography of a Pioneer* (Cincinnati, 1857), 150; Meacham, Journal, 20 February 1792, PLDU; Ormond, Journal, III: 53, PLDU; Obadiah Echols, *The Autobiography of Obadiah Echols* (Memphis, 1870), 117.

6. Norman, Diary, 247–48, 444, 636, 815, 888; see also, 10 February 1794, 25 June 1793, and 414, SHC; James Jenkins, *Experience, Labours, and Sufferings of Reverend James Jenkins*

(Columbia, S.C., 1842), 58–59; John Brooks, *The Life and Times of the Reverend John Brooks* (Nashville, 1848), 119.

7. William Watters, *A Short Account of the Christian Experience, and Ministerial Labours, of William Watters* (Alexandria, 1806), 12, 16; James Ireland, *The Life of the Reverend James Ireland* (Winchester, Va., 1819), 57; Echols, *Autobiography*, 60, 87. See also John Taylor, *A History of Ten Baptist Churches* (1823; 2nd ed., Bloomfield, 1826), 136–37. On the significance of dueling and other physical contests, see Kenneth S. Greenberg, "The Nose, the Lie, and the Duel in the Antebellum South," *AHR* 95 (1990): 57–58, and *Masters and Statesmen: The Political Culture of American Slavery* (Baltimore, 1985), 33–40; Bertram Wyatt-Brown, *Southern Honor: Ethics and Behavior in the Old South* (New York, 1982), 353–58; and Elliott J. Gorn, " 'Gouge and Bite, Pull Hair and Scratch': The Social Significance of Fighting in the Southern Backcountry," *AHR* 90 (1985): 18–43.

8. Strickland, *Life of Gruber*, 62; James Finley, *Autobiography of the Reverend James B. Finley; Or, Pioneer Life in the West*, ed. W. P. Strickland (Cincinnati, 1853), 167–68. See also, Brooks, *Life and Times*, 9. Finley's published memoir ranks among the most artful and highly stylized of clerical autobiographies, and as such must not be treated as a reliable source of information concerning his life. He often embroidered and possibly invented events to make certain points about theology, morality, and the morphology of conversion intended to educate, edify, or reassure his reading public. Since he regularly sacrificed autobiographical accuracy to those didactic goals, there is reason to doubt the veracity of this account of his own conversion. But that makes his treatment of this episode all the more telling, since his intention was to describe and dispel the fears common among southern men who came under conviction, which, from his long experience as a pastor, he knew well.

9. Edward P. Humphrey and Thomas H. Cleland, *Memoirs of the Reverend Thomas Cleland, D.D.* (Cincinnati, 1859), 22, 36, 54–55. Cleland's use of marital metaphors here is, if not singular, a striking departure from the imagery most commonly used by his evangelical male contemporaries to describe their conversions, which were more typically either familial (i.e., allusions to being adopted as a son of God), or, even more often, martial, as I discuss below. Female evangelicals also compared themselves to children or warriors when describing their spiritual experience, although they were equally likely to draw on sexual or marital imagery, casting themselves as brides of Christ or ravished lovers. (See Chapter Three, n.41 and n.45 in this chapter.) For a fuller discussion of the fear of evangelical conversion as "feminizing," see Philip Greven, *The Prostestant Temperament: Patterns of Child-Rearing, Religious Experience, and the Self in Early America* (New York, 1977), 125–126.

10. Ware, *Sketch*, 108; Beverly Allen to Charles Pettigrew, 17 November 1784, *Pettigrew Papers*, ed. Sarah McCulloch Lemmon (Raleigh, 1971), 35; William W. Bennet, *Memorials of Methodism in Virginia* (Richmond, 1871), 292, 482; Jenkins, *Experience*, 124; Ireland, *Life*, 85. See also, Meacham, Journal, 5 July 1789, PLDU. On the importance of appearances among southern white men, see Greenberg, "The Nose, the Lie, and the Duel in the Antebellum South," 62.

11. Adam Wallace, *The Parson of the Islands* (Philadelphia, 1861), 57, 87; Taylor, *History*, 149; Finley, *Autobiography*, 168; Young, *Autobiography*, 157–58; see also Jeremiah Jeter, *The Recollections of a Long Life* (1891; reprint, New York, 1980), 43, 44.

12. Strickland, *Life of Gruber*, 70–71.

13. Norman, Diary, 572, SHC; Meacham, Journal, 12 July 1794, PLDU; George Paschal, *History of North Carolina Baptists*, 2 vols. (Raleigh, 1930–55), II: 226. The clergy were so sensitive about drawing congregations that consisted mainly of women or African Americans that they underscored such occurrences in their journals. In the 1780s, Benjamin Abbott, for example, recalled a Methodist class in Maryland with twenty white

312 + Notes for Chapter 5

women and one black man, while Jeremiah Norman reported "tollerable number of Women but few men at Preaching" at one appointment in the 1790s, and in 1810, John Early recorded preaching to "a number of women and a few men." Nelson Reed also noted several occasions, usually during bad weather, when only blacks attended his preaching. (Benjamin Abbott, *The Experience and Gospel Labours of the Reverend Benjamin Abbott . . .*, ed. John Ffirth (New York, 1805), 98; Early, Experiences, VI:56, VHS; Norman, Diary, 408, SHC; Reed, Diary, 17 March 1779, CHDC, RLUC.) But diary entries also suggest that it was uncommon for audiences to be so heavily weighted toward white women or African Americans, and that preachers generally expressed surprise when few men were in attendance.

Church membership, of course, was another matter, and within those ranks, women outnumbered men. While women made up about 60 percent of the white membership of Baptist churches during the decades around 1800, they were even more heavily represented among early Methodists. The records of a Methodist church in Edenton, North Carolina, one of the few that exist for the opening decades of the nineteenth century, indicate that only 31 of the 115 white members admitted during the 1810s were men, just over one-quarter. Moreover, male members were either expelled from or rescinded their affiliation with the church (that is, they withdrew rather than being dismissed because of moving) at a far higher rate than female members. Nearly one-third of all white men admitted to membership between 1810 and 1839 left the church as a result of expulsion or withdrawal, but just 11 percent of all female members. (Church Record Book, Edenton Methodist Church, SHC; the most careful recent study of gender and church membership is Stephanie McCurry, *Masters of Small Worlds: Yeoman Households, Gender Relations, and the Political Culture of the Antebellum South Carolina Low Country* [New York, 1995], 160.)

14. Norman, Diary, 16 March 1794, 7 November 1795, 396–97, 411, 560, 647, 843, 872, SHC; Robert Simpson, ed., *American Methodist Pioneer: The Life and Journals of the Reverend Freeborn Garrettson, 1752–1827* (Rutland, Vt., 1984), 225 (entry for 20 June 1783). Janet Moore Lindman's statistical study of Virginia Baptist church records confirms that white male members had both the highest rate of being accused of violating church discipline and the lowest incidence both of being convicted of those charges or, if suspended or expelled, being restored to church fellowship. Their lower rates of conviction probably reflect both the domination of the disciplinary process by other white men and, perhaps more important, the recognition that if convicted, white male members would be lost to the church permanently. (Janet Moore Lindman, "A World of Baptists: Gender, Race, and Religious Community in Pennsylvania and Virginia, 1689–1825 [Ph.D. dissertation, University of Minnesota, 1994]," 226–28; similar conclusions for the later nineteenth century appear in Jean Friedman, *The Enclosed Garden: Women and Community in the Evangelical South, 1830–1900* [Chapel Hill, 1985], 14.)

The churches also sought to regulate their members' business dealings, and men, far more often than women, were subject to discipline for fraud, usury, and other sharp practices, almost invariably in cases involving other men. Such interventions were less common in the eighteenth century than were church efforts to monitor the behavior of men both within their households and within settings of male leisure, but these actions stirred resentment among laymen such as one Brother White who, infuriated when church arbiters decided against him in a land dispute, "abruptly rising from his seat desired the church to *erase* his name out" (Red River Baptist Church Records, 1 August 1807, SHC).

There is evidence, too, that the Baptists sought to control the political behavior of their male members. One North Carolina association in 1786 advised its members that they had to consult with the brethren before holding any public office, whether elective or appointive, a practice some male members still observed as late as the 1830s. Similarly, a North Carolina church in 1793, while acknowledging that the Bible did not forbid men accepting "worldly commissions" still vowed that if "we see any bad consequences attending it shall think it our duty to check it" (Paschal, *History of North Carolina Baptists*, II: 243; Flat River Baptist Church Records, June 1793, SHC).

15. Young, *Autobiography*, 93; Paschal, *History of North Carolina Baptists*, II: 226n. Some men were so sensitive about submitting to disciplinary authority that they even kept their wives who had been censured from humbling themselves before the church; see Flat River Baptist Church Records, November 1799, SHC.

16. On this point and the importance of honor to all classes of men everywhere in the South, see Wyatt-Brown, *Southern Honor*, passim; Edward L. Ayers, *Vengeance and Justice: Crime and Punishment in the 19th-Century American South* (New York, 1984), 26–28; Greenberg, "The Nose, the Lie, and the Duel in the Antebellum South," 57–58; Steven Stowe, *Intimacy and Power in the Old South: Ritual in the Lives of the Planters* (Baltimore, 1987), passim; and Richard Rankin, *Ambivalent Churchmen and Evangelical Women: The Religion of the Episcopal Elite in North Carolina, 1800–1860* (Columbia, S.C., 1993), 100–101. Misgivings about evangelical manliness were not limited to the South, although, arguably, it became most pronounced in that region because of both the centrality of primal honor and slavery. For Britain, see Lenore Davidoff and Catherine Hall, *Family Fortunes: Men and Women of the English Middle Class, 1780–1850* (Chicago, 1987), 112; on the American North, see Paul E. Johnson and Sean Wilentz, *The Kingdom of Matthias: A Story of Sex and Salvation in 19th-Century America* (New York, 1994), esp. 91–107.

17. Jenkins, *Experience*, 121; Philip Gatch, *Sketch of the Reverend Philip Gatch*, ed. John M'Lean (Cincinnati, 1854), 109; Wilson Thompson, *The Autobiography of Elder Wilson Thompson* (Cincinnati, 1867), 65–69. On the significance of biracial religious gatherings, see Mechal Sobel, *The World They Made Together: Black and White Values in Eighteenth-Century Virginia* (Princeton, 1987), 180, 189; Lawrence W. Levine, *Black Culture and Black Consciousness: Afro-American Folk Thought from Slavery to Freedom* (New York, 1977), 22, 29; Donald Mathews, *Religion in the Old South* (Chicago, 1977), 185, 191.

    Evangelicals also spoke of being edified by private religious conversations with blacks, particularly black men. The Methodist preacher Benjamin Lakin, for example, recorded in his diary meeting with one African American who "spake so feelingly and powerfull of the work of Grace in his soul that it much affected me" ("Journal of Lakin," 14 November 1795). In 1762, Col. James Gordon, a Presbyterian, noted having "much conversation with Hubbard's Dick, whose piety I have a great opinion of" (Gordon, "Journal of Col. James Gordon," WMQ, 11, ser. 1 [1903], 227).

18. Haskins, Diary, 11 August 1783, 21 November 1784, CDHC, RLUC; William M. Wightman, *The Life of William Capers, D.D.* (Nashville, 1858), 124–28; Jenkins, *Experience*, 120–21; John Travis, *The Autobiography of John Travis, A.M.*, ed. Thomas Summers, D.D. (Nashville, 1856), 101–102; John S. Moore, ed., "Richard Dozier's Historical Notes, 1771–1818," *Virginia Baptist Register*, 1402, 1414, 1415; Clark et al., eds., *Journal and Letters of Asbury*, 1 April 1789; Henry Boehm, *Reminiscences, Historical and Biographical, of Sixty-Four Years in the Ministry*, ed. Joseph B. Wakeley (New York, 1865), 90–92. See also, Sobel, *World They Made Together*, 212; Albert J. Raboteau, *Slave Religion: The "Invisible Institution" in the Antebellum South* (New York, 1978), 134–35; Mathews, *Religion in the Old South*, 193; Sylvia R. Frey, *Water from the Rock: Black Resistance in a Revolutionary Age* (Princeton, 1991), 268–69.

19. Haskins, Diary, 11 August 1783, CHDC, RLUC; Smith, Journal, 29 November 1795, in Richard H. Collins Papers, DC, RLUC; Moore, ed., "Richard Dozier's Historical Notes, 1771–1818," 1414. See also Rankin, Diary, 121, CHDC, RLUC, and Reed, Diary, 26 August 1781, CHDC, RLUC.

20. Moore, ed., "Richard Dozier's Historical Notes, 1771–1818," 1402, 1414, 1416–17, 1424.

21. Meacham, Journal, 20 August 1789, PLDU; Wightman, *Life of Capers*, 126.

22. Taylor, *History*, 202; Brooks, *Life and Times*, 19–20.

23. For examples, see Wightman, *Life of Capers*, 74–76; Albert M. Shipp, *The History of Methodism in South Carolina* (Nashville, 1883), 233–34; Early, Account, 12 September 1813, SHC; Ormond, Diary, III: 9, PLDU.

24. Williams, Journal, 11 May 1771, CHDC, RLUC; Christiana Holmes Tillson, *A Woman's Story of Pioneer Illinois* (Chicago, 1919), 80; John Dabney Shane Interview with Benjamin Snelling, Kentucky Papers, Draper MS, State Historical Society of Wisconsin, XII: 111–12; Meacham, Journal, 27 April 1792, PLDU.

25. Taylor, *History*, 94, 108, 139; Raboteau, *Slave Religion*, 134–35. There has been some dispute among historians about the connection between slavery and honor, with Kenneth S. Greenberg and Edward L. Ayers arguing for this linkage and Bertram Wyatt-Brown questioning its existence. As the preceding pages indicate, my findings support the position of Greenberg and Ayers. See Greenberg, *Masters and Statesmen*, passim, and "The Nose, the Lie, and the Duel in the Antebellum South," 57–58; Ayers, *Vengeance and Justice*, 26–27; Wyatt-Brown, *Southern Honor*, 15–17.

26. Flat River Baptist Church Records, June 1823, SHC; Jenkins, *Experience*, 110. See also, Sobel, *World They Made Together*, 207–209, 210–12; Lindman, "A World of Baptists," 177, 201; Jewel Spangler, "Salvation Was Not Liberty: Baptists and Slavery in Revolutionary Virginia," *American Baptist Quarterly* 13 (1994): 229; Frey, *Water from the Rock*, 268–71. As Jewel Spangler points out, the number of ordained African Americans among the Baptists grew steadily after 1800, but only because the number of black aspirants to church office increased, persisting in the face of white resistance.

    The African-American clergy remained a prominent presence for longer among southern whites in the western country. There was a "curious neighborhood" on the border between Kentucky and Tennessee visited by the itinerant Jacob Young, where the local Methodist society at the opening of the nineteenth century was headed by a slave preacher who had also converted all of its members. He was illiterate, but overcame that difficulty by listening to his master read the Bible on Saturday evenings and then choosing and memorizing his text for the Sunday sermon, which drew "a large congregation." As late as the 1820s in Kentucky, a free black named Uncle Phill traveled and spoke to racially mixed groups because, as John Taylor remarked, "his preaching [is] acceptable wherever he goes" (Young, *Autobiography*, 90; Taylor, *History*, 94–108, 139).

27. Wightman, *Life of Capers*, 124–28; Jenkins, *Experience*, 120–21; Travis, *Autobiography*, 101–102; Bennet, *Memorials of Methodism*, 532–33; Taylor, *History*, 94, 108; Boehm, *Reminiscences*, 90–92.

    White preachers also slipped into their published memoirs allusions to the personal failings of popular black preachers. White Methodist clergymen, for example, confided that Harry Hosier had succumbed to the evils of pride and drink in mid-career, while the Baptist John Taylor disclosed that Asa, a slave preacher, had failed to detect the sincerity of his sister Letty's conversion. Bear in mind, however, that white preachers were equally forthcoming about the deficiencies of clergymen of their own race.

28. The Separate Baptists bore the brunt of both popular and civil opposition in the South; Regular Baptists did not escape unscathed but aroused less resistance because their preachers applied for licenses and their meetings were less enthusiastic than

those of the Separates. For the persecution of the early Baptists, see Wesley M. Gewehr, *The First Great Awakening in Virginia, 1740–1790* (Durham, 1930), 115, 119–23; Rhys Isaac, *The Transformation of Virginia, 1740–1790* (Chapel Hill, 1982), 161–63, 172–77.

For examples of early evangelicals eschewing physical violence in favor of verbal reproof, see "Salem Diary," in *Records of the Moravians in North Carolina*, ed. Adelaide Fries (Raleigh, 1922–69), II: 680; Bennet, *Memorials of Methodism*, 181.

29. Chester Raymond Young, ed., *Westward into Kentucky: The Narrative of Daniel Trabue* (Lexington, Ky., 1981), 190.

30. Robert Baylor Semple, *A History of the Rise and Progress of the Baptists in Virginia* (Richmond, 1810), 36; Williams, Journal, 3, CHDC, RLUC; Ireland, *Life*, 165.

31. Rachel Klein, *Unification of a Slave State: The Rise of the Planter Class in the South Carolina Backcountry, 1760–1808* (Chapel Hill, 1990), 45; Paschal, *History of North Carolina Baptists*, I: 462–69; Leah Townsend, *South Carolina Baptists, 1670–1805* (Florence, S.C., 1935), 163, 176–81; Young, *Westward into Kentucky*, 42; Padgett Creek Baptist Church Records [1784–1837], 17, SCL; John Dabney Shane Interview with Josiah Collins, in Kentucky Papers, Draper MS, State Historical Society of Wisconsin, XII:102; Taylor, *History*, 12–15, 25. Some southern Baptist churches passed resolutions guaranteeing that male members would not be disciplined for fighting with the rebel forces, among them the Dutchman's Creek congregation in North Carolina, which assured their brethren that "whether joyn or not they should be used with brotherly love and freedom for the futer [future]" (Dutchman's Creek Baptist Church Records [1772–1787], 5–6, SHC).

32. For example, the Methodist itinerant William Watters attended a sermon preached by an Anglican parson in Virginia who declared the Methodists "to be a set of Tories, under a cloak of religion. That the preachers were sent here by the English ministry to preach up passive obedience and non-resistence [*sic*]. . . . He concluded . . . by declaring that he would, if at the helm of our national affairs, make our nasty stinking carcasses pay for our pretended scruples of conscience" (Watters, *Short Account*, 49). For Wesley's views, see *A Calm Address to Our American Colonies* (Bristol, 1775), passim; see also, Gewehr, *First Great Awakening in Virginia*, 157–58; James D. Essig, *The Bonds of Wickedness: American Evangelicals and Slavery, 1770–1808* (Philadelphia, 1980), 44.

On the political views of Methodist preachers, see George A. Phoebus, comp., *Beams of Light on Early Methodism in America: Chiefly Drawn from the Diary . . . of Rev. Ezekiel Cooper* (New York and Cincinnati, 1887), 13; Jesse Lee, *A Short History of the Methodists, in the United States of America; Beginning in 1766 and Continued Till 1809* (Baltimore, 1810), 60, 62, 64–66, 73; Watters, *Short Account*, 52, 68, 70, 73; Freeborn Garrettson, *The Experience and Travels of Freeborn Garrettson* (1790; 2nd ed., Philadelphia, 1791), 84, 102; Bennet, *Memorials of Methodism*, 99. Jesse Lee recalled that English itinerants were "all of them averse to the war, some of them decidedly hostile to the American cause." Unlike Rodda, most were more circumspect in their public pronouncements, insisting that they aimed to save souls, not meddle in politics. Even so, politics and religion intermingled in the minds of preachers like Thomas Rankin, who saw the revolutionary crisis as a "judgement" on Americans "who have waxed fat and forgot the rock from which they were hewen"—that "rock" connoting at once the deity and the British empire. (Lee, *History*, 72–73; Rankin, Diary, 2 October 1774, 1 January 1775, CHDC, RLUC.)

33. Keith Mason, "Localism, Evangelicalism, and Loyalism: The Sources of Discontent in the Revolutionary Chesapeake," *Journal of Social History* 56 (1990): 23–53; Ronald Hoffman, *A Spirit of Dissension: Economics, Politics, and the Revolution in Maryland*

(Baltimore, 1973), and "The 'Disaffected' in the Revolutionary South," in *The American Revolution: Explorations in the History of American Radicalism*, ed. Alfred F. Young (DeKalb, Ill., 1976), 273–316. For instances of Methodist harassment during the Revolution, see Lee, *History*, 64–44, 77; Garrettson, *Experience*, 102, 115–16, 127, 141–41, 162–63, 171–73, 201–202; Phoebus, *Beams of Light*, 13; John Dabney Shane Interview with Samuel Gibson in Kentucky Papers, Draper MS, State Historical Society of Wisconsin, XII: 124.

34. Reed, Diary, 1 June 1780, 20 September 1780, 8 May 1781, 20 May 1781, 9 June 1781, 12 June 1781, 17 June 1781, 24 June 1781, 24 June 1781, 1 July 1781, 2 July 1781, CHDC, RLUC. Other itinerants inspired whig loathing for the same reason. In 1777, a Virginia militia officer demanded "to know my mind respecting fighting," and found little assurance in Freeborn Garrettson's reply that "God had taught me better than to use carnal weapons against the lives of human creatures . . . that if he did not learn to fight with other weapons, he would go to hell" (Garrettson, *Experience*, 69).

35. Gatch, *Sketch*, 45; Garrettson, *Experience*, 127; Lee, *Short History*, 66. Women often defended itinerants from mob attacks after the war as well; see Henry Smith, *Recollections and Reflections of an Old Itinerant* (New York, 1848), 309; Shipp, *History*, 229–30.

36. Frey, *Water from the Rock*, 255–59; Meacham, Journal, 12 May 1791, 25 August 1795, PLDU; Early, Account, 16 July 1812, SHC. O'Kelly's charges so unnerved Meacham that he took to scouring Asbury's private journal for seditious sentiments, but finally came away reassured that "the whole tenor" evinced "his Patriotic Spirit as a Minister of the Gospel."

    Southerners may also have wondered at the readiness of both Methodists and Baptists to condemn local Fourth of July celebrations, even though preachers emphasized that they opposed only the drinking and other unseemly revels attending such commemorations. A scandalized Jeremiah Norman even ended his courtship of one young woman after hearing reports of her attending the festivities in 1800. (Norman, Diary, 977, SHC.)

37. Early, Experiences, VI:49, 114, VHS; Early, Account, 31 March 1812, SHC; Norman, Diary, 551–52, SHC; Jenkins, *Experience*, 170–73; Joshua Lacy Wilson to Sally Wilson, 17 February 1808, Joshua Lacy Wilson Papers, CHDC, RLUC. See also, Smith, *Recollections*, 307–308.

38. Finley, *Autobiography*, 364–65; Bennet, *Memorials of the Methodism*, 644; Strickland, *Life of Gruber*, 65.

39. Brooks, *Life and Times*, 42–43; Early, Account, 20 September 1811, SHC; Early, Experiences, VI:61, VHS.

40. Early, Account, 10 January 1812, SHC.

41. Even the most casual examination of clerical memoirs published during the first half of the nineteenth century reveals that ministers routinely "recycled" into print the stories of their life and times that they had been relating orally to various audiences for several decades. The tenor of those published recitations is replete with the confidence that can only result from prior success. Although the analysis that follows necessarily focuses on printed sources, the importance of oral performances in influencing lay opinion cannot be emphasized enough, because such presentations surely reached a wider audience, particularly in the more remote and less literate western country. For the changing style of pulpit discourse, see David S. Reynolds, "From Doctrine to Narrative: The Rise of Pulpit Storytelling in America," *American Quarterly* 32 (1980): 479–98; for a discussion of literacy and the circulation of devotional literature in the early nineteenth century, see David Paul Nord, "Religious Reading and Readers in Antebellum America," *Journal of the Early Republic* 15 (1995): 241–72, as well as "Sys-

tematic Benevolence: Religious Publishing and the Marketplace in Early Nineteenth-Century America," in *Communication and Change in American Religious History*, ed. Leonard I. Sweet (Grand Rapids, Mich., 1993), 239–69.

42. Wightman, *Life of Capers*, 13, 18; Stith Mead, *A Short Account of the Experiences and Labours of the Reverend Stith Mead* (Lynchburg, Va., 1829), 23–25; Finley, *Autobiography*, 15, 17–19, 20–21. See also, *Georgia Analytical Repository* (May/June 1802), 26. The preoccupation with the Revolutionary generation's heroic legacy was ubiquitous in early-nineteenth-century America; for treatments of this theme, see George B. Forgie, *Patricide in the House Divided: A Psychological Interpretation of Lincoln and His Age* (New York, 1979); Michael Paul Rogin, *Fathers and Children: Andrew Jackson and the Subjugation of the American Indian* (New York, 1975); Marvin Meyers, *The Jacksonian Persuasion: Politics and Belief* (Stanford, 1957). Southern evangelicals shared that common fascination but were more broadly drawn to military conflict of any kind.

43. Abbott, *Experience*, 25; Peter Cartwright, *Autobiography of Peter Cartwright, the Backwoods Preacher* (Cincinnati, 1856), 25, 27; Brooks, *Life and Times*, 11; Edward Stevenson, *A Biographical Sketch of the Reverend Valentine Cook, A.M.* (Nashville, 1858), 13–14; Finley, *Autobiography*, 113, 183; David Purviance, *A Biography of Elder David Purviance* (Dayton, 1848), 273; Shipp, *History*, 233–34.

44. Taylor, *History*, 149; Humphrey and Cleland, *Memoirs of Cleland*, 54; for the use of military metaphors, see Abbott, *Experience*, 566; Ware, *Sketches*, 169–70, 172, 174; David Dailey, comp., *The Experience and Ministerial Labors of Reverend Thomas Smith* (New York, 1848), 102; Early, Experiences, VI:55, VHS; Early, Account, 6 September 1807 and 15 May 1813, SHC; Finley, *Autobiography*, 184; Young, *Autobiography*, 41, 62, 74, 264; Cartwright, *Autobiography*, 30–31, 37; Jenkins, *Experience*, 146–48; Boehm, *Reminiscences*, 119; Watters, *Short Account*, 48; Charles D. Mallary, *Memoirs of Elder Edmund Botsford* (Charleston, 1832), 102–103.

45. James Jennings to Edward Dromgoole, Edward Dromgoole Papers, 11 March 1807 and 15 April 1807, SHC; Alfred Brunson, *A Western Pioneer: Or, Incidents of the Life and Times of the Reverend Alfred Brunson* (Cincinnati, 1872), 205; Brooks, *Life and Times*, 66; Finley, *Autobiography*, 294. Note, too, that the same recourse to martial imagery appears in the writings of evangelical women. The letters of Sarah Jones, an eighteenth-century Virginia Methodist, draw on metaphors of warfare as frequently as the language of familial affection and sexual transport to convey the quality of her private religious experience. On one occasion she wrote to the preacher Jeremiah Minter that "I feel Sampson strong, Caleb's spirit, and Joshua's resolution," and in another letter urged him "in the name of Daniel's God [to] try to storm this Sodom." "What makes a general triumph?" she asked rhetorically. "Honour. What brings honour? Daily conquest; hard fighting, and victory in every battle" (Sarah Jones to Jeremiah Minter, 1 December 1788, 2 January 1790, 21 July 1790, in Sarah Jones, *Devout Letters*, ed. Jeremiah Minter [Alexandria, Va., 1804]). For the importance of martial imagery in the evangelical tradition, see Greven, *Protestant Temperament*, 116–17.

As John Boswell points out, a military ethos has permeated Christianity since its inception, appearing most prominently during the medieval and early modern eras among the Benedictine and Cluniac monastic orders and the Society of Jesus. Its persistence is sustained by bibliocentrism, because, as he notes, "Not only was the Old Testament . . . filled with accounts of military conquest on the part of "God's people" . . . but even the New Testament has more terms drawn from military experience than from any other single aspect of life . . ." (*Same-Sex Unions in Premodern Europe* [New York, 1994], 156–58).

What I wish to emphasize, then, is that the use of military imagery and ritual and invocations of the Revolutionary legacy were unique to southern evangelicals only in the extent to which they dominated their strategy for recruiting and maintaining converts. Virtually every group in early-nineteenth-century America looked for legitimacy by casting their goals as fulfillments of the Revolution's promise, and northern temperance reformers, among others, made some use of military symbolism in their campaigns. (See William Breitenbach, "Sons of the Fathers: Temperance Reformers and the Legacy of the American Revolution," *Journal of the Early Republic* 3 [1983]: 82.)

46. Taylor, *History*, 151–52; Jeter, *Recollections*, 155; Shipp, *History*, 144: Finley, *Autobiography*, 31–33, 302. See also, Thompson, *Autobiography*, 256–71. For other Methodist and Baptist accounts of converting military officers, see Gatch, *Sketch*, 86; Jenkins, *Experience*, 83, 89; Ware, *Sketches*, 166–67; Shipp, *History*, 164; Bennet, *Memorials of Methodism*, 400–401; O. P. Fitzgerald, *A Biography of John McFerrin* (Nashville, 1889), 28–29, 37; *Georgia Analytical Repository* (September/October 1802), 110–11.

47. Smith, *Recollections*, 56, 100–101; see also, Abbott, *Experience*, 95; Brunson, *Western Pioneer*, 287; Finley, *Autobiography*, 187, 291.

48. Bennet, *Memorials of Methodism*, 487; Susannah Johnson, *Recollections of the Rev. John Johnson and His Home* (Nashville, 1869), 254–59; Travis, *Autobiography*, 36.

49. Phoebus, *Beams of Light*, 117; Finley, *Autobiography*, 252–53; Young, *Autobiography*, 295. See also, Travis, *Autobiography*, 48.

50. Brooks, *Life and Times*, 18–19; Brunson, *Western Pioneer*, 303–305; Cartwright, *Autobiography*, 90–92, 236–37.

    Brooks's apprenticeship for the ministry also included serving among the guard at camp meetings, a duty, to his disappointment, less than replete with episode. He "would meet with very rough looks and words, and some times the threat of blows, but to my regret the last never came. Oh how I did want one of them out in the woods a little while; though often challenging to a walk, I could never get one; the challenger would back out by saying this is no place for such as that."

51. Thompson, *Autobiography*, 144–50; Finley, *Autobiography*, passim; Young, *Autobiography*, 3.

52. Harriet Martineau, *Society in America*, ed. Seymour Martin Lipset (New York, 1962), 352.

53. On the access of evangelicals to courthouses for preaching, see Frey, *Water from the Rock*, 251–52. Southern colonial authorities also identified the early Baptists with political subversion. In the summer of 1771, for example, Virginia officials stopped several Baptist preachers and searched their saddlebags for "treasonable papers." Meanwhile, North Carolina's royal governor, Thomas Tryon, opined that the Regulators, a backcountry insurgency, were "a faction of Quakers and Baptists" (Semple, *History*, 34; Paschal, *History of North Carolina Baptists*, II: 361).

54. Bennet, *Memorials of Methodism*, 536–39.

55. Ibid., 561–63; see also, Early, *Account*, 26 July 1811, SHC; Early, Experience, III:38, VI:61, VHS; Wallace, *Parson of the Islands*, 79; Jenkins, *Experience*, 165.

    Equally indicative of the evangelical effort to woo the good opinion of magistrates is their response to an episode in which a young Ohio gentleman whipped two Methodist preachers for calling him a liar. On that occasion, Francis Asbury heeded the advice of the state's governor, himself a former Baptist minister, who warned against trying to prosecute the assailant, plainly because he believed that taking legal action would only alienate local magistrates. The governor explained his reasoning: the attacker was "a high-minded young man . . . and would not brook an insult from any body; and as they [the preachers] began with him, he thought they got no more than they deserved . . . [and] to let it pass" (Young, *Autobiography*, 204).

56. Norman, Diary, 863, SHC; Early, Account, 17 September 1811, SHC. See also, John Logan, *Sketches, Historical and Biographical, of the Broad River and King's Mountain Baptist Associations from 1800 to 1882* (Shelby, N.C., 1887), 26. James Jenkins, for example, objected to the clergy holding office and lamented the active role taken by some Methodist clergymen in the Nullification crisis of the 1830s, yet Jenkins himself accepted an appointment as justice of the peace (*Experience*, 179–80, 202); on the mingling of evangelical religion and politics in the South Carolina low country during the Nullification debates, see also, McCurry, *Masters of Small Worlds*, 150–58).

    The best accounts of the ambivalence of antebellum southern clergymen about entering the realm of politics are Anne C. Loveland, *Southern Evangelicals and the Social Order, 1800–1860* (Baton Rouge, 1980), 111–24, and Mitchell Snay, *Gospel of Disunion: Religion and Separatism in the Antebellum South* (New York, 1993), passim. While Loveland emphasizes that most evangelical clergymen played "only a limited political role," Snay advances a stronger case for their increasing prominence in political affairs, especially by the middle decades of the nineteenth century. Snay's judgment is supported by Richard Carwardine, who argues for the growing intensity of evangelicals' moral engagement in politics as the Civil War approached. (*Evangelicals and Politics in Antebellum America* [New Haven, 1993], passim.) See also, Brooks Holifield, *The Gentlemen Theologians: American Theology in Southern Culture, 1795–1860* (Durham, N.C., 1978), chapter 2, and Larry Tise, *Proslavery: A Defense of Slavery in America, 1701–1840* (Athens, Ga., 1987), 163–70.

    It should be noted, too, that nineteenth-century southern preachers and politicians projected remarkably similar public images, emphasizing their impressive physiques, martial valor, and physical courage; see Nichole Etcheson, "Manliness and the Political Culture of the Old Northwest, 1790–1860," *Journal of the Early Republic* 15 (1995): 59–77.

57. Brunson, *Western Pioneer*, 283–87; Cartwright, *Autobiography*, 123–24, 134–36; Thompson, *Autobiography*, 216–21. See also, Young, *Autobiography*, 242–44. A particularly inventive postbellum Methodist biographer, O. P. Fitzgerald, carried these patriotic themes a step further by arguing that the "moral force" of the American Revolution had never been spent but only assumed a new shape in post-Revolutionary Methodist expansionism. 'The soul of the civil revolution seemed to animate the religious revival; the fires of 1776, refined into a holier flame, kindled anew in the West. . . . It was a martial metempsychosis" (Fitzgerald, *McFerrin*, 39).

58. Robert Paine, *Life and Times of William McKendree* (Nashville, 1880), 158–60; see also, Jenkins, *Experience*, 157–58. Even evangelical accounts hint at the continuing friction with militia bands. On the day before McKendree had extended the olive branch to the Illinois major, he "had raised a company of lewd fellows of the baser sort to drive us from the ground" and they had encamped there overnight "to prevent us from doing any harm." At first James Finley also suspected that a militia company's offer to protect a camp meeting "might perhaps be a mere ruse to get us into difficulty" (Finley, *Autobiography*, 294–95). For evangelicals' association of military life with immorality and infidelity, see Taylor, *History*, 47; Jenkins, *Experience*, 16; Finley, *Autobiography*, 278; Mallary, *Memoirs of Botsford*, 59; Young, *Westward into Kentucky*, 130; *Georgia Analytical Repository* (September/October 1802), 137.

59. Bennet, *Memorials of Methodism*, 438, 658–59; Wightman, *Life of Capers*, 52–54; Brooks, *Life and Times*, 40; John F. Wright, *Sketches of the Life and Labors of James Quinn . . .* (Cincinnati, 1851), 107–108.

60. Bennet, *Memorials of Methodism*, 438; Young, *Autobiography*, 169; Wallace, *Parson of the Islands*, 79–80; George Brown, *Recollections of an Itinerant Life: Including Early*

Reminiscences (Cincinnati, 1866), 60–61. Preachers sometimes even plucked young men to serve as guards from the ranks of potential troublemakers.

61. Brown, *Recollections*, 56–57; Brooks, *Life and Times*, 109; Echols, *Autobiography*, 120. In research preliminary to the present study, I reconstructed the social profile of those men who converted during the so-called Great Revival (1800–1805) in one up-country Baptist congregation, Bush River, in Newberry County, South Carolina. This exercise revealed that the only distinctive characteristic of those male converts, beyond their relative youth and lack of strong ties to the church through other kin, were close familial relationships (as sons, nephews, younger brothers) with older men who enjoyed local fame because of their military service during the American Revolution. This case study pointed out to me the possible salience of the relationship between male anxieties centering on martial prowess and susceptibility to evangelical conversion. Whether more extensive research of other churches will bear out this finding is a task to which I commend scholars more youthful, energetic, or both. ("The Origins of an Evangelical Consensus in the Old South: From the American Revolution to the Great Revival," unpublished paper.)

62. Young, *Autobiography*, 52, 74, 105.

63. Early, Experiences, III: 40, 42, VHS. Joseph Carson, Early's contemporary, recounted a similar episode: A young man who believed that Carson had insulted him from the pulpit demanded "satisfaction" and "gave me a blow which had well nigh sent me backward, but I recovered and finding that I must defend myself, I seized him by the arm and led him out of my way" (Bennet, *Memorials of Methodism*, 536).

64. David Sherman, *A History of the Revisions of the Discipline of the Methodist Episcopal Church*, 3rd ed. (New York and Cincinnati, 1890), 165–66; Cartwright, *Autobiography*, 230–31. Gentlemen also spurned peremptory forms of address, as Early reminded the scion of another elite family who presented him with a letter of complaint from his father: "I told him to tell his father that if he had sealed his letter and directed it to me as a gentleman ought to have done I should have felt myself bound to have answered him accordingly, but as it was I should treat him with silence." Joseph Carson also underscored his aspirations to gentility by insisting that other men treat him with due politeness. Around 1810, after disarming a young gentleman who threatened him with a knife, Carson extracted the dramatic apology that "If I don't behave like a gentleman while I stay on this camp-ground, you may cut my throat" (Early, Account, 17 September 1811, SHC; Bennet, *Memorials of Methodism*, 561–63).

As Bertram Wyatt-Brown points out, when the South's masters came to acknowledge the clergy as gentlemen later in the nineteenth century, a tacit agreement evolved that they could refuse challenges to duel without losing face. (*Southern Honor*, 354.)

65. For examples, see Brooks, *Life and Times*, 32–36; Brown, *Recollections*, 36–37; Young, *Autobiography*, 80–81, 100; Thompson, *Autobiography*, 249–56; Collins, *Autobiography*, 93.

66. Johnson, *Recollections*, 150–53; on the protocol of dueling, see Greenberg, "The Nose, the Lie and the Duel in the Antebellum South," 62–63.

67. Valerie I. J. Flint has written eloquently of the similar process by which early medieval Christian churchmen sought conversions by incorporating some elements of pagan magical practices; see *The Rise of Magic in Early Medieval Europe* (Princeton, 1991), passim.

68. For the early enmity between evangelicals and Freemasons in the South, see Norman, Diary, 438, 450, 641, 775, SHC; Early, Account, 19 December 1807, SHC; Paschal, *History of North Carolina Baptists*, II: 470–71; Townsend, *South Carolina Baptists*, 114; Logan, *Sketches . . . of the Broad River and King's Mountain Baptist Associations*, 26.

Compare the opposition expressed there with Susannah Johnson's boastful account of her Methodist husband's acceptance among Masons a few decades later in the western country. (*Recollections*, 224, 236.) For the best exploration of the national phenomenon that Richard Carwardine has described as "the interpenetration of the worlds of the evangelical and the professional politician," during the antebellum period, see his *Evangelicals and Politics*, 50–54; see also, Jean Baker, *Affairs of Party: The Political Culture of Northern Democrats in the Mid-Nineteenth Century* (Ithaca, 1983), 271. On revivals within the Confederate Army, see Drew Faust, "Christian Soldiers: The Meaning of Revivalism in the Confederate Army," *Journal of Southern History* 53 (1987): 63–90.

Fragmentary evidence suggests that the Methodists had succeeded in attracting a larger proportion of white males as members by the middle of the nineteenth century. By the 1840s, for example, the percentage of men belonging to the Methodist church in Edenton, North Carolina, had risen to 36 percent of all white members, compared with only about 25 percent in 1810. Stephanie McCurry has similar findings for low-country South Carolina Methodists, whose white membership was about 40 percent male by the 1850s. (*Masters of Small Worlds*, 160–63; Church Record Book, Edenton Methodist Church, SHC.) But the dearth of Methodist church records for the period before 1800 makes it hazardous to generalize about evangelical success in attracting white male members, and the Baptists, for whom better records exist, registered no significant gains among white men over the period covered by this study. Of course, as I argue above, membership statistics provide only the crudest measure of popular religious affinities and, in this instance, cast little light on the more important question of whether the South's masters had actively embraced evangelicalism. On the other hand, impressionistic evidence confirms mounting rates of male "adherence" to evangelical faiths—that is, a greater willingness to entertain the teachings of Baptists and Methodists.

69. A number of historians have noted how primal honor and evangelical piety met in the South's response to the sectional controversy of the 1850s. (See Bertram Wyatt-Brown, "God and Honor in the Old South," *Southern Review* 25 (1989): 283–96; Snay, *Gospel of Disunion*, 145–46; and Edward R. Crowther, "Holy Honor: Sacred and Secular in the Old South," *Journal of Southern History* 58 (1992): 619–36. My findings, of course, suggest that this fusion of value systems was under way decades earlier, arising first in response to religious rather than political imperatives.

70. Church records typically specify those occasions when male offenses like drunkenness and fighting took place in private homes, usually because such breaches also entailed the physical or verbal abuse of wives, children, slaves, or other relatives. (See, for example, Red River Baptist Church Records, 14 March 1814, 17 October 1823, SHC.) The more numerous instances of men engaging in such pastimes at public gatherings are also identifiable, either because a number of fellow-revelers are cited at the same meeting or because the records place offenders at the scene. For the case of William Morrow, see Red River Baptist Church Records, June 1792, SHC; for related examples, follow in the same records the discipline of Giles Connell (1804–1806), James Hicks (1795), and Jesse Gardner (1823–25). There is also evidence to suggest that nineteenth-century churches increasingly shielded the reputations of those men whom they did cite for crimes related to marital matters by considering their cases in sessions composed exclusively of the brethren, rather than bringing them before the church as a whole.

My conclusions concerning the shifting patterns of evangelical discipline are based on an analysis of the records of three Baptist churches in different parts of the South:

Bush River in South Carolina, Flat River in North Carolina, and Red River in Tennessee. The records of the Carolina churches date from the late eighteenth century, and indicate that citations of white men for offenses against relatives and household members made up between one-fifth and one-quarter of all disciplinary cases involving that group between the 1780s and 1805. By contrast, such offenses comprised only about 9 percent of all disciplinary actions initiated against white male members of all three churches between 1806 and 1830. Citations of the same group for offenses such as drinking, fighting, cursing, or competing in games of chance, all in the company of other men, did not decline over the same span of time, but either held constant, in the case of Bush River, or increased, as in the case of Flat River. In all three churches, such offenses were the largest single category of citations against white male members, accounting for about 60 percent of the total number of disciplinary cases between 1806 and 1830. This calculation actually understates the mounting concern of evangelical churches about the public behavior of white male members, because it does not factor in numerous citations involving the white brethren for offenses such as doing business on the Sabbath or acting dishonestly in financial transactions with other men. (Bush River Baptist Church Records, SCL; Flat River Baptist Church Records, SHC; Red River Baptist Church Records, SHC.)

71. To be sure, the southern clergy did not organize campaigns against drinking and dueling as effectively as their northern counterparts; see Wyatt-Brown, "God and Honor in the Old South," 294–95.

72. Red River Baptist Church Records, 18 February 1816, SHC.

73. The salience of this cultural division between evangelical and nonevangelical men has been described vividly by historians of the later South; see especially, Ted Ownby, *Subduing Satan: Religion, Recreation, and Manhood in the Rural South, 1865–1920* (Chapel Hill, 1990), passim. My purpose here is to establish its emergence and unexpected persistence as a result of specific historical circumstances.

74. Wyatt-Brown, *Southern Honor*, 14–15, 45–48.

EPILOGUE

1. The term "popular evangelicalism" has recently come into currency among some historians who use it to distinguish churches like the Baptists and the Methodists from denominations like the Congregationalists and the Presbyterians, whom they designate as "bourgeois evangelicals." I tend to be wary of both terms, because it has yet to be demonstrated that the social composition of membership among early national Baptists and Methodists differed significantly from that among Congregationalists and Presbyterians. It is equally questionable whether the "popular evangelicals" were any more egalitarian than the "bourgeois evangelicals" by the opening of the nineteenth century.

Nathan Hatch has advanced the most forceful argument for viewing early Baptists and Methodists, among other religious groups, as radically democratic and egalitarian, although echoes of that thesis appear in an earlier study by Rhys Isaac. The most eloquent critics of that view are Rachel Klein and Stephanie McCurry, while Paul Johnson, who shares their position, has formulated the most perceptive overview of the entire debate in a review of Hatch's book. (See Nathan Hatch, *The Democratization of American Christianity* (New Haven, 1989); Rhys Isaac, *The Transformation of Virginia, 1740–1790* (Chapel Hill, N.C., 1982); Rachel Klein, *The Unification of a Slave State: The Rise of the Planter Class in the South Carolina Backcountry, 1760–1808* (Chapel Hill, 1990); Stephanie McCurry, *Masters of Small Worlds: Yeoman Households,*

Gender Relations, and the Political Culture of the Antebellum Southern Low Country (New York, 1995); Paul Johnson, "Democracy, Patriarchy, and American Revivals, 1780–1830," *Journal of Social History*, 24 (1991), 842–50.

2. For the best book-length studies of contemporary evangelical groups, see Randall Balmer, *Mine Eyes Have Seen the Glory: A Journey into the Evangelical Subculture in America* (New York, 1993); and R. Stephen Warner, *New Wine in Old Wineskins: Evangelicals and Liberals in a Small-Town Church* (Berkeley and Los Angeles, 1988). The most balanced and sustained journalistic coverage is that of Gustav Niebuhr, the religion editor at *The New York Times*.

3. For a thoughtful report on this group, see Joe Conason, Alfred Ross, and Lee Cokorinos, "The Promise Keepers Are Coming: The Third Wave of the Religious Right," *The Nation*, October 7, 1996, 11–19.

APPENDIX

1. James Finley's acerbic observation about how Methodists collected membership statistics doubtless applied to the Baptists as well: "The careless manner by which the preacher in charge too frequently arrives at the numbers in society cannot be too severely censured" (*Autobiography of the Reverend James B. Finley; Or, Pioneer Life in the West*, ed. W. P. Strickland [Cincinnati, 1853], 254–55).

2. See Edwin Gaustad, *Historical Atlas of Religion in America* (New York, 1962), and Roger Finke and Rodney Stark, "American Religion in 1776: A Statistical Portrait," *Sociological Analysis* 49 (1988): 45, 47.

3. Patricia Bonomi and Peter Eisenstadt, "Church Adherence in the Eighteenth-Century British American Colonies," WMQ, ser. 3, 39 (1982): 273–74; Morgan Edwards, "Materials toward a History of the Baptists in North Carolina," *North Carolina Historical Review* 7 (1930): 368–69.

   A simpler formula for determining church membership is suggested by Roger Finke and Rodney Stark, who, based on the work of Rufus Babcock and Herman Weber, two early-nineteenth-century Baptist and Presbyterian church historians, fix the average number of church members per congregation at seventy-five. To arrive at total membership involves multiplying the number of congregations by seventy-five. In my view, the numbers that result from this formula are too high. (Roger Finke and Rodney Stark, "American Religion in 1776," *Sociological Analysis* 49 [1988]: 42.)

4. Gaustad, *Historical Atlas of Religion in America*, 89.

5. Bonomi and Eisenstadt, "Church Adherence in the Eighteenth-Century British American Colonies," 249–53.

6. John Asplund believed that among the Baptists "three times as many attend meeting as join the church," while David Benedict, another nineteenth-century Baptist historian, put the ratio at 7:1. Both could be right, Benedict if children under sixteen are counted as adherents, and Asplund if the figure for adherents is restricted to the population sixteen and over.

   There are bad as well as good ways to measure church adherence, and one of the worst is the approach used by Roger Finke and Rodney Stark. They begin with the mistaken assumption that adherence to any religious group that did not count children as members can be calculated simply by adding the number of children under sixteen to their total number of church members. The problem with that approach is that large numbers of adherents were *adults* (sixteen and over). Bonomi and Eisenstadt make precisely that point, which renders their estimate of church adherence in all of the eighteenth-century colonies (56–80 percent) far more reliable than Finke and Stark's incredible projection of 17 percent for 1776. ("How the Upstart Sects Won America: 1776–1850," *Journal for the Scientific Study of Religion* 28 [1989]: 29–30.) Finke and Stark appear to be unaware of Bonomi and Eisenstadt's work; their recent study, *The Churching of America, 1776–1990* (New Brunswick, 1992), rests on the same flawed premise about adherence.

Index

Abbott, Benjamin, 39, 72, 136, 233, 311*n*3
abortion, contemporary evangelical
    denunciation of, 256–7
adherents, numbers of, 265, 323–4*n*6
African Americans
    Afro-Christianity of, 6, 50–2
    child spirituality among, 80, 284*n*4
    churches formed by, 68, 281*nn*51–2
    in church government, 168
    church membership of, 5, 13, 23, 46,
        262–5
    church oversight of, 301*n*57
    contemporary evangelical preaching by,
        257
    ecstatic religious responses of, 49–50, 78,
        198
    extended families of, 299*n*46
    free, 68, 218
    male-female ratio of church
        membership among, 217
    preaching by, 217–25, 314*n*26
    Ripley refused pulpit by, 306–7*n*34
    segregation from whites in worship,
        67–9, 217–18, 255
    white apprehensions of converts among,
        47–52
    witchcraft, belief in, among, 63, 65, 74
    women visionaries among, 165, 175, 203
    see also slaves, slavery
"African poison," 63
age, attitudes toward, among early
        southern whites, 99, 102, 291*n*41
agriculture, "safety-first," 45, 295*n*24
Allen, Beverly, 213
Allen, Richard, 307*n*34

American Indians
    in memoirs of preachers, 233
    Shakers and, 150, 157
    shamans of, 65
    white captives of, 150, 299*n*45
American Revolution
    Anglican loss of strength in, 22–3
    evangelicals in, 86–7, 226–30,
        315–16*nn*31–5
    evangelicals' later attitude toward, 233,
        238, 241–2
    Methodism's appeal to veterans of,
        243–4
    moral force of, in Methodism, 319*n*57
Anderson, Elizabeth Owen, 127–8, 294*n*13
angels, 55, 278*n*32
Anglicans, see Church of England
Anthony, Joseph, 15–16
apparitions, 57–8, 74, 278*n*37, 279*n*39
    see also devil
Arianism, 198
Arminianism, 268*n*3
Arminian Magazine, 282*n*56
Asa (slave preacher), 175, 202, 314*n*27
Asbury, Francis
    African-American preachers and, 218,
        219
    during American Revolution, 228, 230
    becomes bishop, 102
    on church governance, 100
    covenant brotherhood introduced by,
        147–8
    death of, 114
    familial titles encouraged by, 145–6
    feminine appearance of, 213

Christine Leigh Heyrman was born in Boston in 1950. She received her B.A. at Macalester College in 1971, and her Ph.D. from Yale University in 1977. She has taught at the University of California at Irvine, Yale University, and Brandeis University. Since 1990 she has been Associate Professor of History at the University of Delaware. She is the author of *Commerce and Culture: The Maritime Communities of Colonial Massachusetts, 1690–1750* (1984) and (with four others) *Nation of Nations: A Narrative History of the American Republic* (3rd edition forthcoming).

A NOTE ON THE TYPE

This book was set in Minion, a typeface produced by the Adobe Corporation specifically for the Macintosh personal computer, and released in 1990. Designed by Robert Slimbach, Minion combines the classic characteristics of old style faces with the full complement of weights required for modern typesetting.

Composed by Creative Graphics, Inc.,
Allentown, Pennsylvania
Printed and bound by Quebecor Printing,
Martinsburg, West Virginia
Designed by Anthea Lingeman